THE PEOPLE'S WAR

JAPANESE SOLDIERS FRATERNIZING WITH THE EIGHTH ROUTE ARMY
AFTER A BATTLE

THE PEOPLE'S WAR

by

I. EPSTEIN

With six full-page woodcuts carved specially
for this book by
CHEN YIN-CHIAO

Foreign Languages Press

First published by Victor Gollancz LTD, London, UK, 1939.

Home Page:
http://www.flp.com.cn
E-mail Addresses:
info@flp.com.cn
sales@flp.com.cn

ISBN 7-119-03471-5

Foreign Languages Press, Beijing, 2003

Published by Foreign Languages Press

24 Baiwanzhuang Road, Beijing 100037, China

Printed in the People's Republic of China

PREFACE

Huang Hua

It is a great honor for me to write a preface for the new, PFS (China Society for People's Friendship Studies) 50-book series under the general title of **Light on China.** All these books were written in English by journalistic and other eyewitnesses of the events described. I have read many of them over the seven decades since my student days at Yenching University. With some of the outstanding authors in this series I have ties of personal friendship, mutual regard, and warm memories dating from before the Chinese people's Liberation in 1949.

Looking back and forward, I am convinced that China is pursuing the right course in building a strong and prosperous country in a rapidly changing world with its complex and sometimes volatile developments.

The books in this series cover a span of some 150 years, from the mid 19th to the early 21st century. The numerous events in China, the sufferings and struggles of the Chinese people, their history and culture, and their dreams and aspirations were written by foreign observers animated by the spirit of friendship, equality and cooperation. Owing to copyright matters and other difficulties, not all eligible books have as yet been included.

The founder of the first Chinese republic, Dr. Sun Yat-sen wrote in his Testament in 1925, "For forty years I have devoted myself to the cause of the people's revolution with but one end in view: the elevation of China to a position of freedom and equality among the nations. My experiences during those forty years have convinced me that to attain this goal we must bring about an awakening of our own people and ally ourselves in common struggle with those people of the world who regard us as equals."

Chairman Mao Zedong declared, at the triumphal founding of the People's Republic in 1949, "The Chinese people have stood up." Today, having passed its 53rd anniversary, we see the vast forward strides that have been taken, and note that many more remain to be made.

Many foreign observers have traced and reported the real historical movement of modern China, that is: from humiliation — through struggle — to victory. Seeking understanding and friendship with the Chinese people, their insight and perspective were in basic harmony with the real developments in China. But there have been others who viewed China and the Chinese people through glasses tinted by hostile prejudice or ignorance and have invariably made irrelevant observations that could not stand the test of time. This needs to be better understood by young people and students, at home and abroad. The PFS series *Light on China* can help them gain an overview of what went before, is happening now, and will emerge in the future.

Young students in China can additionally benefit from these works by seeing how foreign journalists and authors use fluent English to record and present historical, philosophical, and socio-political issues and choices in China. For millions of students in China, English has become a compulsory second language. These texts will also have many-sided usefulness in conveying knowledge of our country to other peoples.

Students abroad, on their part, may be helped by the example of warm, direct accounts and impressions of China presented by their elders in the language that most readily reaches them.

Above all, this timely and needed series should help build bridges of friendship and mutual understanding. Good books long out of print will be brought back to strengthen the edifice.

My hearty thanks and congratulations go first to ex-Premier Zhu Rongji, who has been an effective supporter of this new, PFS series. They go to all engaged in this worthy project, the Foreign Languages Press, our China Society for People's Friendship Studies, and others who have given their efforts and cooperation.

Chairman Mao Zedong has written: "So many deeds cry out to be done, and always urgently. The world rolls on, time presses. Ten thousand years are too long. Seize the day, seize the hour."

The hour has come for making these books available to young people in China and abroad whose destiny is to build a better world together. Let this series add a small brick to that structure.

Beijing, Autumn 2003

CONTENTS

LIST OF ILLUSTRATIONS

CHAPTER I

This Land is Ours!

C HINA'S modern history began when her common people first stood up and said: "This land is ours!"

It has always been a dangerous thing to say.

Back in the eighteen-fifties, after China had suffered her first defeat at the hands of the foreign Powers and had been compelled to cede Hongkong and a number of concessions and to open her coastal ports to foreign trade, the leaders of the great Taiping peasant rebellion had said it to the Manchu imperial Government. Ten years of war and twenty million lives were the forfeit, yet the Mandarins kept the land. Only the aid of foreign guns and foreign volunteers, like Franco's, enabled them to do it.*

In 1900, the "Boxers" said it, after China had lost, in quick succession, Annam and Tonking to the French, Formosa and Korea to Japan, Tsingtao to the Germans, Port Arthur to the Czar, and Weihaiwei to Great Britain. The "Boxers" were misled, betrayed, and destroyed. The Chinese people are still paying for the perfidy and cowardice of their rulers at that time.

---

* The imperial army was re-armed and re-organized under the direction of General "Chinese" Gordon, who was later to perish at Khartoum. Another prominent "volunteer" of the period was Frederick Townsend Ward, an American.

1

Western and Japanese trained intellectuals said it throughout the next ten years. They fought and suffered and agitated; they lost their newspapers, their homes, and their heads. There had been revolutions in Russia and Turkey. In China, the party which was later to be called the Kuomintang was formed. In 1911, with the aid of other groups, it overthrew the Manchu dynasty and laid the groundwork for a new stage in Chinese history. (The last emperor and ministers of the dynasty now grace the puppet Court of "Manchukuo".)

The rebellious South-west said it when a traitor President of the Republic signed, in 1915, the Twenty-one Demands designed to give Japan virtual overlordship in China. Within a year the President, Yuan Shih-kai, had tried to make himself Emperor, had seen the death-blow given to his hopes, and had died.

1919. For the first time, the students shouted it in the streets. The Treaty of Versailles, fruit of idealism and guardian of self-determination, had turned over to Japan the province of Shantung, previously filched from China by the Germans. A Japanese-bought government acquiesced. (Several members of this Government are now "Ministers" in Japan's puppet show at Peiping.)

Students fell under police bullets in the streets of Peking and were buried in the earth which they had refused to see signed away without their consent. There had been revolutions in Russia, Germany, Austria, and Hungary. In China, industry had developed rapidly during the War, and with it a labour movement. The Chinese Communist Party was founded in 1920.

In literature, young writers revolted against the barren classicism of the past and put down in writing for the first time the everyday speech of the people. With a few thousand characters, anyone could now read. Without being laughed at as a boor ignorant of classical forms, he could write — as he spoke. Anyone could understand a book or newspaper read aloud.

The Washington Conference and the Nine-Power Pact forced Japan to disgorge part of the concessions which she had extorted from China while the Western Powers were fighting each other in Europe. Meanwhile, in North

China, rival militarists battled to decide whether Japan or Great Britain would have first call on the country's resources. The Kuomintang and the Communist Party, both of which had said for the Chinese people, "This land is ours!", were illegal in the territories of these war-lords. (Now Chang Tso-lin, the Japanese-backed war-lord, is dead, killed by his patrons when he waxed too independent. The other, Wu Pei-fu, sits amidst wine-bottles and books of poetry in Peiping, deciding whether or not to head a puppet State for the Japanese.)

The Kuomintang entrenched itself at Canton in the South. The Kuomintang was aggressively nationalist. A party of industrialists and intellectuals, its aims were to break the stranglehold of foreign-dictated tariffs which was crippling Chinese industry, to destroy the feudal landholding system which paralysed modern industrial growth, and to unite the country by driving out the Northern militarists — defenders of feudalism and tools of foreign intrigue.

The immediate aims of the Communists, a workers' and peasants' party, were the same. Like the Kuomintang, they were interested in breaking the hold of the foreign Powers on the country; interested in the development of industry and a stronger working class; interested in the destruction of feudalism and feudal militarism throughout the land.

The Kuomintang led the rising urban middle class. The Communist Party, although organized only a few years before, had demonstrated its ability to lead and to organize the workers in the cities and the peasants in the villages. Dr. Sun Yat-sen, father of the national-revolutionary movement in China, realized that only by the joint action of these classes and of the two parties could the aims of both be attained. In 1923, an alliance between them was concluded. Together they crushed a revolt in Canton which was headed by a feudal Kwangtung militarist and the compradore of the British Hongkong and Shanghai Bank, which backed the rebels as a bulwark against "Communism". (To-day, the militarist, Chen Chiung-ming, is dead — but his followers fought in the invasion of South China as Japanese hirelings. The compradore, Chan Lim-pak, was Japan's first choice for puppet mayor of conquered Canton.)*

The Southern alliance went for support to the people:

"This land is ours," said the students, and although British rifles shot them down in Shanghai and Canton, a nation-wide movement continued to say it.

"This land is ours," said the workers, and in a general strike they paralysed Hongkong and tied up British trade in China's ports.

"This land is ours," said the peasants as they smashed the power of the landlord and usurer in their villages and, gun on shoulder, marched in the revolutionary army against the strongholds of the Northern militarists. The rotten structure of feudal China tottered as they advanced.

Dr. Sun Yat-sen died in the spring of 1925.

Two years after his death the alliance between the parties, between all groups thwarted by the backward state in which China was being kept, broke down. The Kuomintang exchanged the support of the workers and peasants for a bloc with the landlords and compradores. No longer could the common man say that the land was his — for the land was in pawn. The Communists perished under the knives of executioners or retired to mountain fastnesses, where they continued to organize the disinherited.

Then followed ten of the saddest years in China's history. Because the great drive of the Southern armies ended not in the dethronement of feudalism but in a compromise with it, new civil wars between generals were fought. Because the common man continued to rebel, countless armies were thrown against the strongholds of the Communists, whose very existence was regarded as the inspiration for his rebellion.

---

* The first great action of the Chinese working class against the pressure of reactionary feudalism and foreign imperialism, the general strike of 20,000 workers of the Peking-Hankow railway in February 1923, was led by the young Communist Party. The strikers demanded only the right to organize unions. For this, 200 of them, and also a progressive lawyer who had volunteered to defend them in court, were brutally massacred by the police of British-backed Wu Pei-fu, who suppressed the strike. 1923 also saw the organization of the first Peasant Unions in the vicinity of Canton.

From the point of view of the Japanese, the situation was perfect — and they took advantage of it. It was easy for them, in 1931, to wrest Manchuria from a China which had just emerged from a great civil war and was now beginning a new campaign against the Red Republic in Kiangsi — a China estranged, for internal political reasons, from the only other country bordering on Manchuria — the Soviet Union.

From the beginning, the people of Manchuria refused to accept slavery. Although the main armies had withdrawn, tens of thousands of soldiers, hundreds of thousands of armed peasants and workers, and a number of generals continued to resist the conquerors. While in China south of the Great Wall the generals still fought the people, in Manchuria all who opposed the invader were united. The names of the Manchurian militarists who joined the Japanese have vanished in a haze of obloquy. The generals who resisted became national heroes — known throughout the world. Who has forgotten the elusive Ma Chan-shan, his stand on the Nonni River, and the chase he led the Japanese through the Manchurian forests?

No troops moved into Manchuria from the South. The Nanking Government placed its hopes in the League of Nations, of which both China and Japan were members. The League produced only moral lectures.

The Manchurian volunteers fought on alone.

In 1932, Japan struck at Shanghai. Who has forgotten the exploits of the heroic Nineteenth Route Army which held them there for two months?

During the fighting, the Chinese Soviets in Kiangsi published an offer to join forces with any military unit marching against the Japanese.

A Sino-Japanese truce was signed in Shanghai. The Government, confident that the Japanese would now be satisfied with Manchuria, turned to its old pursuit of "internal pacification." New definitions of "treason" were invented. To say that it was possible to fight the Japanese before the suppression of the Communists was treason. To agitate for the return of Manchuria — treason. To collect money for the volunteers — treason.

The anti-Japanese heroes of the Nineteenth Route Army, withdrawn from Shanghai, were sent to Fukien to fight the Red Army. They fought for a year. Then they rebelled and formed a new government. The revolt did not gather strength and collapsed after Nanking's planes had bombed Foochow. The planes had been bought by popular subscription — for use against Japan.

The Japanese encroached further upon North China. The Shanghai "truce" was followed by the Tangku "truce." Henceforth, a part of the North was to be turned into a "demilitarized zone." That is, Chinese troops were not to be permitted to enter, but Japanese troops, by virtue of that holy script, the Boxer Protocol, could move as they liked along the railways. The Tangku capitulation gave Japanese aircraft the right to survey the territory to see that this unilateral demilitarization was fully carried out.

In the summer of 1935 came another humiliation. The Ho-Umetsu "agreement" was stuffed down the throat of supine China. By its terms, Central Government troops were expelled from the provinces of Hopei and Chahar. No units of China's ruling party, the Kuomintang, could function in these provinces — not even in the great cities of Peiping and Tientsin. Anti-Japanese patriots were to be prosecuted. A regional administration was to be created, employing Japanese "advisors".

The Chinese army was away chasing the Communists on the borders of Tibet.

Japanese officials and the Japanese Press openly discussed the forthcoming separation of five northern provinces — Hopei, Chahar, Shansi, Shantung, and Suiyuan — from the authority of the Central Government. Shansi has coal reserves sufficient, says the *Encyclopaedia Britannica*, to last the whole world for a thousand years. Hopei is rich in coal, wheat, and cotton. Chahar and Suiyuan have iron, hides, and wool; Shantung, coal, cotton, and wheat. These provinces, said Japanese theorists, would form an economic bloc with Japan and "Manchukuo" and provide raw materials for the Imperial dream of world conquest.

But the dreams of the Japanese were never to materialize. Then and there, this new encroachment met from the Chinese people the resistance which the Chinese Government had not dared to make. On December 9 and

16, 1935, thousands of Peiping students, braving the carbines of Sung Cheh-yuan's police and the machine-guns which the Japanese threatened to turn against them, paraded through the ancient city with slogans which were to become the watchwords of the National Salvation Movement, then of the Sian revolt, and finally of the United Front for National Resistance. In 1935, however, "Down with Japanese Imperialism" and "Stop Civil War to Fight Japan" were rank treason, and a number of students paid for their boldness with their lives. Japan was officially a "friendly Power" — and to suggest that civil war existed was heresy. The endless campaign against the Red Armies was not civil war but a punitive expedition against "bandits".

Nonetheless, the Peiping demonstrations and the wave of protest they aroused throughout the country checked the immediate plans of the Japanese. To shoot down these boys and girls would have been dangerous (history showed that the entire nation had begun to move after the massacres of students in 1919 and 1925), and the fever into which their patient had suddenly been thrown made the Japanese surgeons pause before undertaking another operation on the body of the Chinese giant. It was necessary first to calm him down and to administer more anaesthetic.

But it was too late for anaesthetics.

Through the students of Peiping, the people of China had said to the Japanese: "This land is ours, and you will not take it without war." To their own Government, they had declared: "This land is ours. You shall not sign it away."

The Peiping "agreement" of June 1935, concluded between China's Minister of War, General Ho Ying-chin, and the commander of the Japanese North China garrison, General Umetsu, was the last instrument of capitulation the Central Government was to sign.

Half a year after the student demonstrations came a real test for China's unity. The military leaders of Canton and Kwangsi had long nursed ambitions of attaining national power. Now they prepared to march against Nanking and to muster support throughout the country by waving the anti-Japanese banner. The Peiping events had shocked and disquieted Japan.

But this new development did not worry her particularly. She sat back and hoped — for civil war.

She even discreetly and in devious ways gave comfort to the incipient rebels of the South, though they marched under anti-Japanese slogans. What matter what they shouted, so long as they fought, and China's painfully accumulated store of armaments and her carefully trained divisions of regulars were wasted in the struggle?

But the students who had cried "Down with Civil War" in the streets of Peiping had not done it, as was charged by the authorities, merely as a veiled attack on the Government.* They had expressed the deep-rooted conviction of the entire Chinese people that in the face of the Japanese danger all internal strife must stop. And despite its slogans, the Southern adventure did not result in a civil war. On the contrary, the people of Kwangtung utterly refused to support it — and without a struggle the diarchy of years was ended and the South was brought under the administration of the Central Government.

That summer, the Red Army marched into Shansi province with the slogan: "Chinese Must Not Fight Chinese. We Demand an Anti-Japanese National Defence Government!"

At the same time, a significant incident took place when the Japanese sought to extend their feelers to Chengtu, in the Far West. They sent "investigators" to visit the city preparatory to opening a consulate there — something they had insisted on despite the fact that they had no trade in the region and that the Central Government had strenuously objected to their doing so. The investigators never came back. Demonstrators in the streets of Chengtu

---

* At the time of the demonstrations, Professor Tao Hsi-sheng, of the Peiping University, published a statement to the effect that the student upheaval was financed from Moscow. This became a stock joke in Peiping, and the students themselves laughingly claimed that the allegation was highly useful to them — since the printers, long unpaid, who were producing their propaganda materials, agreed to grant them credit after reading it! What no one knew was where the learned professor had obtained the money to pay for the full-page newspaper advertisements in which he made his charges. But a guess may be hazarded on the strength of the fact that, to-day, three years later he is in the camp of Wang Ching-wei and one of the chief proponents of the Japanese brand of "peace in East Asia". History finds its own.

tore them to pieces.

In the autumn, the Japanese organized a mercenary Mongol army to invade the province of Suiyuan. Instead of negotiations, capitulation, and a Chinese withdrawal, they met resistance. Chinese forces, which included Central Government troops, won an important victory at Pailingmiao. The whole country went wild with enthusiasm. "We are not afraid of the Japanese," said the puzzled, matter-of-fact, professional soldiers of the Suiyuan garrison. "But what are we to do with the delegations? Every day more of them come. How are we to feed them? Where are they all from, all these students and workers and women and members of the professions who come with gifts in their hands?"

"This land is ours!" felt the people of North China. "Why should we not pay tribute to those who defend it?" The lesson was not lost on the troops. They had not been bothered with delegations and with volunteer ambulance units when they had fought in the civil wars. No one had called them heroes. They were of the disinherited, and now, for the first time, they too began to feel: "This land, and all these people — are ours."

In Shanghai, Tsingtao, and Tientsin, there occurred a development of tremendous importance. More than a hundred thousand workers in Japanese textile mills walked out in a general strike.* The demands of the strike were economic, but its background was political. A hundred thousand Chinese workers were demonstrating their solidarity with the fighters in Suiyuan. "Why should we be exploited by the invaders of our country?" was their slogan.

The strike lasted a month. Although the authorities attempted to suppress it, as they did all popular movements at this time, the entire Chinese people recognized it as an event of the greatest national significance. In

---

* Among forward-looking circles in China — the importance of the strike as the first participation of the great mass of the people in the anti-Japanese struggle was immediately recognized. At a round table discussion with a group of six young Chinese journalists in Tientsin during the last days of 1936, which had witnessed the South-western and Sian crises, I asked everyone to reply to the question: "What was the outstanding event of the year in China?" Three of my six friends replied — "the anti-Japanese strikes".

Tsingtao, the Japanese landed marines to terrorize the strikers — half-starved cotton operatives, the majority of them women. Then every patriot in China realized that these ragged workers were leading the battle of the whole nation. They who were most exploited, whose every day of lost earnings meant hunger, were standing firm against the national enemy. In Shanghai, the strike did more than anything else to accelerate the formation and strengthening of the united front of patriotic Chinese of every class against Japanese encroachment. The All-China National Salvation Association formed a committee to defend, aid, and comfort the anti-Japanese strikers. On the committee were a prominent magazine publisher, the dean of Shanghai University's College of Law, and two other jurists, a writer, an educationalist, and a noted banker. It was an augury for the future.

The Government, whose waverings were by this time crystallizing more and more towards a policy of resistance, was appalled by the growing wave of popular anti-Japanese activity which threatened to force its hand. Taking up the challenge, it threw the whole committee into prison on a charge of "endangering the safety of the Republic", for which death was the maximum penalty. The arrests stirred all Chinese society. In the highest ruling circles, General Feng Yu-hsiang, Inspector-General of the army, and other important officials openly voiced their disapproval. The anti-Japanese united front grew in scope and strength.

In the meantime, fighting had ceased between the Red Army and the "Bandit Suppression" troops of the North-west. The Communists marched with anti-Japanese slogans, and their "suppressors" were Manchurians whose one wish was to come to grips with the enemy who had driven them from their homes. But in theory the anti-Red campaign still continued. There was an effort, a last effort, to make it continue in practice. New troops arrived — and were defeated. An order was issued transferring the Manchurians, who would not fight, to another section of the country. The result was spectacular. Generalissimo Chiang Kai-shek, who came to see that the war against the Communists was really carried on, was imprisoned by the Manchurian troops and confronted with the United Front programme. This programme included

THIS LAND IS OURS!

a demand for the release of the "Seven Leaders" arrested in Shanghai.

According to the evidence of Madame Chiang Kai-shek herself, the then current version that the Communists had connived at the kidnapping was entirely incorrect. Hurriedly summoned for consultation, they insisted that the Generalissimo be freed. By doing so they proved the sincerity of their offers of co-operation with the Central Government against Japan and their insistent demand that an end be brought to any and every kind of civil war.

Thus a major and tragic internal military struggle was avoided, and the Generalissimo returned to Nanking to receive one of the most enthusiastic welcomes in Chinese history from three-quarters of a million people who saw in his release the end of civil strife.

During the crisis all patriotic Chinese had registered a number of unanimous and instinctive reactions.

They had opposed the demand of certain ambitious Nanking generals, anxious to get rid of the "rebels" and Chiang at the same time, for an immediate punitive expedition. (The Japanese had given tacit offers to suspend all provocations if such a campaign was launched, had withdrawn the marines landed to suppress the strikers in Tsingtao, and had even promised military co-operation in any action against the North-west. Oh for another civil war in China!)

They had sympathized with the programme of national unity advocated by the Manchurian leaders, while completely condemning the kidnapping.

They were tremendously relieved by the safe return of the Generalissimo, and they rightly interpreted the peaceful solution of the crisis as a sign that henceforth the only fighting the Chinese army would do would be against the Japanese.

Chiang Kai-shek, having gone through the experience of being made a prisoner by Government troops, released through the influence of the Reds, whom he had regarded as his worst enemies, and almost done to death by the bombers which his most "loyal" generals were all too ready to unleash over the place of his captivity, had ample reason to re-examine his own position and policies. He seems to have clearly realized at last that the whole basis of his power had changed. It became evident that the continuance of the line which he had tried to force upon the Manchurian troops at Sian would inevitably lead to endless civil war, increasing Japanese encroachment, and popular dissatisfaction so widespread that it would threaten his power. On the other hand, he could, by putting himself at the head of the popular movement against civil war and for effective anti-Japanese resistance, consolidate his position on a political basis far firmer than the doubtful loyalty of a few personal henchmen and the conventional allegiance of bureaucratic groups between which he held the balance of power. He could become in a real sense the leader of the country, the symbol behind which all sections of the population would rally. After Sian, he began to move in this direction. The succeeding months were to show that both from the point of view of his own position, and of the interests of the nation, his choice was a wise one.

"This land is ours!", all political groups had declared in response to Sian. "It is ours in common, and no single individual or clique can sign away its integrity, squander its energies in civil war, or deny our right to participate in the defence of our common heritage." The enemy was at the gates. Only by the united effort of all parties linked in a democratic federation could China survive. The experience of the 1927 revolution had shown the rewards of such unity. The years of civil war and national humiliation had been the penalty for its abandonment, the suicidal result of efforts to suppress by force the aspirations of the people.

The first condition of real unity was internal democracy, giving every group the opportunity to truly develop its power to contribute to the country's struggle for survival.

The Chinese people had long realized this. The result of Sian was that the Government and army also were brought face to face with the pressing demands of the hour.

Three factors were responsible for the forging of the unity against which Japan has now baffled in vain for almost two years:

The first was the growing conviction among all classes in China that further capitulation before Japan spelled ruin for every section of the Chinese people. Ruthless Japanese encroachment laid the groundwork for this conviction. United Front propaganda gave it form and a programme of action.

The second was the consistent adherence by the Communists to the policy of democratic anti-Japanese unity which they had been elaborating since the invasion of Manchuria. The Sian incident, in which the Manchurian armies, having captured Chiang Kai-shek, called them in for consultation, gave the Communist leaders the power to decide the fate of the man who for ten years had done his utmost to exterminate them. Yet they unhesitatingly insisted on his release and return to power, not as a quixotic gesture, but because any other course would have led to civil war at a moment when all China, with the exception of hopeless reactionaries and simple traitors, was crying for unity.

The third factor was Chiang Kai-shek himself. His imprisonment and the events which followed it opened his mind to facts regarding the situation within the country of which he must to some extent have been kept ignorant by those who had surrounded him. An astute politician who had built the edifice of his power in the past by bringing under his banner every potentially-dangerous group whose hostility could be tempered by the sweets of office, he saw that he had left out of this carefully erected structure the strongest political force of all — the democratic and national aspirations of the Chinese people themselves. Japan was driving him to the wall. He saw clearly that for China's survival and his own it was necessary to go with the tide and not to oppose it. He made his choice and has kept to it unwaveringly.

The whole country adopted a new slogan: "Support the leader against Japan." The old Kuomintang slogan had been simply "Support the leader." The two additional words contained in embryo the whole meaning of the transformation wrought in Chinese politics. Chiang Kai-shek had been "leader" unconditionally, but, as the Sian incident showed, his power had been built on sand. Now, after Sian, he had become really a leader, with all parties, including the Communists, putting themselves under his orders. But to this leadership a condition was attached. It was to be leadership against Japan — leadership in harmony with the life-interests of the great

Chinese people. Chiang Kai-shek had been the chief of a military dictatorship, sitting uneasily atop a boiling cauldron of internal contradictions. He was now the highest commander of a united people in its struggle for existence.

Of course, the transformation did not come overnight. The heritage of the past was sloughed off slowly and painfully. The liberation of political prisoners began, but many remained in jail, including the seven leaders of the National Salvation movement. Anti-Japanese publications were still occasionally suppressed. Efforts to organize the people for patriotic activities still met with official suspicion and obstruction. These things took long in disappearing.

But although the results of Sian did not become completely apparent until the outbreak of the war six months later, it was evident to all informed observers that the turning-point had come.

To the Japanese, the events of 1936 must have appeared unutterably alarming. First, on the eve of the New Year, their scheme for the separation of the five Northern provinces had been thwarted by the student demonstrations in the streets of Peiping. A civil war for which they had waited with bated breath had failed to materialize, resulting only in a new increase in the power of the Central Government. An attempt to swallow Suiyuan as six counties in Chahar had been swallowed was staunchly resisted. The strikes in the cotton-mills had given notice that the masses of the great cities had begun to move. Finally, the greatest crisis of all not only failed to destroy the unity that had thus far been achieved but, on the other hand, had made it complete — with resistance to aggression as its foundation and cementing principle. A day before the Generalissimo's release, the Japanese had rejoiced at the prospect of a great upheaval, in the course of which they hoped to use the power of the Central Government to smash the rising popular movement. They had hoped that the civil war would end with Nanking finally and hopelessly committed to capitulation. Within twenty-four hours, they saw all prospect, not only of capitulation, but even of compromise, recede into the distance. The unity they had feared and fought against for twenty years had finally come to China.

In the Northern provinces, the results of this change were immediately felt. Sung Cheh-yuan, chairman of the semi-autonomous Hopei-Chahar Political Council, had been passively resisting for over a year all Japanese proposals for "economic co-operation" — meaning the exploitation of North China's resources by the Japanese and for the Japanese, but financed by Chinese money. The Japanese had been confident of their ability finally to threaten Sung into satisfying part, at least, of their demands, but this confidence was based on the assumption that he would continue to play a lone hand, with the Central Government too timorous to back him up in a crisis. Now things were changing. For the first time since 1935, the military and political weight, not only of Sung and his 29th Army, but of China as a whole, was again opposed to the Japanese bid for control of the North. And China as a whole was in a highly different condition from that of two years before. All the painstaking Japanese efforts to achieve the demoralization of the local army and administration had gone for nothing — and in place of "independence", North China was fast returning to the orbit of Nanking.

For circumstances such as these, Japanese wisdom knew only one remedy: to provoke a conflict, strike a blow — then watch carefully for the result. If Sung should capitulate or fail to get backing from the Central Government, profound demoralization would set in within the Chinese camp, and there might even be a renewal of civil war. If, on the other hand, Nanking would regard the provocation as a challenge to a test of strength and send its troops north, it would be clear that only a heavy military defeat could check China's growing strength in unity. Japan did not anticipate any great difficulty in inflicting such a defeat in the shortest period of time. The plan was foolproof.

This was the genesis of the "incident" at Lukouchiao (Marco Polo Bridge) which precipitated the war.

What has happened since has shown that even the wisdom of the Japanese war-lords has its limitations. It has shown that even the world's best spy service cannot help a clique of international housebreakers to understand the rebirth of a people, the unconquerable strength of millions of human beings fighting for their homes.

For almost two years now, Japan has fought against the Chinese people by methods resembling those of Genghis Khan more than those of any modern conqueror. She has taken a number of cities. On almost every front she has, by the force of her superior armaments, repeatedly pushed back the Chinese army. But she has never annihilated its main force, which remains intact for an ultimate counter-offensive.

The decaying feudal heritage of the past, on which she based her hopes for a quick conquest of China, has indeed brought her a few easy victories. But greater by far than the number of such triumphs has been the number of cases in which she has encountered unexpectedly strong resistance both from the army and the people. And wherever popular resistance has once begun, it has not died, but, on the contrary, has grown, despite all the savagery and terror with which the Japanese have hoped to suppress it. This has been because, wherever they have gone, the invaders have proved by their behaviour that normal life is impossible for the population until they have been driven out. But now there is more than this — there is more than desperation. The people fight because they know, from successes already achieved, that they can cope with the enemy. And they fight because in many areas they have built, in the midst of the struggle, a life better than they knew before, in which rents and taxes have been lightened and the common man has come to rule himself. It is not only for what they possessed before the war that the people of China are fighting: it is also for what they have gained, and for the new confidence that by their own efforts and struggles they can gain much more.

That is why the Japanese will not win this war. That is why China's four hundred millions, with a new consciousness of their great power and their great potential wealth, are at last arising to struggle for their own existence and to build for their own future.

With blood and with sweat, with new energy and with new confidence they say it — no longer in small and hunted groups, no longer in one section of the population rather than another — but unitedly as one people in the face of one common threat which menaces the existence and the future of all:

"THIS LAND IS OURS!"

CHAPTER II

Songs of Resistance

"Arise, all who will not be slaves
Our flesh and blood will be the new great wall."

SUCH are the first lines of the "March of the Manchurian Volunteers". Inspired by the heroic struggles of the people of Manchuria to free themselves from the Japanese yoke, this stirring chant has captured the heart and imagination of the whole country. From the front lines to the great cities, and from the cities to the remotest villages, every Chinese knows it and every Chinese sings it.

The history of the "March of the Volunteers" is the history of the rising tide of resistance to Japanese aggression. Both its music and its words sprang from the depths of the Chinese people, from the dark Chinese reality of the period of capitulation.

Nieh Erh, composer of the "March", was a natural genius; and his appearance in the Chinese musical world was a portent, a flash illuminating the tremendous talent lying hidden in China's masses of lowly and oppressed. Born in the distant South-western province of Yunnan, Nieh Erh early took up the Chinese worker's heritage of hunger and bark-breaking toil. First he was a coolie, then a soldier. In 1933, he made his way to Shanghai. Somehow,

17

he acquired a mouth-organ, and through much labour and great love made himself a complete master of this modest instrument. His playing won the appreciation and encouragement of a Shanghai moving-picture director, who provided him with an opportunity to study the piano and the violin. With his almost savage application to work, Nieh Erh became a competent performer within a few months. Then he took up composition. In 1934, he wrote "The Great Road", theme-song of the moving-picture of that name.

"The Great Road" was a pioneer effort in cinematographic realism in China, a portrayal of the solidarity, power, and fighting spirit of the people whom Nieh Erh knew and from whom he had sprung. "On the great road we shed our sweat and our blood together" sing his toilers along the highway.

"Together, together we strain at our loads.

Together we fear neither iron nor pain.

All forward together! Our battle is common!

The great road to freedom together we'll tread!"

Nieh Erh's talent made him a singer. His utter artistic integrity, his organic loyalty to the masses which had given him birth, made him a singer of the people. It was logical that he should write the people's hymn of resistance.

But Nieh Erh was never to see the Chinese people answer his call. He was never to hear his songs on the lips of millions of fighters for China's liberation, fighters at last "Together", but without Nieh Erh.

In 1934, the pressure of censorship made impossible the further progress of the realistic cinema. Nieh Erh left Shanghai for Japan, where he hoped to continue his musical education. After a few months in Japan, he planned to go to the Soviet Union to study the new music of that country. He was tremendously optimistic and productive in those days. Then he went swimming at the seaside resort of Kuganuna and was drowned. The circumstances were mysterious, and the state of the body suggested that he might first have been stunned and then thrown into the stream. He was only twenty-four when he perished.

Nieh Erh is dead, but he continues to sing in a million voices.

The words of the "March" were written by Tien Han, most vital and talented of China's new dramatists. Tien Han has suffered for his early championship of the cause of resistance. For more than two years he languished under arrest in Nanking. Released after the outbreak of the war, he was quickly given a part in the Chinese Army's newly-organized Political Department, the potentially all-important organ whose function is to teach the soldier that he is fighting for the people, and the people that the army, long an alien force, is now theirs. To-day Tien Han heads the Arts Section of the Department. Under his guidance, the new theatre that he founded has taken its place as an important factor of resistance, with scores of mobile troupes carrying the message of struggle to the army and the people. In his department, too, work the creators of China's magnificent war posters.

When I first heard the "March of the Volunteers", it was still forbidden. It was four months before the outbreak of the war, in Tientsin, in North China, a city already controlled in all but name by the Japanese army and its secret service.

I had heard vaguely of a "mass singing movement" which had been launched in connection with the work of the All-China National Salvation Association in Shanghai. The whole idea had sounded strange. Apart from the wordless work-chants of the coolies and interminable falsetto arias from ancient operas — the Chinese did not ordinarily sing. In *Red Star Over China*, Edgar Snow has told how the Chinese Red Army sang its way across the 8,000 miles of the epic Long March, but few knew this at the time. This particular "singing movement" had as its most active promoter a young Y.M.C.A. secretary named Liu Liang-mo, who had been educated in a Shanghai mission college and had later attended a Christian conference in California. I had visions of an earnest young purveyor of spirituality and "pep" scanning through horn-rimmed glasses the horizon of the growing movement for popular resistance to see whether it offered possibilities of planting new Y.M.C.A. glee-clubs.

Then a friend told me that Liu had come to Tientsin from Suiyuan, where he had taught his songs to the troops who had held the Japanese and their Mongol mercenaries at bay through the winter's fighting. That afternoon he would inaugurate the mass singing movement in the gymnasium of the local Y.M.C.A. Would I come?

From the street, before I reached the building, I heard the harsh, passionate, and emphatic strains of a new type of Chinese song. It was the kind of song one has to hear only once to remember. Its abrupt, triumphant phrases were like those of a last-minute fighting speech delivered by a tense and hoarse-voiced commander to determined men on the eve of an attack. The doors of the hall were open. Inside, about four hundred people stood and sang. They were ordinary people from the street — students, petty clerks, workmen, schoolchildren, newsboys, and even ricksha pullers, who stood near the door keeping an eye on their vehicles outside. With serious faces they repeated the separate phrases of the song they were being taught. Then they sang two phrases at a time. Then a whole stanza, of which every line was a slogan, an embodiment of the things they had all thought, but to which they had not known how to give common expression — an outburst of feelings long suppressed.

"A crisis has come for the people of China

And now each of us is driven to give one last cry —

Arise! Arise! Arise!"

Lin Liang-mo was completely absorbed in his work. Young, slim, and finely-drawn, he seemed to be listening to and prompting each singer separately, while at the same time he himself never stopped singing. He seemed two men — one singing, like his audience with relieved passion at being able at last to utter the "one last cry" of every Chinese; the other disciplined and methodical, teaching and listening.

This man was no mere organizer of glee-clubs, rejoicing in a successful sing-song. He was a portent. He was developing not a bright idea of his own, but a new way of expression for the latent source of power and dawning consciousness of his people.

In the city, the Japanese had 4,000 troops and an equal or even greater number of spies. It was not surprising therefore that now, on its very first day, they should put in an appearance on the scene of this "dangerous" activity. And they did — two zealous and unmistakably Japanese detectives — brown, broad-shouldered, squat, slightly paunchy men approaching middle age. They walked in with a blatant show of having come in quite by accident, yet so evidently thinking, "This is all uninteresting, except that it may give us a chance to get at you with a rubber truncheon, which will really be absorbing and enjoyable," that the singing in their vicinity began to waver. Some of their neighbours began to look first at the door and then at their broad backs, in wistful calculation of the chances of reaching the one while the other remained turned.

Liu saw them too, but he avoided the appearance of having done so. He kept on singing phrase after phrase, which the hall repeated after him addressing himself especially to the group around the detectives whose flagging enthusiasm he stimulated by energetic gestures. In this way he finished the song. Then he turned quite away from the Japanese, the tension of the song disappeared from his face and figure, and he addressed his audience almost casually in easy conversational tones: "The doors of this hall are wide open to anyone who wants to come in to learn to sing our songs. I assume that every friend who comes in does so for this purpose. If anyone does not sing, he must be here for some reason of his own — perhaps to try to disturb us. I will now ask everyone to look at his neighbour and see if he is singing." For just an instant he looked hard at the Japanese, then, straightening up, began the "March of the Volunteers", which his hearers already knew.

Everyone looked at his neighbour and within a few minutes the gaze of all four hundred was fixed on the square, pudgy figures of the detectives, while the "March" rang out proudly:

"Millions are as one,
Braving enemy cannon,
Onward!
Braving enemy cannon!
Onward, Onward, Onward! On!"

The Japanese grew red, fidgeted, looked away from the hundreds of eyes. Finally their lips began to move, reluctantly forming the Chinese words, "Arise, all who will not be slaves" as they pushed their way towards the door.

The meeting went on for another hour on a rising note of enthusiasm. When it ended, Liu had recruited ten young men, who, after several hours of personal instruction from him, were ready to organize and head permanent groups of their own.

Collar open, and his face and body showing clearly the exhaustion of which there had been no sign during the four hours on the platform, Liu smiled at me over the cup of tea he was gulping down. "That was a critical moment for all our work here. You know that we are technically not anti-Japanese and we use no songs in which the word 'Japanese' occurs. This is the only basis on which we are tolerated. If I had said nothing to-day, the people would have drifted away. Such a flop at our first meeting would have been fatal. They are not used to free action of any kind, and they have learned to be afraid of the Japs. Any appearance of being cowed or even passive would have nullified the effect of the songs. You cannot shout patriotic slogans, then fade away in the face of the enemy. On the other hand, if I had spoken out boldly, I could easily have got them to throw those fellows out. But then there would have been an 'incident', demands, arrests, new humiliations. That too would mean the end of our work here. And that wouldn't do, the work must go on.

"The work must go on. You do not realize how important an instrument an easily-learned song is. Many of our people do not read. Anyone making speeches to them would be arrested. But the song carries the slogans of resistance from mouth to mouth. Mass singing brings with it a consciousness of strength and unity. And nothing can stop the spread of a song. In a few days these ten boys will have created ten new singing groups. Each group will produce new enthusiasts who will lead groups of their own. They will know what they are singing, and why."

He introduced me to the new group-leaders, one by one, "This one is a student. This one will go on teaching in the Y.M.C.A. This one is a railway worker; this one a textile worker; this one a street peddler; this one —"

As I was leaving, he pressed my hand and said, "You understand, when the time comes our groups of singers will be ready to become groups of fighters."

During the preceding six months Liu had been working in Shanghai, in Fukien, in Peiping and Tientsin, and then the Suiyuan war zone.

A few days after Liu's departure I was walking along the street. A workman walked by swinging his tools and whistling, "The March of the Volunteers". One heard it more and more often as the weeks went by. "What is that song?" Europeans asked. "All the Chinese are singing it."

What the pudgy detectives and their superiors did about all this is not recorded, but it was obviously too late for truncheons.

* * *   * * *

As the movement grew, new songs appeared — songs for workers, peasants and soldiers, songs for students and songs for women. There were good songs and bad songs, but all were sung because so great was the demand that the composers and librettists could not keep up with it. The whole country sang.

From the stifling atmosphere of the Japanese-dominated cities of North China the youth poured out in the fields and hills on camping and hiking trips. On summer days, thousands at a time marched out of Peiping into the nearby Western Hills, where they scrambled up the steep slopes and held meetings and sang songs. A few months later, many of them, fighting partisans now, were to swoop down from these same slopes on isolated Japanese detachments.

In a hundred places, where no organizer had been able to penetrate, the new songs fought the battle of the united national front, fired the imagination of the youth, and directed its energies toward the national struggle. The Y.M.C.A., for instance, was one such old skin bursting with new wine.

For years the Government had banned all independent organizations of the youth, fearing "dangerous thoughts" The Y.M.C.A., on the other hand, was encouraged, petted, and given all facilities. Over its portals was written "No politics enter here", and into it the middle-class youth, Christian and non-Christian, was sent to cool its hot blood in athletics and organizational detail.

Because there was nowhere else to go, the middle-class youth had poured into the Y's. And on their heels came history and the abhorred "politics". In the halls of the Y.M.C.A.'s and the Y.W.C.A.'s young men and women, harassed and spied upon elsewhere, enjoyed the extra-territoriality of undoubted respectability. Here they could talk and think. Thus it was that patriotic songs drowned the hymns, political courses began to displace lectures on Christian ethics, and young social workers, whom the Y.M.C.A. had taught the importance of plan and detail in the organization of clubs and camps, began to turn their talents to the organization of resistance.

It was the same with the Boy Scouts and the athletic societies, all originally created to regiment the youth, to keep it under observation, and to wean it away from the urge to think independently on national problems. But the United Front had no boundaries. So pressing and so evident was the necessity for national unity in the struggle for self-preservation, that even these organizations, created to recruit faithful guardians of the economic and political monopoly of the well-to-do minority, burgeoned with the militant movement for resistance, which was officially condemned as radicalism, and even as "treason".

But nothing could obscure from the eyes of these young men of the middle strata, these sons of officials and merchants and officers and professional men, the facts of their own position. Time was when the future held out to them, at least, the prospect of safe jobs and steady advancement within the Government structure. But now? What would be the future of the budding engineer if Chinese industry was destroyed and the country became the object of Japanese exploitation? What would happen to the student in the military academy if the national army retreated farther and farther, until it was finally reduced to the status of a Japanese-dominated police force against the Chinese people — the inevitable result of further capitulation? The duty-free influx of Japanese goods would kill the manufacturer. Could the future teacher look forward with equanimity to teaching from specially-prepared texts the virtues proper to an enslaved race? Before the eyes of all was the plight of every class of Chinese under the Japanese heel in Manchuria and East Hopei. For the middle class, as for the myriads of China's toilers, the future became a choice between degradation and struggle.

Months before freedom of speech and the Press came to China, the fighting song awakened greater and greater numbers to the circumstances of their position.

Later, Liu Liang-mo told me of a case in which this was graphically illustrated. "Just a few days before Marco Polo Bridge," he said, "I was leading a group of middle-school students in a three-day camp in the Western Hills near Peiping. The first night, over the camp-fire, I called on every individual student to sing his favourite song. The boys were a mixed group, socially, and the songs they sang reflected their background. The smart young sons of officials and foreign-trained professionals crooned hits from the latest American movies. Sons of small Peiping shopkeepers and clerks sang old romances or patriotic songs. Then one boy got up who was a refugee from Manchuria. He sang two songs — a melancholy air, called 'The Sungari River', describing with all the pain of loss the beauty and the wealth of the mountains, fields and forests of the North-east — and then, passionate, the banned militant song of the Manchurian exiles, 'Tahui Laochia Chu' (Win Back Our Old Home).

"He sang with his heart, and tears glistened in the eyes of some of the boys. Our middle-school students are extremely sentimental. It is easy to move them to demonstrations of feeling. After he had finished, there was silence. Then one student got up, an angular, strongly-built boy from North Kiangsu, the son of a military official. 'That is a traitorous song,' he said harshly. 'Our government has banned it and the whole agitation for the return of Manchuria. We shall fight Japan when we are ready. Such sentimental appeals are calculated to rush us into war before we are prepared. They sabotage our whole plan of resistance. We know these patriots — they sing of the national danger to mask the activities of enemies of the Government. You North-easterners talk of fighting the Japanese and restoring our old frontiers. But all you have done was to kidnap our leader and bring the whole country to the brink of ruin.'

"Although he was repeating almost exactly the arguments by which the reactionaries justified their attempts to suppress the patriotic movement, he was obviously sincere. The strength of his protest impressed some of the boys. But it could not convince them because, living in Peiping, they had seen the Central Army retire before Japanese threats and they had felt the effects of the constant concessions made to the invader.

"The Manchurian got up. He was shaking with anger and humiliation. ' You say that it is treason for us to want to return home, to win back our lost provinces for China. What if your home were burned and you, instead of me, had come back to territory still in our hands, hoping to join with all other Chinese to win back your homeland? And what if I got up and said to you, "We are preparing. If the enemy waits ten years before attacking us here, then we shall be able to repel him. As for your home, it is lost. Even to sing about your love for it is treason"? If I told you this, you would eat tears and bitterness. You would feel as I feel. You would begin to hate not only the enemy. You would begin to hate me also. Is this how you want to unite the nation? Don't think that I alone feel this way. Look at Peiping, our greatest cultural centre. It is going the way of Manchuria. Once it is lost, will it be treason for its people to remember Peiping? Is it treason for our oppressed brothers wherever the Japanese chose to come to think that their duty as patriots is to win back their homes. It is not only Manchuria you are renouncing by this policy — it is our entire Fatherland.'

"He sat down. Many of the boys were crying. One of them got up and shouted, 'Tahui Laochia Chu! Win back our old home!' Sixty voices repeated it. Chang, the student who had attacked him, went back to his tent.

"Two days later young Chang came to see me. 'I have been thinking very hard,' he said, 'and now I know that they were right. We may lose more territory and still survive. But if we forbid our people to remember and to fight, then we are lost. We must not become divided on the question of fighting the enemy. We are all Chinese. But we must do more than shout. I, what can I do, for instance?'

"I asked him to help me with the organization of singing groups. That night, around the camp-fire, he got up and proposed a song — 'Win Back Our Old Home'. The boys were terribly moved, and we had a general discussion, at which I explained that we all wanted unity under the Government — but unity by consent based on common resistance to the national enemy, not unity by coercion while our country capitulated. It was a very successful meeting. Many of the boys undertook to organize groups.

"On the night before we broke camp, the fighting began at Marco Polo Bridge. We held a last meeting at which many students spoke on the meaning of the attempt to take North China by force. We all agreed that the decisive moment had come, that China must fight now.

"I have not seen young Chang again, but he has been writing constantly. During the days before the fall of Peiping, ho organized three groups there — not only to sing but to help the 29th Army. At the battle of Nanyuan he helped bring in the wounded under fire. Now he is back home in North Kiangsu, 100 miles from Shanghai, in the rear of the Japanese. He began by organizing singing groups months before the enemy came. Now he is a district magistrate and commander of a large guerrilla detachment. He is only nineteen, but he is one of the most effective leaders in the district. Once every two or three months a letter comes from him by someone who has managed to get through the lines. He always writes enthusiastic detailed reports of the strengthening of the people's movement in his district, and he never fails to mention that camp-fire meeting."

Of the singing leaders in the North, some are with the guerrillas, some are publishing illegal newspapers in occupied territory, some have perished, and some have come South to work in the army and in the people's organizations. None are passive in the face of the struggle.

Liu Liang-mo himself has set whole cities and provinces singing. But song promotes itself, and there are more urgent things to be done. The plight of the wounded is one great crying need, and in the inferno of Shanghai, under constant bombing in Soochow, and finally in fire-devastated Changsha, he has led groups of worker-students to the fronts of greatest suffering.

Tien Han too works among the ruins of Changsha. The city was destroyed by the hands of the garrison commander, who, once one of the master jailers of progress in China, committed the cowardly crime of burning down the city while the enemy was still 100 miles away. He was executed, and Tien Han is one of those in charge of the rehabilitation of the blasted home of 300,000 people.

As for Nieh Erh, his songs have conquered the country.

"Together" was the watchword of his "Great Road" — and now the people of China are marching together along the great road of national liberation.

"Arise, all who will not be slaves," he sang, and now battalion after battalion of China's millions rises and goes out to battle, singing as a battle-cry the song that was written to rouse a people oppressed and lethargic.

No one will say that Nieh Erh remained inactive in the great struggle — even though Nieh Erh is dead.

CHARTER III
Defiance

W HY did the Japanese attack Marco Polo Bridge on July 7, 1937?

All neutral observers have given only one answer. They did it to test the nature and power of the China that had emerged from the political changes of the past year. The regional administration in the North had begun to meet the paper demands of the Japanese with paper refusals. Behind it stood Nanking. Would Nanking stand behind it when the demands were backed with guns?

This was the basic secret of the Chinese political situation which Japan set out to unearth. It was a secret that spies could not secure, a piece of information to be ferreted out only by well-staged provocation. Tokyo knew long before Hitler and Mussolini that provocation pays. At least when the victim is weak and reluctant to try conclusions. Provocation had won Manchuria. It had created "demilitarized zones", an "autonomous State", and numerous acknowledged Japanese "special interests" throughout China. The last two times the technique had been attempted, it was true, things had not turned out so well. Peiping's 10, 000 students had ruined a neat plan to separate all North China from the authority of the Central Government. And when Japan tried to nibble piece-meal what it had proved impossible to swallow all at once,

28

she had found from the resistance in Suiyuan that it would take more than nibbling. Very well, this time she would try a real show of force.

The Japanese troops in North China at this time numbered about 10,000 — considerably more than they were allowed to keep by the Boxer Treaty. In the beginning of July these troops were turned out for grand manoeuvres. Instead of conducting their exercises on the Peiping-Mukden Railway, along which, by the terms of the same treaty, certain Powers were permitted to station troops, they chose the neighbourhood of Lukouchiao (Marco Polo Bridge) and the district town of Wanping. This town was to be the object of their "hypothetical" attack. Despite the patent illegality of the whole proceeding, the Chinese authorities made no protest. This must have irritated the Japanese, who, as later events showed, were determined to work up an incident there, come what may.

Marco Polo Bridge is not only historically interesting for its association with the great Venetian traveller, or architecturally notable for its marble lions and thirty noble arches. It is also strategically intriguing. It lies on the Peiping-Hankow railway, the only avenue along which Chinese Central Government troops could be rushed directly to Peiping in case anything untoward happened in the city. In the old Imperial days objections had been raised to the jangling to which the shunting of trains and movement of freight from one to another of the three railways converging on Peking would subject the delicate nerves of the Son of Heaven. So a loop line had been built from the Peking-Mukden railway to the Peking-Hankow railway to take the inter-railway traffic past the capital. One terminus of the loop line was the Marco Polo Bridge.*

Possession of Marco Polo Bridge would not only give the Japanese an opportunity to stop Chinese national troops from coming up to the Chinese city of Peiping: it would also give them a direct route to Central China for Japanese troops from "Manchukuo".

---

* For much of the material on the incident I am indebted to Mr. Shusi Hsu's *How the Far Eastern War Was Begun.*

The bridge and the town beyond it were, indeed, a brilliantly-chosen hypothetical objective for the summer manoeuvres. The way to make sure that men engaged in mock warfare will absorb and profit from the tactical lessons the experience is intended to teach is to approximate as far as possible the conditions of actual hostilities. In the Japanese manoeuvres in North China in the summer of 1936, this excellent rule was followed to the letter. The operations were carried out on an earnestly coveted piece of territory belonging to another country. And they were real.

On the night of July 7, Peiping was awakened by the firing of field artillery. Its people emerged from their houses on the morning of the next day to find the city under strict martial law, several of the gates closed, and sandbag barricades being thrown up in the streets.

What had occurred? Another "incident", and one with a typically Japanese flavour. A Japanese unit engaged in the manoeuvres had allegedly found that one of their number was missing. They demanded that they be allowed to march into the district town of Wanping at the far end of Marco Polo Bridge and conduct a house-to-house search until they found him. The Chinese troops on duty had refused. The Japanese tried to force the bridge. Fighting ensued. The Japanese retired and trained their guns on the town, which they bombarded for five successive hours. By morning there were 200 dead and wounded in Wanping. But the Chinese defenders stood their ground. Marco Polo Bridge remained in their hands.

The missing Japanese soldier later turned up. What his name was, how he returned to his unit, and whether he existed at all are items of information which have never been published and rest securely in the archives of the Japanese army. He was a true "unknown soldier" of Japanese imperialism.

High Chinese and Japanese officials rushed to the spot. A "truce" was arranged — both sides to withdraw from the bridge. But instead of withdrawing, the Japanese brought up more men. There were renewed clashes, and still the Chinese soldiers did not concede an inch, but gave back blow for blow. Eleven Japanese troop-trains were ordered from Mukden to Tientsin. Two arrived on January 10. During the next three weeks the trains came in at the rate of several a day, carrying endless streams of men, arms, and supplies. Meanwhile the Chinese local authorities had accepted terms for settlement which provided for abject Chinese apologies, the thorough-going suppression of patriotic activities, and the withdrawal of Chinese troops from Marco Polo Bridge "on account of the fact that their close proximity to the Japanese troops stationed at Fengtai easily causes incidents". This was the official Japanese text.

On July 15, the Japanese announced that they would insist on the expulsion from the Peiping-Tientsin area of the Twenty-ninth Army, the only Chinese Army stationed there.

Things had clearly got out of the "local incident" stage. The Central Government at Nanking announced that it would not authorize the Northern authorities to make any further concessions. To back its words, it began sending troops northward along the Peiping-Hankow railway. However, to show that the door was not closed to negotiation, these troops were concentrated a full 100 miles south of Peiping.

The Japanese replied with the most impudent statements one government has ever made with regard to another with which it continues to maintain relations. They declared to the foreign Press that they would not tolerate "interference" by the Chinese Government in the "local" affairs of North China. To Nanking they sent a virtual ultimatum to "cease immediately its provocative activities". They failed to reply to the proposal by the Chinese Ministry for Foreign Affairs that the question be discussed through diplomatic channels following the withdrawal of both Chinese and Japanese troops.

From all parts of China, a roar of protest went up. The poorly-armed defenders of Marco Polo Bridge had stood up successfully to repeated Japanese assaults. Would not the whole nation back them up? No more retreat, said the voices of China's people. No more humiliation. No more surrender to blackmail. Every Chinese conscious of national problems expected and demanded of his Government that it make a decisive stand.

At Kuling, on July 17, General Chiang Kai-shek announced the Government's decision that the time to make such a stand had come. There would be no further surrender. The Japanese would not succeed in their game of bluff. If they tried to push China to the wall, China would fight.

"There are some people", he said, "who imagine that the Lukouchiao incident was sudden and unpremeditated. But already a month ago there were indications that it would occur....

"The only way we could have avoided it would have been to allow the foreign armies to come and go freely within our territory without limitation while our own army remained bound by restrictions imposed on its movements. We would have had to allow others to fire at our soldiers and not reply to their fire. No nation with respect for itself can endure such humiliation.

"The Manchurian provinces have been lost to us for six years. Then there was the Tangku agreement. Now the point of conflict is Marco Polo Bridge, at the very gates of Peiping.

"If we allow the bridge to be occupied by force, the city that was our capital for 500 years, the political, cultural, and strategic centre of the North will be lost. Peiping will become a second Mukden and the provinces of Hopei and Chahar will share the fate of Manchuria. If *Peiping becomes a second Mukden, what is there to prevent Nanking from becoming a second Peiping?*"

The Japanese had wanted to know if Nanking would be "stubborn" about North China. Chiang's speech was a clear answer.

Negotiations of a kind were still going on in the North, and Chiang Kai-shek did not exclude the possibility of compromise. But it would have to be a compromise involving no further humiliation for China. Anything else the Chinese people would not accept.

"Any kind of settlement", he said, "must not infringe upon the territorial sovereignty and sovereign rights of our nation. We will not allow any illegal change in the status of the Hopei and Chahar Political Council [the regional administration] which is fixed by the Central Government. We will not agree to the removal by outside pressure of local officials appointed by the Central Government. We will not allow any restrictions to be placed on the position now held by the 29th Army."

If the Japanese did not meet these conditions, there was only one way out for China.

"We are a weak country. But if we are driven to the limit of endurance there is only one thing we can do — to throw every last ounce of the energy of our nation into the struggle for national existence. And when that is done, neither time nor circumstance will permit our stopping midway to seek peace. We should realize that to seek peace after war has once begun would mean to accept terms spelling the subjugation of our race and the complete annihilation of the nation. Let our people realize the sacrifice involved in struggle. But we must bear all and fight to the bitter end in expectation of the final victory. For should we hesitate and vainly hope for temporary safety, we shall perish for ever."

The decision as to whether such a struggle would be forced upon China rested with the Japanese Army.

On July 22, another compromise was reached in the North and approved by Nanking. On July 26 the Japanese occupied Langfang, just half-way along the railway line from Tientsin to Peiping.

There was no further "weakness" from the Central Government. On July 28, General Chiang Kai-shek issued another statement to the nation in the course of which he said:

"The limit of endurance has been reached. The Government has the responsibility of defending the territory and sovereign rights of the country and of protecting the people. The only thing it can do now is to... lead the entire nation in a struggle to the bitter end. I am confident that the final victory will be ours."

For seven years the nation had clamoured against the suicidal policy of permitting the aggressor to painlessly acquire more and more of the country's territory and resources. During those years China had trodden a path of humiliation that had set her best minds and her youth crying out in protest. A yawning gulf loomed between the Government and practically all sections of the people except the officials on its pay-roll.

But now the head of the Government spoke the feelings of every Chinese.

"Fight to the bitter end!"

"Throw every ounce of energy into the struggle!"

"The final victory will be ours!"

These words from the Kuling speech lived on as popular slogans throughout the war. They were displayed on posters, blazoned on the banners of troops going out to battle, and written defiantly on walls in the occupied areas to blister the eyes of the Japanese.

They represented a policy to which there could be no opposition, for which there could be only support.

In the days following the rupture of negotiations in the North, Chiang Kai-shek's former worst enemies came to confer with him for immediate joint measures of struggle against the Japanese. The armistice which had existed between the Kuomintang and Communist Party for several months became a fighting alliance, the conditions of which were published shortly afterwards. These conditions were the result of conversations held in Kuling between Chiang and Lin Pai-chu, President of the Soviet region in Shensi, Kansu, and Ninghsia. From the far South-west came Generals Li Tsung-jen and Pai Chung-hsi, outstanding military leaders in the revolutionary campaigns of 1925-7, who had since been building themselves a Spartan "state within a state" in the mountainous province of Kwangsi. They controlled an army which had the reputation of being one of the best fighting forces in China and was to prove that the reputation was not undeserved.

* * *   * * *

Meanwhile, on July 28 and 29 respectively, Peiping and Tientsin had fallen to the enemy. The Japanese got Peiping and Tientsin cheaply.

The Central Army never reached Peiping and Tientsin. The 29th Army was not equipped for resistance. It had no artillery and little conception of defence against modern arms. Due to the fact that its activities were under the strict surveillance of the Japanese, it had, during the period of negotiation, scrupulously abstained from erecting even such lines and defences as could be put up during this short space of time. Moreover, General Chang Tze-chung, Mayor of Tientsin and commander of one of the army's three divisions, played the traitor in those days and handed over the administration of Peiping to the enemy. Later he was to redeem himself.

Nevertheless, the 29th made a stand in Nanyuan, where the Peiping garrison was quartered. A bloody battle was fought there, in which Japanese tanks, airplanes, and artillery took a toll of thousands. Practically the entire Chinese 132nd Division was wiped out, together with its commander, General Chao Teng-yu. General Tung Ling-ko, vice-commander of the entire 29th Army, also perished. At Nanyuan, Peiping students fought shoulder to shoulder with the soldiers. They had been devoting the summer to three months' military training in the encampments of the 29th Army. Many friendships had arisen between students and soldiers. Now the soldiers and their student comrades were facing the enemy together.

In Peiping, people from all walks of society quickly organized themselves to help the army. Women scraped bandages. Young men and girls carried food out to the battlefield and brought in the wounded. The heroism of the men who fought at Nanyuan was so impressive that even Europeans living in Peiping risked their lives to drive out to the scene of the fighting and bring back car-loads of wounded, on the roofs, on the fenders, on every part of their cars that could carry an extra man. Some of these Europeans saw how the Japanese infantry — arriving on the field when there was nothing left there but the dead and dying, kicked the wounded Chinese soldiers to death where they lay.

While the men of Nanyuan fought, Peiping was handed over to the enemy behind their backs. General Chang Tze-chung, who worked the deal, was commander of the 29th Army's 38th Division. He was an able soldier, and in 1938 had fought the Japanese on the Great Wall. Not long after the army was shifted to garrison duty in the rich Peiping-Tientsin area, he was given the post of Mayor of Tientsin. It was a fat job for a poor divisional commander, with many people coming to ask for favours and bearing gifts. The Japanese bore the best gifts. General Chang had come to office with the reputation of an anti-Japanese fighting man. Before long he was president of the air-line company the Japanese had formed to enable them to fly a passenger service (with military planes) all over North China and Inner Mongolia. After this he took a trip to Japan, as a guest of the Government. He lived in the best hotels and was given the best in food, wine, and women. Did he like this? Then he was taken to parades of Japan's military might, with weapons of annihilation — heavy guns, aerial bombing, and gas — convincingly demonstrated. Or perhaps this — was what he preferred? When they were through with him, General Chang's simple soldier's ears were wide open to the incessant stream of convincing arguments in favour of "Sino-Japanese co-operation" which his kind hosts poured into them.

To General Chang's shocked surprise, his Division would not go over with him. It denounced him, elected a new commander, and followed the rest of the 29th Army.*

One day before the disgrace of Peiping, Tientsin fell.

What was the position of Tientsin? There was a river. It was freely navigated by Japanese destroyers and gunboats. There was a railway. Japanese troop-trains had been pouring in along it for days, and the station was constantly full of Japanese troops. The Japanese had a large concession. They had two sets of barracks, one inside the concession and one outside the city limits. The barracks were built like fortresses, surrounded by pill-boxes and barbed wire. On July 28 there were perhaps 3,000 Japanese troops in Tientsin.

Chinese troops were not allowed in Tientsin at all. According to the Boxer

---

* General Chang Tze-chung, however, went back to his division. A few weeks before the fall of Peiping, he slipped out of the city alone on a bicycle, disguised as a peasant. He cycled until he found Chinese army outposts, then announced his identity and gave himself up. At the time, it was stated in Nanking that he would be shot. Another story was that he had been allowed to re-enter the army as a private soldier. In any case, he was seen by foreign correspondents on the Tientsin-Pukow railway front early the following spring — again in command of a division, one of the best on that front. To them he spoke frankly of his role in Peiping and his desire to atone for it. In March, he helped win the important Chinese victory at Linyi, which prepared the way for the triumph of Taierhchuang in the beginning of April. During recent months Chang Tze-chung has been twice decorated. He is regarded as one of the boldest and most successful field commanders in the Chinese army, and his name often appears in news from the front.

Protocol they could not approach within 20 miles of the city. The armed forces of China in the city of Tientsin consisted of several hundred police.* Moreover, considerably less than half the area of Tientsin was under Chinese control. British, French, Japanese, and Italian concessions cut into the areas where Chinese authority operated. The German, Russian, Austrian, and Belgian concessions had been returned to China, but on each of these was foreign property important enough to be regarded as a vested interest by some one of the Powers. Besides Japan, Britain, France, the United States, and Italy kept garrisons in Tientsin. In case of "trouble" each would guard its own concession. America had no concession. Her barracks were situated in the former German area, where many Americans lived and which American troops patrolled in emergencies. The American army also guarded the Standard Oil Company's installations in the former Belgian concession.

In Tientsin 600 men of the Peace Preservation Corps fought 3,000 Japanese for thirty-six hours. Armed only with rifles and machine-guns, they managed to cut the Japanese in one barracks off from those in the other and to isolate completely the Japanese troops in occupation of the railway station. Japanese artillery fire and aerial bombing failed to dislodge them, failed even to put them on the defensive. Their reply to air bombing was to send a detachment to attack the Japanese airfield and destroy the planes; and the attackers actually got to within a few hundred feet of their goal before they were forced to turn back by fierce machine-gun fire, leaving half their number dead on the ground. When their concentrations were dispersed, they broke up into units of three or four, barricaded themselves in houses, and waited carefully for Japanese soldiers to come within range of their rifles. They fought with reckless courage and cool calculation, these 600 men, and they had the Japanese in such a welter of fright that the young captain from Tokyo who acted as spokesman at the barracks pale-facedly told foreign correspondents,

---

* There were the ordinary traffic police and the "Peace Preservation Corps" or civil guards, who were armed with rifles and machine guns and performed the function of a garrison. The men who fought the Japanese belonged to this body.

"We may all be massacred to-night."

And it is true that things would have gone badly for the Japanese had the ill-starred 38th Division, which was wandering commander-less somewhere near the city, been there to take advantage of the condition to which the 600 khaki-clad policemen had reduced the enemy.

At the sound of brisk rifle-fire on the morning of July 28, all Tientsin put on a countenance of hope. For years the Japanese had walked like masters in the city. From high to low there was no one who had not felt the iron heel of their increasing domination. By smuggling in their cheap goods they had ruined the native cotton industry — then bought up the plant. Most of the industrial workers in the city were working for Japanese masters, for lower wages than they had received before. The Japanese flooded the city with opium and heroin. There was hardly a family that had not had one of its members fall victim to the deadly drug — and which did not curse the Japanese for it. The small merchant hated the Japanese for his smuggling and under-selling; the intellectual — for his restricted freedom. Thousands of refugees from Manchuria, thousands of others who had relatives there or in the nearby districts of East Hopei, knew the dark reality of life in the "lost territories". The people of Tientsin did not need anyone to tell them the personal penalties of national humiliation. For three years they had been slowly sinking into the pit of slavery with nothing to protect them but the game of political obstruction played by the local authorities to head off the Japanese, the courageous voices of the Peiping students — with the echo they raised throughout the country, and their own sullen hatred.

But now the National Government had proclaimed its will to fight. And the first shots had rung out in Tientsin. A city that for three years had tottered on the brink of slavery was striking the first blow in self-defence. No Chinese, in Tientsin on the morning of July 28, spoke of the scores of Japanese troop-trains that had come rumbling through the city during the past weeks. No Chinese spoke of the fact that there was no military base near Tientsin able to cope with the enemy forces. But every Chinese friend one met on the streets that morning shouted joyfully, "Do you hear those shots? We have begun to fight!"

It was a feeling so new and so sudden in this land of capitulation that everything was expected to change at once. The first rifle-shots followed by gunfire, suggested the beginning of a large-scale battle. Had the 38th Division entered the city? Had the Central Army by some miracle arrived?

Six hundred policemen were fighting the Japanese army. Six hundred policemen who had been summoned by their commander, General Li Wentien, and told: "The Japanese are planning to take over the city. Our Government has declared its decision to fight. Therefore it is our duty also to fight."

Never was anyone in such a terrible position as the Chinese police and militia in territory partly controlled by the Japanese. Any Japanese tough could manhandle them, yet they could not resort to arms. Japanese and Korean "ronin" could poison the people with heroin, beat them, and take their women. The police could not interfere. Rather, it was their duty to see that the people did not react in a way that might give rise to an "incident". Sometimes the police were assigned as guards to customs stations outside Tientsin to keep a watch for smugglers. They had explicit orders. If the smugglers were Japanese and submitted peacefully to search, they were to search them. If they got rough, they were to leave them alone. If the Japanese attempted to beat up the customs staff, the police were to protect them — presumably by getting in the way and taking the beating. On no account were they to hurt any Japanese. Now at last they could use their rifles. One can see why they fought well.

By noon the Japanese were heavily bombing the area where the Chinese Government offices were situated. Besides the Government buildings, several blocks of tenements were destroyed. The policemen had attacked the Japanese air-field and been repulsed with many losses. But they had succeeded in isolating Japanese units in three different parts of the city.

Waves of mass feeling swept the people of Tientsin. When Japanese airplanes appeared, shots rang out from attic windows in all parts of the city. Every Chinese who possessed arms shot at them, in spite of the fact that there was no chance of scoring a hit. Once a plane dipped, seemed in trouble. Huge crowds ran along the streets cheering towards the spot where they expected it to come down. Over every house in the city and concessions, Chinese flags fluttered.

The heroic audacity of the 600 and the upsurge of wild joy among the people created an unforgettable sense of untried power suddenly let loose. Surely there was something behind the 600. Surely the resistance, so daringly begun, would lead to further swift, bold blows from unexpected quarters. The common people of the city expected it. The Europeans, infected by their enthusiasm, framed and discussed elaborate theories about the general plan of the Chinese counter-attack — of which the 600 were the spearhead. The Japanese were simply frightened. "We may all be massacred to-night," said their spokesman. No Japanese spokesman had ever made such a "statement" before.

Towards the end of the day, the Japanese managed to out-flank the main force of the 600. They tried to do it by marching through the French concession. The French refused to permit this. Then the Japanese remembered the Rome-Berlin-Tokyo axis. The Italian authorities let them throw a pontoon bridge over to their concession and march through to the rear of the Chinese. Later, when some of the Chinese police were retreating past the concession, Italian sentries shot at them. They were coming too close, they explained, and endangering the neutrality of the concession. Two French soldiers were stranded in the railway station with the besieged Japanese troops. The Japanese shot one of them in the shoulder, threatened the other. No love was wasted between French and Japanese.

Throughout the next night no one in the city slept. All listened for the heavy firing that would herald a large-scale Chinese counter-attack for which the stand of the 600 had prepared the way. It is hard to recapture the tension of those hours. Now and then there would be a burst of machine-gunning. Perhaps that was it? A field-gun fired... now...? But then everything grew quiet again. The night passed. There was no counter-attack.

The 600 had fought uninterruptedly for thirty-six hours. Now less than half of them were left. Throughout the morning the Japanese hunted them like wild beasts. About thirty passed over into the French concession and let themselves be interned. They came with their arms, walking erect. The bodies of those who were trapped were to lie rotting for days in the August sun, purposely left where they fell by the Japanese.

In the afternoon all was quiet. Foreign journalists were again summoned to a Japanese Press conference. "Gentlemen," said the neat British-trained captain, who only a day before had been talking of being massacred, "to-day we are bombing Nankai University."

Nankai University was one of the finest in North China. It owned a handsome campus and existed partly on American endowments. Its Institute of Economics had produced a number of pioneer studies on Chinese rural and industrial life. Unfortunately, Nankai's students were patriotic. The Japanese did not like Nankai University.

"Why?" asked the foreign correspondents in unison.

"Because, gentlemen, the outrageous Chinese are keeping troops there. " The "outrageous Chinese" was not a personal aberration of speech. It was the official phrase used by Japanese spokesmen to designate, in English, the Chinese army.

"No," said one correspondent, "I didn't see any there when I was there this morning."

"But the buildings are very strong. They are very suitable to fortify. The Chinese will use them."

"How do you know?" — newspapermen are an impudent and discourteous race.

"If I were the Chinese commander," said the captain, spluttering slightly, "I should use them."

"But still, is this any reason to bomb a world-famous educational institution?"

"Gentlemen, Nankai University is an anti-Japanese base. We must destroy all anti-Japanese bases."

"What do you mean?"

"Nankai students are anti-Japanese and Communistic. They are always making trouble for us."

"But, Captain, there are no students on the campus. It is now the summer vacation, and the place is deserted."

The captain became really angry. He said, "Gentlemen, I am a military man. I inform you that to-day we are destroying Nankai University. It is an anti-Japanese base. All Chinese universities are anti-Japanese bases."

"Then the Japanese army will bomb all Chinese universities?"

"You will please excuse me."

The Japanese bombed Nankai. Their planes flew over it in squadrons, so low that they could almost lay their bombs on the campus. The magnificent library and all its contents were destroyed with the other buildings. After the bombing was completed, Japanese soldiers came on the scene with straw and kerosene and set fire to all that the bombs had not destroyed. This was their revenge on the student movement.

Yesterday, all Tientsin had watched the fight of the 600. To-day, the whole city watched the systematic, inhuman, punitive bombing of the books. The exaltation of the day before was succeeded by leaden despair. People did not look one another in the eye. The explosions of the bombs dropped on Nankai came regularly, like heavy hammer-blows. The bodies of the fighters lay rotting in the sun.

In the office of a friend there was a young Chinese. He was a boy from an East Hopei village who had come to Tientsin knowing only a few hundred characters. He had begun by dusting and cleaning. But he was a man who was always active and could never be satisfied with any level of knowledge. He discovered a night school and paid one of the eight dollars a month that he earned to study in it. He had learned to read and write well and had taken up English. Now he could read and write English. He had become a typist. All this he had accomplished in two years of hard work.

On the day of the fighting, he had disappeared. Now he was back sitting at his desk with his head in his hands.

He turned to us: "Where are our airplanes? Where are our troops?"

"They couldn't have come up so quickly," we said.

"Then what about us?" he shouted. "This morning the Japanese took over three thousand rifles in the old German concession. Why did six hundred men have to fight the Japanese? Why didn't they give a rifle to me? That would be six hundred and one. And the three thousand rifles to three thousand others? That would have made three thousand six hundred. Do you think we do not know how to use rifles? Everyone knows. Who has not fought bandits in the villages. And even if one doesn't know, it's easy enough to learn. You saw our people in the streets yesterday. We are many, and we want to fight. And those rifles were lying there. For whom were they keeping them?"

"Where were you yesterday?" we asked him.

He looked at us. "I have two friends in the night school. They are workers at the electric-light plant. Yesterday we tried to get out to the fighting. We thought we might be able to pick up some guns. But they wouldn't even let us out of the French Concession." And he bit his lip in annoyance.

The Japanese were "mopping up". They were hunting and shooting young men in the area of yesterday's fighting. Especially were they looking for "shave-headed students". By this, they meant students who had been undergoing military training during the summer and had had their hair close-cropped like soldiers. Standing near the railway station, I saw them bring in a number of prisoners roped together. Several were policemen, some ordinary civilians, one — evidently — a "shave-headed student". The Japanese produced a rising-sun flag and kicked the prisoners to their knees before it. The prisoners struggled. The Japanese used the butts of their rifles and beat them to the ground. Then they kicked them up and marched them off again. They shot them against a wall, a few hundred yards away.

* * *   * * *

While the 600 fought in Tientsin, another battle was going on at Tungchow, capital of the Japanese puppet "State" of East Hopei. This "State" was an outgrowth of the demilitarized zone created by the Tangku capitulation of 1933. It was headed by Yin Ju-keng, a Chinese traitor.

East Hopei had an "anti-Communist army" of 30,000 "Peace Preservation Corps" trained by the Japanese. The annual revenue of its administration was $25,000,000, derived chiefly from smuggling and the drug trade. Smuggling was ingeniously carried out. Yin, being "autonomous", did not recognize the customs tariffs of the Chinese Government, and let Japanese goods pay one quarter of the regular duty if landed on parts of the coast which he controlled. The Chinese Government, not recognizing Yin's "autonomy", could not open customs stations on his borders. If a rake-off was paid to Yin, smuggling became quasi-legal.

The Japanese regarded East Hopei as a model of what North China would become under their administration. Here was a miniature prototype of "peace in East Asia". True, it was a peace that smelt of the opium pipe. In a report submitted to the League of Nations, Miss Muriel Lester stated that she found 570 drug dens in one East Hopei city of 200,000 (Tangshan). But this too was profitable.

And the people were "happy". The schools had been purged of nationalist ideas. Anti-Japanese thought had been eradicated. A Chinese armed force, absolutely "loyal" to the rising sun, had been created.

Then, on the morning of July 28, East Hopei blew up. A total of 400 Japanese soldiers and civilians in Tungchow were wiped out after several hours of resistance. They were destroyed by the "loyal" army they had taken five years to create. And the cream of that army, the pro-Japanese "Anti-Communist Officers' Training Corps", led the revolt. The first object of their wrath was the "Special Service Mission" of the Japanese army, spiritual guide and sponsor of the State, centre of espionage, coercion, and intrigue. No one in the mission escaped.

What had happened?

In East Hopei, as elsewhere in North China at the time, the shadow and the substance of things did not coincide. Thus, although this region — whose borders extended to within nine miles of Peiping — was completely controlled by the Japanese, a garrison of 800 Chinese troops was allowed to continue at Tungchow. They belonged to the 89th Independent Brigade of the 29th Army. Their presence can be explained in this way. Tungchow was not part of the "demilitarized zone". To turn the Chinese troops out of the city would have precipitated an incident. At that time the Japanese wanted, no incident. The troops stayed. The Chinese also wanted no incident. They allowed the illegal stationing of 500 Japanese soldiers at Tungchow and the institution of the East Hopei "Government". Each pretended the other was not there.

On July 27, the Japanese decided that they needed their 500 troops elsewhere. Tientsin was seething. In Peiping, the battle of Nanyuan loomed.

But they could not leave the Chinese troops in their rear. So, with the aid of their "Peace Preservation Corps", they disarmed the 29th Army garrison. There seems to have been no resistance. But the Japanese were not content with disarming the Chinese soldiers. They herded them into a corner of the city wall — and machine-gunned the defenceless men until not one of them was left alive.

The men of the "loyal" East Hopei Army were compelled to stand by and witness this butchery of their Chinese brothers, with whom they had walked and talked and smoked only a few days before.

That evening, part of the Japanese garrison withdrew to Peiping. They had now no scruples about leaving Tungchow. The Chinese soldiers were dead. The "Peace Preservation Corps" would preserve the peace.

Then, according to an official Japanese propaganda pamphlet: "Whatever their motive, the Tungchow peace guards turned traitor to the State which they had served and the people with whom they had been connected by vows of friendship until only a few hours before."

The Japanese began to feel doubtful about the East Hopei pattern for peace in Asia. They began to lose confidence in the possibility of using Chinese to fight Chinese anywhere, at any time.

"Gentlemen," said the little captain at the Press conference, "we have had terrible, terrible news from Tungchow. The outrageous Chinese have massacred hundreds of our people. You shall see for yourselves. The Japanese army is arranging an airplane."

The captain looked serious, "I do not have to impress on you, gentlemen, the barbarous nature of the Chinese. We Japanese regard the dead as gods. We dispose of the remains immediately by burning, and we worship the spirits of the dead. Even Chinese dead — we respect. More than they do themselves."

On the next morning the captain rang up, very agitated. "It is raining so hard. The airplane will be available to-morrow."

The bodies of Japanese secret-service agents, of Korean drug-smugglers, and of women done to death with their men-folk by the rebellious traitor troops at Tungchow lay in the rain — awaiting the eyes and cameras of foreign correspondents. The bodies of 500 Chinese soldiers, shot down in cold blood after having been disarmed had been removed, presumably with respect, certainly with dispatch.

The next morning it rained again. "To-morrow," promised the captain.

And the next morning. And the morning after that.

The dead, "regarded as gods", lay and waited. It was August. It was hot.

On the fifth morning the sun shone, but the airfield was too slippery to permit a take-off. "To-morrow," promised the captain.

It was a week before he gave it up.

Around the railway station in Tientsin, along the roads near the Japanese barracks, lay the bodies of the fighting policemen. They were not too pretty to see. Among them, occasionally, a fresh corpse lay, white and red. A "shave-headed student" perhaps. Japanese soldiers and flies moiled around them. The soldiers took each other's pictures. An occasional young soldier paled and held his nose.

Unofficial representations were made to the Japanese by the concession authorities. Would they please...? The bodies were rolled into the Haiho river. They floated down the stream as, months ago, the bodies of workers had floated — shot by the Japanese after having built their fortifications. Two hundred bodies within a few days had come down then — bodies of strong young men. Other bodies floated down. In Japanese heroin dens, emaciated human wrecks died. They too went into the river. So long as North China remains enslaved, the Haiho will continue to carry to the sea these by-products of Japanese imperialism.

* * *   * * *

Great numbers of Chinese were moving into Tientsin's foreign concessions. Among them were thousands of students from Peiping. Some wished to stay — but the majority were looking for transportation to the South. Long queues formed at shipping offices. Every vessel bound for Shanghai carried twice or thrice its normal load.

I met a friend, a Chinese newspaperman. "What are you going to do?" I asked. He and a number of others were staying. China's best newspapers had been published in Tientsin. Now there was only the organ of the Japanese. My friend was looking for European or American backers to lend their names to a paper to be published on the concessions. This was necessary before the concession authorities would allow it to appear. He had not found anyone.

"But we cannot let a million of our people go without *our* news," he said. "Look at this."

He handed me a mimeographed rice-paper sheet entitled, *Broadcast News.* It was a closely-written transcript of the official Government information from Nanking. There were also other items. One described guerrilla activities around Peiping and ended with a stirring appeal to the people of North China.

"Worth staying for, isn't it?"

For months afterwards, *Broadcast News* was the only source from which Tientsin Chinese could learn what their Government and army were doing, apart from the foreign newspapers, which few could read. The thin paper sheets were pasted up on walls. They found their way everywhere, even into the folds of the Japanese organ which was sold all over the city.

When, in response to Japanese protests, the police of the concessions began to tear down the posted copies of the paper, *Broadcast News* issued an appeal to its readers, "Fellow countrymen with radios. When you listen to our national capital in the evenings, turn on full volume and open your windows so that all our brothers may hear."

Concession police, coming up to disperse the crowds which formed spontaneously at certain times, stopped to listen.

*   *   *   *   *   *

The Japanese began the organization of a puppet administration. For this administration they brought out of retirement political, physical, and moral degenerates of all kinds. They organized a "Self-defence Force" of White Russians. Headed by a Japanese officer, Major Taki, this group staged a raid on the Soviet Consulate in Tientsin. They stalked about armed and terrorized personal enemies and other "white" groups not in favour with the Japanese.

*   *   *   *   *   *

Suddenly I received a visit from a "shave-headed student". I had known him in Peiping as an active worker in the National Salvation movement. He was shabbily dressed and very tired. At the time of the Lukouchiao incident, he told me, he had been undergoing military training. Then he had fought at Nanyuan. "Thirty comrades came on the train with me," he said. "We disguised ourselves and spread out through the different cars. Ten are girls. Can you find us a place to live in the concessions?"

I did some frantic telephoning. We parcelled out the students among several friends.

"Do you know anything about boats sailing to Shanghai? Are they being searched?"

I looked at him: "Running away?"

My friend did not look like a student. He was country bred, and the deep tan of months of summer life in camp had enhanced the natural healthy brown of his skin. Now his teeth broke out, snowy white, in a broad grin. He shook me by the shoulder. "Wake up, Lao Hsiang. You don't mean to say that you too think that because Peiping and Tientsin have fallen and the Japs have what they want, everything is over. You know what we call that now — the North China blues. Running away? We are not going to America. And so long as we continue active, wherever we go in China will be the front, because this time the whole country will fight. If we go to the rear, it is only to find work for the front. But just so you don't worry about us, I will tell you what we plan to do. Ten of us are going to Nanking to join the army. Five will go to Yenan — to the Red Army University — to study guerrilla methods. Some of the girls want to do nursing, and two of them are going to Yenan too. The rest of us have our homes in this province. We will go back to our villages. Perhaps there will be something to be done there. And some day we'll all come back here."

He smiled. "Well? Will your conscience let you find out if there are boats we can take? And don't forget to get a ticket for yourself. I think you too had better 'run away'. The war is not only not over, but it hasn't even begun. Why don't you come and see it?"

CHAPTER IV

*Birth of an Army**

O N July 8, 1937, a day after the "incident" on Marco Polo Bridge, an old Manchurian peasant woman went shopping in Peiping. She was a small, thick-set, brown-skinned old woman, with her meagre hair so tightly brushed back that her scalp shone through the thin strands. She was a black-eyed, square-jawed old woman, and she bargained lustily with the store-keeper, speaking so loudly that he drew his head in between his shoulders and looked cautiously around to see if anyone was within hearing. The old lady passed a bundle of bills over the counter. In return, she received a number of heavy paper-wrapped packages which she deposited carefully in her market basket.

The old woman went home to a houseful of people — her husband, an old man of seventy, two sons, two daughters, and five young men who were their friends. When she arrived they closed the doors and all crowded around her. She pulled her purchases out of the basket and began unwrapping them, laying them out neatly on the bed. They were shiny, well-greased pistols —

---

* This story of the First People's Anti-Japanese Allied Army, later to become the Fifth Army of the Hopei-Chahar-Shansi Border Area, is based on information I obtained in the course of personal interviews with Madame Chao and Wu Hsin-min (a member of Chao Tung's original six). An autobiographical article by Chao Tung in the *Sing Tao Jih Pao* and Chinese materials on the Border Area provided additional detail.

50

eight Mausers and two Brownings.

This houseful of people and this minuscule arsenal formed the initial strength and armament of a partisan army which within a year was to number 10,000 rifles. The old woman's eldest son was Chao Tung, future commander of the army. He had already behind him a record of six years of guerrilla leadership in Manchuria. The other young men were his comrades in arms, also Manchurian partisans. The old lady herself, temporarily in charge of the "army's" ordnance, purchasing department, and commissariat (many bowls of rice for six strong young fellows), was to become famous throughout China and the world as Madame Chao, "Mother of the Guerrillas".

The money to buy arms and organize a unit had come from several sources. Admiral Shen Hung-lieh, mayor of Tsingtao, had given some. General Ma Chan-shan, once the greatest thorn in the side of the Japanese in Manchuria and now about to organize a spectacular army of guerrilla cavalry in Inner Mongolia, was another supporter. There were constant contributions from Manchurian exiles in Peiping, organized into the North-eastern National Salvation Association. These people had lost their original homeland to the Japanese. Now they were about to lose their second. Small wonder that the Manchurians were in the forefront of the struggle against the invader.

The six young men, the old woman, and a representative of the association, put their heads together. The arms must leave the city immediately. When the enemy encircled Peiping or took it, it would be too late.

Even now it was difficult. The city was under martial law. Every gate of the ancient walls was heavily guarded by the 29th Army, and civilians caught carrying arms would have an unpleasant time. Much thought was given to this question. It was learned that the buses running to the universities outside Peiping were not being searched. Two of the young men took pistols out that way. Meanwhile, rickshas bearing old Mother Chao and her daughters left the city through the West Gate. When the sentries approached, the old lady told them off in a few well-chosen words. Did they have nothing better to do than to bother an old woman and two young girls? The rickshas passed through uninspected. Around the waist of the old woman, two pistols were securely strapped. Each of her daughters carried two more. Under the seat of old Mother Chao's ricksha was a box containing 1,000 rounds of ammunition.

All the arms were concentrated at Tsinghua University, eight miles from the city.

Every detail in those early days called for much thought, infinite resourcefulness, and determination. The group left Peiping on July 20. It numbered six armed men. Six young civilians with pistols were not safe in the countryside. If the Japanese caught and searched them, they would certainly be shot. If they fell into the hands of Chinese troops, they might easily be executed as Japanese-paid gangsters — because the Japanese were using hundreds of plain-clothes men to stir up trouble in and around Peiping. Village guards would try to disarm them. In the first place, they might be bandits, and in any case their arms were useful. Through decades of civil war the Chinese peasant had come to know the value of a gun in troubled times. Unarmed, he was at the mercy of bandit gangs and demoralized war-lord troops. The backwash of retreating armies swept over his village and left him without his horse, his cart, and his crop. With a few rifles he could keep the storm away — and it rolled on toward some other point, less effectively defended.

The group evolved an explanation of its status. The six young men were geological students going into the hills for a tour of investigation. They dressed the part, they carried maps, and the guns were to protect them from the unruly elements wandering through the country in these unsettled times.

They made their way towards Tayangcheng, a village near Peiping, with whose headman they had previously made connection. This headman gave them eight rifles. From Peiping came sixteen comrades — twelve former partisans from Manchuria and four students of North-eastern University. Two peasants joined the group. They were now twenty-four. They had ten pistols and eight rifles.

Neither for love nor money would any of the neighbouring villages part with a single rifle. There was only one place to get arms for the six men who still had none — from the enemy. So, on the second day of its existence, the newly-formed unit drew for the first time on the classic source of supply of the Chinese partisan movement. Six miles away, they heard, there was a post of about twenty members of the "Peace Preservation Corps" of the East Hopei puppet Government, under a Japanese officer. The partisans decided to disarm them. But when they came to the post they found only three badly frightened men, who instantly surrendered their guns. This was the first "battle".

Negotiations with the Japanese had begun. For several days there had been no fighting at Marco Polo Bridge, and the excitement in the countryside was subsiding. During a week of wandering, the unit tried to establish connections with the population. The peasants listened to the speeches of the student partisans. They saw a small unit of armed men, mostly Manchurians, who spoke of the struggle against Japan. But the Japanese had not yet come into the villages, and the fighting had stopped. The peasants were sympathetic but cautious. They did not want to be hunted across the countryside as "bandits" by the Japanese and the 29th Army together after "peace" had been made. Some of the partisans began to get discouraged. They spoke of returning home. But the majority were in favour of continuing and making their way into the puppet State of East Hopei, where the people already knew the bitterness of slavery and would be ready to rise.

In the village of Yungan — "Eternal Peace" — they were almost wiped out. The people had greeted the unit warmly, but the gentry of the village, who had made their peace with the Japanese, were worried. To them the appearance of the partisan group was a harbinger of evil ranking only with banditry and agrarian revolt. One of the gentry, a Mr. Chang, had dealings with Korean drug-dealers and the Japanese secret service. He informed a nearby post of East Hopei troops under Japanese officers that anti-Japanese partisans had quartered themselves in the village of Eternal Peace. This was on July 28, the day of the Tientsin fighting, and one day before the battle of Nanyuan.

Wu Hsin-min, one of Chao Tung's original six, told me the story of the fight that followed:

"At first we had stationed outposts at the entrance to the village, but then it started raining. We thought there was no use letting our comrades get wet for nothing, so we called the outposts in. We had not come into contact with the enemy and had no idea that they knew of our existence. And, of course, we didn't know that that dog Chang had informed on us.

"Shortly before dawn about fifty Japanese and traitor troops surrounded the courtyard in which we were sleeping and began showering us with hand-grenades. Four of our men were killed outright. Two were wounded. One, who happened to be outside, was caught and stabbed to death at once.

"There seemed no way we could get out. But one side of the courtyard was taken up by a shack which had no back door. We thought they would not bother stationing a guard behind that. So, while some of us shot it out with them, the rest weakened the mud and brick wall of the shack from below. Then we all put our shoulders to it and pushed, and the whole shack came down on top of us.

"We scrambled out and ran, shooting as we went. A few of their men, all Chinese, were loitering on that side. They were completely bewildered, and instead of trying to stop us they ran about shouting meaningless orders at each other. I remember one fellow waving his arms and yelling, 'Take them alive! Take them alive!' Perhaps they were secretly glad to see us get away. Anyway, before they could make up their minds, we had run off in different directions, making toward the hills."

Before digging themselves out of the ambush, the partisans had agreed to disperse and to re-unite at Miaofengshan, a "holy mountain" west of Peiping which every May is the scene of picturesque mass pilgrimages beloved of European and American tourists. Eighteen men met at the appointed place. They were bedraggled and discouraged. Six, who had their homes near by, left the group immediately. The rest debated whether to bury their arms and go back to Peiping. Finally, they decided that only Chao Tung should go into the city, to see what the situation was and, if possible, immediately get more arms and recruits. They did not know that Peiping had fallen.

For two days Chao Tung did not come back. Two more men were sent after him. Of the nine partisans who remained on the mountain, three or four had once been bandits in Manchuria. Now they itched to return to their old vocation. They were hungry and ragged. It would do no harm, they argued, to expropriate some merchant travelling along the road. But the others, including the four students, attacked them fiercely. "You can get out if you want to become bandits," they said. "But you will not take any arms with you. These arms were bought to be used against the Japanese." The tension within the little group grew. The demoralization which had followed the ambush at Yungan was fast reaching an ugly climax. It had driven six partisans home. It had set others thinking of banditry. The students were nervous from the unwonted excitement of battle and the humiliation of defeat. They were hungry and stiff from unaccustomed exertion. Was it any use? But they did not show what they thought.

What decided whether that little army of twelve would continue or collapse was something outside itself, something that was going on in the fallen city of Peiping. While the partisans were ranging the hills in search of arms, their supporters had not been idle. The anti-Japanese movement of the Manchurian refugees had provided inspiration for the initial effort. Now it added its powerful voice to the voices of the ragged students who, out on a windswept hillside, were trying to persuade their demoralized comrades to give up the promise of rich loot from unarmed Chinese for the dangers and uncertainties of barehanded struggle against the military might of Japan.

Chao Tung and the other two men returned to the mountain. With them came old Mother Chao and a delegate of the North-eastern National Salvation Association. They brought quantities of bedding. The bedding was unwrapped. Out came three machine-guns, twenty rifles, four pistols, and thousands of rounds of ammunition. They had taken all this through the city gates, now guarded by puppet troops, with Mother Chao proudly sitting in a ricksha astride the machine-guns. It was just after the Tungchow mutiny, and the Japanese were not providing their puppet troops with arms. Two men had tried to search the bedding. One look at the muzzle of Chao Tung's pistol had been enough.

Within the next twenty-four hours, twenty students from North-eastern

University made their way out of the city and up the mountain.

They sat on the mountainside and talked. The partisans told of their adventures and troubles. Mother Chao told of hers. She had bought the arms for $2,000 given by a prominent Manchurian resident and $1,000 which she herself had collected in small contributions. Her terms with the arms dealer were part payment in advance. But the dealer did not often have old women as customers. Here was a chance, he thought, of making some money out of this dolt of a peasant. All that was necessary was to give her a good fright, and she would forget all about the arms. He had drawn her into a corner and said menacingly: "I know that your son is a partisan. If you don't pay everything at once, I will tell the Japanese." And old Mother Chao had replied, loudly and clearly: "Of course, my son is a partisan. He has been a partisan in Machuria for six years. We are not afraid to die. If we were, do you think we would be doing this work? So you can tell the Japanese. That will not help them to catch my son. But when they arrest me, I will tell them who has been supplying the partisans with arms, you traitor's soul. And they'll catch you easily enough." Recreating the mood with the words, the old woman indignantly scolded the fighter sitting nearest to her, and he looked as sheepish as though he, and not the contemptible arms dealer, was the object of her wrath.

The laughter of the partisan band, only yesterday a miserable remnant, echoed through the hills.

There had been other troubles, not so easily faced. Four of the men killed at the Village of Eternal Peace had been former Manchurian partisans, refugees with their families in Peiping. Now their wives and mothers came to Mother Chao weeping: "Our breadwinners are gone. What shall we do now?" And some of them said, in pain and bitterness: "Why wasn't your son killed? Here are four of us, and it is our sons and husbands that are dead." The old woman could not face them, and moved to another place. Then the Manchurian Committee took a hand in the matter. They went to the families and said: "You have frightened Mrs. Chao away. Now who will do the work she has been doing, risking death every day? Who will avenge your menfolk?" So the families took what help the Manchurians could give them and old

Mother Chao came back to buy arms as before.

While the unit was encamped on the mountain, it constantly sent scouts through the Western Hills looking for arms. Disbanded soldiers and police roamed the countryside and were glad enough to sell their rifles for a few dollars. A few joined the partisans and told them where arms were stored in secret caches in fields and cottages. Now the unit no longer suffered from the typical disease of guerrilla formations — the surplus of men over arms. It had forty members, at this stage mostly students, and almost twice as many rifles.

A general meeting was called at which the detachment adopted the name of the "First People's Anti-Japanese Allied Army". A little grandiloquent, perhaps, for forty men, but many Manchurian partisan armies had begun with less. Chao Tung was elected commander. Under him were three other officers — Sun Ming-hao, Yin Fu-hsiang, and Liu Feng-wu, all former Manchurian volunteers. There were no student officers. It was decided that all recruits without military experience would serve in the ranks for at least two months before being given any position of command.

The detachment decided to make its presence known to the people of Peiping, who were plunged into depths of despair by the treacherous handing over of their city. At the beginning of August it set out to attack the Second Model Prison, where 600 prisoners were held, many of them political offenders in imminent danger of execution by the Japanese.

Here is the story of the raid, as told to me by a participant:

"We approached the prison at night, some from the front and some from the rear. At the same time, we stationed outposts at two of the city gates so that we should be told if any Japanese troops appeared. I was with a group which was sent to tackle the main gate of the prison.

"Some of us knew Japanese. This gave us an idea. We got hold of a street urchin, gave him ten cents, and told him to run towards the prison and shout: 'Japanese officers arc coming! Japanese officers are coming!'

"A few minutes later we came up, speaking all the Japanese we knew as loudly as we could. When the gatekeeper opened up, we drew our pistols and made him surrender the keys. Meanwhile, some of our men had found the telephone lines and cut them. Others disarmed the guards.

"Then Chao Tung stood up in the middle courtyard of the prison and shouted so that all the prisoners could hear him: 'We are not Japanese! We have come to save you! Break down your doors! We are the anti-Japanese partisans from outside Peiping!'

"We began to open the cells as fast as we could. Meanwhile, the prisoners had picked up the trestles of their beds and every other heavy object they could get hold of and were breaking their way out of those we had not reached. When we opened the armoury, we found three machine-guns, thirty-five rifles, a number of pistols, and much ammunition.

"I was guarding the front gate with a machine-gun. The prisoners poured out into the main courtyard, where Chao Tung addressed them. 'You were rotting in jail,' he said. 'Many of you would have been killed. Now you can be useful to the Chinese people. Fight the national enemy!' We distributed the thirty-five rifles to the likeliest of the prisoners and left immediately. It would have been dangerous to stay any longer."

The forty partisans, with 570 prisoners in tow, marched out of the city. It was a weird procession. The prisoners were all dressed in white convicts' uniforms, and some were chained. Some had been confined for so long that they could hardly walk. Many were ill. This strange parade passed through one of the main gates of the city with a police guard atop it — but the police guard was appalled by such numbers and retired to telephone frantically to headquarters. Meanwhile the partisans and convicts disappeared in the darkness, towards the friendly hills.

In Peiping and Tientsin the news of the opening of the Second Model Prison was whispered from ear to ear. To the population it meant: "Everything is not over." To isolated anti-Japanese fighters preparing to carry on their work under conditions of enemy domination it brought a message of encouragement: "You are not alone. Already the work of others can be seen."

In the hills, a meeting was held. Three hundred of the former prisoners, including all the "politicals", joined the detachment. The situation within the small army underwent another swift change. Again there was an acute shortage of arms. The personal composition of the unit was also altered, with the student element in the minority. The detachment numbered 350 men now. Supplies, food, finance, all presented new problems.

The partisans remained close to Peiping, near that tourist Mecca, the Summer Palace. Old Mother Chao came out regularly with more weapons in her market-basket and with news of how the army's "rear" and financial base was being organized in the city. She would get into a ricksha at her own door-step every morning and ride straight out to her son's headquarters. No one suspected her as yet. Mother Chao had a new duty now. She was acting as recruiting agent in the city. Students came to her and, at a safe distance, followed her to the detachment's hideout. They came in groups of two or three from the middle schools and universities. Some of these students had spent the previous year in Shensi, in the guerrilla training-schools operated by the then Red Army.

A Japanese truck rode unsuspectingly by a partisan outpost near Peiping's Te Sheng gate. The outpost, composed of released prisoners, opened fire and killed two of the guards. From the truck, the partisans got two rifles and a pistol and several hundred blankets and canteens. "We made up packs and really began to look like soldiers," a partisan told me. "We stopped worrying about how we would sleep in the open when the autumn came. We saved several hundred dollars for our friends in the city who would have had to buy us winter equipment." The Japanese shut and sandbagged the Te Sheng gate. They set about trying to discover what kind of enemy this was that refused to recognize their rule, opened their jails, and attacked their transport.

The detachment had been in existence for a month. From six, its membership had increased to 400. Three weeks before, it had been a pitiful remnant. Now it was the chief anti-Japanese force in the neighbourhood of Peiping.

A second general assembly, held at this time, established a headquarters and a Political Department for the unit. What was this Political Department? It was a body created by those who had entered the detachment to fight the Japanese to see that, whatever happened, it would continue concentrating on this task. In the course of its short life, the unit had undergone startling changes of personnel. The Political Department was to be a guarantee that it would never change its aims. It was composed mainly of students, and at its head was Kao Peng, a graduate of North-eastern University, who, before the war, had been the underground representative of the All-China National Salvation Association in oppressed Manchuria.

How did the Political Department begin its work? Kao Peng gathered the forty students in the detachment and assigned them to various units. They lived the lives of ordinary partisans and established ties of personal friendship and understanding with men who had been soldiers, peasants, or even bandits. They explained to them from the facts of their own lives the necessity for resisting the Japanese. Many of the partisans had come into the unit with very vague ideas of its aims. They could be fertile soil for any "leader" trying to seize control of the detachment for purposes of banditry or personal aggrandizement. The political workers laboured to make the partisans regard any such attempt as national treason. To break up an anti-Japanese armed force was not a personal matter: it was a stab in the back of national resistance and an act of direct benefit to the enemy.

A partisan army can only be a people's army. Without the confidence of the people it loses all the advantages of its position. It becomes a homeless band of adventurers with every man's hand against it. To gain the people's confidence for Chao Tung's detachment was another aspect of the work of the Political Department. The first step was to tighten discipline among the partisans. Nothing was to be taken without payment. The peasants and their homes and fields were to be treated with consideration. A slogan was carried: "The Partisans are the Army of the Lao Pai Hsing."* Everywhere the students made speeches to the villagers, asking for, not commanding, co-operation.

Finally there was "political work among the enemy". In the partisan

---

* Lao Pai Hsing, or "Hundred Ancient Names", is the expression most commonly used in China to denote the common people. Traditionally, there are only 100 surnames in China — and the "hundred names" therefore comprise all Chinese.

battles of the early days, the enemy was seldom Japanese regulars, often Japanese-officered puppet troops. To these the partisans shouted as they advanced:

"Why don't you turn your guns against the real enemy?"

"Chinese must not fight Chinese!"

"Let us win back our old homes!"

This, with a few volleys, was often enough to make them drop their rifles and run, or even to come over to the side of the partisans. The puppet troops had little stomach for their master's wars.

Old Mother Chao sent a letter from Peiping with bad news. Traitors had given the Japanese information about the detachment and its contacts in the city. Her role too had been discovered, and she would have to leave. A few days later she slipped away safely and travelled by a roundabout route to Central China.*

The Japanese set a bloodhound on Chao Tung's trail — Kao Hsien-chang, one of the worst-hated traitors in North China, Kao was a bandit chief and a Japanese agent. For $50,000 he had played Judas to Li Hai-ching, a leader of Manchurian volunteers whom he had invited for "negotiations for joint action against the enemy" and then killed. Now the Japanese promised Kao $100,000 for the destruction of Chao Tung and his unit. As before, Kao arranged a "conference". But this time he issued no invitations. He came himself, with 350 armed men, for a "friendly visit" to Chao Tung's headquarters. Forewarned, the detachment first manoeuvred the puppet unit into a position in which it was split up, then surprised and disarmed it. Kao himself was taken prisoner as he sat in the ante-room of Chao Tung's

---

* Mother Chao went to Chikungshan, a mountain resort on the Peiping-Hankow railway in Southern Honan. She did not remain idle. With the aid of two Manchurian partisans, her husband, and two daughters, she tried to establish a new guerrilla base on the Northern bank of the Yellow River, then threatened by the Japanese. Four thousand "Red Spears" were enlisted and a headquarters established in Weihwei. This guerrilla army fought several successful actions against the Japanese, but later disintegrated due to lack of organization and leadership. Since the beginning of 1938, Mother Chao has been travelling throughout the country raising money for the partisans in North China.

farmhouse, waiting to be received. As a result of a brief skirmish, in which only three were killed and one wounded, the anti-Japanese army captured 300 rifles. The disarmed bandits were released. Kao Hsien-chang was court-martialled and shot.*

A few days later a Japanese aeroplane spotted the partisans at Tienmenchu, in the Western Hills, and flew low in order to machine-gun them. A lucky rifle shot brought it down. That one aeroplane cost the Japanese treasury ten times as much as it had cost the friends of the detachment to supply it with arms and maintain it during the two months of its existence.

Incidents such as this, coupled with the mushroom growth of guerrilla units around Peiping in August and September, prompted the Japanese to launch a campaign of annihilation against the partisans. In the beginning of October they sent three brigades of troops, with aeroplanes, armoured cars, and tanks, into the Western Hills country. Before the incident on Marco Polo Bridge, the Japanese had kept all North China cowed with one brigade. That had been all they needed to force the signing of the capitulation agreements in Tangku and Peiping. Now three brigades were required to pacify a small piece of territory which had been "conquered" months before. This occupation was already proving expensive.

Once again, the partisans were pushed towards the holy mountain of Miaofengshan. To the same place, fleeing from Japanese troops who were closing in from all sides, came twenty-seven other partisan units, numbering 7,000 men.

The wooded slopes of the holy mountain effectively hid the partisans and made the aiming of artillery and aerial bombs largely a matter of guesswork. Planes operating in relays bombed Miaofengshan for days. They destroyed the peak temple, goal of the annual pilgrimage, and the reverberations of the explosions were heard in Peiping, thirty miles away. But the bombing did not kill a single partisan.

---

* Mr. F. M. Fisher, *United Press* correspondent in Peiping, who at this time succeeded in reaching the partisan headquarters, witnessed the entire Kao Hsien-chang episode.

It was when trying to get away from the mountain on which they had been surrounded that the guerrilla units suffered heavy casualties. Chao Tung's detachment was lucky. It managed to slip out through a byway lightly guarded by the Japanese. However, it did not escape without losses. Seven planes followed its retreat and fifty partisans fell victim to machine-gunning from the air. Other groups were less fortunate. A thousand men led by Chang Hung, a former regimental commander in the Manchurian army, walked into a Japanese ambush on a narrow mountain path and lost half their number. Of the remainder, many were dispersed. The remant of the unit joined Chao Tung's group, of which Chang Hung later became chief of staff. Kung Chang-hui's unit of 500 men was reduced to fifty. These fifty also joined Chao Tung. When he left Miaofengshan, he had 1,500 men.

After the detachment's first great trial by fire came its last serious internal crisis. The path of anti-Japanese resistance was hard and long. The path of banditry was always profitable, seldom particularly dangerous, and might lead, if one's gang was important enough and manageable enough, even to a puppet generalship. The detachment was pledged to the path of resistance. Chi Tsang-wu, an ex-bandit and one of its battalion commanders, chose the path of banditry. He worked carefully and slowly. By feats of personal strength and courage and by much boasting he built up his own prestige. By impeding in every respect the political work of the students, he tried to make sure that his men would know no law but his word. At every step he tried to isolate the students from the partisans. By sneering at their personal softness and their inexpertness in carrying arms, he hoped to build up a similar attitude on the part of his men. It was easy to see where this would lead.

The students went to Chao Tung and insisted that Chi be removed. They pointed out that his presence in the detachment would inevitably line up behind him the ex-bandit elements who might otherwise be saved for the anti-Japanese struggle. The behaviour of his men in the villages had already begun to break down the confidence of the people in the good faith of the partisans. Chi smoked opium and swaggered about like a bandit chief, with his flunkeys at his heels. The peasants watched him anxiously. They had seen his kind before.

Chi Tsang-wu heard of the students' petition. He did not know that he was in a new kind of army. He called in the students in his battalion and invited them to sign another petition: "We, the students and political workers serving in Chi's battalion, ask that he retain his command...." They refused. He became furious. "I am your commander. I order you to sign." But they did not sign and continued to insist on his ejection. As a result, Chi was moved to another position.

Among the commanders of the detachment who had served in the old war-lord armies, Chi organized what he called the "Power Party". In their units, these officers tried to reproduce the bad old system of personal allegiance and terroristic discipline. In the councils of the detachment, the members of the "party" pressed for constant increases in the power of the small army. "We need more guns, more men, and more money," they said, and they advocated greater demands on the detachments' supporters in Peiping and forced requisitions from the population in the villages. Most of all they hated the political workers. "When a soldier disobeys, we beat him. This makes him fight better," they declared. "When the enemy appears, we shoot at him. That is what an army must do. What is the use of speeches? These students only lessen our power and impede our growth."

When the students saw the growth of the "Power Party", they began to work hard to counteract its influence. They applied themselves to military exercises to show the men that they were not only talkers but also fighters. They sought to distinguish themselves in skirmishes. They knew that in order to isolate these swaggering would-be warlords, they would have to inspire the men not only with sympathy but also with confidence. In this they succeeded.

When the "Power Party" finally made its attempt to seize the detachment and turn it into a bandit army, it found that it had no supporters. Chi Tsang-wu was shot. Several of his followers were disarmed and thrown out of the unit. A number of students were promoted to commanding rank.

For years the war-lords had suppressed the popular movement. Now the psychological vestiges of war-lordism fought on the side of the Japanese against the rising people. But the partisan movement in North China easily cleansed itself from this corroding influence. The era of the war-lords was past.

The detachment retired to Nankow Pass, where the Great Wall comes nearest to Peiping. Here, at the end of August, a great battle had been fought. Now a group of bandits, working with the Japanese, was terrorizing the population of the devastated countryside. The detachment attacked and dispersed them and captured two machine-guns and many rifles. The people were quick to show their gratitude. They fed the partisans and took care of their wounded.

With 1,500 men, Chao Tung's detachment was now the largest in the vicinity of Peiping. But it was not the largest in the province of Hopei, in which a total of at least 20,000 partisans were already up in arms against the invader. Throughout the preceding months small groups had joined to make large ones. Large ones were establishing contact with each other to form "allied armies". Already the Hopei People's Self-Defence Army under another Manchurian, Lu Cheng-tsao, was in control of many districts in the central part of the province. It was composed of former soldiers and militia, railway workers and peasants. A group of 1,000 had sprung up near the town of Taming, in the south. It had a political corps of 200 students conducting propaganda among the people. In Tzehsien, on the Hopei-Honan border, a detachment of 4,000 partisans maintained a district government. In the Taihang mountain range, on the triple border of Hopei, Honan, and Shansi, Dr. Yang Hsiu-ling, who had been quietly teaching in an engineering college in Tientsin, established a guerrilla base which after eighteen months is still a constant source of trouble to the enemy. In North-eastern Shansi the advance guards of the Eighth Route Army had laid the foundations of the Shansi-Chahar-Hopei Border Branch Military Area. They had already established connections with Lu Cheng-tsao's armies in the rich heart of the province, where they sat astride the Peiping-Hankow railway.

Meanwhile, in Peiping and Tientsin, the North China National Salvation Association had reorganized itself into the North China People's Anti-Japanese Self-Defence Committee. On November 10, the Committee held a meeting in Tientsin, attended by representatives of many partisan groups. Shortly afterwards their delegates came to Hankow to report to the Central Government and seek official recognition and support.*

Such was the picture presented by the "occupied" areas in Hopei after the people of the province had had three months in which to organize their welcome to the bearers of peace and tranquillity made in Japan.

At the end of November, a messenger came to Chao Tung's headquarters in the mountains near Nankow. He brought a letter from Chu Teh and Peng Teh-huai, commander and vice-commander of the former Red Army, now the Eighth Route Army of the National Government. They wrote that they had heard of Chao Tung's detachment and that they hoped it would consent to co-ordinate its activities with those of the regular forces and partisan units of the Eighth Route in the interests of more effective struggle against the enemy.

On December 10, the detachment held a conference at Fuchiatai. It was decided to start immediately westward — for Wutaishan — the "five holy mountains" of Chinese Buddhism which stand starkly at the frontier of Hopei and Shansi. The cold weather was coming and the partisans needed a base. Chao Tung had visited the five mountains and knew the magistrate of the district town at their foot.** Besides, at Wutaishan they hoped to find the national army, represented there by a part of Lin Piao's famous 115th Division, which had remained there after the main headquarters of the Eighth Route Army, established at Wutaishan in September and October, had moved to South Shansi.

---

* These particulars are from an interview with one of the delegates, Miss Liu Ching-yang, at Hankow, in December 1937.

**This patriotic magistrate, Sung Shao-wan, was to become chairman of the Shansi-Chahar-Hopei Border Area.

But they encountered the Eighth Route Army long before they got to Wutaishan. Crossing the Great Wall into Chahar, they found the three districts of Yuhsien, Laiwang, and Kwanlin held by one of its regiments, commanded by Yang Chien-wu. Commander Yang directed them to Fuping, in Western Hopei. Here partisan detachments from all over the province were concentrating to discuss plans for joint action.

Nieh Yung-chan, commander of the border military area of Shansi, Chahar, and Hopei, met them at Fuping. Nieh was a man of great talents and much experience in China's struggle for liberation. He had studied in France, Germany, and Russia. In 1926, he had been secretary of the political department of the Whampoa Military Academy, which produced the military leaders of the revolutionary campaigns of 1925-7. After the split between the Communists and the Kuomintang he had worked in the Kiangsi Soviets and the Red Army. Now that the United Front was reconstituted he had the authority of the National Government to raise the people of the occupied territories to struggle against the invader.

The detachment decided to stay in Fuping for training. It remained there for over a month. Standard systems of military and political instruction were adopted. The military training concentrated on developing physical stamina and the technique of night fighting and the rapid attack. Political education was combined with general education, since many of the men were illiterate. It was based on the programme of the United Front and emphasized self-discipline and the necessity of maintaining the closest contact with the people.

The daily schedule comprised an hour and a half of running and mountain-climbing before breakfast, an hour each of class-work in military tactics and political education between breakfast and lunch, and several hours of intensive arms drill in the afternoons. Evenings were devoted to lectures, theatricals, and mass singing. This programme was followed by all the units concentrated in and around Fuping.

The following pay scale was put into operation for the various ranks:

Commander of Army   .   .   . $5.00 a month

Regimental Commander	.	.	.	$4.00 ,,
Lower officers	.	.	.	$3.00 ,,
Rank and file	.	.	.	$2.00 ,,

Promotion was on the basis of experience and ability shown in the course of actual fighting. It did not necessarily take place from grade to grade. A common partisan could be promoted to company commander on his showing in one battle. A commander could be unceremoniously reduced to the ranks if he failed to discharge his responsibility. But such changes were not arbitrary: they were made by joint decision of the military and political leadership of the unit concerned.

Tactical training was carried out through practical exercises and miniature "wars" in the class-room sandbox. The partisans were fascinated by this sandbox fighting, and spent hours off duty outflanking and "annihilating" each other's counters while they varied the topography of the sandy battlefield. The fighters were trained to discuss and analyse each action. Henceforth, after every engagement the partisans would go over it point by point, searching out the reasons for victory or defeat.

Hitherto, the "First Allied Anti-Japanese People's Army" had been a wandering band of men who wanted to fight the Japanese and had moved about building up its strength and armament. Now, with a force of 1,500 fully armed men definitely committed to the anti-Japanese struggle, it was faced with a number of new questions. Technical and political problems were closely linked. Fifteen hundred men needed a base of operations, a place from which they could draw supplies and recruits and which they would have to defend. How would they maintain themselves in such a base? By bleeding the people white, like a bandit gang or an old war-lord army? Or by linking themselves inseparably with the people and becoming their armed vanguard against the cruellest robber horde that had ever ravaged the North China countryside — the Japanese army with its record of murder, pillage, and rape? Then there was the problem of offensive operations. Would each partisan unit continue to operate independently on the flanks of the enemy, or would all unite for concerted action to cut the Japanese lines of communication and tie up the enemy forces in the rear at a time when they were most needed for major actions on the main battle-fronts?

Chao Tung's detachment and the other partisan detachments that came to Fuping found sane and sensible answers to all these questions. They were not given generally-worded lectures. The Eighth Route Army placed at their experience its rich fund of practical experience in guerrilla warfare and popular organization, tried and tested in many campaigns. They saw with their own eyes how in two short months in Western Hopei, it had welded unbreakable links between the people and the armed forces of the area and ensured — not through coercion, but through organization and co-operation, that larged armed formations were kept supplied with recruits, material, and food. Fuping was in constant radio communication not only with the headquarters of the Eighth Route Army in South Shansi, but also with the Shansi command and with the Central Government in Hankow. It was in a position to co-ordinate the military activities of the partisans.

A United Front working arrangement was quickly reached between Nieh Yung-chen at Fuping and a number of partisan leaders who had gathered there. The civil administration of all areas behind the Japanese lines which had been recaptured by the partisan forces would immediately revert to the central authorities, represented on the spot by a "Border Government of Shansi, Chahar, and Hopei". The partisan detachments would be assigned to guard and to develop their activities from certain definite areas. They would follow the lead of the Border Government in matters of general civil and military policy, but would have considerable autonomy in local matters and the internal affairs of their units.

This was in December 1937, six months after the outbreak of the war, in territory which newspaper maps had long designated in block letters as "under Japanese occupation".

On January 15, 1938, by special authorization of the Central Government, the frontier administration was formally inaugurated at Wutaishan. At that time it already controlled forty-two districts behind the Japanese lines. Its military forces totalled 100,000 partisans in the three provinces.

Shortly afterwards, Chao Tung's detachment, now the Fifth Branch Army of the Frontier Military Area, set out for the eight districts in Western Hopei which it had been assigned to garrison. Very soon now, its numbers would swell almost tenfold, to more than 10,000 men. Few of the new recruits would be soldiers. Almost all would be peasants and working-men fighting in defence of their homes and their land.

The detachment was destined to reconquer much territory and fight many battles. On July 7, 1938 — anniversary of the outbreak of the war it sent 1,000 men to appear once more before the walls of Peiping. For a day, it retook Marco Polo Bridge. In a daring raid on the city power plant, it plunged Peiping into darkness. Sandbag barricades were erected in Peiping's streets and, just as a year before, guns boomed and squads of soldiers patrolled the city enforcing martial law. But now it was the invader who was on the defensive. Its work done, the detachment withdrew. The foray towards Peiping was a political demonstration, result of the Border Government's decision to "commemorate the anniversary of the war by bold blows against the enemy." To the Japanese, to the people of Peiping, to the foreign embassies, and to all the world, it said: "North China is still ours." The Japanese shuddered in anger and irritation. When would this end? The people of Peiping took new heart. In the foreign embassies, radio transmitters buzzed.

But all this would be later. Now the detachment was just beginning the new phase of its career.

The picturesque band of partisans whose fortunes and personnel fluctuated after every skirmish belonged to the past. A whole historical period separated the first rumblings of protest in the hills around Peiping from the planned defence of the new frontier areas in which bases for an anti-Japanese counter- offensive were being built in accordance with a systematic military, political, and economic plan. Only six months had passed. During these six months the stalwart people of North China had given birth to many warriors.

They were beginning to give birth to armies.

Of these the army of Chao Tung was only one.

CHAPTER V

Trial by Fire

"THIS time the whole country will fight," my student friend had said in a tone of complete conviction during the days of deepest despair in Peiping and Tientsin. "The front will be everywhere."

Events moved quickly to prove that he was right. Twelve days after the fall of the two cities, major forces of the Japanese army and crack Chinese Central Government troops clashed at Nankow Pass, on the Great Wall, some thirty miles north-west of Peiping. And within a fortnight the great battle for Shanghai had begun — a heroic three-month struggle that won for China the sympathy and admiration of the world.

For the Japanese, the Shanghai "incident" was the logical sequel to Marco Polo Bridge and to their whole previous policy. When threats and political pressure had failed to win them domination of the North, they had applied force. And when the Central Government at Nanking replied to force with defiance and preparation, instead of surrender as before, the Japanese re-solved to strike at what they considered the main citadel of the Government's power.

By winning Shanghai, the Japanese could deal the Chinese Government a staggering blow. Industrially and financially, the city was China's richest base. In it were concentrated fully 70 per cent of her modern industry and a large part of her currency reserves. As a port, Shanghai was China's chief gateway to the West. Through it flowed the greater part of her foreign trade. Militarily, Shanghai commanded the approaches to Nanking, both by river and railway.

Shanghai was also the centre of British, American, and French influence in China. All three countries had capital investments, as well as trading interests in the city, and in certain parts of it (the International Settlement and the French Concession) they enjoyed administrative control. Britain's stake in Shanghai was particularly large. In no other city outside the Empire had she invested so much capital. After the capture of Shanghai the Japanese hoped to have the whip hand not only over Nanking, but also over the chief economic rival of their imperialism in China. They fully anticipated that Britain would support China in attempting to ward off an attack on Shanghai. But they also believed that once the great city was safely a hostage in their hands, she would hasten to make terms; and that the powerful British influence on the Chinese Government then would be used to force Nanking into a quick "peace". This was precisely what had happened after the first "Shanghai War" in 1982, when the heroic three-month resistance of the Nineteenth Route Army had been terminated by a "truce" of capitulation dictated largely by British interests.

This truce, which closed the first battle of Shanghai, left the Japanese in such a favourable situation for the second that they did not for a moment doubt their ability to quickly take possession of the city. By its terms, Chinese troops were banned from the area, leaving a feeble garrison of 3,000 "Peace Preservation Corps" — as at Tientsin. The Japanese, on the other hand, were given the right of free movement on the "Extra-Settlement Roads" situated on Chinese territory bordering on Hongkew, a part of the foreign-administered International Settlement which they had long favoured as a residential area. In 1932, the most stubbornly defended Chinese positions had been situated on these roads, and their consolidation had cost the invaders long efforts and many casualties. Now they were dominated by an all-but-impregnable fortress, bristling with guns and capable of resisting the heaviest shells and bombs — the newly-constructed steel and concrete barracks of the Japanese Naval Landing Party at Kiangwan.

As at Tientsin, the heritage of the unequal treaties imposed on China by the Western Powers during their period of imperialist expansion created a situation most favourable to the invaders. In Tientsin, the Boxer Protocol had closed the city to Chinese troops. In Shanghai, the Japanese were able to create a strong base within the International Settlement. As in North China also, resistance was hampered from the first by the fruits of concessions made by the Chinese Government during the years of capitulation. These have already been described.

The Naval Barracks was not the only Japanese stronghold in Shanghai. In strategically important streets of the International Settlement, canny Japanese citizens had for years been building themselves little modern "homes" of the strongest materials, with interesting thick concrete slabs for roofs. Schools for Japanese children, Japanese-owned factories, and even a "scientific experimental station" on one of the outside roads which a friendly Chinese Government could not refuse to accommodate on its territory, were all advantageously situated and solidly constructed. In their capacious cellars, guns, shells, and food-supplies awaited "the day".* It was only after a month of war, when most of the surrounding structures in these once-peaceful streets had been carried away like so much chaff, that the squat, solid efforts of the Japanese architects, arranged according to the plans of Japanese tacticians, could be recognized for what they were by even the most inexperienced eye. But by then there were artillery pieces on their well-buttressed roofs and machine-guns peering out everywhere from behind their sturdy walls.

Repeated manoeuvres of the Japanese Naval Landing Party (the Japanese garrison in Shanghai, which numbered 5,000 at a time when China kept only 3,000 armed police in the city) were held in areas where hostilities were expected. Since they were carried out in the early morning, usually between

---

* One wonders in how many cities of the Western world, fascist gentlemen (aided, no doubt, by expert advice) are similarly building and stocking up against *their* "day".

three and five o'clock, even some of the prepared points could be used after the streets had been well cordoned against observers. The Japanese capture of Shanghai was rehearsed by many successive garrisons, all of which later came back as reinforcements to apply their experience in the real war. But these elaborate rehearsals did not prove as useful as anticipated, because once again unexpectedly strong Chinese resistance upset the Japanese plan.

That Shanghai would be the scene of new provocations if the Japanese bluff was called in North China was not doubted by anyone. Remembering 1932, the people of the city began to prepare for the worst in July, when it was first indicated that the Marco Polo Bridge skirmish might lead to general hostilities. The Chinese Government too began its military preparation to prevent Shanghai from going the way of Peiping and Tientsin. But it did not violate the 1932 truce agreement, and while the Peace Preservation Corps in the city began to erect defences, no regular troops entered the city until the reinforcement and movements of the Japanese marines made it evident that the attack was about to begin.

Already on July 24, Shanghai had been alarmed by an incident strikingly similar to that which had led to the first clash on Marco Polo Bridge. The Japanese Navy suddenly announced that a bluejacket named Miyazaki had been kidnapped, and that drastic action would be taken if he were not immediately pro- duced. Japanese patrols were sent into Chinese territory to search for him and the situation grew ugly. But the incident ended when a Chinese boatman at Chinkiang turned Miyazaki over to the authorities, after having pulled him, dripping, out of the Yangtze, in which he had tried to commit suicide. Questioned, he confessed that he had violated discipline by going to a brothel other than those designated for the use of His Imperial Japanese Majesty's Navy, had been seen by a superior, and had deserted rather than face the consequent penalties. Of this "incident" not even the Japanese Navy could make a cause *de guerre*, especially since negotiations were proceeding in the North and the future course of the Sino-Japanese conflict had not yet become clear.

In August, Japanese preparations for action at Shanghai became obvious and unmistakable. All Japanese residents in Hankow and other Yangtze ports were evacuated by their river flotilla, whose vessels did not return to their stations, but remained concentrated at Shanghai. On August 9, the same day that this fleet arrived, there occurred in the port city a real provocation in the Imperial manner. Sub-Lieutenant Oyama and Seaman Saito of the Naval Landing Force sacrificed their lives to create a "pretext" — the sacred talisman without which the Japanese never act, and which, being a methodical people, they always prepare in advance. Driving out to the Chinese military airdrome at Hungjao, they replied to the challenges of sentries by opening fire and killing one of their number. Other sentries quickly shot the Japanese. Two days later an armada composed of five cruisers, nine destroyers, nine gunboats, an aircraft-carrier, and a number of transports sailed into Shanghai. At the wharves owned by Japanese commercial shipping companies they discharged men, munitions, supplies, trucks, tanks, and all the paraphernalia of a well-equipped expeditionary force. Needless to say, such a force cannot be assembled and cross the Sea of Japan all in the space of two days, even at the behest of outraged Imperial dignity.

The Japanese Embassy was still open in Nanking. On the day of the arrival of the armada, it demanded that the Chinese Government withdraw the "Peace Preservation Corps" from Shanghai, which Japan thus hoped to win without having to fight for it. The Chinese Government replied not to Japan but to the whole world. Publicly announcing the measures it was taking in self-defence, it did not withdraw the Peace Preservation Corps, but began hurriedly to reinforce them with regular troops of the crack 88th (Central Army) Division.

On August 13, the first guns boomed at Shanghai, and a large- scale modern battle burst like a bomb in the vitals of this great city, in which 4,000, 000 people lived and worked. Within a day, while a tremendous human cataract of refugees poured into the French Concession and the non-Japanese sections of the International Settlement, acres of homes, shops, and factories were turned into a battlefield. Into Chapei and Kiangwan, the guns of the newly-arrived Japanese armada poured a ceaseless stream of steel while Chinese soldiers and Japanese marines attacked and counter-attacked, fought and died by thousands in the long grey streets. Before long all the weapons at the disposal of both sides had been brought into play. Japanese seaplanes dumped death on the Chinese lines, and the pursuits and bombers of China's air force, for the first time in the history of the service, flew out to meet a foreign enemy.*

August 13 marked the end of the North China "incident", the Shanghai "incident", and all other incidents. From now on there could be no further talk of "localization" of the hostilities. Regardless of the fact that diplomatic relations between the two countries were still on a "normal" basis, a general war between China and Japan had begun. Two days after the fighting broke out at Shanghai, Japanese airplanes carried out their first bombing of Nanking, capital of the Chinese Republic.

In July, the heroic defence of Marco Polo Bridge had inspired the entire Chinese nation with pride and confidence and had caused the Government to put itself at the head of a people clamouring for resistance. Since then, Peiping and Tientsin had fallen almost without a struggle. Now, at Shanghai, the Chinese army had come to grips with a better-armed Japanese force on a three-mile battle front every inch of which was subject to the point-blank fire of hundreds of naval guns. Would the Chinese soldiers stand firm against such punishment? Or would they give way, leaving China's greatest city in the hands of the enemy?

The Chinese army did not give way. Throughout August and for two

---

* Two tragedies marked this first flight. On August 14, Chinese bombs accidentally killed about 2,000 Chinese and several foreigners in the streets of the International Settlement. One, which fell on the Palace Hotel, was aimed at the Japanese cruiser *Idzumo*, which was anchored near by. The others dropped from the damaged bomb-rack of a Chinese airplane which had been hit, according to an official investigation, by Japanese anti-aircraft fire. It must be noted that the *Idzumo* and other vessels lay near the German, Soviet, and British Consulates and that the responsibility for endangering the Settlement lay, according to all neutral opinion, with the Japanese, who were using it as a base. In a protest to the Municipal Council of the Settlement, Mayor O. K. Yin pointed out that Japanese anti-aircraft guns had been mounted on the roofs of Japanese banks and other buildings even in the Central District, not involved in the hostilities.

months thereafter, it continued to hold the city. Against the fury of Japanese steel and high explosives it set up the "new great wall" of flesh and blood of which Nieh Erh had sung. With its own inadequate technical equipment it struck back at the invaders, delivering telling blows. In this, it was effectively assisted by the air force, whose young cadet pilots participated in the Shanghai operations and successfully beat off Japanese aerial attacks on Nanking and Hangchow. At the end of the first week of hostilities, thirty Japanese aeroplanes had been brought down, partly by the efficient ground-defences of the capital, partly by the machine-guns of the new-winged youth of China.

In the aerial warfare of those early days, the Chinese definitely had the upper hand. It is hard to exaggerate the importance of these initial victories, especially for civilian morale in the rear. People who had seen Japanese raiders brought down in flames on their first flight over the cities in which they lived were not likely to have any paralysing fear of them in the future.

After Marco Polo Bridge, the Chinese Government had for the first time voiced bold defiance of Japanese attempts to swallow the North. Now, after Shanghai, it threw down the challenge to all the aims of Japanese policy in China.

While armies fought at Shanghai and Nankow Pass, Nanking was the scene of political and diplomatic developments which showed clearly that Chiang Kai-shek's call for "war to the end" had been seriously meant. The Japanese had sought to dominate China without fighting.

The armies of the Central Government were now engaging them on two fronts.

They had done everything in their power to turn provincial military leaders against Nanking.

Now commanders from all over the country flocked to conferences in the capital, with offers to lead their armies against the common enemy. They came by airplane from the remotest provinces, regions that until a few years before had been a by-word for inaccessibility. Many of them had previously paid only lip-service to the Central Government, and some, like Lung Yun,

Governor of far-off Yunnan, were visiting the capital for the first time. Outstanding among those who came to pledge their fullest co-operation in the national struggle were the leaders of China's two most formidable military forces apart from the Government's own German-trained divisions. They were the Kwangsi generals — Li Tsung-jen and Pai Chung-hsi — for years rebelliously autonomous; and the leaders of the Red Army against which the Nanking forces had waged civil war for a decade. Li Chi-shen, Chen Ming-shu, Chiang Kwang-nai, and Tsai Ting-kai, commanders of the famous Nineteenth Route Army, which had defended Shanghai in 1932 but had later been demobilized after rebelling against the Government's policy of capitulation, also returned to Nanking to offer their services to the nation.

The efforts of all the groups which had been working at cross-purposes during the era of capitulation were now united in the face of the Japanese attack. Chiang Kai-shek had constructed long military roads throughout the country in the course of his campaigns against the Chinese Soviets and the consolidation of his authority in the Western provinces. Now hundreds of thousands of troops from the distant South-west were marching along these roads to the fronts of war against Japan. The Kwangsi generals had built up their military machine largely in the hope of overthrowing Chiang. Now their hardy soldiers were already in the trenches at Shanghai and in Shantung. The Red Army, in its battles with the better-armed Government troops, had achieved almost legendary skill in the tactics of manoeuvre and surprise. Within a very short time it was to show that these tactics could be equally effective against the Japanese.

The Japanese had attempted by every means at their disposal to isolate China from the Soviet Union. The basis of Tokyo's constant demands that China adhere to the "Anti-Comintern" Pact had been the hope that in the event of a Soviet-Japanese war, China would aid Japan, or at least remain neutral. Until the war came, there were also benefits to be gained from Sino-Soviet estrangement. Without fear of trouble in her rear, Japan could pursue unhindered her provocations on the Soviet border. At the same time, she could nibble "friendly" China at her leisure.

Now, on August 21,* a pact of non-aggression was signed between China and the U.S.S.R. This pact was devoid of military significance and was no different from the many similar treaties in force between the Soviet Union and its other neighbours. But it had not been signed before because Japan had been trying to bring Nanking into line with the Berlin-Rome-Tokyo axis, and Nanking, while declining the honour, had not wished to do anything openly to provoke Japan. In the circumstances of August 1937, the signing of the Sino-Soviet Non-Aggression Pact was a fact that fell into line with the resistance on Marco Polo Bridge, Chiang Kai-shek's speech at Kuling, and the answer, blow for blow, to the Japanese attack on Shanghai. It meant that henceforth China would protect her own integrity and interests both militarily and diplomatically. If the Japanese answer to this "outrageous" turn in the Chinese Government's policy was to attempt to wipe that Government off the face of the earth, China was prepared to meet the challenge.

What Japan had feared above all was the national-revolutionary unity of the Chinese people. To prevent this unity had been the essence of her policy for twenty years. And in the era of capitulation she had constantly bullied the National Government into suppressing popular anti-Japanese movements and intensifying its war against the Red Army which had long since proclaimed the recovery of the lost territories to be the chief object of its activities. More than this, she had even offered to loan her troops to Nanking for "joint operations" against the Chinese Soviets, an offer which, if accepted, would have given Japanese forces the right to proceed to any place in China where they happened to perceive a red herring. This offer had been renewed during the Sian Incident, when the Imperial Army announced its anxiety to "rescue" Chiang Kai-shek from his kidnappers.

However, the constant Japanese encroachment had only served to unite the country instead of splitting it. After Marco Polo Bridge, Kuomintang and Communists had laid the ground-work of a formal alliance to replace the truce that had obtained since Sian. The terms of this alliance were to be:

---

* Formally announced, in Nanking and Moscow, on August 29.

1. The reorganization of the North-western Soviet Office into the Border Region Government founded on universal suffrage and the principles of democracy; submission of lists of official personnel for appointment by the Central Government;

2. The reorganization of the Red Armies into the National Revolutionary Eighth Route Army;

3. The Communist Party to issue a declaration pledging wholehearted co-operation with the Kuomintang for national salvation;

4. Chiang Kai-shek to issue a reply recognizing the legal position of the Chinese Communist Party.*

The public announcement of the reorganization of the Red Army (which was actually accomplished on August 22) was made on September 10. And twelve days later the two statements contemplated in the last two points of the agreement were officially published.

"Only with internal unity can we successfully repulse the onslaught of Japanese imperialism," stated the manifesto of the Communist Party's Central Committee. The party's present aims, it declared, were three in number. The first was the fullest prosecution of a national revolutionary war for the recovery of the lost territories. The second was the realization of democratic reforms. The third was the improvement of the living conditions of the people. This policy was based on Dr. Sun Yat-sen's Three People's Principles, which had formed the foundation of the first revolutionary alliance of the two parties in 1924, and which the Communist Party now declared to "represent the needs of China to-day".

In the interests of anti-Japanese unity, the party announced that it had given up its previous policies of working for the overthrow of the Kuomintang, organizing Soviet administrations, and confiscating the estates of landlords. It declared that the existing Soviet Government was already in the process of

* As given by Lin Pai-chu (Lin Chu-han), who negotiated these points with Chiang Kai-shek, v. *Annual Report of the Border Region Government* (of which he is President). I have listed his three points as four.

reorganization on the lines agreed upon at Kuling. The Red Army, now the Eighth Route National Revolutionary Army, was placed under the control of the Central Military Council of the National Government.

The Generalissimo's reply acknowledged the Communist declaration point by point. Chiang Kai-shek termed the action of the Communist Party "an outstanding example of the triumph of national sentiment over every other consideration". In a subsequent paragraph, he defined the attitude which the Chinese Government would now take towards its former opponents. "To all citizens who are followers of the Three People's Principles", he wrote, "the National Government will extend its hand, irrespective of their former actions or beliefs.... Likewise, the National Government will be glad to accept the support of all parties which desire to come under the leadership of the Kuomintang in the struggle for national existence."

Political prisoners were released, first in Nanking and Shanghai and later throughout the country. Not only the breach between the parties, but the tragic gulf that had for years divided the people of China from their Government, was at last being bridged. On the Shanghai front, representatives of all parties and all groups of the population were already working in the Anti-Enemy War Work Association, which rendered valuable services to the armies holding up the Japanese advance. The reconciliation of the Kuomintang and Communists acted as a stimulus to renewed effort in every field of national endeavour.

Among the first to greet the reconciliation was Madame Sun Yat-sen, widow of the founder of the Kuomintang, the father of China's national revolution. "Throughout his life", she wrote, "Dr. Sun advocated the principle of joint struggle for the existence of China. That is why he held that the Kuomintang and Communists should work together. The Communist Party is a party which stands for the interests of the working classes, both industrial and agricultural. Dr. Sun realized that without the keen support and co-operation of these classes, the mission of completing the national revolution could not easily be carried out. If the co-operation with the Chinese Communist Party which Dr. Sun advocated had continued uninterruptedly until the present time, China would by now have been a free and independent power. Past events are a good lesson. During the present crisis, all former differences should be forgotten. The whole nation must join together in opposing Japanese aggression and fighting for the final victory."

For many years the Chinese Soviets had been a dark mystery, not only to the West, but to great numbers of people in China itself. In the official Press, one read of "extermination of bandits" and the repeated deaths in action of Chu Teh and Mao Tze-tung, who somehow always seemed to turn up to be "killed" again. That a well-organized Soviet Government and a 100,000 strong Red Army existed was not generally believed. From the "Communist brigand" version promoted by the Government, to the "spontaneous and unorganized agrarian movement"* of spurious theoreticians the "explanations" permitted by the censorship were one great mass of unfounded and often maliciously inspired misinformation. On such documentary evidence as was available from the Soviet areas and accounts published by the Communist movement abroad, hostile propagandists and feckless wiseacres poured streams of inky "disproof" and "scepticism".

The books of Agnes Smedley were classed as slightly unbalanced fiction; and the accounts of Edgar Snow, who had actually "been and seen", were received as undoubtedly first-hand though somewhat suspect evidence.

Now, with the reconciliation, new legends sprang up. The Communists had never been Communists at all and had now "surrendered their principles". They had been Communists all the time and still were, and had entered the United Front in order, by wily and devious ways of their own, to undermine and destroy the National Government. The Chinese Soviets had "finally decided to liquidate their movement completely... and by the summer of 1936 had drifted so far from their original principles that they were actually more friendly to landlords and capitalists than the Kuomintang." In fact, they were reactionaries. This last "interpretation" appeared under the auspices of one of

---

* The Trotzkyist view.

the most earnest followers of the egregious Mr. Wang Ching-wei.*

Early in September, I managed to locate the two Eighth Route Army representatives in Nanking, whose presence and address were still being kept secret from inquiring newspapermen by professionally "discreet" publicity officials who were slow in adjusting themselves to the new situation and regarded the United Front as a hush-hush arrangement of which only their own carefully denatured version should be allowed to reach the world. Thus I was fortunate enough to secure for American newspaper readers an authoritative Communist interpretation of the new phase of Chinese political development in which the co-operation of the country's two great parties had been substituted for struggle between them. I also did my duty by the *United Press*, which was pleased that I had obtained the first foreign Press interview with the "secret Red negotiators" in the capital.

So deeply underground were the Communists in Kuomintang China before Sian, that in spite of the fact that I had lived in the country since childhood, I had never until this time knowingly met a member of the party. Now, about to see the legendary leaders of the Red Army, I was excited and curious. Sitting in the prim waiting-room of the delegation, under what still

---

The Facts About Communism in China, prefaced (and judging from the style, written) by Mr. T'ang Leang-li, chief propagandist for Wang Ching-wei and once China correspondent of the *Daily Herald*. Tho truly remarkable author of this pamphlet further states that "it is to be assumed that they [the Communists] will be incorporated in the body politic in the same way as their comrades in Germany and Italy (!) have been absorbed.... Germany formerly had a trade union movement which next to the British was the strongest in the world; a Communist party second in strength only to that of Russia; a Social Democratic Party which was the wealthiest labour party in the world.... All these powerful and active political groups have been completely absorbed in Germany under the Nazi regime, and when China is no longer exposed to the danger which now threatens her from without, it will be found that the reformed Communists will similarly co-operate [sic] earnestly and effectively with the Kuomintang.... If the German Government", he goes on, "had been made aware [of the new Communist Programme] it would not have been so easily induced to sign... the anti-Comintern pact [with Japan]." This limpid masterpiece is dated April 1938, i.e. after Hitler's recognition of "Manchukuo". Fortunately, Mr. Wang Ching-wei is no longer able to develop these conceptions, in Chungking, and his avowed followers, members of the "fifth column" of Japanese imperialism in China, have ceased to write China's foreign publicity.

seemed the fantastically unreal constellation of portraits of Sun Yat-sen, Mao
Tse-tung, Chiang Kai-shek, and Chu Teh, I composed mental pictures of stern-
visaged, unapproachable, fanatic veterans of ten years of bitter struggle and
the epic Long March.

The door opened, and I was greeted by a gangling, bespectacled En-
glish-speaking intellectual in blue student uniform and a handsome smiling
officer in khaki. Their warm handshakes and forthright manner put me immediately at my ease. For two hours, we discussed the birth of the United
Front and the new line of the party. Every question that I put was frankly
answered. Half-way through the interview the air-raid siren wailed the approach of enemy planes, and we ended our conversation hunched in a deep,
dank, half-finished dugout, crowded with people and dimly lit by a low-
powered electric bulb hanging from a hank of wire which seemed to come
from nowhere.

I liked these young Communists tremendously and was struck by their
utter absence of officialism, but I was disappointed at having met only two
obvious "indoor workers" and subordinates, and not the battle-scarred heroes whom I had prepared to encounter. Taking leave of them in their sunny
courtyard filled with open-faced, blue-uniformed boys and girls, I asked them
their names. "Yeh Chien-ying," said the officer, "former chief of staff of the
Red Army". "Chin Pang-hsien (Po Ku)," said the tall "student", "former Chairman of the North-western Soviet Government". These, and the young soldiers who stood around and had served me with tea, were the iron men of the
Red forces who had vanquished strong enemies and bitter hunger, rushing
rivers, and snow-peaked mountains. These were the fighters of the Eighth
Route Army, who were to write many glorious pages into the annals of China's
struggle against Japan, and before another year was out, to continue their
"Long March" to lost Manchuria.

The notes I took of that interview perished in the sack of Nanking. But I
still have the brief interpretation of the Communist Party's position which I
later wrote on the basis of it for the *United Press*. This interpretation cast
some light on points which were then being hotly discussed by the world

Press:

"Refuting the suggestion that their party has 'surrendered to the Kuomintang', Chinese communists maintain that their own Marxist principles dictate the fullest co-operation, both during the war and during the subsequent period of national reconstruction, with the Government they once fought.

"The national war against Japan, they believe, is revolutionary in nature. They state that Marxist theory differentiates between the nationalism of oppressor states imposing their will upon others and that of oppressed peoples fighting for national liberation. The former is regressive — the latter, progressive. Furthermore, the communists believe that the country-wide struggle against Japan will teach every Chinese to connect his own personal fate with wider national issues, and therefore to aspire to take a hand in the political shaping of a new democratic China. The Communists advocate mass organization based on this new consciousness of the people.

"This view has caused the Chinese Communists to make the struggle against Japan the cornerstone of their activity and agitation. Apprehending that the intensification of social strife at this juncture might throw the propertied classes into the camp of peace, or even the arms of the Japanese, Chinese Reds are now advocating the co-operation of all classes in the interests of the war. Having adopted this policy, they are branding as traitors those opposed to such co-operation. To them, the use of revolutionary slogans and traditions to create a state of disunity which would facilitate the victory of the imperialist Japanese is the lowest form of political trickery, and they denounce as Trotzkyists all those who try in this way to break up the national front of all classes and parties which they advocate.*

---

* It is not to be supposed from this that the Chinese Communists try to hold back the masses from attempts to better their livelihood. On the contrary, they continually advocate the lightening of the people's burdens in the councils of the Government, practice the land-reform and rent reduction programme outlined in Dr. Sun Yat-sen's *Three People's Principles*, and encourage mass pressure to shift the material burden of the war to the shoulders of the rich.

"Communist leaders have assured me that their party has not been, and will not be dissolved. Its members are giving everything to the anti-Japanese struggle not because they have 'reformed', but because they consider that it is their duty, as Communists, to do so."

At Shanghai, the Chinese army was demonstrating to the invaders and to the whole world that it could fight. What was going on at Nanking indicated clearly what it was fighting for. The battle now was not to decide whether Japanese aggression would progress to achieve China's subjugation, or be held to the positions which it had already consolidated. This had been the question in 1932. In 1937, the dynamic factor was the awakening of the Chinese people. Even before the hostilities began, the Chinese Government had begun to move cautiously to capture the initiative from its imperialist adversary. Now the Chinese diplomatic and political counter-offensive was in full tide. Point by point, the entire structure of Japan's continental policy had been challenged.

Held up on the Shanghai front, where their discomfiture was a spectacle for all the world, faced with the defiant consolidation of a China which they had tried first to blackmail and then to beat into submission, the Japanese took up the Fascist cowards' weapon of civilian bombing. Already on August 26, when Foreign Minister Hirota had announced to the world that "Japan's only course now is to beat China to her knees so that she no longer has the spirit to fight", his words had been punctuated not by victories of the Japanese Army and Navy but by the exploits of the Japanese Air Force, which on that same day destroyed six schools and a hospital and killed 200 sleeping workers in their beds at Paofutang, slum section of the capital. Now the Japanese spokesman in Shanghai grandiloquently declared that the Japanese air fleet would proceed to "destroy Nanking" as a punishment for the defiant attitude of the Chinese Government.

Two days' "warning" was given to Nanking. Women and children were evacuated from the city. Those who had work to do stayed, as before. Spain had proved, and China now confirmed, that the Fascist recipe for beating whole peoples into submission did not work. Not only Chinese, but nationals of other countries working in the capital, refused to leave their homes. When the American ambassador announced his withdrawal, on the orders of Washington, to a gunboat on the river, his action was regarded as desertion by everyone in Nanking. The right to expect safety at all points away from manifest military objectives belonged to every human being living in the city, Chinese or foreign. The only available defence of this right was to "stay put", to keep on working, and place the responsibility for whatever happened on the shoulders of the Japanese. Washington's order to its ambassador to withdraw from clearly-marked embassy buildings at the behest of a treaty-breaking invader whom the United States did not recognize as a combatant, was placid acceptance amounting to direct condonation of Japan's criminally insane project of indiscriminately wiping out a great city from the air. Within a day, America had become the most unpopular country, next to Japan, in the Chinese capital. As representative of the *United Press*, I saw my news sources dry up. Chinese friends declined to visit our office, which was temporarily housed in the embassy.

American citizens living in Nanking came in with signed denunciations of their Government's policy. Admiral Yarnell, commander of the American Fleet in China, took the law into his own hands and declared that the U.S.S. *Luzon*, stationed at Nanking, would not leave the city to carry away the ambassador or for any other purpose. It is to be supposed that the State Department was unequivocally given to understand the results of its unfortunate order. In any case, before the actual severe bombings had begun, Mr. Johnson was back in his embassy, which he did not leave again.

So much for the "warning". During the last week of September 1937, Japan showed the horrified world the meaning of the fact. On September 22, sixty-five Japanese airplanes raided Nanking, dropping bombs in thirty different places. Many were killed in the crowded South City. A hundred refugees from the Shanghai war zone, lodged in a camp on the water-front, were wiped out by a bomb. Meanwhile Canton, to which no warning had been given, also began its martyrdom. In four raids within twelve hours, over

2,000 men, women, and children were slaughtered. "Foreign observers are puzzled over the nature of the Japanese objectives, as not one Government building or military establishment was hit," cabled Renter's correspondent. The Japanese aviators were not puzzled. Their purpose was to terrorize, and their objectives were the civilians in Canton's crowded streets. In Hankow, previously thought to be out of the range of enemy aircraft, 800 citizens were killed and 860 houses levelled to the ground on September 24.

Luckily, Nanking was not Canton or Hankow. Had it not been a new city of wide roads and great open spaces, the punishment to which it was subjected would have cost tens of thousands of lives. For five days, despite startled international protests, squadron after squadron of Japanese airplanes attacked the capital. On September 25 alone, ninety-six machines participated in the raids. Among other places, they bombed the great Red Cross hospital, filled with wounded from the Shanghai front.

But resistance and life and work went on. Anti-aircraft guns banged away at the raiders, and occasionally one would be brought down — plummeting earthward like a comet with a tail of fire and black smoke from its flaming gas tank, or floating to earth in hundreds of charred bits after the explosion of its bombs had pulverized it in the air. Every time this happened, cheers went up from the whole city, and crowds rushed, oblivious of the danger, to the fallen machines. Following the people on one such expedition through the narrow side alleys of the Confucius Temple district, a remnant of medieval Nanking in the streamlined modern capital, I came upon Madame Chiang Kai-shek, clambering over the smoking fragments of fallen bomber. As Secretary of the Air Commission she made it her business to personally investigate the results of every raid.

The great wave of popular organization for war service which was to become one of the outstanding features of life in China during the next year had already begun to rise in Shanghai. But in the capital months passed before it gave any sign of existence. Nanking was a military and bureaucratic city, frigidly proud of its massive buildings and new boulevards. Everything in it was meticulously regulated, every military contingency provided for.

When the enemy bombers came, its smartly-uniformed police and gendarmes and well-trained, disciplined first-aid units knew what to do. The streets were cleared in a few minutes. The people were herded into dugouts which had been built since the war in great numbers. Cars and trucks, carefully camouflaged, were parked under the leafy shade of roadside trees. Everything was smooth, orderly, and self-sufficient. There was one strange thing about the new Nanking, at first appearance. Not only was there no popular organization, but there seemed no basic population. Where were the butcher, the baker, and the candlestick maker, the worker and artisan and ever-present Chinese beggar? Did they not live there, or had they too, by some mysterious municipal zoning ordinance, been regulated away?

The explanation lay in the fact that there were two Nankings. There was the arrogant new capital. And there was the down-at-the-heel decaying ancient city on which it was superimposed, a city which had never really recovered from its sack during the Taiping rebellion, a catastrophe which had left it with a tenth of its original built-up area and perhaps a quarter of its original population. Even this remnant was unceremoniously shoved aside when the ground-plan was being laid down for the capital — and the new boulevards cut mercilessly through homes and shops. Nanking was transformed into a great garrison town of smart officers with gold-mounted dirks at their belts, officials with Packards and sleek fur collars, carefree young aviators who marched arm in arm down its main streets, and brisk business men in American suits. The original inhabitants were left unmolested only in the teeming South City. Elsewhere they had been evicted, and existed under bridges or in miserable lean-tos on empty lots which were sometimes a few steps away from the rear entrances of the most imposing Government buildings, but were carefully screened from the streets. Official cars roared proudly along the gleaming asphalt ribbons which formed the capital's thoroughfares. The people walked humbly along their dusty sides, or calmly tilled their fields and tended their cattle in the interstices of the great city, whose buildings were still so scattered over its vast area that they might have been flung out at random by some giant hand.

Now, when the ordeal came, it was the new, official, slightly Prussian Nanking that opposed its careful organization to the terror from the skies. Alone of all the cities in China, Nanking had prepared for air raids even before the war. Air-defence posters had been displayed in its streets for years. Huge concrete models of aerial bombs stood in its main squares "to educate the people". It had good anti-aircraft guns, well-trained gunners, and strong searchlights. Every time enemy planes attacked Nanking, they paid. The number of their machines which returned was always less than that which had started out.

For Nanking's step-children, the evicted poor, hundreds of new public dugouts were provided. And they needed dugouts. From Spain to China, Fascist bombs have an affinity for the poor. Aimed at ministerial buildings standing in spacious grounds, they almost always miss their targets. But from the slums of Barcelona to the miserable shanty-towns of Nanking, every bomb falling among the poor has brought holocausts. And everywhere that a palace has had a shack for a neighbour, the bomb has fallen on the shack. Before the bombings the dispossessed Nanking of the poor had had nothing to do with Nanking the near-Prussian capital. But now the new spaciousness of the city saved lives. Dugouts preserved the people from splinters. Gendarmes who had previously pushed them about and tried to keep them out of the sight of foreign dignitaries who came to admire the elegance of the capital, now told the poor how to protect themselves against death from the air. Every enemy plane brought down by the guns of the new Nanking marked a victory, above all, for the toiling population, the chief victim of the Japanese air terror. In Nanking, as elsewhere, the struggle made all classes allies against the national enemy. The success of one was the success of all.

There were thousands of refugee students in Nanking, the same students who had crowded the trains from Peiping, the steamers from Tientsin. They had come eager for service, and they complained that the Government had no plan for utilizing their energy and enthusiasm in the war of liberation. Crowds of them besieged the offices of the Eighth Route Army, asking for admission to the famous anti-Japanese university which forged intellectuals into fighters in cave class-rooms in the loess cliffs of Yenan. Only a few of the applications could be handled. The university was already full. Daily, the bespectacled Po Ku told scores of young people: "The fight is everywhere. You must not make your activity dependent upon whether you can or cannot be admitted to the university. There is so much to be done. It is your duty to find a place for yourselves in which you can apply all your energies to the struggle, wherever you are."

On September 18, anniversary of the Japanese conquest of Manchuria, Nanking saw its first popular demonstration. A few northern students made speeches in the streets and decorated the dignified walls of Nanking with new placards — not the striking, well-executed productions which already dominated the chief gates and squares of the capital, but hand-drawn on cheap paper, carefully and passionately. In one of Nanking's main theatres, an exhibition was held of posters by Shanghai artists mature in technique and burningly sincere in content. There were hundreds of them, impressively demonstrating the creative explosion generated by the war. Only a few months before, this fighting anti-Japanese art had been prohibited. Now the artists could speak with their hearts to the whole nation.

On September 18, I heard for the first time over the great 75-kilowatt metropolitan radio station, Nieh Erh's "March of the Volunteers" — a song long prohibited in Nanking, and which I had last heard in the Japanese-dominated North. All China was beginning to sing it now.

A day or two later, in the auditorium of a Nanking middle school, I attended a dramatic performance by the Peiping and Tientsin Student Union. The union's dramatic groups planned to go out into the country, and the stage-sets were accordingly simple, using only the resources which could be found in any village. The one-act plays were powerful and moving. One, "A Night in Peiping", showed a group of students heroically carrying on an underground printing-plant in the occupied capital of China's culture. Another, "Defend Marco Polo Bridge", vividly reproduced the outbreak of the war. The student actors knew their material. They had all been participants or eyewitnesses of the situations it dealt with. While one boy was demonstrating how national propaganda could be presented through the medium of the old "Big Drum" minstrelsy, the recitative ballad style used by Chinese storytellers and dear and familiar to the peasantry, Japanese planes attacked the city. The scream of power-diving planes, the thud of bombs, and the crack of anti-aircraft guns brought the audience to its feet, prepared for panic. But the performance did not stop. The student singer went on. "At Marco Polo Bridge", he sang, "we heard the big guns of the enemy." A bomb 200 yards away shook the building. "But we were not afraid and returned every blow of the Japanese dwarfs with a blow of our own." Another bomb came down. "We can hear the bombs of the enemy now," chanted the student. "But we will not stop fighting till we have driven him back into the sea." The audience now listened to the singer more than to the bombs. Everyone kept his seat. After half an hour, the raid ended. The young student stopped his sing song recitation, laid down the cymbals with which he had marked the ends of the periods, and looked suddenly tired. The audience applauded wildly.

This was how the new dramatic art of China grew, how it gave courage and inspiration while it experimented, in the fire of battle, with new methods which would bring it closer to the people.

In the audience, that day, were not only students, but high officials and social leaders of the capital. Among them were Shao Li-tzu, Minister of Publicity, and Yen Pao-heng, chief secretary of the New Life Movement. These men had their cars outside, ready to take them to concrete bombproof shelters. But they too had kept their seats listening to the simple, powerful appeal of the student artist who fought the national battle with song, and understood his duty as a fighter — not to relinquish his weapon, but to wield it more vigorously when the enemy attacked. The "Big Drum" recitative was for peasants and artisans. Cultured Chinese did not listen to "Big Drum" singers. But now a university student was giving all he had to the mastery of this "uncouth" technique, and the content of his recitation was such that it evoked in sophisticated scholars and jaded officials the same fighting response that it was designed to draw from the common people. Such were the times, and such the circumstances.

Before I left, the singer gave me his card and telephone number. He promised to call on me. A few days later, I tried to get in touch with him in the school building in which the refugee students were housed. "You will find him", a girl told me, "at the headquarters of the gendarmerie." The gendarmerie had discovered that the Peiping and Tientsin Students' Union was not properly registered and had put its leaders under restraint. It was a week before they were set free.

This was Nanking under the bombs. Defiance of Japan. Political unification. The concrete basis of the United Front, and the popular United Front movement beginning to grow and make all sections of Chinese society conscious of the strength to be drawn from unity in the struggle. At the same time, a retention of the old arrogant police conception of government. On the one hand, recognition of the popular forces. On the other, the persistence of suspicion of every movement not officially initiated and the automatic functioning of the old mechanism of suppression. But the popular awakening was beginning. And the old oppressive mechanism, designed to keep the people subdued during the period of capitulation, was on its way out. A year previously, the students would have been imprisoned for long periods, or they might have disappeared altogether. Now they were released within a few days, after a gendarme captain had "spoken to them like a father".

The Japanese attempt to terrorize the Chinese Government and people by the terrible air-raids on Canton, Hankow, and Nanking took the lives of thousands of citizens, but it failed entirely in its object of breaking the national will to resist. On September 25, the day on which ninety-six enemy air-planes dropped tons of high explosive on the capital and massacred 600 of its inhabitants, Chiang Kai-shek gave an interview to foreign Press correspondents. Calling on the Powers to support China's struggle and stating flatly that no country which was a signatory of the Nine-Power Treaty and the League Covenant could consider itself neutral, he declared:

"The Japanese raids on Nanking will not affect the military situation.

"The Japanese blockade of our coast* also will not stop us from fighting, although it will hurt the trade of the Powers which have failed to stand up to the aggressor in the Far East. Whether the massacre of civilians here and in other cities will terrorize us into submission, you can judge for yourselves from what you have seen. All it will do will be to give the Chinese people, and the peoples of the world, a fuller realization of Japan's barbarism. Our resistance cannot be crushed. China will hold out, no matter bow long this war will last, because she possesses incalculable and inexhaustible power and resources."

Once more, as on all occasions since July 17, Chiang Kai-shek voiced the mind of the Chinese people, their demand that the Powers carry out their contractual obligations, and the courage and confidence which made them determined to continue the struggle until the final victory. The "inexhaustible power and resources" of the Chinese nation had not yet been brought into the arena to any appreciable extent. But the words were prophetic, and, far to the North, at Pinghsin Pass (Pinghsinkuan) in the mountains of North Shansi, the prophecy was already becoming fact. There, on September 25, the day of Chiang Kai-shek's interview, the Eighth Route Army, employing guerrilla tactics, wiped out the Japanese Sakai detachment** of 3,000 men. But the victory was not won by the Eighth Route alone. On the eve of the battle, its political organizers called together thousands of local peasants and distributed rifles among them. The people participated in the fight and helped to win it. Pinghsinkuan was a landmark in the history of China's resistance. While on the Eastern Front the Chinese forces were holding Japan with the available military resources amassed by Nanking through years of effort to create a modern army, Pinghsinkuan was living testimony that the "inexhaustible power" of the Chinese people was not a thing of words alone. Already its potentialities were being realized, to the confusion of the invader.

---

* On August 26, the Japanese naval spokesman at Shanghai announced the imposition of a blockade on the entire China coast from Chinwangtao to Pakhoi.
** Part of Itagaki's Fifth Division.

As I telephoned Chiang Kai-shek's interview and, some time later, the news of Pinghsin Pass, to the Shanghai office of the *United Press*, my colleagues there could hear the pandemonium of bombs and anti-aircraft guns which split the air and shook the foundations of the capital. And I, at my end of the wire, heard clearly the thud of Japanese guns hammering away at the unbroken Chinese lines in Shanghai.

By the end of September the battle for Shanghai had entered its second stage. For a fortnight after August 13, the fighting had been concentrated on a three-mile front in the heart of the city. Every yard was hotly disputed. The guns of the Japanese navy made the urban districts of Chapei and Kiangwan a hell of high explosives and jagged steel. Not only artillery, machine-guns, rifles, hand grenades, and airplanes were used along this short line on stubborn flesh and blood. Both sides employed that most effective weapon in street fighting—the torch. Whole blocks of buildings were burned down to smoke out enemy positions, and to form fiery walls for concealment or protection from flank attacks. Before the fires had time to properly die down, Chinese soldiers and Japanese marines rushed forward to fight to the death for the possession of the waste of smouldering embers which they left in their wake. The Chinese soldiers welcomed such hand-to-hand encounters. At Shanghai they discovered that in close fighting they were more than a match for the Japanese. Repeatedly, they jeopardized the enemy positions and forced their way deep into Japanese territory in Hongkew and Wayside. But the Japanese could throw much more death, in steel parcels, from afar, and thus prevented the turning of these gains into victory.

On August 27, the Japanese army came to reinforce the navy which had fondly hoped to win for itself alone the glory of capturing Shanghai. Landing near the confluence of the Yangtze and Whangpoo, the soldiers sought to establish contact with the marines in the city. But the cup-shaped Chinese cordons established around the two Japanese forces long made this impossible.

It was only on September 15, that the month-long struggle of the Japanese to establish a *place d'armes* sufficiently extensive to permit the landing of large numbers of men and their deployment into a regular line, was crowned with success. On that day, the Chinese line moved away from the river-banks, out of the range of point-blank naval fire. In place of the two cup-shaped cordons, a continuous forty-mile front was established. This did not affect the situation in the city. The Chinese line had simply swung around on a fixed pivot, like a door swinging on a hinge. The pivot, or doorpost, was the North Station of Shanghai. Fighting in the heart of the city continued. The struggle was still one of greatly superior technical power over flesh and blood. The naval guns could still reach the entire Chinese line. The only difference was that before September 15, they did not even have to bother to take aim. They could see every position and knew its exact location, so that they could fire point-blank during the day or night, and always be sure of killing Chinese soldiers. Now they had to locate the lines before they could be sure that their barrages were taking effect.

The Chinese army at Shanghai fought against terrific odds, but it had behind it in the city three million compatriots and active sympathizers. The slogan of co-operation of the army and people was not fully achieved in Shanghai in the sense of direct personal contact and co-operation between soldiers and civilians such as was to develop during the next year in the partisan areas in North China and the lower Yangtze valley. But from the beginning of the battle, all classes of the population helped the army in every way they could. Dance-halls, theatres, and restaurants were turned into hospitals for the wounded. Thousands of women volunteered as nurses. Boy scouts made daily trips into the battlefields, bringing back the injured. Chambers of commerce, provincial guilds, and social organizations of all kinds gave great sums of money for necessary supplies and "comforts". A general war-work committee undertook to provide the army with anything it required. The headquarters of one of the sectors asked for 8,000 gunny-sacks, which it urgently needed for sandbags. The Committee was notified, issued appeals by telephone, placard, and radio, and had collected many more than the required number within three hours. Children collected cigarette tins and empty food cans. These were filled with metal scrap and converted into improvised hand-grenades. Soap, towels, padded vests, pencils and paper, books and magazines — all these important alleviations of the life of men at the front were sent to the lines in hundreds of thousands, being delivered personally by representatives of the groups donating them. Tens of thousands of people kept up regular correspondence with individual soldiers in the trenches. Entertainments and educational courses were organized for the wounded and convalescents. School children visited the hospitals to write letters for the illiterate.

The most active element in the general war-work committee (Shanghai Anti-Enemy Rear-Work Association) was the old National Salvation Association, now re-named the Cultural Workers' National Resistance Federation. This association was the first real United Front organization in China. It had arisen after the great Peiping student demonstrations of 1935, and had led a semi-legal existence until the outbreak of the war. A landmark in its history had been the union of representatives of all classes of the population to support the great anti-Japanese general strike of textile workers a few months before the Sian crisis. This activity had led to the arrest of seven of its leaders, who were first accused of "acts endangering the safety of the Republic" — a capital crime — then held in prison for months through indecisive trials. Shortly before the outbreak of fighting in Shanghai a broad United Front committee had been organized to obtain their release. Soon afterwards the Government set them free of its own accord, and the new committee, with some of the released leaders again actively participating, threw itself into intensive war work.

Within a month, the Federation had created hundreds of branch associations in the city, with an aggregate membership of more than 100,000. Patriots throughout Shanghai were organized into sectional, street, and block units. The Central Committee concentrated and directed the work of all. It was in contact with the city offices of all the armies fighting on the Shanghai front and consulted them as to their needs. Every week it issued a new set of instructions, laying down a concrete plan of work for the next seven days. Every unit devoted its energies to this plan. For instance, when padded vests were called for, the units organized their production in their respective sections, in consultation with all the residents. The rich inhabitants of every street provided materials and, where these were available, paid for the hire of sewing-machines. The workers' wives sewed. Winter garments were being made in every house and on every doorstep in Shanghai. Tens of thousands of warm uniforms flowed to the army from the innumerable lanes and alleys of the great city. When the central organ called for letters to the soldiers, countless thousands poured in. Any call for volunteers immediately met a city- wide response.

For groups of soldiers and civilians wishing to improve their value in the struggle, the Association provided lecturers on all phases of the national crisis from the relative wealth of China and Japan to the tactics of guerrilla warfare. Writers, teachers, and journalists who continued to carry on their own work, conducted special classes for many hours every night. Often military units asked for educational and propaganda workers to be sent to them. Many groups were formed, groups which were later to become the political departments of the detachments to which they were assigned or of partisan formations which grew up around Shanghai following the fall of the city. No one spared himself in this work. Propagandists worked directly behind the firing-line. Day and night disappeared. Chien Yi-shih, one of the most beloved and active leaders in this field, led a group of twenty young men to help Chang Fa-kuei's army in Pootung and worked under such pressure that he broke down and died after a few weeks. Propagandists worked among soldiers and civilians, men and women, the wounded and refugees.

Some of the propaganda groups formed at that time have since carried on their activity on many fronts and won national fame. The women's dramatic group of Miss Hu Lan-chi, composed chiefly of girl textile workers, is with the partisans along the Yangtze. Another group, led by the dramatist Hung Shen, was to form the nucleus of the dramatic section of the Political Department of the National Military Council in Hankow and Chungking. Two more went, after the fall of Shanghai, to the Eighth Route Army in the North-west, where they are part of Ting Ling's famous War Service Group. A group of Customs employees left their jobs and went South to work among the peasants and fishermen of Kwangtung. Liu Liang-mo, the man who taught millions to sing, led a party of twenty young men to Soochow, Nanking, and Changsha. The cultural world of Shanghai organized itself into a fighting army to aid in the defence of its city. When the city fell, the army split up into detachments which are the backbone of China's cultural rebirth in all parts of the country. Many Shanghai professors teach in the Lu Hsun Academy of Arts in Yenan. Tu Chung-yuan, National Salvationist publisher of Shanghai's great *Life Weekly*, who once spent two years in prison for attacking the Japanese, has led many members of the association to edit newspapers and open schools in distant Sinkiang.

With many of the printing-houses destroyed and paper stocks low, Shanghai's progressive journalists nevertheless increased their production tenfold. It was necessary to educate the army and people as quickly as possible for the great struggle in which so much depended on full understanding of the issues by its every participant. Workers, soldiers, and students jammed the lecture-halls and clamoured for textbooks and reading matter of a kind which had not been produced before because of the ban on anti-Japanese literature. To solve this problem, several newspapers and periodicals were established. Kuo Mo-jo, one of China's leading writers who had just returned from a ten-year exile, founded the *National Salvation Daily News*, which became the official organ of the Cultural Workers' Association. After the fall of Shanghai, Kuo became chief of the Propaganda Section of the Political Department in Hankow and Chungking, while his paper, under the editorship of Hsia Yen, translator of Gorki into Chinese, moved first to Canton, then to Kweilin. Many small periodicals were merged into the Joint Wartime Publications. *Resistance*, a paper appearing every three days under the editorship of Chao Tou-feng, one of the released "Seven leaders", attained a circulation of 100,000 copies. Another edition was published in Hankow, where the matrices were flown by airplane. The older progressive magazines *World Culture*, *Women's Life*, and the *People's Weekly* improved their content and gained tremendously in circulation. All these publications still exist in other parts of the country.

The National Salvationist "Life Bookstore" issued 20,000 four-volume sets of "Wartime Textbooks" for illiterates and semi-literates, selling for two or three cents a booklet. Between the beginning of the war and the fall of Shanghai, six books were issued in the "National Salvation Series". They included Chiang Kai-shek's speeches, Madame Sun Yat-sen's *China Will Never Be Conquered*, and Hu Yao-tzu's *War and Diplomacy*. The people of Shanghai bought edition after edition of *General Resistance*, by Pan Han-nien, resident representative of the Eighth Route Army, *Two Months on the Northern Front* by Li Kun-po, another of the recently released leaders, and *The Brussels Youth Conference*, by China's delegate, Chien Chun-jui "The Mass Library" produced Socialist classics: Plekhanov's *Questions of Marxism*, Engels' *Anti-Duhring* and *Theses on Feuerbach*, and a number of other works in editions of many thousands. It also published pamphlet translations of the following articles in the *Great Soviet Encyclopaedia*: Philosophy, Formal Logic, Historical Science, and Social Forms. Two editions of 3,000 within as many months were issued of a translation of R. Palme-Dutt's *World Politics*. Collections of articles by Chang Chiang, famous war correspondent of the Ta Kung Pao, a booklet on political work in the old Red Army, and *Sketches of Partisan Life* describing guerrilla warfare in the North, each went into editions of tens of thousands. The "Black and White Series" (from the Black River — Amur — and the White Mountains of Kirin, in Manchuria) told of struggle against the Japanese in the lost territories.

Stormy growth was also witnessed in the graphic arts. The poster, woodcut, and cartoon comprise a whole front in the history of China's anti-imperialist struggle. The development of this "front" has been a record of ceaseless effort, privation, and suppression. Even when he was able to sell all his work, the Chinese graphic artist was so poorly paid that, to make ends meet, he had to produce at least a finished piece of work every one or two days. But the artist who put his pencil at the service of the people's movement rarely sold his productions. He had to work nights, in secret, after earning his keep by heavy toil at some other trade. He had to hide his tools, and as often as not destroy his previous woodblocks for fear of discovery. For many years, persecution and arrest were his lot. Small wonder that when the war began, and the chains that had bound this vigorous art were loosened, it leapt into the fight for national liberation philosophically disciplined and with its mind made up regarding the work that lay before it. New artists arose. Vigorous experimentation in technique continued. But the graphic arts worked, from the first shot fired at Marco Polo Bridge, only in and for the struggle. Every patriotic newspaper was rich in cartoons, every large city placarded with posters, every propaganda pamphlet richly illustrated with woodcuts. In Shanghai the artists published *Manhwa* (The Cartoon), a fighting weekly representing all mediums of graphic art.

The first months of the war richly vindicated those who had for years contended that only along the path of anti-Japanese struggle would China find awakening, liberation, and growth. Not the oft-predicted ruin, but a new birth accompanied the first blows the united Chinese nation struck in defence of its independence. Shanghai in the fire of battle witnessed more cultural gress in three months than in the previous three years.

The people of Shanghai not only cared for the wounded, supplied the army, and educated themselves for conscious participation in the national war: in many cases they gave their troops military aid and themselves participated in the fighting.

Among workers, artisans, and shop clerks representatives of the Central Government formed a corps of sharpshooters and secret agents to act as snipers and to spy on the Japanese movements. This corps included coolies in the Japanese employ and municipal servants of the International Settlement whose work took them into the Japanese-occupied areas. During the Shanghai battle, 3,000 of these men were enlisted under Tai Li, head of Chiang Kai-shek's secret service. Towards the end, 500 of them perished from one Japanese bomb as a result of information given by a traitor. They were killed in a building in which they were taking shelter during daylight preparatory to dispersing as soon as darkness fell. The Japanese bombed the building and destroyed it with all its occupants.

There were hundreds of cases, too, of spontaneous participation in the struggle. Some of these became widely known.

Early in the battle there was an occasion when the men of the Chinese 88th Division broke through the Japanese lines and approached the Wayside Wharf. They were guided in this successful attack by a number of Hongkew workers. When the workers came to them and proposed that they carry out this action, the officers were suspicious and would have nothing to do with the scheme. To prove their good faith, the workers themselves attacked Japanese outposts, and came back with reports of success and 200 rifles which they had captured and which they offered to hand over to the Division. Finally, when the surprise attack which they had advocated was made, the workers participated in it rifle in hand.

Shanghai's great industrial district of Yangtzepoo was in the fighting zone, and the factories were closed, leaving many thousands of operatives idle. These men formed voluntary labour battalions and offered their services to the army as carriers and trench-diggers.

When the Japanese made their first attempt to land at Pootung, across the Whangpoo from Shanghai proper, the boatmen of the thousands of sampans clustering in the river themselves evolved a plan for repulsing them which they took to the army. When the ruse that they proposed was approved, they changed clothes with thousands of soldiers who rowed their boats out as usual, landed behind the Japanese without the latter being aware that anything was wrong, and cleared Pootung within a few hours.

In Pootung too there occurred an instance in which a Japanese worker gave valuable assistance to the Chinese forces. He was an old warehouse keeper, an employee of the Japan-China Cotton Mill. Before the hostilities, the Japanese army had hidden a large supply of arms and ammunition in the warehouse under his charge. Early in October, the old man made his way to Chang Fa-kwei's headquarters on the Pootung side and offered to guide the Chinese to the arms hoard. He had sympathized with them from the beginning, he said, and had long wanted to do what he was doing now. But it had seemed a hard step to take, and he had debated the matter back and forth in his mind. Then he had received news that his grandson, who had only just begun his military service, had been killed in Shanghai a few days before. The death of the boy in what he had from the first regarded as a cruel and senseless adventure decided him. He felt that it was his duty to hit back at the militarists who were wasting the young blood of his country. The old Japanese remained with Chang Fa-kwei's army and retired with it when it left Pootung.

Arrested in the city itself, the Japanese advance took the form of a broad enveloping movement by the right flank, consisting of the army forces which had landed on the banks of the Whangpoo and the Yangtze. The movement was slow and painful, taking two months to cover some ten miles of territory. At every step it was resisted by Chinese detachments which demonstrated marvels of heroism against superior odds. Typical of the unyielding stand of the Chinese soldiers was the story of the garrison of Paoshan, in which a whole battalion fought a desperate rear-guard action as a result of which it was completely annihilated, only one survivor remaining to tell the tale of the siege.

The line established by the Chinese forces on September 15 remained unbreached until the beginning of October. During these three weeks of deadlock, the defenders not only held off the Japanese but recovered some of the positions captured by the enemy earlier in the battle. Thus, the Municipal Civic Centre, imposing nucleus of an ambitious scheme to build a Greater Shanghai away from the European and Japanese-dominated International Settlement, fell once more into Chinese hands. But until mid-October there were no decisive changes in the general situation, both sides being busy with accumulating forces for a major encounter to decide the result of the whole Shanghai campaign.

On October 19, the Japanese, who now had 150,000 men massed on the Shanghai front, began their long-heralded "Big Push" with the objective of finally encircling the city. The immediate aim of this new general attack was the occupation of Tazang, a small market town about six miles north-west of Shanghai, popularly known as the "chicken village" because it was the city's chief supplier of fowls. The "chicken village" became the scene of an epic struggle. This struggle was to decide the fate of Shanghai and, the Japanese thought, of the whole war. In the operations incident to its capture, they hoped to crush the power of the Chinese army. And they hoped to do it quickly, before the opening of the Nine-Power Conference at Brussels, belatedly called to consider the attitude of the Western Powers towards their illegal incursion into China. Nothing succeeds like success, and the Japanese hoped to silence the haranguers in Europe by presenting them with a *fait accompli* on the actual theatre of war.

To achieve this, the Japanese concentrated large forces of infantry, a total of 700 artillery pieces, and 150 bombing planes to batter the eight-mile sector of the Chinese line which lay between them and Tazang. On October 24, all 150 bombers concentrated on the little village itself in the most savage aerial bombardment in military history, not excelled by any that had occurred in Spain. By October 26, after seven days of ceaseless fighting, their right flank had advanced some five miles. On October 27, Tazang fell into the hands of the Japanese. But the 50,000 troops which they bad hoped to trap and annihilate by completing the encirclement of the Chinese positions within Shanghai had already begun their orderly retreat. On October 30, the Chinese left the northern sections of the city and the railway station which had hitherto been the pivot of their line. They left behind them the eight- mile wall of flame of burning Chapei, surely one of the most spectacular conflagrations in world history, and the 500 men of the famous "Lost Battalion" who entrenched themselves in a reinforced-concrete warehouse and for four whole days withstood the massed artillery of the entire Japanese army in the port city. The story of the "Lost Battalion" and of how a young girl guide crossed a shell-torn no man's land to present its members with a Chinese flag which fluttered for days over lost Chapei, is known to the entire world.

The Chinese army retreated from Shanghai in good order and fought rear-guard actions in the western suburbs which prevented the Japanese from completing their encirclement of the city for more than a week. To completely clear the Shanghai area of the defenders, the Japanese had to land a new force at Kingshanwei, near Chapoo, on the northern shore of Hangchow Bay. This landing was practically unopposed, and by November 8, the Japanese advancing from this direction presented such a menace to the Chinese right flank that another retreat had to be carried out.

Shanghai, China's most populous city, chief port, and greatest industrial centre, fell into the hands of the enemy. Having got their hands on it, the Japanese began directly to apply the tenets of policy which they had tried to stuff down the Chinese Government's throat for years.

Economic co-operation? The Japanese army systematically looted every building still standing in the occupied area. Throughout the fighting their bombers had made special efforts to wipe out factories and thus destroy China's independent industry. Now every scrap of machinery was knocked down and shipped to Japan as scrap metal. If ever Chinese capitalists had been disposed to accept Japan's protestations that she was fighting not their interests but only the political line of the Kuomintang Government, the weeks following the occupation of Shanghai, when the Japanese troops roamed like a horde of scavenging jackals through the desert they had created, quickly dispelled any such illusion.

Anti-Communism? Everyone who opposed the Japanese was *ipso facto* a "Communist". This included not only workers and peasants but also the Chinese ruling class, which, after much wavering, had finally refused to accept the role of compradore and policeman for the war-lords of Tokyo.

Emancipation of the Peoples of Asia from White Imperialism? To foreign Powers, Japan sang a different tune. She maintained that she was defending joint interests of all imperialism against an "anti-foreign" Chinese Government. But both in China and the West, even those who would have liked to believe her could not. Nothing could obscure the character of the Japanese drive to establish for themselves a place in the sun. The objects of this drive were to reduce China to an enslaved agricultural appendage of Japanese industry by violence and terror; and to drive Western interests, whose possessors were too preoccupied in Europe to lift a finger in their defence, out of the country by threats and blackmail. This was Japan's role in the campaign for the re-division of the world which she waged in co-operation with the Fascist robber-states of Europe, her allies in the Anti-Comintern Pact. The bumper crop of "incidents" which began immediately after the retirement of the Chinese forces from Shanghai concretely illustrated every phase of this policy and made the aims of the Japanese apparent even to the dullest observer.

After the occupation, practically the entire Chinese population of Shanghai remained in the International Settlement and the French Concession, where it had taken refuge early in the fighting. Although they were under foreign administration, these areas now became an "island" of fighting China away from the main body of the country. Under the pressure of the Japanese and in conformity with the demands of formal neutrality, the British and French authorities progressively forbade all patriotic activities. The great Shanghai newspapers, with the exception of those which had acquired foreign protection, were closed. The official *Central News Ageney* discontinued its service. But the people's network of resistance which the United Front of the three million Chinese in the city had established in the fire of battle, was indestructible. In a hundred ways, it continued to do its share in the national struggle. The collection of funds for the Government and the fighters at the front did not stop. Young men migrated to the interior to carry on the struggle as partisans, propagandists, and workers and engineers in China's new industries. When the Japanese staged a "victory parade" through the streets of the Settlement, they were greeted with bombs. Traitors who worked with the Japanese were destroyed by patriotic terrorists who usually managed to escape arrest because they enjoyed the sympathy of the population and of the Chinese members of the Settlement police force. Anti-Japanese literature continued to be published and distributed, surreptitiously but universally. To this day, Shanghai remains one of the greatest political and intellectual centres of Chinese resistance to Japan.

The heroic defence of Shanghai had given the world new respect for China and her army, and had opened its eyes to the weaknesses of Japanese military power, which had taken three months to solve the relatively simple problem of capturing the city in predominantly favourable strategic circumstances. Politically, Shanghai was a great victory for China. It had given even the waverers in the country a degree of confidence and consciousness of their own strength which would never have been theirs if the record of retreat in the North had been repeated on the Yangtze. It had allowed time for the consolidation of the internal changes which had been brought about as a result of the war, and for the training of considerable numbers of reserves. Internationally, it had enabled China's Finance Minister, Dr. H. H. Kung, to obtain substantial credits for arms purchases during his trip to Europe,* from which he returned in October. It had convinced the foreign Powers not only that their interests in China would receive no consideration in the event of a Japanese victory, but also that China was not too weak a horse to be cautiously backed. While they failed to decide on any concrete measures of assistance, they formally condemned Japan's aggression through the League of Nations, the Nine-Power Conference at Brussels, and the strong pronouncements of President Roosevelt. Shanghai also helped China to win the sympathy and solidarity of the peoples of all countries who had been kept fully informed of the first great battle of the Sino-Japanese war, which had been fought in a great international port in full

---

* The list of loans secured by Dr. Kung is given as follows (in Chinese dollars) $135,000,000 from Great Britain; $23,000,000 from Swiss and Dutch groups against currency silver; $50,000,000 from the Czechoslovakian Skoda works, etc.

view of the entire world.

Militarily, however, the defence of Shanghai had proved too expensive. Some of Nanking's best units, such as the 87th and 88th Divisions and the superbly trained and equipped Salt Revenue Guards, were completely annihilated. The total losses of the Chinese forces certainly exceeded 300,000 men. Chinese strategists had at first greeted the Japanese operations at Shanghai as a welcome division of their forces which would make it more difficult for them to advance in the North. But as the struggle progressed, China too had had to withdraw well-trained troops from all parts of the country to replace the heavy losses she had suffered. The Japanese offensive in the North had been resumed in October, and on November 8, the day of the final evacuation of Shanghai, the army of General Itagaki had fought its way into Taiyuan, chief city of Shansi province, the natural fortress that dominated the Northern provinces.

The concentration of all available man-power on the short Shanghai front had also made possible the easy landing of the Japanese at Hangchow Bay. This landing accelerated the Chinese withdrawal beyond all expectations. With all the forces at their disposal, assisted by intensive aerial bombing, the Japanese pressed forward in pursuit, and did not allow the retreating army a moment's rest as it struggled to drag itself and its supplies back through a morass of rice-fields, sodden from recent rains. "They fly through the air while we crawl through the mud," a tired officer said to me in Nanking. It was impossible to man the strongly fortified Soochow-Quinsan "Hindenburg" line with these depleted and exhausted units, and the new troops which should already have been there, to let the retiring divisions pass through their lines for rest in the rear, had not had time to take up their positions, due to the unexpected rapidity of the retreat. The great chain of fortifications which Nanking had built on the insistence of its German military advisers was never defended. Spies had informed the Japanese of the gaps which still remained in its construction, and of what points were garrisoned by inferior troops. By the middle of November all that lay between the enemy and the capital was a Chinese army in full retreat, rapidly losing value as a fighting organism. In acknowledgement of the fact that Nanking was directly menaced and that there was no immediate prospect of halting the advance of the Japanese armies, the Chinese Government transferred its military headquarters to Hankow, its official seat to distant Chungking.

To the Japanese, this was disquieting. They had hoped that the Chinese would admit that the game was up and remain in Nanking to negotiate peace. Nevertheless, they believed that they had won the war, and that the new confidence which China had gained as a result of the long defence of Shanghai would disappear when they advanced upon the capital. Foreign Governments, which had been impressed by the slowness of Japanese progress in the port city, were also unprepared for the sequel. The European and American Press now paid tribute to the great effort China had put forth in Shanghai, but suggested that in this effort she had expended all her strength and that there was nothing left now but "an honourable peace".

Was this to be the end of a second "Shanghai war"? Had China's resources for struggle been exhausted? The Nanking Government was the same as that which for six years Japan had kept cowed by threats alone. It had begun resistance with great confidence, but now its armies were in flight. Would it strive to preserve what was left by a second Shanghai truce and reverse the political development of the past year?

The Tokyo Government and its "anti-Comintern" allies evidently thought so. While the Japanese army and navy pushed on towards Nanking, they opened their first great political offensive for the conclusion of "peace in East Asia".

CHAPTER VI
Decision

THE evacuation of Nanking began on November 15. The new Nanking and the old poured in an indistinguishable stream down the broad thoroughfares of the capital and through the bottleneck of its North Gate leading to the Yangtze. Fine automobiles and bullock-carts, officials' wives escorting pianos and furniture, and coolies with shoulder-poles from which a bundle of bedding hung at one end, a baby in a basket from the other, all were hurrying away from the threatened city. Against the current, moving from the Yangtze towards the front, marched division after division of stocky, broad-faced, straw-sandalled, peasant soldiers, the great circular umbrella hats which they wore over their helmets daubed bright yellow and green for camouflage, their sturdy chests bedizened with heavy potato-masher hand grenades. Soldiers camped on the great squares. The gleaming asphalt of the boulevards was broken up for trenches and tank-traps. Here and there, among the soldiers, moved small groups of long-gowned civilians with rifles — new recruits, *franc-tireurs*, future guerrillas.

The massive Government buildings, the new "banking circle" and great hotels, and the blue-roofed mausoleum of Sun Yat-sen, standing high on Purple Mountain, all lost their somewhat blatant newness and stood desolate and disregarded, a thing apart from all this unusual activity.

110

The tens of thousands of poor who had chosen to remain in the city because they had nowhere to go, crowded, carrying their belongings, towards the new "safety zone" from whose sanctuary many of them would be dragged out — the men to be shot, the women to be raped, after the Japanese occupation.

The ship on which I travelled up-river to Hankow had been chartered by the Government for the evacuation of official personnel. Designed for a few hundred passengers, it carried 3,000. High functionaries crowded together four or five in a two-bunk cabin. Clerks and runners filled the lower-class cubicles and the decks. In the steerage and the holds, wounded soldiers lay piled across each other, seeing comfort in proximity, chattering with fever, pain, and cold. In the midst of this mass of humanity, white-clad stewards went through the motions of peacetime "service", carried full-coarse dinners on trays to the cabins, and addressed those who looked as if they were of that rating as "Sir".

We were spared the fear of airplanes. Throughout the four-day run, clouds hung low over the Yangtze, there was constant driving sleet, and one almost prayed for the risk of bombs and a warm sun in preference to safety in frozen misery.

I slept in the ship's tiny post-office. The postal clerk had been a lover of Nature. He had left as his heritage six canaries hung in a row of cages above the bunk, many jars of silkworms, starving now that they had eaten all their mulberry leaves, and several tiny lattice-work baskets of chirping crickets.

Evidently, he had also shown hospitality to the scores of rats which at night ran over the faces of myself and my companions in the cabin — a Kuomintang representative from the Chinese community of Antananarivo, Madagascar, who had been attached to the Overseas Ministry, and the little daughter of the ship's cook, who during the day strode around, smiling and cheerful, singing at the top of her lungs the ever-popular "March of the Volunteers".

When we arrived at Hankow, we found, flowing along the Bund, the continuation of the evacuation parade down the main arteries of Nanking. The same faces, the same mixture of types, the same bundles of belongings.

Living accommodation was next to impossible to get. I obtained a barn-like room at an improvised hotel which had come into being to house, and rob, the flood of new arrivals, paid an outrageous price, and after a day, may the Lord forgive me, submitted to the persuasion of the manager and gave up my barn to an official who said he had come to rent it for Mr. Wang Ching-wei.

Nanking had been a bureaucratic ivory tower, a new Forbidden City, arrogant and remote from the earth. The triple city of Hankow, Wuchang, and Hanyang, the commercial and industrial, as well as administrative centre of Central China, had no such pretensions. It was grimy, practical, and unbelievably crowded. In its streets, the local population mixed with thousands upon thousands of refugee invaders who had converged upon Wuhan from Shanghai, from Nanking, and from the lost North. These "refugees" included great numbers of active anti-Japanese fighters in all fields of Chinese life who had come to this city because they expected it to be the new centre of resistance. In Nanking, the officials could work in their stately buildings as if they alone existed in the world. In Hankow, they had to conduct their business from holes and corners, rented apartments and poky hall-bedrooms. Instead of towering above the people, they were dwarfed by the massed humanity of the city which was to be China's effective capital for the next eleven months.

In Nanking, we had watched the slow depletion of the lengthily and carefully trained crack troops of the Central Government, handsomely uniformed and, although altogether inadequately provided with heavy armaments, individually equipped as well as the soldiers of any other army. In the streets of Hankow, beginning from four o'clock in the morning, a chorus of harsh middle-Yangtze voices rasped out a sharp "One, two, three, four", beating time for the muffled tramp of thousands of cloth-soled feet. The voices, and the feet, belonged to workers, shop apprentices and peasants, carrying rifles and uniformed in cheap blue denim. These were the men of China's new army, a force of armed citizens who were soon to prove that they could fight as well as any professional soldiers.

An ancient Chinese proverb stated baldly and brutally: "Good iron is not used to make nails. Good men do not become soldiers." But now, under the standard, "Struggle to the end", slogan-writers had brushed "Good men must join the army" in huge characters on Hankow's walls.

When airplanes had flown over Nanking, they had usually belonged to the enemy. In Hankow, the drone of aircraft could be heard for twenty-four hours of the day. Swift Curtis-Hawks, built in the American assembly plant which had come to Wuchang from Hangchow, did breath-taking stunts in their test flights over the Yangtze. And often, in those early days, the entire population of the city craned its collective neck to catch a glimpse of giant grey, taper-winged, four-engined aerial fortresses rumbling overhead, or strange short-nosed pursuits darting about with incredible speed. These new planes came from the U.S.S.R., the only country in the League of Nations that had thus far taken seriously the Geneva admonition to its members to render individual aid to a China fighting against aggression.

In the streets of Hankow one could see volunteers, foreign aviators who had come to help the pilots of the Chinese air force fly the units of their new aerial fleet. Some walked with an air and a swagger, gentlemen of fortune from all over the world. Others, sturdy, shock-haired, and dressed in leather jackets, strode along in groups, like workmen returning from a factory. They were the volunteers from the Soviet Union — proletarians of the air. Soviet, American, and French, the volunteers fought their first battles for China over threatened Nanking, where Japanese raiders, certain that they would encounter no opposition from China's depleted air force, suddenly found a new air force, strong opposition, and death.

* * * * * *

Against the background of the Japanese break-through on the Shanghai-Nanking front and the new preparations for resistance in Hankow, the heart of the country, the anti-Comintern block, launched its campaign for a Sino-Japanese "peace". This campaign was not the first foreign-inspired "peace movement" in China, and in order to understand it, it is necessary to survey briefly the attitude of the Western Powers towards the Far Eastern conflict.

The repercussions of the Chinese war of resistance on the international arena were interesting, and understanding of them was of extreme importance for China. When Marco Polo Bridge began to assume the menacing proportions of a prelude to war, the Western Powers automatically assumed an attitude consonant with the development of their respective policies since 1932. Great Britain had long since discounted North China in her political strategy, and had concentrated on strengthening her financial ties with the Central Government and investing large sums in South China and on the Yangtze. She hoped for a "peaceful" solution of the northern conflict, so long as the consequent capitulation was local and did not involve any form of all-embracing Sino-Japanese economic bloc. The official American attitude was one of general sympathy with China, but for practical purposes it could be summed up as follows: "This is none of our business."

After the attack on Shanghai the position changed. In Shanghai, Britain had invested £180,000,000, of which £100,000,000 was sunk in Yangtzepoo, the industrial area of the Settlement which the Japanese used as a base and which from the beginning became part of the city's battlefield. From the outset of the three-month fight for the city, the Tokyo Government and its forces manifested their disregard of British interests and their determination to hammer Nanking into complete submission — which meant the abandonment of Western participation in China's development. Because of this, the British commercial community in the country, which had been more than a little pro-Japanese in 1932, was staunchly pro-Chinese in 1937. The United States, with the first guns of Shanghai, re-affirmed its isolationist position. Americans in threatened areas were asked to evacuate (they indignantly refused), there was talk of withdrawing all American forces from China (the army garrison at Tientsin was, ultimately, removed), and "neutrality" reached its peak in the order to Mr. Johnson to leave Nanking. The revision of this policy was heralded, on October 5, by President Roosevelt's Chicago speech, and the State Department's announcement on the next day branding Japan as an aggressor and violator of the Nine-Power

Pact. America's investments in China were only one-fifth of Britain's.*
But her traditional insistence on the "Open Door" had demonstrated her
conception of the ultimate importance of the Chinese market, and the growth
of Sino-American trade in the months before the war confirmed her in that
belief. Moreover, with practically no military commitments outside her own
territory which could compare with Britain's, she could, once she adopted a
policy, throw all the weight of her great power behind it.

Of the European "anti-Comintern" Powers, Germany had by far the
greater interests in China. After the War, she had been favoured by successive Chinese Governments because it was considered that economic relations with a defeated and militarily weak industrial State were attended with
no risk of imperialist penetration. German firms supplied machinery to the
remotest provinces and had offices there. The Sino-German Eurasia air lines
spanned the country from north to south and from east to west. German military advisers reorganized the Chinese Army, acted as salesmen and demonstrators for German equipment, and left their ideological stamp on a whole
generation of Chinese officers which grew up in the anti-Red campaigns.
Mussolini had an aerial mission in Nanchang and had once presented an
aeroplane personally to Chiang Kai-shek. But Italian activity (during their

---

* Foreign capital investments in China Proper in 1935 were: Great Britain U.S. $1,000,
000,000; Japan U.S. $500,000,000; U.S.A. U.S. $200,000,000.
The British investment was thus twice the Japanese, five times the American.

China's Foreign Trade in 1936 (percentage)

	Exports.	Imports.	Trade Turn-over.
British Empire	30.8	21.2	25.1
Total of which—			
(United Kingdom)	(9.2)	(11.7)	(10.6)
(Hongkong—mainly tranship-ment)	(15.1)	(1.9)	(7.5)
United States	26.4	17.6	22.5
Japan	15.2	16.6	16.0
Germany	5.5	15.9	11.5

Shanghai was both the *locale* of the greatest British investments and the greatest port
for her foreign trade.

many-year sojourn in China, the aircraft experts assembled only a few machines) and influence both remained weak, while Germany forged forward to the position of Kuomintang China's chief "friend" before the War.

Germany was distressed by the Japanese attack on China. In the first place, it threatened her own commerce in the country. Even more important, she foresaw that the tying up of large bodies of Japanese troops in the country would make Japan a less effective ally against the Soviet Union. Because of these facts, Germany found it possible at this period to argue that her pact with Japan was aimed only at "Communism" (meaning the Soviet Union), and did not in the least prevent her from continuing to be a "sincere" friend of China. With the aid of the capitulationist faction of Wang Ching-wei, and the anti-Soviet and anti-United Front elements in other groups, she carried on her triple policy, of alienating China from the Soviet Union, breaking up the co-operation between the Kuomintang and Communist Party, and working, in the role of "honest broker" trusted by both sides, to save the forces of her ally for the greater objectives of the Rome-Berlin-Tokyo axis.

Italy's interests were more directly parallel to those of Japan. She wanted the Far Eastern hostilities to continue, hoping that the attention of the British Fleet would thus be diverted from the Mediterranean. In this case, if Great Britain wanted a safe passage for her fleet to East of Suez, she would have to pay for it by substantial concessions in Mare Nostrum.

The outbreak of hostilities was a grave setback to the year-long joint efforts of Germany, Italy, and Japan to force Chiang Kai-shek into the anti-Comintern block. It smashed their previous strategy, forced their spokesmen within the Chinese Government to refrain from open activity, and precipitated serious latent contradictions between Tokyo and Berlin. By the time they had reached a new basis of joint action in the Far East, the initiative in the work of establishing "peace" had, to their great chagrin, been taken over by Great Britain, which in October 1938 inspired the Brussels Conference of signatories of the Nine-power Treaty.

The form of international consultation on the Sino-Japanese conflict had been the subject of a spirited passage at arms in Geneva. The Soviet Union,

France, and New Zealand, wanted to keep all action within the framework of the League of Nations. Had the Powers consulted under the provisions of Article XVI, a decision adverse to Japan would carry with it the obligation of all League members to apply sanctions against the aggressor. That such action would have the support of the United States, which had just formally condemned Japan as a treaty-breaker, was a reasonable supposition.

Britain did not want to punish Japan. Her aim was to bring about a dictated truce, as she had once done at Shanghai, to be reached through third-Power mediation. A peace could still be satisfactory to Great Britain if it left Japanese troops in North China and included Chinese concessions which did not affect British spheres of influence. To achieve such a peace, consultation between the signatories of the Nine-Power Pact was a likely instrument. The list of consultants would not include the Soviet Union. It would include Japan, which would make a unanimous decision impossible. It would be headed by the United States, who, as the originator of the Nine-Power Treaty, would strive to make it a success. Consultation under the Nine-Power Treaty did not obligate the consulting powers to any action specifically directed against the aggressor and was envisaged, rather, as the imposition of mediation upon both parties.

After attempts to broaden the basis of the consultation by inviting the Soviet Union and Germany to participate, the Conference began its deliberations. Japan and Germany did not attend. China stated flatly her determination to carry on the struggle, unless a peaceful settlement was based on unconditional restoration of occupied territory and full respect for her sovereignty. Throughout the discouraging weeks which followed the fall of Shanghai, she did not waver in her resolution, which was repeatedly stressed by Dr. Wellington Koo at Brussels and Generalissimo Chiang Kai-shek in Nanking. Finally, the conference adjourned, nominally for a time,* after passing a weak resolution urging "peaceful settlement", against the vociferous opposition of Italy, a country which all through the conference had been

---

* At the time of writing (April 1939) strenuous efforts are being made to revive the Nine-Power Conference.

stating Japan's case.

In their effort to sabotage all international consultation on the Far Eastern war and capture the initiative of "settlement" for themselves, the anti-Comintern Powers arranged a division of labour, with Tokyo, Rome, and Berlin each doing that share which was most consonant with its interests and inclinations. An acute Chinese observer thus summed up their activity at the time: "The three Fascist states, Germany, Italy, and Japan, each have a function to perform. Japan will accelerate her aggression in China. Italy will become Japan's loudspeaker at the Nine-Power Conference. Germany will start a peace movement to counteract its effect."*

So it happened. The collapse of the Nine-Power Conference was immediately followed by phenomenal activity by the three Fascist Powers and their under-cover agents in China. Rumour-mills got to work all over the world, prophesying Chiang Kai-shek's imminent capitulation. Japanese armies hastened towards Nanking. Wang Ching-wei, safe in Hankow, made despairing speeches, growing lyrical over the spectacle of the last solitary Chinese fighting to the end against irresistible Japanese aggression. The German ambassadors in Hankow and Tokyo shuttled back and forth with terms of capitulation. German news correspondents whispered to their foreign colleagues:

"Watch Wang Ching-wei, he is the coming man in China." With unprecedented zeal they interviewed every responsible Chinese official in Hankow and Nanking, asking each one for a statement on the possibilities of peace and putting in a good word for the schemes of the Pact.

The journalistic probing and bludgeoning which preceded the flight of German Ambassador Trautmann from Hankow to beleaguered Nanking to present Japan's demands to Chiang Kai-shek himself constituted a classic of Nazi-Fascist thoroughness. By the end of November there was a round dozen of German and Italian correspondents in the two cities, all desperately

---

* Chang Nai-chi, banker and National Salvation leader in the Shanghai *Shun Pao* (quoted from *Pacific Digest*).

canvassing. On December 1, a big "journalistic" gun was fired from Italy, where one of Wang Ching-wei's oldest followers, Chen Kung-po,* had just arrived on a "goodwill" mission. An article in the *Popolo d'italia* of Milan, written in the turgid style of Il Duce himself, advised China to sue for peace.

On December 2, Dr. Oskar Trautmann flew from Hankow to the capital to present the Japanese peace conditions conveyed to him by Herr von Dierksen, his colleague in Tokyo. The smokescreen thrown out at the time for the benefit of naive right-wingers in China and abroad stated that these conditions were:

1. A definite assurance from Japan that she had no territorial ambitions in North China and merely desired economic co-operation;
2. China to participate in the anti-Comintern pact;
3. Japanese troops to be withdrawn from Chinese territory.**

Strangely enough, Dr. Trautmann could not convince the Generalissimo of the acceptability of these apparently "magnanimous" terms, and came back to Hankow disappointed. Chiang Kai-shek's refusal to consider them was definite, so definite that four days later even Wang Ching-wei was getting back into step by declaring in Hankow (again to the indefatigable *Transocean*) that China would have no truck with any peace negotiations, but would prepare for a long war.

The real Japanese demands were officially published by the Chinese Government six weeks later. They stipulated, that before peace could be concluded, China would have to recognize "Manchukuo", suppress the anti-Japanese movement and the Communist Party, enter the anti-Comintern bloc, allow the establishment of puppet-administered "demilitarized zones in nec-

---

* Chen, on a general European tour, spent most of his time in Germany and Italy. As official Government representative, he was supposed to persuade them to change their attitude towards China. Actually, Mussolini took a definitely pro-Japanese stand, and Rome recognized "Manchukuo", while Tokyo recognized the Italian conquest of Ethiopia, shortly after he came. In December 1938, Chen fled the country to follow Wang, whom he had been sent to persuade to return.

** V. China Weekly Review's *Japan's War in China*.

essary localities", conclude an economic agreement with Japan and "Manchukuo", and pay an indemnity to Tokyo. Of withdrawal of the Japanese forces there was not a word.

The Japanese advance towards Nanking continued. With every few kilometres gained, Tokyo issued new threats, while the German newspapermen in Hankow probed again and again the possibilities of capitulation. "Would China continue to resist?" "Would Generalissimo Chiang Kai-shek resign from office?" "Did China see any hope in going on fighting after the fall of the capital?" The replies were not very satisfactory to the axis Powers. From every quarter came assurances of maximum effort in the forthcoming new phase of the struggle. Military control of all branches of the Government was intensified. Young men were mobilized for military training all over the country. Kwangtung alone gave notice of the enlistment of 300,000 men.

The Japanese army broke into Nanking on December 13. The retreating defenders suffered thousands of losses in their attempt to cross the rapidly flowing Yangtze. Some could not retreat at all. Built for defence, the massive walls of Nanking proved a death-trap when some gates were rendered impassable by enemy artillery and others were choked with piled-up masses of trucks, carts, horses, and human bodies. Entering the city, the Japanese shot thousands of disarmed soldiers, violated the refugee zone, and raped, tortured, looted, and killed in an orgy of destruction unparalleled in recent history,* On the people of Nanking they wreaked vengeance for China's refusal to submit to colonial slavery. To the world, they exhibited the moral ugliness of all wars of imperialist conquest and the complete lack of discipline of their own army.

Simultaneously with the capture of Nanking, there occurred the *Lady-*

---

* For authenticated foreign eye-witness accounts of the horror of Nanking see H. J. Timperley's compilation *What War Means* (a bad title for a good book). All wars mean suffering. But only the wars of predatory imperialism, such as Japan's aggression in China, mean bestial and indiscriminate terror. The Chinese people's war of national liberation, like all wars against oppression throughout history, means no such thing. There are wars and wars — wars of the jungle, and wars of growth and progress.

bird and *Panay* incidents, in which the British gunboat was damaged and the American sunk. These deliberate provocations clearly demonstrated to all groups in Britain and the United States the inevitable consequences of further weakness in the face of the Japanese threat to their interests in China.

On December 16, from his new headquarters at Wuchang, Chiang Kai-shek broadcast a message to the nation, analysing the tasks facing China and pledging himself to the continuation of resistance:

"Since the beginning of our armed struggle", he said, "our total casualties in dead and wounded on all fronts have exceeded three hundred thousand. These losses are unprecedented in the history of China's opposition to foreign aggressors.

"The basis of China's further success in prolonged resistance is not to be found in Nanking, nor in the great cities and the towns, but in the villages all over the country and in the fixed determination of the people. So long as Japanese aggression continues, fathers should teach their children to resist, brothers should encourage each other to rise and fight. If the endeavour of the whole people is directed against the enemy, the enemy will be doomed.

"We must not be influenced by temporary victories or reverses. Rather should we grasp the real meaning of resistance and strengthen our conviction that the final victory will be ours.

"In the course of China's national revolution, armed resistance against Japan is inevitable. Externally, China desires independence. Internally, she seeks an existence free from oppression. Our armed resistance is, therefore, a war of democracy, as enunciated in Dr. Sun Yat-sen's *Three Principles of the People*. It is a war against the brutal forces of imperialism, a battle for survival and freedom. No nation ever wins liberation without paying a heavy price. Such suffering is unavoidable and cannot be rejected if the nation is to live. Moreover, we must realize that to advance the national revolution, China must pursue the war of resistance to the end. No matter how the present situation may change, we must not surrender, but march onward. To fight on may not lead to early victory, but to capitulate is to accept extinction.

"China is fighting for the cause of international peace and justice," he concluded. "Although sanctions have not been enforced against Japan, her guilt as an aggressor has been universally recognized by world opinion. No matter how the international situation may change, we must not yield to disappointment. And we must renounce any inclination to depend on others. We ourselves have accepted the battle, and we must make sure that the cause for which we fight shall not perish."

The moment was the most crucial, the announcement the most important, since the July days in which China first cast down her challenge to Japanese imperialism. After the military disaster of Nanking, after the disappointing floundering of the Nine-Power Conference and the "peacemaking" intrigues of the Fascist Powers, this re-statement of China's fundamental position heralded a new era of confidence, a new growth of the fighting power of the Chinese people. Like Chiang's July speech, it evoked new demonstrations of support all over the country.

The National Government's defiance of Japan had brought unity to China. Now its re-affirmation of unyielding determination to carry on the fight with all the energies of the Chinese people until the aim of final victory was attained brought in its train the further consolidation of this unity.

Responding to Chiang Kai-shek's speech, the Central Committee of the Chinese Communist Party issued a new manifesto.

This manifesto reviewed the losses and gains of the six months' warfare which ended with the fall of Nanking. It announced complete solidarity with Chiang's insistence on continued struggle, which it declared to be in perfect consonance with the policy of the Communist Party with regard to the war. On the basis of this unity of views, it called for the extension of unity of action between the Kuomintang and the Communists.

Not the temporary loss or retention of any point or any section of Chinese territory, not the question of military and material resources was the determining factor in the final outcome of China's struggle for liberation. The determining factor was "the firm unity of our 450,000,000 fellow-countrymen and their perseverance and confidence in the prolonged and difficult struggle". Not only the might of Japan's arms threatened the existence of the

Chinese people, but also any and all tendencies which would further her political strategy of "using Chinese against Chinese"... "the plot by traitors, enemy spies, and Trotzkyite bandits to create dissensions... and to destroy the unity of our national strength, especially at a time when this unity has not reached its full height".

Then came the crucial declaration of policy:

"At the present grave moment in our national crisis, the further unity of anti-Japanese forces throughout the nation is the main factor needed to save the situation. The fundamental method of consolidating these forces is the realization and extension of the anti-Japanese national United Front. And the fundamental requirement for the realization and extension of the national anti-Japanese United Front is the stabilization of the close co-operation between the Kuomintang and the Communist Party. What the Central Committee of the Chinese Communist Party considers to be glad tidings for all our fellow-countrymen at the present moment is that *both the Kuomintang and the Communist Party not only realize the necessity of further unity but are determined to continue their co-operation. The Chinese Communist Party has not merely joined hands with the Kuomintang to save the nation during the war, but is determined to co-operate harmoniously with the Kuomintang to reconstruct the nation after the war has ended in victory.*" (Italics mine — I.E.)

The manifesto ended by proposing that the Kuomintang, Communist Party, and other anti-Japanese forces co-operate to accomplish "six urgent and important tasks" to mobilize "the military, intellectual, financial, and material power of the whole nation for prolonged resistance"; politically, organizationally, and militarily to strengthen existing armies, form new armies, and unite all under one unified command, with uniform discipline, equipment, treatment and tactics; to stabilize and strengthen the National Government of United China by the democratic representation of all anti-Japanese elements, improvement of administrative personal and elimination of corrupt elements; to carry out a "National Defence Economic Policy" beginning with the establishment of an adequate war industry; to mobilize and arm the people both in unoccupied China and the enemy's rear, eliminate traitors, and mobilize the

Chinese overseas; and to extend international propaganda with the purpose of enlisting a greater degree of aid from friendly peoples.

It ended with a statement of conviction that "our great Chinese nation, with its 450,000,000 people and the sympathy and support of the world's democracies, will certainly defeat Japanese imperialism, which is hated by the Japanese people themselves and jealously watched by the foreign Powers".

The Kwangsi generals Li Tsung-jen and Pai Chung-hsi, General Chang Fa-kwei, commander of the "ironsides", and other military leaders once opposed to Nanking issued similar declarations, advocating the maximum united effort of the entire people in the struggle and expressing full confidence in the final victory.

New armies from all over the country took up positions on China's many fronts. The country was divided into several war zones, with the ablest generals in command. The welcome lull which ensued when the Japanese failed immediately to push westward along the Yangtze towards Hankow was fully utilized. Booms were laid down to block the river. New positions were constructed. The period of weakness on the North-eastern front continued, the Japanese crossing the Yellow River to capture Tsinan. In the South-east, Hangchow fell into the hands of the enemy, who repeated there the atrocities of Nanking. But in Shansi and Western Hopei, reorganized Chinese troops and partisans affiliated with the Eighth Route Army were already counter-attacking. And on all fronts, troops were being re-disposed and strengthened in preparation for new campaigns.

Industry was placed under military control. A hundred thousand men were put to work on a new military road connecting China with the Soviet Union.

Dr. Sun Fo, chairman of the Legislative Yuan, left for the U.S.S.R., England, and France to enlist support for China's continued resistance.

In the boldest direct blow so far struck at Japan's economic interests in China, Chinese troops at Tsingtao blew up enemy-owned industrial plant valued at 300,000,000 yen.

In Hankow, the new capital of resistance, representatives of all anti-

Japanese political tendencies conferred on measures of joint action. The commercial city became a living political centre. It had the administrative importance of Nanking, and much of the intense cultural life of wartime Shanghai. Everywhere, the keynote was preparation for struggle.

China had undergone her trial by fire. She had made her decision.

She would fight on — and she would win.

CHAPTER VII
Appraisal

AT the New Year, the first period of military operations was over. On three fronts, Japanese armies rested, their geographical objectives achieved. On the Northern battle line, one column of their forces had reached the Yellow River and had crossed it to take Tsinan. In the West, they had taken Paotou on the Inner Mongolian plain and Taiyuan, capital of mountainous Shansi. In East Central China, they held a triangle bounded by Shanghai, Nanking, and Hangchow. By all the rules of the military textbooks, they now controlled the entire North China plain — the rich five-province paradise of which they had long dreamed. Moreover, they had occupied and chastised (with many refinements of terrorism) the seat of the Government which had dared to oppose their conquering march. The greatest doorway of China's trade, the political capital of the country, and the great "Hindenburg line" of defences which had been designed to make that capital impregnable, all were in the hands of the invader.

True, these conquests had not been bought cheaply. Japan had dreamed of a short war resulting in China's subjugation within three months. But Shanghai alone, despite the greatest efforts, had held her forces for that period, and now almost six months had passed. She had wished to accomplish her aim with an army of fifteen divisions. Some of her military leaders, like Katsuki, commander-in-chief in North China, had even said (before the war) that one would be enough. But already she had put twenty-six* divisions into the field — a total of perhaps half a million troops. Well, it had been worth it. The Imperial Army was victorious. The enemy would capitulate and Japan assume her predestined role of undisputed mistress of East Asia.

But the Chinese Government did not capitulate. Having lost North China, the original apple of discord, and Nanking, the seat of its own power, it should — by all the rules — have sought for peace. It broke these rules and continued to hurl defiance at the Japanese. "No matter how the present situation may change," said Chiang Kai-shek a week after the fall of the capital, "we must not surrender, but march onward. To capitulate is to court certain national disaster." These were not the words of the commander-in-chief of a defeated army.

More than this, they were not the words of the leader of a defeated nation. "War", wrote old Clausewitz, father of Prussian strategy, "is simply a continuation of diplomacy by other, violent, means." Japanese diplomacy had long attempted to terrorize China and make her an obedient protectorate of Japan. It had failed. Then "other means" had been tried. They had evoked not submission but increased resistance. So they had been applied more ruthlessly and on a grander scale. Japanese armies now controlled the home of China's ancient civilization and two great centres of her modern development. But there was no surrender. "Other means" too had failed to achieve the objects of Japanese policy.

Japan invaded China because she could not subjugate her by the cheaper methods of diplomacy and provocation. The fact that she was driven to strike was in itself a reflection of China's growing strength. Japan admitted this strength, and she struck to destroy it before it grew too great. "We must now beat China to her knees, until she has no spirit left to resist," Tokyo's Foreign Minister Hirota had declaimed. Fine words, but all that they meant was that where the threat of Japan's power had once sufficed, the full weight of her

---

* Neutral military observers in Hankow considered this Chinese estimate to be accurate.

military machine was now needed.

If the New China had been merely the metropolitan opulence of Shanghai, the newly developed industries of the coastal fringe, and the monumental architecture of Nanking, Japan would indeed have succeeded in her aims. Both Japan's confidence of victory and the waverings of many Chinese groups were the results of the mistaken belief that this was really so. But Japan and the defeatists had reckoned without the great resources inherent in China's tremendous territory and 450,000,000 people. Political unification had made these resources available to the Central Government for the purpose of national resistance. Now the Government's determination to continue the war inspired the people to support it with new confidence. And the Government itself drew new strength and faith in victory from the ever-increasing army of conscious fighters for national liberation which demanded its guidance in the struggle.

Hankow, at the opening of 1938, was a city of self-criticism and progress. It was a city in which past mistakes were appraised and new plans were made for the future. On New Year's day, it became definitely clear the Japan's peace overtures had been finally rejected, and that further German efforts at mediation were bound to fail. The reorganization of China's Government was announced. Chiang Kai-shek gave up his civil post and turned his attention more exclusively to the affairs of the army. China's communications were put under military control. The membership of the National Defence Council was increased from thirty to seventy-five. Among the new members were Shen Chun-ju, grand old man of the National Salvation Movement, and Mao Tse-tung and Chou En-lai, leaders of the Chinese Communist Party, which had long advocated protracted resistance leading to China's final victory. The General Headquarters was strengthened by the removal of wavering elements. Provinces at the front and in the immediate rear were put under military governors.

Ten days later, the Japanese Imperial Conference, sitting in Tokyo, acknowledged the failure of Japanese arms to beat the Central Government of China into submission. Its decision, as announced by Premier Konoye on

January 16, read as follows: "The Japanese Government will not recognize the Nationalist Government as the other party in negotiations for a readjustment of Sino-Japanese relations, but will pursue military operations to overthrow that regime in the expectation that a new Chinese regime will emerge and become party to such parleys." In reply, the Chinese Government repeated its determination to continue fighting. It published the Japanese peace conditions which it had rejected in December.

At the same time, China recalled her ambassador to Japan, who, through six months of war, had been sitting in Tokyo writing "strong protests" against incidents like the violation of diplomatic immunity involved in the detention of a vice-consul's baggage at a Japanese port. The last grotesque remnants of "normal relations" between the two countries were now swept away. Practically, as well as symbolically, this was a clearing of the decks. The continued residence of the ambassador in Tokyo had been more than all overpunctilious observance of legality, more even than a humiliating survival of the days when Japan's acts of war against China were "incidents" and hostilities ended with Chinese apologies and concessions. The retention of the technical framework for "diplomatic settlement" had been a reflection of an irresolute belief in the possibility of negotiations. Now it was clearly recognized that such a "settlement" could only mean surrender. And China had no intention of surrendering. So the last channel of direct contact with the Japanese Government was abolished, as the Chinese people had long demanded.*

Internally, the Kuomintang, Communist Party, and all other groups favouring continued resistance, moved more rapidly towards real unity. The Kuomintang Government had demonstrated its determination to fight on. Through six months of war the Communist Party and the Eighth Route Army had shown the nation how much could be achieved by the wholehearted and disciplined carrying out of the slogan: "Everything for the war." Old hatreds and suspicions began more and more to give way to the growing realization

---

* A subordinate official, however, remained in charge of the Embassy premises in Tokyo until July 1938 — a year after the outbreak of the war.

that the free initiative of all groups was the first condition for the development of a many-sided and effective struggle.

Kuomintang, Communists, and adherents of other groups worked together in the new Political Department of the General Headquarters, established at the time of the reorganization of the Government. This department was created to enable China to take full advantage of the revolutionary nature of her war of resistance. Every honest Chinese supported the war. It was the function of the Political Department to organize this support and make it do work. Through army, divisional, and regimental political departments, the soldiers of China would be taught the aims of their struggle. In the rear, workers, peasants, students, tradesmen, intellectual workers, and professionals — all would be organized into national associations to aid the war. Every honest and progressive person throughout the world sympathized with China's fight and abhorred Japanese aggression. It was proposed to extend and improve China's international propaganda. In Japan's colonies, Korea and Formosa, unrest was brewing. The Japanese people themselves had no stake in the war. For them, too, propaganda was to be prepared.

The Political Department was headed by General Chen Cheng, Vice-Minister of War, and formerly one of the chief commanders in the campaigns against the Red Army. His assistants were Chang Li-sheng, a prominent Kuomintang politician, and Huang Chi-hsiang, a member of the "Third Party" (Social Democrats), once proscribed by the National Government. The propaganda section was placed under Kuo Mo-jo, famous Chinese left-wing writer, who had spent ten years of exile in Japan. In the Great Revolution of 1925-7, Kuo had headed the Political Department of the entire Nationalist army. All talents were represented in the department. Tien Han, who had written the words of the "March of the Manchurian Volunteers", was art director of the propaganda section. Hung Shen, another dramatist, supervised the production of patriotic plays. Yeh Chienyu, dean of the vigorous modern Chinese school of cartoonists, was in charge of poster work. The aesthetic writer Yu Ta-fu, who had lived long in Japan, headed the sub-section producing propaganda for the enemy. The best actors, directors, and camera-men of

China's young motion-picture industry now worked in the Political Department's Studies, producing films to arouse the people to take part in resistance.

On January 9, I was present at a meeting held to celebrate the opening of the first Communist daily in Hankow, the *New China Daily News*. Despite the fact that the newspaper was avowedly the official organ of the party, the speakers included many non-Communists and members of the Kuomintang. Representatives of all sections of Chinese society welcomed the appearance of the daily. "We hope it will criticize the Government's failings and help it with practical suggestions for the carrying out of resistance," said the sixty-year-old jurist, Shen Chu-ju, oldest of the "Seven Leaders" of the National Salvation movement, who had been arrested in the previous year, now a member of the National Defence Council. "We will look to your paper to interpret the social meaning of the war and expose every tendency towards capitulation," said Dr. Teng Chiu-ming, a professor of Kwangsi University. Chang Hai-meng, an official of the Legislative Yuan, declared: "I am an old member of the Kuomintang, and I say frankly that we have not carried out the will of Dr. Sun Yat-sen. To-day, we need the aid of the Communist Party to recapture the national revolutionary spirit of 1925. The Communists know how to organize the people. If we could not beat the Northern militarists without the organization of the masses, how much more do we need their aid to defeat the Japanese invaders."

Wang Ming (Chen Shao-yu), a member of the political bureau of the Chinese Communist Party and once China's delegate to the Comintern, spoke frankly on the nature and aims of the new organs. "Our editor, comrade Pan Tse-nien, is a Communist, and we will expect him to follow the line of the party in all respects. But this need not worry anyone. The line of the party to-day is the line of the Chinese people. Its problems are theirs. The newspaper will discuss all the difficult questions connected with organization for resistance. It will frankly point out weaknesses and tendencies dangerous to China. The national United Front of the Chinese people already exists. It would be false to deny that some friction between the various groups forming it also continues to exist. By frank discussion, our newspaper will help to remove misunderstandings and to strengthen the unity of all parties in the fight for a new, regenerated China."

The establishment of the *New China Daily News* was an event of great importance. Many times, during the following months, points of dispute between the Kuomintang and the Communists were the object of polemics between their organs. Free discussion took the place of armed struggle and police terror. An attempt by paid hooligans to wreck the offices of the newspaper was universally condemned by public opinion throughout China.

Democracy had not yet come to China. In the Political Department, disputes over methods and the division of functions long continued to shackle initiative and impede real work. The new freedom of the Press was still subject to attacks. But the important thing was that a beginning had been made in mobilizing the people where nothing had been done before. A free Press was coming into existence where there had been none before. The united front was meeting difficulties. But that was because, from an arrangement on paper, it was turning into a thing of flesh and blood. It was natural, under these circumstances, that the obstacles in its way should also assume concrete form. But the unity of the Chinese people was stronger than those who sought to impede it. At the time, January seemed a month of erratic ups and downs. From the perspective of a year we can see that the march was inevitably forward.

As the rear moved toward the free co-operation of all parties under the leadership of the National Government, so the front moved toward greater co-operation between armies under a unified command. During the first six months of the war, many positions had been lost as a result of independent actions by generals who did not recognize each other's authority. Now stern measures were applied to enforce obedience to orders and to suppress the remnants of war-lord "autonomy". Already in December, General Li Fu-Ying had been shot in Shansi for retreating from a point which he had been ordered to defend. Now mandates were published rewarding successful commanders and punishing officers and civil officials who had been remiss in their duties. A number were sentenced to death or imprisoned. Thirteen divisional commanders were dismissed from their posts for inefficiency. General Han Fu-chu, governor of Shantung, had long held the position of a semi-independent buffer between the Japanese and the Central Government. This had been a convenient arrangement during the era of capitulation. But now he had tried to maintain this position in the course of the national war. He had retreated from Tsinan, allowing the Japanese to take the provincial capital without firing a shot. He was promptly arrested, court-martialled, and executed.

The public announcement of Han Fu-chu's conviction stated that he had been found guilty on five counts. First, he had disobeyed the orders of his superiors. Second, he had imposed the sale of opium upon the people. Third, he had used force to collect extortionate taxes from the population of his province. Fourth, he had seized public funds for his own use. Fifth, he had confiscated the arms which the people kept for self-defence. In other words, General Han Fu-chu had behaved in the manner of a typical provincial warlord of the old school. Now he had been tried and shot, the first general in modern China to be executed on such charges. Two years earlier his behaviour would have been regarded as "normal". There had been many like him. But he had made the mistake of continuing in the old ways when all China was fighting for democracy and national liberation. The volley that killed him sounded the end of the war-lord era. It underscored the meaning of the national united front. From this front even old-style provincial militarists were not excluded. If they did their duty as soldiers and as Chinese they would enjoy, for the first time, the support of their people. If they he not fulfil this duty — the fate of Han Fu-chu was a warning. Past enmities were forgotten, past crimes forgiven, when the Chinese people rose to defend their national independence. But for anyone attempting to sabotage this struggle there would be no mercy. The life of a nation was at stake.

Military unification was not only a matter of penalties. If in some cases it had to be imposed with a firm hand, in others it had been achieved through voluntary co-operation and had already shown important results. Troops from all over China had fought at Shanghai and in Shansi, and there had not been a single case of refusal to obey orders to travel thousands of miles to the front. Armies organized by war-lords as local tax-collecting and monopoly-defence machines left their bases to fight bravely against the national enemy. In Shansi, the advance of the Japanese after the fall of Taiyuan had been effectively checked by the co-operation of central and provincial troops, the Eighth Route Army, and the armed people.* In the national war there was room for everyone, and everyone fought together. The years of militarist civil wars in China had been studded with sell-outs and betrayals. In the war against Japan, not a single officer had gone over with his troops to the enemy. On the other hand, old fence-sitters like Shih Yu-san, who had once been very close to the Japanese, and Chang Tze-chung, who had been partly responsible for the collapse at Peiping and Tientsin, now fought against the Japanese — and fought well. Manchurian auxiliaries trained by the Japanese themselves deserted to the Chinese side whenever they had the opportunity.

Unification of existing armies was only one phase of the creation of a new armed force of the Chinese people. In January, measures were passed for nation-wide conscription under centralized control. The country was divided into nine conscription areas. The system of conscription by lot was introduced. Forcible impressment of peasants, the usual recruiting method of provincial armies was strictly prohibited.** On the civil side, the Executive Yuan issued orders regulating the creation of committees in every district town in the country to care for the families of soldiers fighting at the front. Families of soldiers were exempted from the payment of surtaxes. They were not to be conscripted for labour service. They could apply for relief in case of

---

* The Shansi provincial Army, and the whole western war zone, was under the command of General Yen Hsi-shan, for many years master of the province. The central troops were commanded by General Wei Li-huang, the Eighth Route Army by Chu Teh.

** This prohibition was effective in areas near the front, but press-gang methods (known as "la fu" — one of the most terrible words in the vocabulary of the Chinese peasant) persisted in Szechuan and other remote provinces. The troops from these areas were consequently the worst and least dependable in the Chinese Army until the practice was corrected.

poverty or disease, and for funeral expenses in case of death. Special benefits were decreed for the families of men crippled or killed in battle. These provisions were not uniformly carried out. Even if they had been, they would have been insufficient. China's front-line fighters deserved more of their Government. But a beginning had been made.

While reorganization was going on in the rear, the front was the scene of preparation for a new phase of military operations. Having occupied Tsinan, the Japanese moved down the Tientsin-Pukow railway. Simultaneously, another army began moving northwards from the other end of the railway, at Nanking. To join these two armies at Hsuchow was the Japanese objective. After achieving this junction, they planned to use their combined forces to drive westward along the Lunghai railway, which roughly follows the south bank of the Yellow River. At Tungkuan, they hoped to make a new junction, this time with the Japanese armies operating in South Shansi. This would accomplish the strategic encirclement of all Chinese forces operating north of the Yellow River, including the troublesome Eighth Route Army.

Japan's objectives at the beginning of the Hsuchow campaign* were fourfold. First, she wished to join her northern and southern fronts. Second, she wanted to annihilate the Chinese armies north of the Yellow River. The third aim was to check China's arms imports by sea through an invasion of South China. The fourth, to drive westward, cutting the roads linking China to the Soviet Union. She was to fail in all but the first of these objects. As for the others, it was only nine months later that she was able to strike at Canton. China westward supply route has become many routes, not one of which has yet (April 1939) been interrupted. It is safe to say that China's armies north of the Yellow River will never be annihilated. For this, China's new methods of struggle were responsible. We have remarked the political regeneration of the country. Let us now consider the new tactics of the Chinese army which

---

* As used here "Hsuchow campaign" includes not only the operations immediately incident to the capture of the town, but the whole phase of hostilities of which the struggle for Hsuchow was the pivot.

were to foil Japan during the year of war.

On January 15, General Chiang Kai-shek carried out a general inspection of the Northern fronts. At Loyang, he conferred with Chu Teh and Peng Teh-huai, commander and vice-commander of the Eighth Route Army. The Eighth Route Army operated in Shansi; and Shansi, first of all the fronts, had shown during the past two months how defeated armies could rally to check and counter-attack the invader. In the Nanking area, the Japanese were resting. Along the Tientsin-Pukow railway, the demoralized army of Han Fu-chu was offering little resistance. But in Shansi, the Japanese were already on the defensive and had lost a large part of their initial conquests. The Eighth Route Army did not claim all the credit for this development. After the fall of Taiyuan, the commanders of all three armies operating in Shansi had foregathered and sworn that they would not allow themselves to be driven across the Yellow River, but would remain in the province, to harass and counter-attack the invader. They had all loyally co-operated, and it was due to their joint efforts that the advance of the Japanese was halted. But the combined mobile and guerrilla tactics which they adopted and, to which they owed their success, were the tactics of the former Red Army, and this army had taken the lead in showing them how these tactics could best be applied.

For ten years, Chiang Kai-shek had known the Red Army as a formidable enemy. Now, through the six months of the people's war of resistance, he had come to know the Eighth Route Army as a loyal and dependable ally against Japan. Through ten long years of civil war, the Red Army had maintained and strengthened its forces in the face of a better-armed and more numerous enemy. Now the entire Chinese army was facing a similar situation. Who better than the Eighth Route Army could advise the correct tactics for it to adopt? The root of the Red Army's successful resistance had been the fact that, wherever it operated, it had enjoyed the full support of the people. In the national struggle against Japan, the whole Chinese army was fighting for the people. It was necessary for it to learn how to seek their aid. Here, too, the experience of the Eighth Route Army was valuable.

The Loyang conversations certainly had considerable effect on the proceedings of the Staff-Officers' Conference, held at Wuchang during the last week of January. Generalissimo Chiang Kai-shek was convinced that in order to ensure co-ordination between the various forces composing the Chinese National Army, it was necessary to raise the authority of staff officers and give them a common plan of action, and these officers were accordingly put through an intensive course on the problems of the Hsuchow campaign.

The Wuchang Conference made a realistic and mature appraisal of the previous errors and new tasks of the Chinese Army. It demonstrated that just as the war of national liberation had brought out the fighting abilities of the Chinese soldiers, so it had raised the level of thinking of Chinese officers.

At the conference, full cognizance was taken of the fact that the war had now become a struggle to the end. Not only the available military forces, but all the national resources of China and Japan were now matched against each other. China had the greater territory, natural wealth, and population. Politically, she enjoyed the great advantage of fighting a national revolutionary war in which the Government could be certain of the support of all classes of the population. But industrially and militarily — in all the things that confer superior striking power on a nation — Japan was far ahead of China. Her resources were developed to the full, while China's though "incalculable and inexhaustible", in the words of Chiang Kai-shek, were largely potential. Japan brought to the struggle the result of sixty years of industrial growth. But this growth had been based chiefly on imported raw materials accumulated over the same period. It could not reproduce itself. Japan's expenditures were justified only if she attained her objectives, or at least quickly gained effective control of new sources from which she could replace what she had expended. The alternative was collapse.

Politically, too, Japan needed a quick victory. The necessity of fighting this war was by no means clear to her people, to whom it had already brought a fall in living standards, the loss of more than 100,000 fathers, husbands, and sons, and the sacrifice of even the few quasi-democratic political rights which they had previously enjoyed. China's people, on the other hand, fully realized that they were fighting for their existence. The death and suffering the war had brought them they could charge squarely to the armies of Japanese imperialism. Under their own Government, they were making gains, even while they struggled. Their armies, once regarded as a scourge on the countryside, were now manifestly protecting them against Japanese terror and exploitation — the details of which any peasant could hear from any passing refugee. Soldiers treated the people better than ever before. While the last remnants of freedom were disappearing in Japan, the Chinese people were given long-denied rights of liberty of speech, publication, and organization. Where, as in the former Soviet area and the recaptured territories of the North, the people had been consciously made the basis of a democratic administration, their economic burdens had also been considerably lightened.

Strategy is a reflection of social and economic facts. The reflection of Japan's superior industrial strength was the confidence of her militarists in their ability to inflict a "knockout blow" on China. The reflection of her basic poverty was the fact that they were forced to seek desperate means to inflict this blow as quickly and as cheaply as possible. Japan's people had no interest in the war. Therefore, at home the militarists fed them with jingoist propaganda while ruthlessly suppressing their every tendency to begin thinking for themselves. When they put on uniform and enlisted in the army, they were encouraged to forget all questions concerning the ultimate aim of the war by seeking the "pleasures" and profits of the moment in looting, murder, and rape. Disaffection in the army was rigorously punished. Nevertheless, anti-war propaganda was carried on by the braver and more developed, while "epidemics" of mass suicide among the soldiers gave the lie to the official conception of an Imperial Army whose every member burned with enthusiasm for Japan's divine mission.

Documentary evidence in the hands of the Chinese general staff indicated that the Japanese had originally planned to use fifty divisions of troops to defeat two hypothetical enemies China and the U.S.S.R. For China, they had deemed fifteen divisions sufficient. The remaining thirty-five for the Soviet Union.

At the outbreak of the war, Japan had a standing army of twenty-five divisions. Sixteen of these were dispatched to China for the Shanghai and Shansi campaigns. This was already in excess of the original plan, but after Shanghai even this force was found to be pitifully insufficient. So Japan was forced to mobilize fifteen divisions of reserves, of which ten were sent to the front. Thus, at the end of the first period of military operations, Japan had exceeded her plan by eleven divisions. She was eleven divisions farther than she had been at the beginning of the war from her projected "victory" over the joint forces of her hypothetical foes. Moreover, she had suffered 150,000 casualties.*

What were the military reasons for the Japanese failure? The chief of these reasons was her arrogant miscalculation of China's strength. When China mobilized all her resources for resistance, Japan decided to abandon her plan of fighting only in North China and to strike at the lower Yangtze, military and political centre of the country. This was a serious mistake. It divided Japan's forces, forced her to send far more troops to China than she had originally intended, and caused her to expend such quantities of men, money, and supplies, that she was reduced from a first- to a second-class military Power. Knowing her limited strength China, tried to tempt her into greater expenditures. Seeking to conserve her resources, Japan was niggardly about sending needed reinforcements. As a result, her forces had nowhere and at no time been sufficient to destroy any Chinese army. Her flanking tactics, carried out with inadequate forces, were effective in making the Chinese abandon their positions, but not in surrounding them and destroying their strength. In the hands of the pinchbeck military fascism of Japan, the classical tactics of Cannae, Sedan, and Tannenberg, designed for the annihilation of the enemy, became no more than a method of dislodgment and pursuit.

In the first stage of military operations, China had committed errors which allowed the Japanese to take full advantage of their strength. These errors were now frankly discussed at the Staff Officers' Conference. As outlined in

---

* Chinese estimate of Japanese soldiers killed, wounded, or invalided home.

a lecture by Chiang Kai-shek, they were as follows:

Firstly, China had continued to expect that the countries pledged by the Nine-Power Treaty to maintain her independence and territorial integrity would check Japan. Her army had therefore limited itself to defensive tactics. For a poorly-equipped army, the attempt to hold a stationary line is fatal. It gives the better-armed enemy a chance to pick out a weak spot and hammer at it with all his superior armament. Since great numbers of men are needed to maintain sufficient strength at all points of the defended line to withstand such an assault, the defending army is compelled to surrender all initiative, being left without means of counter-attack. It can just sit tight and be shelled and bombed, as the Chinese army was at Shanghai. China's infantry was more eager for contact with the enemy and better endowed for hand-to-hand combat than the infantry of the Japanese. Under the conditions at Shanghai, it was forced to remain passive, while the enemy could use to full advantage his superior strength in aircraft and artillery.

China's second error had been lack of co-ordination. While the Japanese attacked at Shanghai, other fronts had remained largely passive. Their obvious duty had been to counter-attack and thus draw away and hold as large a part of the enemy's forces as possible, reducing his pressure on the Shanghai front, where China's forces were labouring under serious tactical handicaps.

Her third error was a result of the lack of uniformity of command, the treason of Han Fu-chu, and a general misapplication of tactics which were fundamentally correct. To lure the enemy deeply into their territory in order to extend his line and increase his vulnerability was good tactics for the Chinese. But instead of making the Japanese advance expensive by defending designated points along the line, and massing forces on the enemy's flanks for counter-attack, the Chinese forces on the Taitsin-Pukow Railway had in many cases simply retreated. This was not tactics: it was far more like demoralization.

Though placed fourth, the last error was the most important. The Chinese army had not made sufficient use of the sympathy of the people. It had not mobilized the people's strength, the most important auxiliary it could have. The support of the population is the most priceless military advantage possessed by an army fighting for the interests of the people, since it is an advantage which an invading enemy cannot possibly duplicate or effectively counteract. Yet it was in this field, precisely, that almost nothing had been done. Only on the Shansi front had the power of the people been used. Result: the Japanese had been effectively checkmated.

The tactics in which the army of the Chinese Government had been schooled before the war had been taught to it by German military advisers and retired White Russian generals who lectured in the Army Staff College. They were tactics appropriate to an army acting as a police force and punitive instrument against its own people, not to one fighting a national war of liberation. The officers assembled at Wuchang had much unlearning to do, but most of them were beginning to understand the needs of the new situation — and they went about it manfully.

An officer who had attended the Wuchang conference told me later of the new tactics it adopted for the Chinese Army. These tactics were a combination of guerrilla, mobile, and positional warfare.

"What is guerrilla warfare?" he asked. "Guerrilla warfare is a method of using the strength of our people against the enemy. It is best carried out by the armed people stiffened by groups of regular troops specially detached from the army for this work. Guerrillas must attack the enemy everywhere, make him afraid to leave his base, wipe him out where he is weak, attack his lines of communication to impede his supplies and cut off his retreat. The farther the Japanese advance into our territory, the longer their lines of communication, and the greater their vulnerability to guerrilla tactics. If they keep a small garrison at any point, the guerrillas will wipe it out. It is impossible for them to strengthen all points. To effectively guard their communications, they will have to withdraw troops from the fronts where their striking power will be lessened."

The guerrilla would constantly harass and worry the enemy. Every day they would cause him losses. Here 100 men killed, there 200, here a tank blown up, there a bridge destroyed and a train derailed. "At the end", Chiang Kaishek had said, "we will gather all our small success into a great victory."

In an interview given at this time, Chou En-lai, one of the leaders of the Eighth Route Army, had indicated the *impasse* in which the Japanese found themselves. "The Japanese strength in North China is ten divisions," he said. "If they garrison each town with only one company of a hundred men, they will have to use all their forces. But we can easily destroy such garrisons. If the Japanese put a battalion in each town, they will need thirty divisions."

Important as it was, guerrilla warfare was only an auxiliary to the action of the main Chinese Army which the Japanese had failed to destroy or seriously weaken during the first stage of the hostilities. This army would substitute mobile for positional warfare as its main mode of action. Its tactics would change from defensive to offensive.

"When we are holding a line", said the officer, "the enemy can break through at one spot by using his bombers and artillery. We can only sit and take it, and this is bad both tactically and psychologically. A man who is always warding off, instead of giving blows, begins to doubt his own ability to attack. He sees only the enemy's strength, not his weakness. But when we employ our forces in constant manoeuvres and attacks, the enemy, not we, lives in constant apprehension. We know exactly where and when we will strike. The enemy does not."

This did not indicate that positional warfare would be entirely given up. It would be used to hold up the enemy's advance at certain points, giving the mobile arms a chance to strike at his flanks. In this way, key points would be defended. "Hsuchow, for instance," said the officer, "lies at the junction of two important railways. For this reason we must defend it. But it is not like Shanghai, which was a focus of international attention, and whose defence was politically important to us. We will always remember, that our real object is not to defend Hsuchow as such, but to prevent the junction of the enemy forces. Thus, if we lose Hsuchow but prevent this junction by counter-attacks elsewhere, we will have achieved our object. When forced to abandon a position, we will leave enough forces in the surrounding areas to harry the enemy and never let him feel safe in the possession of that point. We may lose many cities; but we will not give up a single section of our country. Even far in his rear, the enemy will continue to feel the pressure of our armed forces."

It was resolved that all officers and soldiers should be lectured on the new tactics and their meaning. Every fighter would be told that China would only now begin to use her strength. The men already had faith in China's cause. They would now be imbued with faith in her military ability to foil the plans of the enemy.

"Everyone understands why we fight the Japanese," said the officer. "We fight because our homes are threatened with destruction, our women with disgrace, and the whole Chinese race with enslavement. There is no need to tell us to fight. No one can stop us from hitting back. All we need to know is how to do it most effectively."

The Wuchang Conference had explained how.

The staff officers who had attended the conference went back to the 202 Divisions of the Chinese Army not only with new ideas, but also with new powers. Their responsibility was not directly to their commanders, but to the national General Staff. Their tactical decisions were made binding for the commanders who held the executive power.

For mobile and guerrilla warfare, the creation of three new armies was decreed. One was to be based on the triple border of Kangsu, Chekiang, and Anhwei, in territory occupied by the Japanese. It would be formed around a core of Communist partisans who had remained south of the Yangtze when the Chinese Red Army started on its great "Long March" to the north-west. This force was destined to become famous as the New Fourth Army. The second would be based on the Kiangsu-Shantung-Honan border. The third, composed of Eighth Route Army men, national and provincial troops, would occupy the Japanese in the mountainous marches of Hopei, Honan, and Shansi.* These armies were children of the people's war. They were United Front

---

* The reason for the numerous "border areas" lies in the fact that China's provinces are usually divided from each other by natural boundaries — most often high mountain ranges. The borders meet, therefore, in mountainous and inaccessible country, easy to defend and strategically commanding the surrounding plains. Throughout Chinese history, these borders have played an exceptionally important part.

armies, and their function was to launch counter-attacks using the new tactics based on the unity and fighting initiative of the Chinese people.

On the Shansi-Chahar-Hopei border, a great new partisan army had already grown up. It had recaptured a total of more than forty districts from the Japanese and restored them to Chinese control. On January 10, with the sanction of the National Government, it set up the first Chinese regional administration to be established in a recaptured area — the Shansi-Chahar-Hopei Border Government. This was China's first real experiment in democratic government under the United Front. It was a model of the new China which would emerge when the entire country had been cleared of the invading enemy.

Meanwhile, popular unity and initiative continued to grow in the rear.

Throughout the country, mobilization commissions were set up. Their function was to recruit and train militia for local defence, conduct wartime propaganda, collect financial contributions, and co-ordinate industries and handicrafts in their respective districts for the production of supplies needed for the front. These commissions were only beginning to exist in many parts of the country, but in some provinces, notably Shensi, Kwangtung, and Hunan, they had already instituted universal military training.

Steps were taken not only to relieve, but to organize and utilize the hundreds of thousands of refugees coming to Central China from the lower Yangtze. A colonization project to absorb 50,000 was instituted in West Hupeh. The colonists were given military training. The skilled workers among them were employed in productive enterprises. Student propagandists were sent to lecture to them on the meaning of the national crisis and the necessity of struggle if they were to regain their homes.

On January 15, representatives of over twenty national educational bodies met in Hankow and established the "Preparatory Committee for National Education During the War of Resistance". The object of this committee was to work out a curriculum of wartime education to be recommended to all schools throughout the country. Meanwhile, student refugees were sent to continue their studies in the distant rear, in the provinces of Kansu, Szechuan,

Kweichow, and Yunnan.*

Students from Peiping and Tientsin who had established a temporary university in Changsha were ordered to leave for Yunnan because of the imminent threat of bombing and invasion. Five hundred of them refused to go. "Wartime education does not consist of constantly moving to the rear," they said. "Our duty is to remain and prepare for the enemy when he comes." They continued to organize the people and conduct propaganda in Hunan. Those of their comrades who agreed to leave walked more than 1,000 miles to their new location. They are hardy folk, these boys and girls of new China.

The sober commercial city of Hankow began to wear a different aspect. In its crowded streets, one could meet active workers for China's liberation from Shanghai, from Nanking, and from the lost provinces of the North. On its walls were countless posters, wall newspapers, and proclamations. Daily they changed, reflecting events in China and in the world. The walls of Hankow were the platform of the people. Whenever there were rumours of capitulation or betrayal, they bore a crop of slogans reaffirming the people's will to resist. When the Chinese air force won a victory vivid placards announced the fact. When Hitler spoke in favour of Japan, the walls bore his features in fierce caricature. When Australian dockers refused to load iron for Japan, proclamations signed by the Hankow Seamen's Union shouted their thanks. China's best-known writers did not disdain to contribute to the wall newspapers of the Cultural Workers' National Resistance Federation which were plastered all over the city. Changed every three days, they never failed to draw huge crowds of faithful readers. China's best artists drew the vigorous posters displayed on every street corner.

Early in February, a series of mass meetings and demonstrations was held to support the London Conference of the International Peace Campaign. On February 7, thousands of women marched with banners through the streets of the city. Among them were the wives of China's leaders, workers from the

---

* Nanking University, the Government's great Central University, Wuhan University, and Tientsin's bomb-blasted Nankai University, are now operating in Szechuan. Peiping's Tsinghua and Peking National (Peita) are in Kunming (Yunnanfu). Many other famous institutions of learning have also moved west.

spinning-mills, newly trained red-cross nurses, members of frontline service groups with pistols at their hips.

February 8 was Youth Day. Five thousand boys and girls gathered at Chungshan Park for a mass meeting. Just as they assembled, Japanese planes appeared over the city. Systematically, the leaders of the meeting directed the young people to places of comparative safety. When the planes had passed over, the meeting reassembled. "Fascist aggression is the enemy of world youth," "Down with Japanese Imperialism," "Long live the Chinese Air Force," they shouted.

February 9 was the day of the workers. Again thousands paraded. There were metal and arsenal workers who produced arms for China's defence. There were textile workers, seamen, and postal employees, and there were truck-drivers and railway-men who had kept troops and supplies moving to the front along China's inadequate transport network in the face of almost super-human difficulties and the relentless and unceasing Japanese air terror. "Brother workers in foreign lands," read their slogans. "We and you together can stop the aggressor." "Help us to fight Japan." "Workers of the world, unite against Japanese imperialism."

On February 12, cultural workers marched to protest against the Japanese destruction of schools and universities. Plays, specially written for the day, were performed. Posters and leaflets drove home the necessity for struggle, the inevitability of China's victory.

The mobilization of China's people was beginning. Daily, the United Front was assuming concrete form in new fields. But there were still many groups which did not understand the essence of the United Front, the free development of all forces having anything to contribute to China's struggle. Competition within the United Front was too often still a struggle for power, not an effort to show fitness for leadership by effective work in the national cause. A strong mass movement was universally recognized as a necessity. But the question was still too often not "how to develop it" but "how to control it". On those who approached the people's movement with this attitude, the movement took its own revenge. Efforts to build up machines for rival cliques failed. Sincere attempts to build up mass organizations for anti-Japanese resistance prospered.

One of the most striking features of life to Hankow in those days was the universal interest in the activities, policies, and leaders of the Eighth Route Army. The record of the army in Shansi was known to all. The former Soviet region had become a model of successful democratic mass mobilization. Its capital, at Yenan, once a sleepy district town in mountainous North Shensi, had been transformed into a great cultural centre — with thousands of youths from all over the country studying in its Anti-Japanese University, Military and Political Academy, and Lu Hsun School of Arts, named after China's greatest modern writer. Every book-store in Hankow displayed hundreds of titles dealing with the history and achievements of the army, the Communist Party, and the Special District. Some of these books and pamphlets were good descriptions and analyses of their subject. Others were ignorantly written by hack writers. But anything in print about the Eighth Route Army would sell, the book-stores shouted for more, and poor writers in need of pocket-money sat up nights compiling new accounts.

There was nothing extraordinary or alarming about this demand for information. It did not mean that the Eighth Route Army was proselytizing at the expense of the Kuomintang, or that the people who read about it were "going Communist". For ten years nothing had been openly printed dealing with an extremely significant and dramatic phase of modern Chinese history and an extremely important tendency in modern Chinese political thought. Now the high walls around what had once been forbidden subjects were broken. Everyone read about the Eighth Route Army, as every student of the Orient had read Snow's *Red Star over China* in the west.

This, and other features of the democratic awakening, caused some Kuomintang groups to think back fondly to the days of police suppression of "dangerous thoughts". Enemies of the United Front, from the notorious Wang Ching-wei to the Trotzkyists (there are Chinese Trotzkyists), launched a new attack on the Communist Party.

On January 17 a band of strong-arm men wrecked the offices of the *New China Daily News*. Newsboys who sold the paper returned, bruised and bloody, telling how they had been set upon and beaten and their papers taken away. On the following days, attacks on the Communists, their publications, and the Eighth Route Army, appeared once more in the Kuomintang Press. One editorial pointed to the German Nazis as China's best friends, and to the Third Reich as a model for her political development. Another demanded the re-introduction of one-party dictatorship and "control of thought". There is only one party in the Soviet Union, they argued, and the Press expresses its views only. How, then, could the Chinese Communist be justified in their objection to the political monopoly of the Kuomintang in China? If the Chinese Communist Party wanted freedom for its Press, why did it not ask the Soviet Union to revise its Press laws?

On February 10, the *New China Daily* printed a reply to these sallies in the form of an interview with Mao Tze-tung, leader of the Chinese Communist Party. In it he pointed out that the Soviet Union had gone through a workers' revolution which had established a dictatorship of the proletariat. To-day there was only one class in the Soviet Union — the toiling people — and only one party to advance its interests. In China, more than one class existed. Under such conditions a one-party dictatorship would represent the dictatorship of one class over the others. For a national United Front in which all classes co-operated against a common enemy, the only feasible political basis was the democratic co-operation of all parties favouring resistance.

Of control of thought, he said: "The principle of control has historically proved itself to be wrong in China." This principle has been tried. It had led to ten years of civil war, which had given the Japanese the opportunity to advance their aggression and launch their invasion.

"On the other hand, it is the principle of the United Front", said Mao Tze-tung, "that has consolidated the whole nation to fight the aggressor." He branded the Press campaign against the *New China Daily* as an attempt to upset the legal status of the Communist Party and to torpedo the United Front. Such attempts will not only destroy the unity of the Chinese people. He concluded, "They will sabotage the national war of resistance."

Other attacks were launched against the Eighth Route Army. It did no fighting, wrote the enemies of the United Front. Money allotted to the army for military expenditures was spent on propaganda, they charged. In reply to these allegations, Chu Teh, the army's commander-in-chief, wrote an account of the army's record in the first five months of hostilities — a record comprising seven major battles and guerrilla warfare over a wide area resulting in the re-establishment of Chinese authority in whole province in the rear of the enemy. The account did not mention the attacks. It was called, simply, "Experience and Lessons Learned by the Eighth Route Army During Six Months of Resistance." Only in the last paragraph, he wrote:

"Lastly, we want to point out the vital importance of the national United Front. The unification of the forces on the north-eastern front in Shansi has shattered the enemy's machinations to drive Chinese to fight Chinese. This is indeed a great political accomplishment. It must be realized that unless unification is universally achieved and strongly maintained, there is still room for the enemy to try their tricks to split our fighting ranks. The unification of the nation, beginning with that of the army, is the secret of victory."

These clear pronouncements exposed and silenced the attackers. In the meantime, Chiang Kai-shek himself had expressed his dissatisfaction with their activities. He had no reason to be dissatisfied with the loyal co-operation of the Communist Party. Moreover, no one knew better than he how much fighting the Eighth Route Army was doing. No one knew better how meagre were the appropriations allowed the army by the Central Government. "I don't care what they use the funds for," he is reported to have exploded angrily. "I have given ten times the amount to other people without it bringing a fraction of the results the Eighth Route Army has achieved."

The attack on the United Front had coupe from the groups in the Kuomintang which still favoured friendship with Germany and Italy. It had come from the groups which Japan hoped would press for the acceptance of her repeatedly proffered terms of capitulation. On February 18, not Mao Tze-tung or Chu Te, or even Chiang Kai-shek, but Hitler himself dealt these groups a blow from which they would never quite recover. On that day he announced Germany's recognition of "Manchukuo" and her sympathy with Japanese aggression in China. In a particularly insulting speech, he declared: "I do not consider China mentally or materially strong enough to withstand the inroads of Bolshevism." All sections of Chinese opinion reacted to these statements with burning indignation. The reaction was strongest not among the progressives, who had all along predicted such a development, but among more or less conservative groups. Capitalists who had lost their factories to the Japanese, bankers who were putting up a successful struggle to maintain the value of China's currency, officers who for years had fought the Red Army began to understand the real meaning of Fascist "anti-Communism" in relation to China's fight for existence.

The Chungshan (Sun Yat-sen) Study Association, an important inner-party organization of the Kuomintang existing for the purpose of theoretical analysis and discussion of questions of policy, issued a declaration calling for greater unity in the national war. "We must consolidate and intensify the United Front," it read. "A joint programme of national salvation must be worked out. All who submit to it must be given work to do, regardless of their party affiliations. The mass movement must be developed. All Kuomintang members and all sincere anti-Japanese workers must be mobilised for mass work."

The mobilization of new groups of the Chinese people went on and the United Front continued to extend its influence. All-China Congresses of Writers and Students were held. Chou En-lai took up the post of vice-director of the Political Department.

On March 1, the Korean Revolutionary Holiday, the walls of Hankow were covered with posters demanding independence for the Korean people. Korean revolutionaries in China issued a manifesto pledging co-operation in the common struggle against Japanese imperialism. On March 27, at the National Congress of Writers, a Japanese author, Wutaru Kaji, mounted the rostrum amidst shouts of applause. He and his wife had braved great difficulties to come to aid China in the struggle against the militarists of their country. In a speech delivered a few days later he said: "When the national revolutionary movement was spreading in China in 1925-7, the people of Japan greeted it with wonder and delight. They organized the China Non-Intervention League to fight the Japanese War Ministry, which was interfering with the movement in China.... During the Manchurian incident and the first Shanghai war, the Japanese people angrily roared, 'Hands off Manchuria,' 'Hands off China.' Did you in China hear those voices? The Japanese fascists are afraid of contact between the Japanese and Chinese peoples.... By using one against the other they hope to oppress both."

Kaji told of the anti-war movement of the Japanese people, of the February revolt of worker conscripts in Kawasaki, centre of Japan's heavy industry, and Chisuma, another suburb of Tokyo. He told of the bloody suppression of demonstrations of peasants and miners in Akita-ken, of the shooting of dock-workers in Kobe.

Shortly afterwards, Waturu Kaji and his wife took up posts in the Political Department, writing propaganda materials for the Japanese troops and lecturing to Japanese prisoners. The United Front against Japanese imperialism is not a united front of the Chinese people alone. China's war of national emancipation is a war of liberation also for the peoples of Korea and Formosa,* and for the oppressed masses of Japan.

Militarily, January and February were favourable months for China. An outstanding development was the increased activity of the reinforced and reorganized Chinese air force. On January 5, Chinese bombers raided Wuhu and destroyed a number of Japanese planes on the airfield there. On January 11, they again flew to Wuhu and bombed Japanese gunboats on the Yangtze. On January 15, an official statement claimed that the Chinese air force had destroyed twenty-four Japanese air-planes and sunk fourteen naval ships in fourteen raids since January. On January 26, Chinese planes bombed the airfield at Nanking. In February too, the Chinese air force scored a number of major successes. On February 3, Chinese bombing squadrons, acting for the first time in concert with counter-attacking land forces, bombed Japanese positions at Pengpu on the Tientsin-Pukow line. On the 18th, twelve out of eighteen Japanese bombers which raided Hankow were shot down after a thrilling air battle

---

* The Formosan Revolutionary League had pledged its support of China's fight early in the war.

watched by everyone in the city. On February 23, Chinese planes struck for the first time at the rear bases of the enemy. In a surprise raid on Formosa they destroyed a power-plant and a number of planes on the airfield. The damage to the power-plant was confirmed by the fact that for three days Hongkong was unable to communicate with the International Radio Station at Taihohu. After February, Chinese planes took part in many engagements on the Northern fronts.

At the end of January, the Tientsin-Pukow railway front, which had been in a state of collapse after the treason of Han Fu-chu, was reinforced by more than 100,000 Kwangsi troops under the command of Li Tsung-jen. These troops stood as a solid wedge in the path of the Japanese columns converging from north and south. The almost leisurely advance of both these columns was abruptly checked. Han Fu-chu's troops, fighting like heroes now that they had confidence in their leadership, counter-attacked the walled city of Tsining, foiling the Japanese plan to drive south to Kweiteh, on the Lunghai railway. On the Southern front, Kwangsi soldiers heroically defended the line of the Huai River, which the Japanese were not to penetrate for a full three months. For the first time, Chinese aircraft supported the armies in Anhwei. Meanwhile, in accordance with the new tactics, Chinese forces launched counter-attacks on the Eastern front, at Hangchow, and in the west, on the Peiping-Hankow railway, and in Shansi. Japanese attempts to wipe out the Eighth Route Army ended in complete failure. Guerrilla activity spread all over the country. From Shansi, General Yen Hsi-shan reported that the Japanese were in occupation of only twelve of the province's 105 districts. On January 13, flying columns of partisans recaptured Kuchow, Yangnien, Feihsiang, and Kwanping in South Hopei. On January 17, Chuansha, in Pootung, twenty miles from Shanghai, was retaken. On February 2, guerrillas in Shansi recaptured Tinghsiang, seventy miles north-east of Taiyuan.

On February 7, a Japanese plot to create an "independent regime" in Canton was exposed and easily liquidated by the Chinese police. The Japanese had approached an old feudal militarist of Kwangtung, General Li Fu-lin, to head the conspiracy. They offered him $200,000. General Li had been a feudal warlord, but he was also a patriotic Chinese. "What shall I do?" he wired the

National Government. "Take the money, we need it," the Government wired back. So Li Fu-lin took the money and continued to associate with the conspirators. When he had accumulated enough evidence of their plans, the Chinese police swooped down. The Pearl River was closed to traffic, martial law was declared, and, under the noses of the Japanese warships which were assembled near the Bocca Tigris forts for a triumphal cruise to Canton, the whole plot was uncovered and destroyed. This was the end of the first Japanese attempt to conquer South China.

Early in February, a strong Japanese column pushed its way down the Peiping-Hankow railway to Sinhsiang, forty miles north of the Lunghai railway and the Yellow River. Chinese troops halted their advance by successful application of their new tactics. They destroyed thirty miles of railway in the path of the Japanese, and dispatched large forces to the Taihang mountains, on the Shansi-Honan border, from which they made constant attacks on the Japanese flanks.

On February 10, the 115th Division of the Eighth Route Army, under Lin Piao, cut the rear of the Japanese on the Peiping-Hankow railway by the lightning recapture of four stations between Paoting and Shihchiachuang in South Hopei. It captured 500 rifles, thirty light machine-guns, and over 100 horses. At Tinghsien, 300 Japanese were killed. At Hsinlo, a supply train was derailed. Partisans tore up the railway lines, destroyed telephone wires.

To drive out the Chinese forces menacing their flanks, the Japanese troops on the Peiping-Hankow railway turned westward into South Shansi. At Lingshih, on the Honan-Shansi border, an important battle was fought. Breaking through the Chinese defence line, the enemy took Linfen, provisional capital of the province. The Chinese forces remained on their flanks and manoeuvred for counter-attack. In the following two months they were to isolate the spearhead of the Japanese advance and recover the greater part of the province.

But, for the moment, the Japanese had achieved their object. Their flank secured, they quickly turned their attention to the Tientsin-Pukow railway front where the opposing forces were massing for decisive battles. Here they hoped to annihilate China's main armies and find victory. But they found something entirely different.

CHAPTER VIII
Counter-attack

D URING the three months following the fall of Nanking, the Chinese Government and people had proved their determination to continue the struggle. The Government had stood firm against every "peace" offer made by Japan. The army had demonstrated its ability to foil the general plan of the Japanese high command. The people, especially in the rear of the enemy, were beginning to participate actively in the war, and guerrilla activities grew in extent and in their influence on the course of military operations.

At the beginning of March, the Japanese decided to abandon operations on the subsidiary fronts and, once and for all, concentrate on the capture of Hsuchow. They would achieve the junction of the Northern and Southern fronts, trap and annihilate the cream of the Chinese Army, unite the entire coast from Shanhaikuan to Hangchow under their rule, institute a puppet government of "all China", and take up positions dominating the approaches to Hankow. The loss of Nanking had failed to paralyse China's resistance. But a resounding defeat at Hsuchow would certainly cause the Chinese Government to sue for peace while it still controlled South China and the Middle Yangtze. To deal a "knock-out blow" was still the ambition of the Japanese Army. With positional, mobile, and guerrilla warfare going on simultaneously on many fronts, it was a little difficult to tell just where the

154

blow should be struck to have the desired effect. After having tested several widely-scattered points, the Japanese decided to administer it at Hsuchow. Here 300,000 of China's best troops were concentrated. Gigantic pincers, converging from north and south and closing on the Lunghai railway west of the city, could trap this force and annihilate it. Surely this would be a *coup degrâce* from which China could never recover. "Tannenberg at Hsuchow" became the motto of the Japanese Army.*

There was no Tannenberg at Hsuchow. A month after the beginning of the attack, the Japanese had not only failed to accomplish their aim, but the northern jaw of their mighty pincers had been all but broken off. The pincers did not close until the latter part of May, when they closed on nothing, the Chinese army having retired. In the meantime Japan had suffered two great defeats, one of which resounded around the world. The despised Northern troops which had melted before the Japanese in Peiping and Tientsin destroyed 4,000 of them at Linyi. A Chinese army composed largely of new recruits trapped and killed 7,000 Japanese in and around Taierhchuang. It was in Taierhchuang, not Hsuchow, that the Japanese found their Tannenberg. And they, not the Chinese army, were the victims.

At the beginning of March the chief sphere of hostilities was in South Shansi and North Honan, along the northern bank of the Yellow River. A lightning Japanese advance had been followed by the stiffening of Chinese resistance. Chiang Kai-shek personally took command at Chengchow, on the Peiping-Hankow railway, on the south bank. Japanese attempts to cross were repelled both here and in West Shansi, where the Eighth Route Army pushed back Japanese units seeking to penetrate into Shensi province.

In the second week of March, Chinese and Japanese troops were racing eastward, along either bank of the river, towards the main front on the Tientsin-Pukow railway. It became clear to everyone in touch with the situation that

---

* At Tannenberg, on August 24-26, 1914, Hindenberg enveloped and crushed the second Russian Army, inflicting 100,000 casualties and taking 96,000 prisoners. The Russians had penetrated deeply into East Prussia. The 20th German Army held their advance, while the First Reserve Army Corps and 17th Army Corps pressed in on their flanks.

the battle for Hsuchow was about to begin.

On March 15, the Japanese began to drive down along the northern section of the Tientsin-Pukow line, on which there had been little fighting during the preceding weeks. They advanced in three columns. The central column pushed down the railway to attack Tenghsien, about fifty miles north of Hsuchow, the right wing operated west of the railway along the north bank of the Grand Imperial Canal, and the left wing east of the railway, pushing towards Linyi (Yichow). It was the aim of the left wing to outflank Hsuchow by cutting the east-west Lunghai railway between the city and the sea.

Chinese forces along the entire front were commanded by Li Tsung-jen, one of the two Kwangsi leaders who had made that province an important military stronghold. His colleague, Pai Chung-hsi, now chief of staff of China's armies, was also in Hsuchow. Together, they worked out a plan to break off and annihilate the spearhead of the enemy advance. Rightly, they anticipated that the central column would not attack Hsuchow directly, but would attempt to approach it by the spur railway which ran over flat country to the Lunghai line. They planned to let the Japanese advance along this railway to Taierhchuang, some thirty miles north of Hsuchow. Meanwhile they would hold the flanks. When the enemy reached Taierhchuang, the flanks would close in, isolating and destroying the entire projecting section of the Japanese line.

It is one thing to make plans, and another to execute them. Since the outbreak of the war, Chinese arms had scored only one major victory — the battle of Pinghsin Pass, in which the Eighth Route Army annihilated 3,000 men of General Itagaki's 5th Division in a mountain defile in Northern Shansi.* Chinese soldiers had proved their ability to fight, and fight well. But Chinese officers had not demonstrated that they were able to co-ordinate the movements of variously trained and commanded provincial troops in complicated manoeuvres. And this was precisely what the Taierhchuang plan called for.

The victorious Taierhchuang campaign was epoch-making for the Chi-

---

* Sept, 23-28, 1937. The battle was won by Lin Piao's 115th Division.

nese Army and nation because it proved that the armed forces of the country, handicapped by inferior armament and lack of uniform, organization, and training, were yet able to out-general and defeat the Japanese in a "classical battle". Its significance was deepened by the fact that one of the divisions which contributed most to the victory belonged to the hitherto weak and frequently defeated 29th Army, while the division that bore the brunt of the fighting and delivered the final blow was composed not of professional soldiers but of wartime recruits from the cities and villages. Finally, it was a victory largely due to the active help of units operating on other fronts and guerrilla formations which concentrated on impeding the enemy's communications and tying up his forces during the most critical period of the operations.

The preparation for the victory of Taierhchuang was the victory of Linyi. Coming from Tsingtao, the Japanese Itagaki and Isogai Divisions arrived on the outskirts of this city on March 15. The Chinese high command decided that the time had come to hold up the advance of the Japanese left flank. Against the 20,000 Japanese and bandit troops* marching on Linyi they threw an equal number of northern soldiers under Pang Ping-hsun and Chang Tze-chung.** The defenders let the Japanese into the town and burned all the surrounding villages. Then they drove the Japanese out again. With the villages destroyed, the Japanese had no place to rest, and once more attacked Linyi, which changed hands three times between March 15 and 19. While Pang Ping-hsun held the enemy around the city, Chang Tze-chung moved north and struck at their left flank. The Japanese were badly battered and forced to retreat ten miles to Tangtouchen. They lost 4,000 men, including three regimental commanders, Colonels Moda, Nakamura, and Nagano. The Chinese claimed the capture of 600 prisoners and a large number of trophies, includ-

---

* Puppet troops under the bandit general, Li Kwei-tang, took part in this operation. They acted as Japanese vanguard and were defeated before the main armies clashed.

** Chang Tze-chung was Mayor of Tientsin at the time of the Lukouchiao incident. He was instrumental in handing Peiping over to the Japanese, but later fled and gave himself up to the Central Government. He has redeemed himself in recent months. His troops, instead of divisional insignia, wear arm-bands inscribed "Down with Japan".

ing several field guns and armoured trucks. Despite the fact that they had suffered casualties equal to those of the Japanese, they pursued them and succeeded in recapturing Tangtouchen, the place to which the Japanese had retired to rest. This victory immobilized the Japanese left flank for almost two months. General Chang Tze-chung was officially pardoned for his part in the surrender of Peiping and commended by the National Government. General Itagaki added to his reputation as the most-defeated Japanese commander.

"This is not a great battle, like Tannenberg and the Marne," said a Chinese strategist to whom I spoke at the time, "but it will go down as one of the major battles of our war. It is the first engagement in which our army has demonstrated that it can not only resist, but also attack under unfavourable circumstances; and not only attack but also pursue the enemy. After smashing the Japanese at Linyi we were able to follow them for a whole day and again defeat them at Tangtouchen. At Shanghai, during the period of positional warfare, we showed that we could hold on. Now, during the period of mobile warfare, we have shown that we can execute staff plans with precision and launch successful counter-attacks. And you must remember that the divisions which fought at Linyi were not the best in our army, while Itagaki and Isogai are both considered crack generals."

The victory of Linyi was won by the combined efforts of all fronts. During the three days of the battle the Japanese centre and right wing, at Tenghsien and Tsining respectively, were kept busy by Chinese counter-attacks. Chinese troops in Honan made sure that no more Japanese troops would be sent away to Shantung, by re-crossing the Yellow River and recovering a number of villages and towns. In Hopei, guerrillas attacked the Peiping-Hankow, Peiping-Tientsin, and Tientsin- Pukow railways deep in the Japanese rear. In Suiyuan, in Inner Mongolia, Ma Chan-shan, doughty old hero of Manchuria, led a cavalry brigade to recapture the town of Tohsien. In Northwest Shansi, the Eighth Route Army destroyed the Japanese at Hochu. As a result of all these diversions, the Japanese skimped on reinforcements for the main front. This made the task of the Chinese command at Hsuchow immeasurably easier.

The stage was now set for the next phase of the campaign — the bottling up of the Japanese in Taierhchuang. On March 23 the Japanese had snapped up the bait held out to them and advanced to the town. Now the Chinese high command waited tensely for the results of the Chinese counter-attack.

To see the battle of Taierhchuang, I left Hankow for Hsuchow in the latter part of March.

Hankow was nervous. It had been worried by Japanese attempts to cross the Yellow River. Now it held its breath as it watched the grim preparations around Hsuchow. Going to the front, I felt a growing apprehension. All through the trip on the Lunghai railway, this feeling persisted. Chengchow, on the south bank of the Yellow River, had been savagely bombed a month before, and was still deserted. The fortifications of Kaifeng, capital of Honan, had been shelled by Japanese batteries. As the train advanced, in clouds of loess dust, across the arid Honan plain, the passengers watched anxiously for enemy planes. Trains coming the other way carried wagon-loads of wounded soldiers. Thousands of refugees stuck like burrs to the roofs and sides of the cars.

When the train arrived at Hsuchow we could hear the sound of guns thudding in the distance. The front was only thirty miles away. On the platform lay a number of dying soldiers. They had been brought as far as the station, but were too far gone to travel. Since they would live only a few hours, they were not taken back to the overcrowded hospitals. All of them were unconscious. The station was deserted.

But the city, surprisingly, was full of life. All the shops were open. Vivid patriotic posters covered the walls. Through the crowded streets, soldiers, militia-men, and civilians bustled about their business. Newsboys cried the papers. Sandwich-men advertised theatrical performances. Women and children walked and played in the city's two parks. Middle-school boys and girls, in neat blue uniforms, distributed handbills. They carried a banner — the banner of the General Mobilization Committee of the 5th War Area. Chengchow had gone through one heavy bombing. It was paralysed with fear and despair. Hsuchow had had more bombings, was closer to the enemy, and might be expected to fall within one or two days if the Japanese broke through at Taierhchuang. Yet the atmosphere was not only incomparably more buoyant and inspiring than that of Chengchow: it breathed more confidence than the atmosphere of distant Hankow. There could be only one explanation for this. In Hankow, they hoped that the Japanese would not break through. But in Hsuchow, they were preparing to crush the audacious enemy who had ventured so near the city. In Hsuchow, thirty miles from the front, they did not for a moment entertain the possibility of defeat.

When I went to interview General Li Tsung-jen, I found that other visitors had preceded me to headquarters. Past grinning guards, three peasants drove a herd of large black pigs straight into the courtyard of the commander-in-chief of the 300,000 troops in the 5th War Area. "What is this?" I asked the young officer who accompanied me. "Peasants bringing gifts to the army," he said. "You can see the Commander-in-Chief after they have gone."

General Li Tsung-jen is a short, square-shouldered, round-faced, twinkling-eyed farmer's son. He is middle-aged, and his short, bristly hair is shot with grey. But he is as full of energy as a steel spring, an aggressive fighting man, genial but short and definite in his statements.

"Why is it important to keep Hsuchow?" I asked him.

"Hsuchow is the critical point of the second period of military operations. It is the key to the safety of the Lunghai and Peiping-Hankow railways, and therefore to Hankow. At this stage, our war area* is the most important. The Japanese will concentrate all their forces to clear the Tientsin-Pukow railway. What they have brought against us now is nothing. They will have to use much more to stand a chance. If they should ever eject us from the city, they will still not be rid of us. The troops in this war area have pledged themselves not to leave it. This does not mean that we will concentrate and allow ourselves to be slaughtered. We will spread out and manoeuvre over a wide territory. We are mobilizing the people, and when the time comes we will use

---

* General Li Tsung-jen was Commander-in-Chief of the Fifth War Area, comprising the provinces of Shantung and Kiangsu, the part of Anhuei north of the Yangtze, and Southeastern Honan.

the power of the masses against the enemy."

I told him of how the atmosphere in Hsuchow had amazed me.

"What seems mysterious to you is really very ordinary. When I came to this war area the enemy were advancing rapidly and the people were in a state of despair. Why was this? The answer can be found in the indictment against Han Fu-chu, the former chairman of Shangtung. You remember that he was executed for retreating without orders, extorting money from the population, and seizing the arms which the people in the villages kept for self-defence. During the last two months it has been different. We have proved to the population that our army was capable of holding off the enemy. We have also proved that to us, the slogan of co-operation between the army and the people does not mean that the people must give everything and the army nothing."

"How have you done this?" I asked General Li.

"A General Mobilization Committee has been founded, composed of representatives of the population, the military command, and the civil government. The mutual duties of the people and army are defined by seven orders which I have issued, and which are posted everywhere for all to read. Without a special warrant from the high command, civil and military officers in this area have no right to demand materials, food, or labour from the people. Conscription is based on the principle of the duty of every citizen to bear arms or otherwise contribute to defence. It is strictly regulated, and any abuses, such as bribery to obtain exemption for the rich, are punished under martial law. Conscription for military service is carried out by lot. It is not permitted for any civil or military organ to confiscate the arms which the people keep for self-defence. On the other hand, it is the duty of the local authorities to train and organize the armed people, to supply them with instructors, and teach them the best way to defend their villages. The duty of the General Mobilization Committee is to develop and co-ordinate the activities of the people and to correct previous errors and abuses. To facilitate this, the entire population of the war area, with the exception of traitors who oppose the national war, has been granted full freedom of speech, publication, assembly, and petition. Civil and military officials are forbidden to interfere with this freedom in any way. I have ordered that, when it is necessary for the army to requisition supplies, they should be taken from the gentry and the well-to-do in the towns and villages, not from the poor peasants. Peasants enlisted for labour service must be as well fed and housed as the troops themselves. Forcible impressment is prohibited.

"The people of Hsuchow are confident because they know what is being done to defend the city and are participating in the work. If they are not satisfied, they can make suggestions to the higher authorities; and they are themselves free to initiate activity which will further strengthen our position. Militarily, the Japanese are stronger than we are. They are better armed, steady, and tenacious, and they frighten away resistance by their barbarous cruelty. That is when the people are not organized. We must be strong as iron against their attacks, moral as well as physical. This can be done if we use our military force to help and encourage the people, and if the people do all in their power to help increase our military force."

"What is the present position at the front?"

"At Linyi, the Japanese suffered great losses in men and munitions. The activities of our guerrillas in their rear make it difficult for them to bring up new men and supplies. The Japanese in Taierhchuang are surrounded. They still have some ammunition, but not much. More than a division of them are cut off, and they are fighting like tigers in a cage. We have captured a large part of their mechanized equipment, so they can't break out. I doubt if reinforcements can save them now."

On the night of April 2, our party started for Taierhchuang.* The train moved slowly, with lights darkened, and all around was pitch blackness. The thudding of the guns came closer and closer. Several hours after we left Hsuchow, a sheet of flame appeared angry red on the horizon. "That is

---

* On the same train were Joris Ivens and John Ferno, who had come to China after making their great documentary film "Spanish Earth", the famous photographer Robert Capa, who had accompanied them from Spain, the American assistant naval attaché, Captain Evans F. Carlson, and a number of Chinese officials.

Taierhchuang," said our adjutant. "It has been burning for three days." We stopped ten miles south of the besieged city and got out of the train to walk to headquarters. For two hours we stumbled through wheatfields in pitch darkness. Our guide was a peasant. "Without the peasants", said the officer, "we could not operate freely in this area. Our army has been here only two weeks and the country is terribly confusing. Every village looks like every other. The people help us greatly. They act as guides, spy out the dispositions of the enemy, and care for our wounded. They do not leave the units even under fire, and many of them have picked up the rifles of the dead and participated in the fighting." The peasant, old and gnarled, walked ahead of us, sucking at his pipe.

That night we slept in the straw in a village barn. Morning came with the booming of guns splitting the clear, sun-drenched air of the North China spring. Our village was square, squat, and walled, with watch-towers standing like solid grey-brick cubes at the four corners. In South Shantung, the villages and watch-towers are Norman in appearance. Many of them were built by Tibetan bannermen who were once settled in the province as a hereditary garrison and brought with them the sturdy rectilinear architecture of their native highlands.

General Sun Lien-chung, commander of the Second Group Army, entertained us at breakfast, in a sunny courtyard in which a peasant woman drove a blindfolded donkey round and round to operate a primitive wheat-mill composed of one round, flat stone rotating against another.* The general was tall, thick-set, and hoarse-voiced, and red-eyed with fatigue. Briefly, he told us of the importance of the town which was being used to lure the Japanese into the trap prepared for them:

"Taierhchuang commands the approaches to Hsuchow by railway and canal. We knew the enemy would attempt to take the town. They need it as a base from which they can attack and to which they can return if their attack

---

* The fact that the peasants had not been expelled from the village where the army made its headquarters was in itself indicative of the new spirit abroad in China.

fails. We too cannot afford to lose Taierhchuang. We need it to frustrate Japanese attacks on Hsuchow. Still more, we need it as a base for counter-attack.

"We are not thinking in terms of defence. The enemy advance guard is now in our hands. The guerillas are cutting their lines of communication and preventing the sending of reinforcements. The cruelty of the Japanese has made the people hate them, and everywhere the peasants are taking up arms. Eight-tenths of Hopei and Shantung still fly the national flag."

An orderly came up with a sheaf of messages.

General Sun turned to go back into the village temple which served him as headquarters. "At a time when the people are doing all this", he said, "how can the army content itself with passive tactics? Just resistance is no longer enough. To-day we must do more than hold up the enemy: we must destroy him."

Here, as at Hsuchow, confidence was high. Within the range of Japanese guns, even between the batteries of the two sides, tall peasants worked in the rich green wheatfields. Before our village and a hundred others like it, army instructors taught companies of blue-clad farm boys how to handle rifles and Bren machine-guns. All villagers between the ages of eighteen and forty-five were enrolled in the self-defence corps. Three or four miles behind the front where two armies were locked in grim struggle, these peasant-soldiers marched and countermarched and fought sham battles over the rolling hills. New village headmen had been appointed, specially trained students who combined the functions of magistrate, militia commander, and principal of the primary school. The school building was made the centre of adult education, patriotic propaganda, and mass organization. Posters and slogans covered the ancient village walls. Long lines of militia-men carried food and supplies to the front and brought back the wounded. Peasants working in the fields kept their rifles stacked close at hand.

"The key to the possession of Taierhchuang", the Chinese chief of staff had told me, "lies in the struggle for the surrounding villages. So long as we hold these villages, the Japanese in the city will feel as cramped and restless as a clumsy man who can find no place to put his hands and feet. From these villages, when the time comes, we will launch the attack which will smash the enemy."

For two weeks, the contending armies had been fighting for the possession of the little railway town. On March 23, the Japanese 5th Division under General Itagaki launched its first attack with two regiments of infantry, two regiments of artillery, and several scores of tanks and armoured cars. General Chih Feng-chen, young commander of the 31st Chinese Division, was ordered to hold them in the city. This division had already met Itagaki at Fangshan in Hopei at the beginning of the war, and in the bitter winter battle of Niangtzekuan (the Queen's Pass) in the mountains of Shansi. It had lost 70 per cent of its original strength, and was now composed chiefly of raw recruits, not professional soldiers but peasants from the fields, workers from the factories, and petty clerks from the shops and warehouses of the big cities. Across the barricades in Taierhchuang, the Japanese shouted to the men of the Thirty-first: "How many men have you left? We were told that we had wiped you out in Shansi." And the Chinese shouted back: "Enough to destroy you here!"

March 23 was a day of bitter fighting. First twenty Japanese tanks advanced against the north wall of Taierhchuang. The Chinese had only forty men and one armoured car equipped with an anti-tank gun outside the wall. The men lay low in trenches. The armoured car waited. When the tanks were a few hundred yards away, the armoured car crossed their path, firing at each one. The men in the trenches waited till the tanks came close, then jumped out and threw bundles of hand-grenades under their wheels and into their ports. Four tanks were destroyed, neatly pierced by anti-tank shells, and nine others were damaged. The Japanese infantry behind the tanks turned to run. The Chinese poured out of the town in pursuit, capturing two field guns, five mountain guns and several anti-tank rifles. The Japanese 63rd Regiment suffered heavy casualties, and its commander was killed. Over the town, a Japanese airplane was shot down. After this encounter, the Japanese tanks did not come carelessly near the Chinese lines. They stood at some distance out in the field, serving as stationary machine-gun nests. The Chinese soldiers lost their fear of tanks. Their army had acquired teeth to crack the shells of these monsters.

The second battle for Taierhchuang began on March 26 and lasted three days, ranging up and down the countryside through the surrounding villages. Both sides brought up reinforcements. The Japanese 10th Division and the Chinese 27th and 30th Divisions took up positions around the city. Heavy guns were moved up and severe artillery duels commenced. The Japanese had forty 15.6-centimetre guns and fifty six 8.8's and "seventy fives". The Chinese had perhaps half as many guns, of 15.5 and 7.5 centimetre calibre. The Japanese fired incessantly, the Chinese only when they had a definite target. With joy, the Chinese soldiers discovered that quite 30 per cent of the enemy shells were duds.* They called these duds "Jiphen hanchien" meaning "Japanese traitors". "Our friends, the Japanese workers are helping us," they said.

Intense Japanese bombardment opened a breach in the city wall of Taierhchuang. On the 28th and 29th they launched attacks through this breach, hoping to take the town. But the 31st Division dug in and held on. The Japanese had been drawn into the trap. They must not pass beyond it.

On the 30th, the Japanese gained a foothold in Taierhchuang itself, and gradually extended their control to two-thirds of its area. Japanese artillery battered the Chinese part of the town. Chinese guns blasted the part held by the Japanese. Chinese and Japanese airplanes bombed the town incessantly. With rifle, bayonet, and hand grenade, the men of the two sides fought each other in the streets. At every ten or twenty yards was a barricade. Piles of corpses grew by every barricade.

Meanwhile, the Chinese 27th and 30th Divisions prepared to close in on the enemy's flanks. During daylight, when the Japanese guns kept up an incessant fire, movement was difficult and the Chinese lay low. Very soon, they knew, the enemy's communications would be cut. Let the Japanese shoot their fill: they would have less ammunition when the final attack came. The

---

* According to foreign military observers, the proportion was the same in Shanghai.

27th Division especially showed great ingenuity in drawing the Japanese fire. It took the windlasses from all the village pumps, stuck them into the ground by their cranks in groups of four, and made them look for all the world like batteries of field guns. Now to attract the attention of the enemy. A real field gun was brought up behind each wooden battery. Quickly, it fired a few shots into the Japanese lines. Just as quickly, it was drawn away. The Japanese commanders scanned the country with their glasses. How clumsy these Chinese were! They left their artillery entirely exposed. Japanese seventy-fives went into action, laying a barrage of several hundred shells. The Chinese did not reply. "Good!" thought the Japanese commanders, "we have disabled them." But a half-hour later the real field gun was brought up again, the line of dummies began to show signs of life. The Japanese were thorough. They laid new barrages, heavier than the previous ones. They wasted thousands of shells. "They didn't even hit a single windlass," a Chinese battery commander told me later, as he laughed about it.

"The night is our opportunity," Chinese officers never tired of repeating. During the day, Japanese airplanes and field guns ruled the battlefields. But all through the night, when the guns had no eyes to see, the Chinese launched attack after attack on their flanks. They moved up stealthily and struck boldly, in small groups. The Japanese did not know where the next assault would come. Hour after hour, they kept up constant machine-gun fire from all their positions. But this did not help. Every morning saw a new section of the line in Chinese hands.

On the night of April 1, the 27th Division raided a Japanese regimental headquarters north of Taierhchuang. They killed the commander and captured many documents. Among the documents was a poem written by a Japanese officer:

"Four hours we fought and took Tientsin,
Within six hours, Tsinan was ours.
This tiny village, Taierhchuang,
Why does it take so long to fall?"

From the same headquarters, they took the diary of an orderly, a common soldier. "Why do we fight?" the soldier had written. "The Chinese people are facing the devil's own tortures. We also are constantly suffering and dying. Heaven alone knows where our bones will whiten and who shall gather them."

On April 2, the town itself again became the scene of heavy fighting. The Japanese increased their strength inside the wall and tried again and again to drive the Chinese out of the town and across the Grand Canal. In street fighting, the men of the Thirty-first were superior to the enemy. During the heaviest Japanese bombings and shellings they crouched behind their sandbag shelters and in the burrows they had dug for themselves along the city wall. Even incendiary bombs failed to dislodge them. General Chih Feng-chen told me wily. "When their planes were using these bombs," he said, "the Japanese, as well as we, had to withdraw from the immediate vicinity. The fragments had a temperature of 2000° and would ignite anything near them. When the planes left, the Japanese would wait for the fires to subside. But our men returned to their positions while they were still smouldering, even though many suffered bad burns. We always got their first, and the Japanese lost, rather than won, by using this weapon." On April 2, also, the Japanese used tear gas, and sneezing gas which turns the mucous membrane of the nose into a raw, bloodshot mass of pain. But they did not dislodge the defenders.

From their rich experience of the relative value of their own and the enemy's weapons, the Chinese soldiers evolved a saying: "Japanese bombing is less to be feared than their guns. Their guns are less effective than their machine-guns. But their machine-guns cannot compare with our grenades. And for us, the big sword is the best of all." The men of the Thirty-first did their best to get close enough to the enemy to use their favourite weapons. After they got past the most difficult obstacle, the machine-guns, they had it all their own way. In street fighting, also, they found the value of the trench-mortar. With trench-mortars they blasted the Japanese out from behind the strongest barricades. "The trench-mortar opens all doors," said the Chinese soldiers.

April 3 was the hardest day. The Japanese now held four-fifths of the town. Their frontal attacks did not cease, and at the same time they tried to outflank the depleted 31st Division and cut its communications with the Chinese forces outside the city. The town was a shambles, with hardly a building left standing. At many points, it was on fire, and a pall of smoke obscured it from view. The 31st Division was reduced to less than half its strength. But these raw recruits, who knew for the first time the hardship and danger of a soldier's life, not only held their ground, but launched repeated counter-attacks. Chih Feng-chen, their thirty-four-year-old commander, moved among them — in leather jacket and slacks — looking more like a student than a general. The veterans of the Division, most of them officers now, showed the recruits how to fight. The Thirty-first lost twenty-four company commanders, killed or wounded. The relative mortality among the younger officers was higher than among the men. Only the best-led and most aggressive fighting units show such figures.

The Japanese could not keep up their pressure. New attacks by the 27th and 30th Divisions, supported by reinforcements, turned their attention once more to their flanks. They had to move men from place to place so as to hold their line where it was most threatened.

During the severe artillery duels of the next two days, I stayed with the Chinese batteries on the right flank of the Japanese. On the 4th, the Japanese were still firing heavily, and shells fell within 100 yards of where our 15.5-centimetre battery spat fire from behind a grey-walled village. The Japanese fired five times to every Chinese one. But on that day, the Chinese shells had more effect. Through a periscope, I saw one land on the road outside Taierhchuang in the middle of a column of marching troops.

On the morning of the 5th, I was sitting on a low hill near the Chinese light field batteries. The shells of the heavy guns farther back whistled overhead, exploding far away. No man's land looked like a giant chessboard with squares of brown and rich green — fallow and planted fields — under the blue sky. Grey, square, squat villages, arranged in pairs along the roads, were the main pieces, and dense green family burial-groves, with tall trees arranged around sober grave-mounds, studded the board-like pawns. The villages concealed batteries. Under the leafy shelter of the groves, munition trucks and staff cars hid from enemy planes. Every grain-stalk-covered hut, every yellow hayrick, concealed death. My hill was covered with shell fragments. Only yesterday, a bombardment had obliterated the vegetation on one side, leaving ugly brown scars. To-day there was less firing. Between the batteries, peasants ploughed the fields, knowing that the shells would fly over them. In a grassy gully which had once been a river-bed, women pastured their cows in comparative safety. Farther down along the gully was a camp of refugees. Young mothers suckled their children. Old men sat on piles of bedding and smoked. Tea was boiling over a fire. The refugees listened to the battle. On the way it developed depended the way they would go: back to their villages — or forward along the weary, bitter road of the homeless.

We heard the drone of planes. The refugees crouched in their gully. We too looked for shelter. Twenty-two silvery bombers appeared overhead. My Chinese companion suddenly clutched my arm. He pointed up at the insignia on their wings. "Ours," he said.

The planes bombed Taierhchuang. They bombed the Japanese positions to the North. In Taierhchuang, there was a flash, a report, a huge pillar of smoke. We learned afterwards that the Japanese munition dump had been hit. It caused great confusion among the Japanese soldiers and made them evacuate an entire section of the town.

Over the Japanese lines, one of the planes wavered. It seemed in trouble. As its companions disappeared in the distance, it lost altitude and began to glide towards the ground. Would it land safely? And where would it land? On which side of the lines?

The plane glided down and came to rest on a fallow field behind a village half a mile from our hill. Soldiers and peasants ran towards it. We also clambered down to see what had happened.

Ten minutes later we were on the spot. The pilot, young, sturdily built, and pale from his experience, stood by the plane. Under his orders, 100 men were covering it with straw and tall stalks of koaling, Shantung's most widespread grain. Already it was unrecognizable. The pilot leaned against a wing and wrote a report to the nearest headquarters.

The plane had landed within easy range of enemy guns. Surely the Japanese had seen it come down. It had been immediately and effectively camouflaged. But the Japanese had shells to waste. Surely they would look for it.

The field guns in our village had stopped firing. They did not want to attract attention now. But from other villages guns fired on. We listened. A Chinese battery fired a salvo. The Japanese did not reply tenfold, as they had always done. Only two shots came back. The Chinese battery fired again. The Japanese did not reply.

For the last half-hour the 100 men on the field had been giving their attention to the plane. Now they all looked at each other. "They have no more shells. They are withdrawing their artillery," everyone said all at once.

When we returned to headquarters village, we found only the peasants. Staff officers, field telephones, the sentries, our baggage — all had gone. A single soldier came out of our farm-house. "Headquarters has advanced six miles," he said. "I have been ordered to guide you there."

Dusk fell as we trudged along the road. Columns of troops, artillery, supplies — everything was going forward. On the arm-bands of the soldiers were divisional insignia we had not seen before. In reply to our questions, they told us that they were from Yunnan. From the borders of Burma and Annam, they had come 3,000 miles by foot, river, and railway to get here. Never before had provincial troops come so far to fight a national enemy. The Yunnanese marched forward singing. They sang the "March of the Volunteers", the war cry of the fighting partisans of snowy Manchuria. A Shantung peasant acted as their guide.

In headquarters, there was jubilation. "We cut off their communications and forced them to retreat," said the adjutant who greeted us. "Eight hundred Japanese in the north-east corner of Taierhchuang are entirely surrounded. We shall wipe them out to-night." The young chief of staff, fresh from the Staff Officers' Conference at Wuchang at which Chiang Kai-shek had lectured, gave us a long talk on the relative fighting strength of China and Japan. He had good news for us. "The commander-in-chief has given you permission to enter the town. I will go with you. We will start early to-morrow morning."

That night, the survivors of the heroic Thirty-first destroyed the Japanese remnants in the town. At six o'clock the next morning, not a single Japanese remained in Taierhchuang. Meanwhile, other units recaptured three villages to the North — Sanlichuang, Yuanchuang, and Liuhachu. Liuhachu had been the seat of the Japanese headquarters. On the right flank, the 27th Division took Liuchuang, Tsanghomaio, and Pienchuang. New troops, which had just come up on the previous day, took Nanlo, Peilok and Chiangshan — on the main road to Yihsien. The Japanese withdrawal was turned into a rout. By morning, there were no Japanese troops within ten miles of Taierhchuang. Only the 27th Division was still engaging the enemy. The other units could not keep up with the Japanese retreat.

On the morning of the 6th, we started for Taierhchuang. As we left headquarters, we saw a plane in the air. It was the young pilot who had made the forced landing the day before. All night he had worked on his machine, while soldiers and peasants rolled and tamped down the field. For two hours he had tried to take off from the soft earth, throwing up columns of dirt and almost turning over. At last he had succeeded.

Taierhchuang was still burning. Its streets were in ruins, with fantastic fragments of walls standing stark and charred. Dead bodies and unexploded shells and grenades lay everywhere. In one place, some city father had planted an avenue of willows along a picturesque creek. Now the creek was filled with corpses, and every one of the willows had been neatly cut down by machine-gun fire. Through the streets, the ragged, haggard men of the Thirty-first were dragging trophies to headquarters — dozens of Japanese machine-guns, hundreds of rifles, swords, and gas masks, and quantities of flags, documents, and tins of food. On the scarred and blackened walls of the town we saw posters — slogans and cartoons in bold brushwork on scraps of white paper: "Drive Out the Enemy!", "Fight Back to Our Old Homes!", "Down with Japanese Imperialism!"

Most of the Chinese soldiers in the city were wearing captured enemy helmets, on which they had substituted the Kuomintang sun insignia for the yellow star* of Japan. Men off duty were eating, sleeping, or washing. They lay on the ground, enjoying the luxury of rest. Many of them had taken off their uniforms, which were covered with dirt and blood. They sat half-stripped, basking in the sun and dangling their feet in the Grand Canal. The men of the Thirty-first were young. Some of them were already bored by inaction. Somewhere, they had got hold of a tennis ball, which they were throwing around, running and laughing.

From one corner of the town came the sound of hundreds of voices shouting slogans. We made our way towards it, stepping carefully over the debris of the morning's battle. From the battered north wall of Taierhchuang flew the Chinese national flag — white sun and blue sky on a red field. Under it stood a girl student in uniform, passionately addressing a crowd of soldiers who stood around. The girl was stocky, red-cheeked, and alive with energy. With every few words, she tossed back her heavy shock of black hair which threatened to get in her eyes. "Comrades of the Thirty-first Division," she shouted in a rich, clear young voice. "For the third time, we have engaged the Japanese devils in a heavy battle. For the second time, we have lost more than half of our men. For the first time, we are completely victorious.

"Comrades, this is only the beginning. We have seen that we can beat them. We must continue to beat them. We have driven them out of Taierhchuang. We must not stop until we have driven them out of Tsinan. Out of North China. Out of Manchuria. Out of our country.

"The final victory will be ours!"

"The final victory will be ours!" roared the soldiers.

"Drive out the enemy!"

"Drive out the enemy!"

"Long live the National Government!"

---

* On their helmets and caps the Japanese wear not the emblem of the rising sun, but a yellow, five-pointed star.

"Long live the National Government!"

"Long live the Chinese people!"

"Long live the Chinese people!"

Hundreds of fists shot up towards the sky.

In the battered Chinese headquarters in the town, we found General Chih Feng-chen, commander of the division. He was sitting in a room stacked with trophies. Around him were Chinese journalists and Press photographers, young men in uniform with pistols on their hips who had been in the town through the last night's battle. There were Chang Kiang, brilliant young war correspondent of China's biggest and richest newspaper, the *Ta Kung Pao*, Lo I of the Communist Party's *New China Daily*, movie cameramen of the Central Political Department's motion-picture studio. General Chih had his arm around the shoulder of the girl student whom we had seen lecturing earlier in the day. Everyone was talking happily.

"Have you many students in your division?" I asked General Chih.

He smiled at the girl. "Yes, we have ninety of them, in the divisional, brigade, and regimental political departments: sixty boys and thirty girls. They came to me last August, when we fought the Japanese at Fangshan. They said, 'Other units are retreating, but you are fighting, so we came to you. Give us work!' I did not know what to do with them, but I couldn't send them away, so I gave them uniforms and rations and let them stay."

"Are you glad that you allowed them to remain?"

"Now I don't know how I would get along without them. They organize joint activities of the soldiers and people, present plays and entertainments, teach the men to sing, read, write, and understand the national struggle, and agitate among the people to help the Army. They are not afraid of anything. Several, including one girl, have been wounded, but they continue to work in the front lines."

"What is the rank of political workers in the division?"

"The students are free to talk and mix with everyone in the division from luggage coolie to divisional commander. But now we are reorganizing the political department in accordance with the rules laid down by General

Headquarters. The political workers will have regular rank and pay. Their function, however, will not change."

He told me of some of the results of the Political Department's work. During the fighting, the people had carried wounded out of the town. They had brought the soldiers food and water. Detachments of young villagers, equipped with the rifles of the dead, had taken part in the fighting. Whenever the Japanese made a move, peasants brought word of it to Divisional Headquarters. Problems of transport, supply, and intelligence, which during the civil wars had presented great difficulty, solved themselves in this national war in which the Army was the fist of an awakening people. For the enemy, these problems became more complicated daily.

"One peasant woman", said General Chih, "passed in and out of the town daily. She would enter by one gate held by the Japanese, and since she carried vegetables and eggs, they welcomed her. Then she would come out and go through the lines to the gate held by us. She told us all their movements and dispositions. On the last day, she reported that the Japanese in the North-east corner of the city were weeping, embracing each other, and writing letters. We knew that their morale was breaking, and attacked immediately. She went back to see what she could find out. This morning we found her dead outside the wall. Evidently they had discovered what she was doing and thrown a grenade at her."

The mascot of the 31st Division was a ten-year-old boy. Three days before, during the heaviest bombardments, he had come to headquarters weeping. The Japanese had sent him to discover the positions of the Chinese guns. He went out and located them. "I am Chinese," the boy told the officers of the Thirty-first. "How could I tell them the truth? So when I saw a gun in the east, I said it was in the west, and when I saw one in the west, I said it was to the east." That day, to the puzzlement of the defenders, the Japanese had wasted 10,000 shells bombarding empty fields. Then the Japanese sent out the little boy again. They did not know whether he had lied to them or the positions had been moved. They threatened the child: "We will kill you if you lie to us." The little boy came to headquarters. He could not go back to the Japanese again because they would certainly shoot him after he deceived them a second time. Fearfully, he told the officers of his predicament. They kept him with them, and now he strutted around headquarters, proudly wearing the uniform cap and puttees which had been given him.

In the afternoon, we passed beyond the town, to the north, along the line of the Japanese retreat. Outside the north wall of Taierhchuang four tanks stood neatly aligned. They had been pierced by Chinese shells as they advanced, and now stood frozen in their tracks. The tanks were of medium weight, and built for two: a driver who also operated one machine-gun, and a gunner who stood up to manipulate the 50-mm. gun and another machine-gun in the revolving turret.

Two miles north of the town, in Shaochuang, we saw twenty heavy trucks, several caterpillar tractors, and 300 dead horses. They had all been destroyed by Chinese artillery. Everything around indicated that the Japanese had left in a great hurry. Hundreds of bodies, barely covered, lay in mass graves near the village. Forty or fifty wooden tablets marked the resting-places of officers from the rank of lieutenant up. The Japanese had not had time to go through their usual procedure of cremating all bodies, although, as some partially burned corpses showed, they had begun to do so. Live shells and thousands of burnished brass shell-cases lay all around. Japan is short of metals, and shells that have already been fired are strictly conserved for refilling. That they now lay around in countless numbers and in utter confusion showed the speed with which the Japanese had fled. In abandoned trenches I found Japanese newspapers full of ferocious caricatures of Chiang Kai-shek and other leaders of the Chinese Government. One soldier had left behind him, in flight or death, a well-thumbed mail-order book of instructions on "How to Dance the Tango", complete with diagrams.

On our way back to Taierhchuang, we stumbled across a Japanese straggler. He had been hiding in a shell-hole, and as soon as he was discovered he began firing at us from his shelter. Our guards shot him down. On him we found a machine-gun drill manual and a record of deposits he had made in a field savings-bank. One week he had saved a yen. The next week, fifty sen. He was a poor man. Two weeks before Taierhchuang he had deposited twenty yen. Perhaps he had robbed a Chinese civilian. He seemed to have had no idea of surrendering, to have been absolutely sure that he would be killed if he allowed himself to be captured. The Japanese Army never spared Chinese soldiers. "If we had known a few words of Japanese, we might have succeeded in taking him prisoner," said one of our men. "It was the same with the Japanese in the city. They would not surrender."

Towards evening we came back to Taierhchuang. An endless file of troops was marching over the pontoon bridge across the Grand Canal. For hours we watched them, long lines of men and supplies stretching like snakes towards the horizon. The 42nd Army passed over, the 30th Division, the 21st Division, the artillery of the 32nd Army. For two weeks Taierhchuang had been an inferno in which men fought and died. Only this morning, the last shots had sounded. Now the battle was over. Taierhchuang was a point in the rear through which men passed in pursuit of the enemy.

Army headquarters had moved again. It was now within a mile of the city. When we came back, tired and hungry, we were greeted with news.

At Hungshanchen, twenty miles to the north, General Tang En-po's 13th Army Corps had captured hundreds of prisoners and many field-pieces.

Between Tehchow and Tsinan, far in the rear of the Japanese, a division of cavalry under Lin Ju-ming had cut the Tientsin- Pukow railway. This was why no enemy reinforcements had come to Taierhchuang. Everywhere in the rear guerrillas, in radio contact with the Chinese Central Command, were tearing up railways and destroying highways. Tsinan itself was entered by guerrilla troops under Sun Tung-hsuan and Tsao Fu-lin. There was fighting in Chefoo and along the Tsinan-Tsingtao railway.

In the Shanghai-Nanking area, mobile units had reoccupied Szean.

On April 5, the rattle of machine-guns was audible in the western districts of Shanghai. Guerrillas were active along the Shanghai-Hangchow railways.

In the north, the guerrilla troops of the Shansi-Chahar- Hopei Border Area were attacking the Peiping-Suiyuan railway in the region of Kalgan,

Nankow Pass, Hwailai, and Suanhua. They tied up two divisions of Japanese troops, who were compelled to give them their undivided attention.

Wherever the Japanese had weakened their garrisons to provide reinforcements for the main front, the armies of the Chinese Government and people had broken through, like flood-waters through the gaps of a dam.

The whole Chinese nation had won the victory of Taierhchuang.

On the next day, the people of Taierhchuang started to come back to their town. They dug among the debris for their belongings, recovered boxes of personal effects from the barricades into which they had been incorporated, and cleared sleeping-places for themselves in their ruined homes. The post office and telegraph administration reopened for business in half-wrecked houses. A train came into the battered North Station. By now the guns could barely be heard in the distance.

We returned to Hsuchow.

Hsuchow, like Hankow, Chungking, Canton, and every other city in China, was celebrating the victory. Its spirit was more buoyant and more confident than ever. Soldiers and people walked with heads erect, proud of their part in the achievement.

The General Mobilization Committee issued instructions to its organizers and propagandists:*

"In addressing the people, explain the significance of the battle. Tell them that we have broken the attack on Hsuchow and laid the foundations for a counter-attack. Stress the way in which we have strengthened ourselves during this second stage of military operations. Tell how Chinese armies on other fronts have helped our victory, and how our victory is helping them. Tell how our spirit of resistance is growing stronger while anti-war sentiment is spreading among the Japanese people.

---

* Condensed from the mimeographed "Theses for propagandists on the celebration of our victory at the front", issued by the General Mobilization Committee in Hsuchow on April 8. Original is in my possession.

"Tell the people the story of the battle. The subjective causes of our victory were our change from passive to offensive tactics, the change from frontal resistance to a strategy of envelopment and annihilation of the enemy, the able direction of General Li Tsung-jen, the co-ordination between the armies on all fronts, and the co-operation between the Army and the people. Explain that the spirit of sacrifice on the part of the Army and the iron determination of the people are due to the correct leadership of the Government of united China. Tell the people that our technical equipment is improving. In this battle our mechanized units inflicted great losses on the enemy.

"Tell the people the objective causes of our victory. The enemy is in financial difficulties. He is trying to win cheaply, to skimp on men and supplies. The enemy's lines of communication are unstable. Our forces have blown up the Yellow River Bridge. Our guerrillas constantly harass the railways and have cut the Tsinan-Lincheng line. Our policy is to force the enemy to unproductive waste of his material. The enemy has suffered severely from these tactics. The Japanese people are tired of war. They realize that it benefits the few at the expense of their sufferings. Read to the people the captured diaries of the Japanese.

"Impress upon the people that Taierhchuang is only the first step. We must realize, that to achieve this first step we did much work and sacrificed many lives. We must celebrate, but not become complacent. This victory is the result of nine months of bitter struggle. We must work much harder and make much greater sacrifices before the final victory will be ours.

"In this campaign, we have realized the importance of co-operation between the Army and people. To continue to successfully defend our war area, we must mobilize all the people in it. Tell the people that all the obstacles in the way of full unity between the Army and population must be overcome."

Leaflets scattered through the city called upon the people to do their part: "Fellow countrymen! The cannon of the enemy have battered at our doors.

We have repelled them but they will come again. There is no time to waste. Organize to do ambulance work at the front. Organize communications units to carry supplies to the firing line. Organize to guard the telephone network, roads, and railways. Those who have money must give money. Those who have strength must give their strength. Most important of all, get into uniform and organize self-defence units. If they come, we must give them a lesson. It is better to die fighting than to be slaughtered defenceless. Unite and fight against the military bandits of Japan. The final victory will be ours!"*

I travelled back to Hankow on a hospital train, the War Ministry's Wounded Soldiers' Train No. 5. This train had once been the crack Shanghai-Nanking Express. Early in the war, it had been adapted to carry the wounded. It had worked on many fronts, and within six months had been bombed more than thirty times. Its windows were broken, its sides patched with many-coloured slats. After the battle, it had gone all the way to Taierhchuang. There it had been bombed again and two members of the crew had been killed. The train's permanent staff consisted of a commanding officer, a medical and dressing staff of five, a pharmacist, an adjutant, a quartermaster, and thirty workers. This crew had been on the train since it began its career. Some members had been killed. Practically all had been wounded, at one time or another, by bomb splinters. The train was equipped to carry 300 wounded. It now carried 900. The 600 men who had no cots, lay on the seats, the baggage-racks, and the floors of the twenty-two cars.

The stoicism of the Chinese soldier is beyond belief. The heavily wounded suffered in silence and died silently. On the trip, we lost about thirty men. The less severely injured crawled around, piled straw for their own beds, made no demands at all upon the crew of the train. I sat up all night, talking to dozens of the men. They had fought all over the country, and they were all

---

* Form of proclamation of the General Mobilization Committee addressed "To the People of the Battlefield".

confident of their ability to handle the Japanese. They cursed the heavy guns of the enemy and spoke of the weakness of the Japanese in close fighting. They all knew the strategic plan for the second stage of military operations. They asked why the League of Nations did not give effective help to China, why America shipped so much scrap iron to Japan. "If all countries helped us with equipment as Russia helps us with airplanes", they said, "we would drive the enemy out quickly. Anyhow the final victory will be ours. But if our arms were as good as theirs, we could win it much sooner."

The hospital train had precedence over all other traffic except urgently needed reinforcements of men and munitions. Every few hours, we made stops to change the dressings of the wounded. Representatives of people's organizations, the Red Cross, and the foreign mission hospitals waited at the large stations with tea, food, stretchers, and fresh bandages. They kept in touch with the train schedules and turned out early, sometimes waiting for hours until the hospital train arrived. In Kaifeng, they had erected about twenty mat-shed dressing-stations along the platform. The Japanese came and bombed the mat-sheds out of existence. The people set them up again. The soldiers continued to receive the attention they needed. When we stopped at Kaifeng, the dressings of 900 men were changed within three hours.

The head of the Army Medical Service, Dr. Lo Chi-teh, told me in Hsuchow that there were eight such hospital trains serving the front. Dressing and casualty clearing-stations were established in Hsuchow, Kaifeng, Chengchow, Sinyang, Chiuyang, and Hankow. In Hsuchow there were two mobile surgical units which moved on trucks and were each composed of two operating teams with instruments and X-ray fluoroscopes, the power for which was provided by small gasoline engines. All this had come into existence since the war, under the most difficult conditions. Despite heroic work, the medical organization was still pitifully inadequate to deal with the enormous numbers of wounded. There was a lack of personnel and the simplest medical supplies. The transport of wounded before they reached the railway was voluntarily organized by the people. The men wounded near the railway lines were lucky. The others arrived late and in horrible condition. "The incidence of infection is proportional to the time taken by the casualty to travel from the firing-line to the dressing stations," said Dr. Lo. Well meant but inept attention killed many men, cost others their limbs. "Often a torniquet applied in the combat zone is not removed or loosened for days while the wounded travel to the rear," he told me. "The limb dies and we have to amputate, although the original wound may not have called for amputation. Frequently, gangrene sets in."

What had already been accomplished, had been achieved in towns and villages which had previously had little or no medical organization, even to take care of their own inhabitants. It was not in Europe that these doctors had to work, but the war-devastated backward heart of China, even normally the "de- pressed area" of this poor country. No one rested on his laurels. Nobody I spoke to was satisfied with his own work or anyone else's. "We must do more, more, more," was the cry. They told the most horrifying stories of dirt, neglect, and ignorance, not to excuse their own deficiencies, but to show what had to be, and would be overcome. It was not only at the front that men fought on and on against terrific odds in the confidence of final victory. And it was not only at the front that the results were beginning to show.

I returned to Hankow, which was buoyant with the news of the victory.

During my absence, the Emergency National Congress of the Kuomintang had been held. The Congress reaffirmed the Government's determination to carry on the war. "In the midst of this struggle," said its Manifesto, "we have also to redouble our efforts to complete the task of national reconstruction." In the course of resistance China would not only expend, but would add to and develop her resources. From the battle, China would emerge stronger than ever before. "The winning of the final victory will not only assure our country of her sovereign rights and administrative integrity, but will also gain for her freedom and equality among the family of nations." General Chiang Kai-shek was elected President of the party.

The Congress made the first formal acknowledgement of China's new birth of democracy. It decreed the founding of the People's Political Council, an organ representing all sections of the population. True, the Council was to be a consultative, not a legislative body. But its formation was a definite step forward along the road from the dictatorship of one party to the democratic collaboration of all. The Congress laid down basic principles of foreign and internal policy. Diplomatically, it resolved to "unite with all the friendly peoples of the world... and with all forces which are against the aggression of Japanese imperialism".

The Chinese soldier would not be an automaton with a gun, but a conscious fighter for his country's liberation. The Congress resolved "to intensify the political training of the army". It expressed confidence in the ability of the people to resist the aggressor. This was shown by its decision "to increase the fighting strength of the people... (so that they may) fight in co-ordination with the regular army". The success of partisan activities in the rear of the enemy was acknowledged and made the basis of another resolution to "commence widespread guerrilla warfare in the regions behind the enemy's lines". Soldiers at the front could fight with greater confidence. The Congress resolved "to grant special privileges to the families of all those who are engaged in the war of resistance".* Official abuses would be remedied, and the Government would "impose severe punishment on all corrupt state servants".

The Congress acknowledged the right of the people to a share in the benefits of wartime industrial development. It resolved to "carry on reconstruction on military lines and at the same time pay due attention to the improvement of the people's livelihood". This fell far short of the realization of Dr. Sun Yat-sen's specific insistence on land reform and industrial democracy in his "Three Principles of the People". But even this resolution represented a solid advance, a victory for the more progressive elements in the Kuomintang. In the struggle that preceded its inclusion, the party's reactionaries and defeatists, led by Wang Ching-wei, had insisted that there could be no talk of bettering the condition of

---

* I have borrowed the characteristic quotations from the decisions of the Congress from an article on "The Fruits of the Kuomintang Congress" by Tao Fen, in the magazine *War of Resistance*, Hankow translated and condensed in the *Pacific Digest*, May 1937. The appraisal of the results of the Congress is my own, and is based on conversations I had with leaders of political groups and people's organizations at the time.

the people in the course of the struggle. "War is sacrifice, and we are fighting to the last man," they perorated, with tears in their eyes. "Every Chinese should be willing to give up not only all economic benefits but also his life." But in spite of these gentlemen, the Congress passed a resolution stressing the nation's duty to those who were actually giving their lives and not talking about it. And despite the tragic utterances and soulful sabotage of the Wang Ching-weis the Congress refused to regard China's war of liberation as a beautiful and noble gesture of futility, but instead stressed the constructive features of resistance and its promise of new life and dignity to the Chinese people.

China's ruling party thus gave clear formal recognition of the objective needs of constructive resistance. It sanctioned the revolutionary developments of nine months of war, and it incorporated into its programme many of the reforms which the people had been demanding and carrying out in the course of the national struggle. All groups of the population hailed the decisions of the Congress as an important reinforcement to the national power of resistance.

The existence of political parties other than the Kuomintang was sanctioned. On April 20, the Chinese National Socialist Party was given recognition. On April 27, the Chinese Youth Party was similarly recognized. Thus the principle of one-party dictatorship passed from the Chinese scene and gave way to the free co-operation of all parties giving their support to national resistance and the reconstruction of the country in accordance with the Three Principles of Dr. Sun Yat-sen.

To strengthen the financial power of the country, a new $500,000,000 National Defence Loan was issued on April 22.*

In all spheres of national life, the victory of Taierhchuang stimulated the people to new efforts, and gave them new confidence in the certainty of final victory.

The dying pro-German, pro-Italian section of the Kuomintang, under the spiritual leadership of Wang Ching-wei, who still hoped to drag China into the camp of the anti-Comintern Powers, continued to hold many important positions in the Government, although it was totally devoid of popular support. The Kuomintang Congress had affirmed the necessity of China's

* The first had been issued on Augnst 26, 1937.

diplomatic co-operation with all friendly Powers and forces in the world. But it had not made any statement differentiating between the Fascist allies of Japan and the democracies from which China could expect help on the basis of both interest and sentiment. This was the result of the activities of Wang Ching-wei and his satellites. By denying that China's struggle was part of the fight of the free peoples of the world against Fascist imperialism, they provided themselves both with a theoretical argument against the growth of democracy at home and a powerful lever with which they hoped to swing China to the "anti-Comintern" bloc. "China's war is national in essence, and has nothing to do with conflicts elsewhere," they said. From this position they hoped to advance to the torpedoing of the United Front, the alienation of the Soviet Union, and final "alliance" with Japan.

Nevertheless, since they had not openly shown their traitorous character, and since the entire Kuomintang had not yet realized the wider implications of resistance, the Wang Ching-wei group retained important posts in the party organization. Wang Ching-wei himself, as an "old revolutionary" and senior statesman of the party, was even given the position of vice-chairman, second only to Chiang Kai-shek. After the fall of Nanking the defeatists and traitors had moaned that China was too weak to fight and must make "peace". Now they began to whisper: "We have won a great victory. Let us call a truce while we are so favourably placed for negotiation." But even the waverers of January now condemned the sabotage of this isolated clique of "revolutionary veterans". Taierhchuang was not only a heavy blow to the Japanese Army: it was a decisive setback to the capitulationist tendencies within the country on which Tokyo had based its hopes of Chinese surrender.

Taierhchuang was a deadly thrust at the much-vaunted prestige of the armed forces of Japan. Already in Shanghai, foreign observers realized with surprise how much they had been prone to over-estimate the power of the Japanese Army. Nanking convinced the world that Japanese discipline did not exist. Taierhchuang and Linyi showed that the Japanese Army could be outmanoeuvred and outfought not only by Chinese troops, but by raw recruits and provincial units poorly trained and equipped even by Chinese standards. This was because the Chinese soldier had something to fight for. It was a lesson to China, to Japan, and to the world.*

After Taierhchuang, the Chinese army continued to pursue the Japanese northward. But it had already exerted its maximum effort, and it still lacked the transport and organization to bring up and dispose large forces with sufficient speed to enable it finally to crush the enemy. The Japanese were given a respite and managed to consolidate their positions at Yihsien. On this unfortunate town, the Imperial Army avenged its defeat in the field. Hundreds of its inhabitants were killed and their houses burned.

Despite the necessity of quickly recouping their position and wiping out the memory of their disgrace, the Japanese were unable to resume their offensive for a full twelve days. During this time they demonstrated their "power" by other activities, far in the Chinese rear. In Changsha, on April 10, Japanese planes bombed the University of Hunan, killing a number of boy and girl students who were enjoying a Sunday afternoon on its picturesque hillside campus. In Canton, they dropped a bomb in a crowd of civilians celebrating the Chinese victory. In the rear of the Japanese, the Chinese people struck back. On April 11, guerrillas were reported to be active around Tientsin. At Minghong, near Shanghai, 7,000 of them fought a pitched battle with the Japanese garrison, the firing being heard in the port city. Higher up the Yangtze, towards Nanking, the Japanese were burning villages and killing the people in savage desperation, as guerrillas picked off their outposts.** In Suiyuan,

---

* At first Japanese spokesmen disposed of Taierhchuang by the simple expedient of denying that it had ever happened. Until April 14, they stubbornly insisted that the town was still in Japanese hands. On that day, the Japanese spokesman in Shanghai finally broke down under the weight of evidence hurled at his head by foreign correspondents and admitted: "Perhaps the Chinese now have Taierhchuang." Immediately after this, he exposed himself to ridicule by saying: "Anyway, Hsuchow was never an objective of the Japanese forces." No!

** On April 14, foreigners in Shanghai saw fourteen truckloads of wounded Japanese soldiers being brought to Yangtzepoo. Mr. Charles Worth, American missionary of Kiangyin, said the Japanese were afraid to venture out of the town except in large groups and armed with machine-guns. Japanese terrorism had reduced the population of Kiangyin from 60,000 to 5,000. Two thousand five hundred Japanese troops arrived in Shanghai from Japan on April 19 to quell the partisans. This is an example of how the fighting people forced the enemy to abandon his policy of economizing his resources and operating only with the troops already in China.

in Inner Mongolia, Ma Chan-Shan's wild Manchurian cavalry recaptured the towns of Holin, Liangcheng, and Chinshuiho. Forty miles south of Peiping, the guerrillas cut the Peiping-Hankow railway, blowing up the bridge at Liuliho. The invaders were driven to frenzy by these ever-present and indefatigable hornets.

By April 19, the Japanese were again ready to strike at Linyi. In a small area in South Shantung they massed a force of 200,000 men, comprising ten divisions, the 2nd, 5th, 6th, 7th, 8th, 10th, 13th, 14th, 101st, and 105th. To achieve this concentration, they practically denuded several occupied areas of troops. The Chinese, taking advantage of this, recaptured many towns in Chekiang, south of the Yangtze, Honan, north of the Yellow River, and all sections of the province of Shansi. North of Hsuchow, fighting raged on a fifty-mile front. Villages and towns were reduced to ashes by artillery and aerial bombardment. Great heroism was shown by soldiers from far-away Yunnan. In a counter-offensive they broke the Japanese line north-east of Taierhchuang. Mobile columns smashed enemy communications around Linyi. On May 4, this new drive of the "irresistible" Japanese army had also been halted. On May 5 the guerrillas delivered their most spectacular blow. They recaptured Marco Polo Bridge on the Peiping-Hankow railway, the spot where the war began, and Wanping, the scene of the first Japanese bombardment. Chao Tung's partisan army took Changping, in the Peiping-Suiyuan railway, twenty-two miles north of Peiping. This stopped Japanese troop movements to and from Shansi. Other guerrillas cut the Tientsin-Pukow railway nine miles below Tientsin, impeding the sending of reinforcements to the Hsuchow battle.

On May 10 the Japanese navy took the almost undefended island city of Amoy in South China, on the Fukien coast. This was played up as a great victory by the Japanese Press, to draw the attention of the people away from the slow progress of the Japanese army attacking Hsuchow.

Finally, in the third week of May, the Japanese pincers began to converge in real earnest. A new offensive was launched south of Hsuchow. General Doihara, Japan's "Lawrence" and prime master of intrigue, drove across the Yellow River north-west of the city. Hsuchow itself was mercilessly bombed.

In one day, 3,004 houses were demolished. Amidst the heaviest fighting of the war, Japanese troops cut the Lunghai railway, advancing with their mechanized units across the flat, dusty Honan plain.

On May 19, Hsuchow fell. Three Japanese columns marched athwart the approaches to the city, their mighty armament poised to destroy the hundreds of thousands of Chinese troops they expected to surround. But they found no Chinese troops, nothing but a few hundred wounded, whom they savagely bayoneted.* The evacuation of Hsuchow had been accomplished with only 1,000 or 2,000 casualties. General Tang En-po's 13th Army crossed the Tientsin-Pukow railway on March 18 and withdrew to North-eastern Anhwei. Provident fog and storm hid its movements from the Japanese and saved it from bombing. General Sun Lien-chung's Second Group Army, comprising the 31st, 30th, 21st, and 22nd Divisions which had triumphed at Taierhchuang moved safely south-westward, smashing through the Japanese cordon after covering the retreat of the other forces. Generals Li Tsung-jen and Pai Chung-hsi, with many divisions of Kwangsi troops, also escaped from the encirclement. Not only infantry but mechanized units and heavy guns were safely withdrawn.** Four divisions, commanded by Generals Yu Hsueh-chung, Fan Sung-fu, Hun Teh-ching, and Sun Cheng, moved east from Hsuchow towards the sea. This was in accordance with the plan for continuing the struggle in the 5th War

---

* The *Japan Times* stated on May 20: "Undoubtedly the Japanese people were greatly surprised to learn that when our forces reached the city walls of Hsuchow there were but a thousand Chinese soldiers to offer resistance" — the "city walls of Hsuchow" are a figment of the imagination. Japanese dispatches described fierce fighting on these walls, and a spokesman in Peiping even produced a diagram showing their thickness at the base and summit. Actually, Hsuchow is not walled. The ancient barrier was razed twenty years ago. "Like unto the walls of Jericho, the walls of Hsuchow fell at the first blast of the spokesman," wrote one correspondent.

The massacre of wounded has been described by the New Zealand novelist Miss Iris Wilkinson ("Robin Hyde"), who was trapped in the city.

** On May 23, a Japanese spokesman in Shanghai partially admitted the failure of the attempt to smash the Chinese army at Hsuchow. "Three or four Chinese divisions succeeded in slipping through a gap in the Japanese cordon around Chinese troops trapped south-east of Hsuchow." A "cordon" which contains a gap through which four divisions, with all their supplies, can "slip" is a thing of fantasy — very much like the "wall" of Hsuchow.

Area. To-day, they still hold North Kiangsu in the rear of the Japanese. They work in close co-operation with strong forces of guerrillas under Li Ming-yang, once chairman of the General Mobilization Committee in Hsuchow. The work of awakening the people in the 5th War Area has borne fruit. In this area, as elsewhere, the Japanese hold only the roads. The hinterland remains Chinese.

On May 20, as Japanese newspapers shrieked the "destruction of the Chinese Army", Chinese airplanes appeared for the first time over the cities of Japan. They dropped not bombs, but leaflets, exposing to the Japanese people the falsehood's of their militarists.

Instead of the Chinese Army, Doihara's 14th Division was encircled and remorselessly battered. It had pushed forward audaciously to Lanfeng on the Lunghai railway. Now it was surrounded on three sides by Cantonese troops which had rushed up from the South. On the fourth side was the Yellow River. Chinese planes ceaselessly bombed the pontoon bridges Doihara's men tried to throw across the river. The Japanese spokesmen in Peiping officially admitted that Doihara's 20,000 men were striving desperately to avoid annihilation. They finally escaped, after suffering heavy losses.

At the end of the second period of military operations, the Chinese had recaptured more territory in Shansi than they had lost in Shantung. The Japanese army in Shansi had been depleted to provide reinforcements for the Hsuchow front. The Japanese forces manning the lines of communication in this province no longer had contact with each other. Their lines of defence were reduced to points. They were fed and supplied with ammunition by airplanes. Systematically, the Chinese armies wiped out one garrison after another. They put up little resistance. An order destined for the Japanese 20th Division at Linfen was dropped by an airplane on the Chinese lines. It read: "In future, we will send you ammunition once a week by plane. You must economize. Decide yourselves where and when to engage the enemy. Reinforcements are out of the question at the present time." Between March 7 and May 10, the Chinese armies in Shansi recaptured thirty-four cities. They claimed to have inflicted 27,780 casualties on the four and a half Japanese divisions in the province.* "Shansi is again practically ours," exulted Chinese spokesmen. The forces operating in Shansi were under the command of Yen Hsi-shan (Shansi provincial troops), Wei Li-huang (Central Government), and Chu Teh (Eighth Route Army). They co-operated in a real united front. The Communist army fought under the general command of Yen Hsi-shan. Yen and Wei lent nine full divisions of their troops to Chu Teh to carry out, under his orders, the strategy that he had planned.

At the end of the second period, Japan, which had started out to conquer China with fifteen divisions, had thirty-one divisions in the country. Since the beginning of the war, a total of 1,100,000 Japanese troops had landed in China. Of these, 250,000 had been killed or wounded. Every day showed that the remaining 750,000 were not equal to the task of both garrisoning the occupied areas and engaging the Chinese Army at the front. This proved the success of the Chinese policy of combining a war of manoeuvre and widespread partisan activity with the defence of designated positions.

The Japanese ambition to conquer China by political means was dead. The capitulationist elements in Hankow no longer dared work openly. They hardly dared to work at all. In Tokyo, Premier Konoye declared that the Japanese Army would fight on "until the Chiang Kai-shek regime was overthrown". There was little else it could do short of withdrawing, but it was a long and doubtful "until". The Japanese war budget had grown to 4,000,000,000 yen. "Japan will obtain reparations from China even if the Chiang Kai-shek regime fails to pay," thundered Foreign Minister Hirota in the Diet. The "if" was quite unnecessary, and the "obtaining" ambiguous. At the end of nine months of war, Japan could not even begin to squeeze any part of her expenditures out of the "conquered" territories, because in reality they were not in her hands.

---

* Japanese casualties, as reported by the various armies, were divided as follows: Taiyuan-Shihchiachuang railway, 980; Tatung-Puchow railway, North section, 1,970; Tatung-Puchow railway, South section, 4,330; Hsianing-Chihsu area, 3,680; Lishih-Shihsien area, 4,990; Wu ares, 11.830. Total, 27.780.

After Nanking, Japan had offered "peace terms" through the Germans. Germany had been playing both sides of the war in a complicated double game. But already in February, Hitler had turned from flattery of China to open support of Japan's adventure. After Hsuchow, Germany threw up the sponge completely. On May 21, the German military advisers, who had built up Chiang Kai-shek's army for civil war against the Communists, were withdrawn from China by order of Berlin. China was finding herself not only internally but internationally.

After the supreme effort of the Hsuchow campaign it was not the Chinese Government that was shaken to its foundations but the Japanese. Not China, but Japan reformed her Cabinet. Not China but Japan introduced stringent compulsory mobilization of all national resources for war. In China, democratic freedom grew. The initiative of the people was the soul and substance of the country's new strength. In Japan, new measures of "political control" were imposed.

There had been no "knock-out blow". Japan was farther from victory than she had been at the beginning of the struggle.

These were the results of the Hsuchow campaign.

CHAPTER IX
The People's War

W E have talked of the beginning of the struggle in North China, the heroic resistance in Shanghai and Shansi, the increasing determination of the Chinese Government and people to carry on the war, and the new proofs China gave of her strength during the second stage of military operations.

"But what of North China?" the reader will ask. "What of the huge areas behind the Japanese lines? Have the invaders managed to turn North China to their own advantage? Are the people of the country resisting their control? And how are they resisting? Of course we know of the activities of the guerrillas. We have heard the romantic story of how a guerrilla army was born. But isn't all this a little thin? Will it withstand the military, economic, and political pressure of Japan when she begins in earnest to consolidate her control over the territories which she has conquered?"

These questions are legitimate. They are important and crucial. Because, despite the difficulties Japan had encountered during nine months of war, her forces had advanced, she had swallowed some of China's richest and most productive territories, and her merchants and industrialists were beginning to follow the banners of her army. The guerrillas? The story of the wandering band of Chao Tung was a proof of the people's hatred of the invader. But such bands could be defeated again, as they were defeated at Miaofengshan.

Perhaps they managed to exist only because the main Japanese forces were busy elsewhere. What the First People's Anti-Japanese Army found at Fuping indicated that partisan warfare was being regulated and planned. But, even so, would all this stand against the Japanese? And even if the partisans did not molest the people, even if it were true that the people hated the Japanese with a deadly hatred, would they forever consent to have their fields become battlegrounds and their villages charred ruins? Was it not necessary for them to gather their harvests and to take their grain to market, however oppressive the regime they were under? Were not the market towns under the control of the Japanese? Continued disorder means starvation to the peasant. Would not the peasant finally consent to buy order, even at the expense of slavery? After all, the Chinese people had been oppressed for centuries. They had been terrorized into submission by forces far less formidable than the Imperial Japanese Army. And Japan's economic weakness? Would it not be remedied as soon as she could exploit the territories under her control? Would she not find it easy to secure foreign loans for the realization of the wealth she had won?

In Hankow, in the early part of 1938, we foreign newspaper-men did not know the answers to these questions. The returned students from America who acted as the spokesmen of the Chinese Government also did not know. If one asked them how China was resisting, they would point to the new tactics of the army, to the decrees ordering the mobilization of the people, to the hatred of the Chinese in the conquered areas for their oppressors, and the sporadic guerrilla attacks on the enemy's line of communications. One had only to press them a little to find that they did not have any real faith in partisan warfare and the awakening power of the people. They saw themselves fighting a brave and desperate battle, a game of chance, with Japan's exhaustion as the stake. How to bolster up China so that her collapse could be staved off longer than Japan's? More arms, more troops, more foreign support — these were the things they thought of. "Japan is born under a lucky star," an official of the Foreign Office told me dejectedly after Anthony Eden had resigned and Hitler had recognized "Manchukuo".

In March, Captain Evans F. Carlson, a Marine officer attached to the American Naval Intelligence, returned to Hankow after a long tour of investigation of guerrilla warfare in North China. Captain Carlson was a man of singular persistence, determined to do his job properly. He had spent three months with the Eighth Route Army and other military groups in Shansi and North-western Hopei. During these three months he had marched 1,000 miles with partisan detachments, had penetrated far into the rear of the Japanese, and had come to within 150 miles of Peiping. What he had seen had been a revelation to him both as a military man and a human being. Captain Carlson was an old soldier, and he had fought guerrillas (whom he long continued to call "bandits.") in Nicaragua. Now, for the first time, he had seen a people in arms. He brought back to Hankow the impressions that he had gathered, replete with facts, and illustrated by photographs. He could not keep what he had seen to himself. He had discovered a new world, a world in which a people fought back after it had been "conquered"; and he thought it important that all those engaged in reporting and interpreting China's struggle should know of his discovery.

Let Captain Carlson tell his own story:*

"I went to Shansi three months ago, because, as a military man, I was interested in seeing a technique of warfare which I had been told was different from the orthodox. Also, I wished to study the economic and social conditions under which it was conducted." Whether the Chinese were effectively disputing Japanese control in the occupied areas, and how "Red" the people were becoming through this process — these, briefly, seemed the questions to which Captain Carlson wished to obtain answers.

So, with the authorization of Generalissimo Chiang Kai-shek and the welcome extended to him by the Eighth Route Army leaders, through whose area of operations he had to pass, Captain Carlson left for the North. "I found

---

* From a talk to European and American Press correspondents in Hankow, March 7, 1938. At that time, Captain Carlson asked to remain anonymous. Since then, he has himself given many public lectures on his observations.

the Eighth Route Army commanders invariably loyal to the Central Government. I was surprised to see how well the United Front works, how fully the Eighth Route, the Shansi troops, and the troops of the Central Government co-operate."

Chu Teh told Captain Carlson that effective Chinese regimes were functioning in the rear of the Japanese, and the captain immediately asked to go and see them. He was permitted to proceed, after signing a paper absolving the Eighth Route Army of responsibility in case anything happened to him.

"The magazine *Time* claims that the Japanese control all the territory within a radius of 700 miles from Peiping," he told us. "But I came within 150 miles of Peiping and was still in Chinese territory. I crossed two railways held by the Japanese — the Tatung-Puchow and Chengting-Taiyuan lines. I convinced myself that practically all the area enclosed by the four railways, the Tatung-Puchow, Chengting-Taiyuan, Peiping- Hankow, and Peiping-Suiyuan, is again in Chinese hands. Besides this, the partisans control seventeen districts in Central Hopei, east of the Peiping-Hankow railway. In Wutaishan I saw schools, hospitals, industrial workshops, and radio stations communicating with Hankow, where all matters of political policy were referred.

"Everywhere", said Captain Carlson, "the people go about their normal occupations. All able-bodied men receive military training, and serve in either the regular army, the partisan detachments, or the People's Self-defence Corps. Every district has a mobilization committee under the magistrate. The regular fighters and partisans, both uniformed bodies, constantly attack the Japanese. The un-uniformed People's Self-defence Groups wearing no uniforms, patrol their villages and towns and examine the credentials of every new person who enters. Farmers in the fields will suddenly ask passers-by for their papers. No spy or traitor can penetrate into the area."

At Putoh, Hopei, the captain saw how the people and the partisans fought the enemy together. A Japanese column advanced on the town. The partisans held up its advance while the people removed all the food in the place. When the Japanese arrived, they did not find even a handful of grain to sustain them. Meanwhile, the partisans surrounded the town. The hungry Japanese had to fight their way back to their base at Pingshan, suffering many losses. "This shows what happens when the people and army co-operate," said Captain Carlson.

Guerrilla warfare in North China consisted not of occasional raids on Japanese garrisons, but of planned operations from a base comprising forty-two districts with a population of 5,000,000. On January 10, Captain Carlson attended the inauguration of the Government of this base, the Shansi-Chahar-Hopei Border Administration, with its seat at Wutaishan. The administration was built on the principle of the United Front. It contained members of the Kuomintang and Communists, officers of the Eighth Route Army and other armies. Its function was to "fight the enemy with military force and compete with him economically and politically". Food production had been increased, and the planting of cotton — which had served Japanese industry — rigorously limited. A comprehensive economic programme, aimed at self-sufficiency for the area, was being realized. Rents, interest, and taxes had been lowered. The administration was organized democratically. The people fought the Japanese not only because "anything was preferable to slavery", but because the conditions they now enjoyed were better than anything they had known before. They were defending not only what they had possessed at the beginning of the war, but what they had gained in the process of the struggle. Even if the Japanese administration promised them life as they had lived it previously, this would no longer satisfy the people. Under the guidance of the Border Administration, they had built something better. This was the meaning of "political and economic competition" and the basis of military resistance.

On this basis, a people's army had been built, a military phenomenon which was new to Captain Carlson, whom it surprised, impressed, and finally delighted. "All military service is purely voluntary," he told us. "Discipline is based on individual volition and sense of duty resulting from common knowledge and acceptance of the aims of the struggle and of each military action. There is no gulf between officers and men, who are not called 'officers and men' at all, but 'leaders and fighters'. The men fight because they have been thoroughly indoctrinated and know that they are defending their common welfare. There is complete confidence among all ranks. Meetings are held before each battle, when the objects and nature of the operation, the duty of each man, and the issues at stake are thoroughly explained and discussed. After an encounter with the enemy, the causes of victory or defeat and their relation to the general aims of resistance are fully analysed. Able fighters are sent to the guerrilla commanders' academy at Wutaishan, where 430 students are now studying."

What impressed Captain Carlson most were the military results of this system. He told us how the men, hardened by intensive physical training and conscious of the importance of maximum effort on the part of every individual, accomplished the seemingly impossible. In one day, the unit to which he was attached marched forty-three miles and climbed eight mountains. Each man carried thirty-five pounds of equipment. And the most amazing thing was the way they won battles, while suffering casualties that were no more than a tenth of the enemy's. On January 6, Captain Carlson witnessed the destruction of thirty Japanese trucks and the capture of much equipment. The Japanese casualties, from a surprise attack with rifles and grenades, were forty. The partisan casualties were four. Many partisan raids, based on surprise and full information of the enemy's whereabouts given by the people, ended in victory without any losses at all on the Chinese side. In Wutaishan, the captain saw large stores of captured Japanese arms, equipment, and rations. "We lived on Japanese food all the time I was there," he said.

This was not propaganda, but the sober account of a trained military observer. "Having witnessed the partisan organization at work, I can say definitely that the areas cut off by the Japanese invasion are not lost to China," Captain Carlson declared. "The new base on the Shansi-Chahar-Hopei border has proved its ability to resist large-scale attack. Each of the eight columns which the Japanese sent against it in December was forced to withdraw. The Japanese cannot conquer such a people. They are like a man trying to plough the ocean."

Not long afterwards, Mr. Haldore Hallson, of the "Associated Press", paid his first visit to the partisan areas of Central Hopei. In all article in *Asia*** he has told of how he reviewed a column of fighters "one mile long and four ranks deep". In the Hopei districts garrisoned by the army of Lu Cheng-tsao, a member of the executive committee of the Border Administration, he saw arsenals turning out rifle ammunition, hand grenades, bayonets, swords, and trench mortars. Garages serviced captured cars and trucks. Radio stations maintained contact with Wutaishan and Hankow. A newspaper issued by the partisans, one of seventeen in the area, was displayed on bulletin boards in 1, 500 villages. Mr. Hanson also testified that all this had been built up on the basis of popular support. The partisans had convinced the people that anti-Japanese resistance was synonymous with the struggle for a better life. "All rents have been arbitrarily reduced by 25 per cent," he wrote. "A moratorium on all debts is being enforced for three years. Land and food are supplied to all refugees entering the Red Area from the war zone. This available land belongs to landlords who have fled to Peiping. The Reds guaranteed owner-ship of the land, but reserve the right to use the property for the duration of the war." From the ranks of the refugees, who had come to the area cowed, discouraged, and half-starved, the partisan army had drawn some of its brav-est volunteer fighters.

Mr. Hanson's use of the words "Reds" and "Red Area" is inaccurate. In this and subsequent articles he has testified to the fact that both the military and political leadership of the partisans was on a United Front basis, with Peiping students, Manchurian volunteers, Eighth Route Army, and new lead-ers sprung from the people co-operating equally. Lu Cheng-tsao, chief com-mander in Central Hopei, was a former Manchurian army officer. Officials were elected by universal franchise. The Kuomintang and Communist Party each had its own open organizations, and the two parties worked jointly in all spheres. Propaganda was solidly United Front. Captain Carlson had estimated the population of the border area at 5,000,000. Mr. Hanson, writing two or

---

* "With the Fighting Guerrillas Behind the Japanese Lines", *Asia*, August 1938.

three months later, gave the figure of 7,000,000. Of these, he quoted a political organizer as saying, 2,000,000 were actively engaged in propaganda or self-defence work, following a brief propaganda campaign. The mass movement was "reproducing its own leadership". By the end of 1938, it was hoped to have every village organized.

Mr. Hanson* also reported the amazing fact that the partisans usually managed to defeat the Japanese while sustaining only a tenth of the enemy casualties. A political worker explained to him that this was due to the familiarity of the partisans with local conditions and to the support they received from the people. This enabled them to keep track of the enemy's movements, attack only when the circumstances were overwhelmingly in their favour, and utilize to the full the tactical advantage of surprise. "Our desire is to restrict our losses to one-tenth those of the Japanese.... At the battle of Poyeh we lost seventeen men, while killing only sixty-odd Japanese. One of our officers was severely criticized by the general staff for that blunder," he said. Mr. Hanson was sceptical. But he was convinced after seeing the piles of captured Japanese arms at Lu Cheng-tsao's headquarters and finding that a large number of partisans were armed with Japanese rifles.

Both of the American observers who have been quoted here agree that the partisan movement in North China has been a factor of political, economic, social, and educational progress. In the process of anti-Japanese resistance, a democratic regime has been built. In the "conquered territory", in the rear of the invading enemy, there has arisen a new Chinese administration founded from first to last on the United Front and carrying out in practice the programme of national liberation, political democracy, and improvement of the people's livelihood propounded by Dr. Sun Yat-sen in his "Three Principles of the People".

In the fire of struggle, the people of the Border Area have not only de-

---

* Captain Carlson and Mr. Hanson had no opportunity to see each other's conclusions or compare notes. The Captain went to the partisan area from Hankow, Mr. Hanson through the Japanese lines from Peiping. They visited widely-separated sections of partisan territory, hundreds of miles apart.

vised means of resisting the Japanese: they have established a strong military base from which the fight can be carried to other areas, and which has, in fact, been constantly expanding ever since its foundation. They have not only founded a strong military base, but they have gained and are exercising the right of democratic self-government, putting an end to the administrative abuses of centuries. This democratic self-government is not only a source of further military strength, but has been used to lighten the terrible economic burdens under which the peasantry of Shansi, Hopei, and Chahar were being crushed into utter slavery and destitution. Men and women who knew only oppression now walk erect as active fighters for a new and independent China, for a new and more abundant life for themselves. And they are doing all this at the same time as they contribute their full share to the defence of the nation, to the recovery of Chinese territory, and to the maintenance and extension of the authority of the National Government of united China. To-day, the Shansi-Chahar-Hopei Border Area is the fighting stronghold of Chinese national sovereignty in the Northern Provinces. To-morrow, it may well serve as the base from which Chinese armies will march to the reconquest of Peiping and Tientsin, of the lost territories of North China, and the rich fields and forests of Manchuria.

But how did all this happen? How was this amazing new democracy built? Where is the source of its power? What guarantee is there that it will not be wiped out in the next campaign of annihilation?

To answer these questions, let us make a brief survey of the history and organization of the Shansi-Chahar-Hopei Border Area, which now consists of no less than seventy districts, with a population of 12,000,000 human beings.

When the first shots of the Sino-Japanese war were fired at Marco Polo Bridge, the Chinese Red Army, recently re-named the Chinese People's Anti-Japanese National Revolutionary Army, was encamped at Yunyang, in Western Shansi. Upon receipt of the news of the new Japanese encroachment, the fighters and commanders were mobilized. Reorganization of the army to meet the new conditions it would be called upon to face was undertaken immediately. Long discussions were held on the strategy to be adopted against the imperialist enemy. At the end of August, the army was re-named the Eighth Route Army, placed under the command of Yen Hsi-shan, head of the Second War Zone, and ordered to march eastward immediately. The main body of the army proceeded to North- east Shansi, while its vanguards pushed into Chahar and North-western Hopei. Chu Teh, the army's commander, set up his temporary headquarters at Wutaishan.*

The leaders of the Eighth Route Army knew that sooner or later they would have to move elsewhere. They knew also that Wutaishan and the entire mountainous area of North-east Shansi were of tremendous military importance. Strategically, they dominated the surrounding plains. If the Japanese captured the area and were allowed to keep it, they would find it easier to consolidate their control of Shansi and Hopei. If, on the other hand, the mountains remained in Chinese hands, they could serve as a base for widespread partisan activities and ultimately for a major effort to dislodge the Japanese from North China.

With these circumstances in mind, the Political Department undertook the construction of a solid anti-Japanese base. They built no Maginot lines — not because they would not have liked to, but because China is a poor country and there was nothing to build them with. They mounted no big guns, because they did not have any. "Our flesh and blood will be the new Great Wall," Nieh Erh, singer of China's struggle, had written in his "Song of the Volunteers". He was right. In revolutionary struggles, unbreakable ramparts can be built of the power of the people. Under Nieh Yung-chen, an old and experienced organizer, the political workers of the army began to build them.

---

* From this point on, most of the facts and figures concerning the Border Area for which I do not give other sources are taken from "The Shansi-Chahar-Hopei Border Area: Model Base of Anti-Japanese Resistance", a long account by the Wutaishan correspondent of the *New China Daily*, which ran through a month's issues of that paper. This account was widely reprinted throughout China and I understand that an English translation is being prepared. My complete confidence in it rests upon the fact that it is fully supported by the reports of foreign observers who have passed through different parts of the area — not only correspondents but also missionaries and occasional business men whose experiences are regularly described in the British press in North China.

First they reorganized the District Governments. When the war reached North-east Shansi in September, many of the magistrates had fled. Others were old, inefficient, and unsuited for war service. All these were replaced by new and progressive men. But some, like Sung Hsiao-wan, magistrate of Wutaishan, were strongly and actively anti-Japanese. These remained at their posts, and ultimately became important figures in the Border Government. When the Government was formed, Sung Hsiao-wan, a Kuomintang man, was elected chairman.

All the workers who could be spared were sent to agitate among the people. It was hard, uphill work. The people of North Shansi were perhaps the most oppressed, the most backward in North China. Wresting their livelihood from barren and ungrateful soil, they were forced to give a large part of the meagre fruits they tore from the earth to feudal landlords and usurers. They were downtrodden, spiritless, and suspicious. When the political workers summoned them to meetings and encouraged them to voice their grievances and demands, they would get up trembling and ask before beginning: "Will we be punished or fined if we say the wrong thing?" Anyone in uniform, they timidly addressed' as "Sir" or "Lord". The atmosphere of soulless oppression was so deadly, that it had destroyed the initiative of every would-be reformer who had previously come to those parts. The political workers found, in one village, a landlord's son who in 1935 had been active in the great anti-Japanese student demonstrations in Peiping. They tried to use him as a propagandist. But two years of living at home had ruined him and left him passive as a pool of stagnant water. Yet this was the place where the impregnable base was to be built. These were the people who would be called upon to withstand the repeated assaults of the Japanese war machine on this coveted strategic area.

Work. Work. Work. From village to village went the organizers, calling meeting after meeting, making speeches, persuading, pressing the reluctant words from the lips of the peasants, urging them to stand up and say what was in their hearts. The new magistrates did not sit in their offices in pompous state: they went out among the people, speaking, organizing.

A traitor was caught. He was taken from place to place, where his story was told and public trials were held. Thus the peasants were taught the meaning of the word spy, the danger of the traitor. The people took part in the trials. They began to look around them, and to detect the many agents the enemy had sent to work among them.

Disbanded soldiers and deserters swarmed through the area. The organizers collected them together, persuaded them, asked them: "If you keep on wandering and looting, and running from the enemy, where will you end?" The people took part in these meetings. They began to have a new concept of the duty of a soldier. The soldiers began to feel shame before the people. Fresh units of defeated and disbanded soldiers were organized.

New magistrates were elected. For the first time, the people were given a voice in determining who should direct their affairs. They began to perceive the meaning of democracy, the fact that they themselves would henceforth be responsible for arranging their common life. They thought and worried, and gave their votes with great seriousness and consciousness of the importance of this new right.

The people were afraid of what would happen when the Japanese would come. If was necessary to prove to them that the Japanese were not so formidable, that they could be fought and beaten. Already, at Pinghsin Pass, the Eighth Route Army had distributed arms to the peasants, who had helped in securing that great victory. Now detachments were sent to engage the enemy to show the people that it could be done. A small group of fighters drove the Japanese out of Fengchih and brought back trophies. A few of the bolder peasants volunteered for these raids, came back, and told their comrades. Fear of the Japanese diminished.

In organizing the villages, the following order was observed. First, the political workers investigated the livelihood of the people. Then they encouraged the peasants to act collectively to demand reduction of rents and interest payments. All rents were reduced by 25 per cent. The iniquitous system of usury prevalent in North-eastern Shansi, under which a debt was doubled after the end of the first year, trebled at the end of the second, and so on, had made many of the toilers debt-slaves for life. Even if they repaid their original indebtedness every year, they still sank deeper and deeper into bondage. Now it was decreed that interest should not exceed 10 per cent a year. This was a veritable revolution. The technique by which these new decrees were carried out was also revolutionary. Although the reduction of rent and interest was ordered from above, the executive power to carry out these orders was vested not in officials, but in the new-born organizations of the peasants. It was their business to see that the landlords and usurers did not demand more than their due, and to bring them to heel if they were recalcitrant. For the first time, the Government was theirs, and the full weight of its authority was behind their demands for a more decent life. There had been no agrarian revolution. The landlords were also protected in the enjoyment of their property, and the usurers kept their money. But for the first time their superior wealth did not mean that they held the monopoly of power. Abuse of their economic status was prohibited. And the inspectors appointed to see that no abuse took place were the peasants themselves, its erstwhile victims.

Only after the Eighth Route Army had thus shown practical its solidarity with the masses, only after the people themselves had been organized to throw off their own burdens and had felt that in organization lay the strength by which they could do it — only then did it ask the people to organize for defence. And the people understood that in defending their country, they were defending a land in which they could at last assert their rights, in which they could live for the first time like human beings and citizens. They flocked to the new military organizations which the Eighth Route Army established, and they brought the arms which they had picked up from the many recent battlefields in the vicinity and carefully stored in their houses. In every village, a self-defence corps was organized, consisting of men from twenty-five to forty-five. The young men from eighteen to twenty-five were trained as partisans. Unlike the self-defence corps, they could be called for service away from home. The most able and enthusiastic partisans could volunteer for the regular army. This was a great honour and many vied for it.

Formerly, the bulletin boards in front of the district governments and their branches in the villages had borne decrees concerning new taxes and notices concerning missing persons. No one had read them. But now crowds gathered about the boards. They read, or listened to the literates among them read, suggestions as to how they could improve their own lives, news of the operations of the army, and notices of mobilization meetings. For the first time, the people of North-eastern Shansi spoke of "our Government", "our army", and "our area".

At the end of October, a great change came about. After only a month in North-eastern Shansi, the Eighth Route Army was ordered south by the central command to help in the defence of Taiyuan. It moved away, leaving in Wutaishan only Nieh Yung-chen with a few political workers, and in the whole area a minuscule military force consisting of one regiment and one battalion of infantry, a service regiment, and a cavalry battalion. "This was the capital with which we had to start business," wrote a Chinese newspaper correspondent who was there at the time. "And our business was a big one — the creation of a vast permanent base in the rear of the enemy."

On October 27, with the approval of the Chinese high command in Shansi, the headquarters of the Shansi-Chahar-Hopei Border Branch Military Area was established in Wutaishan. Nieh Yung-chen was named commander.

Twelve days later, on November 8, Japanese forces driving down the Chengting-Taiyuan railway took the provincial capital. All contact between the new Branch Military Area and other Chinese forces was severed. The area was now solidly in the enemy's rear. Moreover, the Japanese announced that they would now undertake the "mopping up" of all guerrilla bases throughout the province. They re-formed their forces for a campaign of annihilation.

The Eighth Route Army had been in the area for little more than a month. All the great work of popular organization which had already been achieved, had been accomplished in this short period. The people looked upon the army as an unconquerable pillar of strength. But now the army had moved away, and the people were left to themselves. The threat of Japanese attack hung like a thunder-cloud over the horizon.

Here was a challenge to Nieh Yung-chen and his political workers. Under conditions of unprecedented difficulty they had to hammer together an organism capable of withstanding the blow which the Japanese were preparing. The people of the area were getting frightened. "We have no army left," they said. "What can we do with our bare hands?" The area headquarters had an answer. "Organize to defend yourselves!" But who would teach them how? The staff of Nieh's Political Department was pitifully small, and the work had to be carried on in hundreds of villages. So every remaining fighter of the Eighth Route Army was enlisted as an agitator and organizer. From commanders to muleteers, all went into the villages. Their task was not to stay and work intensively. They could not afford to make themselves indispensable. When the Japanese came, they would have to take up their guns. They had to stimulate the initiative of the people themselves, make them organize their own defence. The men of the Eighth Route Army knew that if they could do this, the battle was won. When the people begin to move, things get done with a wealth of energy, initiative, and ingenuity never seen in organization imposed from above; because in organizations created by decree the work is done by a few, whereas a genuine popular movement incorporates the maximum individual efforts of hundreds of thousands. "With confidence in the people and understanding of their needs, nothing is impossible," said the fighters of the Eighth Route. They knew. It was this that had enabled them to survive campaigns of "extermination" over a period of ten years.

The organizers had to work in districts from which the entire administration had fled. A new civil government had to be improvised. It grew up side by side with the Area Headquarters. Sung Hsiao-wan and Wu Yen-kwai, two old magistrates who had stayed, were placed in charge.

The staffs of the telegraph and telephone exchanges had run away. Communications were disrupted.

Traitors and fainthearts went about saying: "Why should we be slaughtered? If we submit to the Japanese, we will be able to live as before. It is true that our life is better now, but what good will that do us if we are dead?" At Wutaishan and Tingshang two newly-formed guerrilla detachments were disintegrated in this way. This, too, the organizers had to fight.

In the midst of all this, the Area headquarters issued a slogan to determine the nature of the work. "Strengthen and extend the Shansi-Chahar-Hopei Border Area." Extend? There were not enough fighters to protect what already existed. "Yes, extend," the political workers answered the doubters. "The partisan movement is like a fish: it needs a large area and a big sea of people from which to draw sustenance and in which to freely develop its movements." Organizers were sent far into Hopei. From the first, they reported encouraging results. Here the people were not labouring under a heritage of darkest feudal oppression, as in Shansi. On the other hand, there was a tradition of peasant revolt, and ten years before, during the Great Revolution, the peasant movement in this part of the country had assumed great proportions. Already many partisan detachments had grown up spontaneously.

Just a month after the Eighth Route Army left North-eastern Shansi, the Japanese launched their attack. Before the Marco Polo Bridge "incident", they had controlled all North China with 8,000 men. Now they sent 20,000 against the new Border Area. Strong columns converged on the area from eight directions, with cavalry, artillery, aeroplanes, and tanks. The great Japanese offensive lasted for two months, at the end of which time it was defeated and the enemy was forced to withdraw. Analysing the campaign late in January, when it was reaching its conclusion, Chu Teh* wrote:

> "A great many battles were fought, and though the enemy had some successes, most of the cities and villages in these areas remained in our hands. In this campaign, the Japanese lost not less than 3,000 men. Our partisan detachment at Yihsien captured a great quantity of war material and a number of field radio installations. We sustained no serious losses. The people of the area, having met the Japanese and seen their barbarity, rose to resist them with great determination.... In all these encounters our brave fighters were carrying on the struggle in isolated groups over a wide area. But they succeeded in drawing the attention of a large en-

---

* Chu Teh, *Experiences and Lessons* (see *Appraisal*, pp. 30-31).

emy force, thus diverting the fighting strength of the Japanese invading army as a whole. Again, in the course of the fighting, we were able to unify the activities of various detachments. In the course of our struggle, the Chinese administration in the area became more consolidated and the strong faith the people had in it greatly increased. Finally, these engagements proved that a guerrilla war can be fought with success (not only in mountainous areas but) also on the plains. In short, an army, even if isolated, cannot be annihilated if it knows how to co-operate with the people.

"In the course of the fighting we were able to unify the activities of various detachments... the Chinese administration in the area became more consolidated and the strong faith the people had in it greatly increased."

How was this done? The *New China Daily*'s correspondent who has given us such a fine account of the Border Area, thus characterized the conclusions which its leaders and people drew from Japanese campaign: "We had learned a lesson. We knew that the enemy would never leave us alone. If we were not well prepared, we would be annihilated."

On December 26, in the very heat of the Japanese offensive, a conference was called in the headquarters of the Branch War Area. It was decided that the future safety of the area depended firstly on an increase in the number of its armed defenders, and secondly, on the training and strengthening of military units, which had already been organized. In the beginning of January, at the first lull in the fighting, all partisan detachments were called to Fuping, in Western Hopei, for training. Flying columns of the Eighth Route Army had first appeared in the vicinity in September. They had organized a number of guerrilla units and worried the Japanese along the Peiping-Hankow railway. Now these units were called together, and independent detachments were also invited to come to Fuping to reorganize and strengthen themselves. Reorganization was carried out under three main heads. The units were encouraged to purge their ranks completely of bandit elements (we have seen how the process of the struggle had forced units like Chao Tung's to do this for themselves if they were to continue to exist). Intensive education was initiated among the fighters, so that they should have a solid knowledge of what they were fighting for and by what methods they could fight most efficiently. Discipline was strengthened. Political Departments were established or, where they already existed, strengthened by the inclusion of experienced organizers from the Eighth Route Army. In every district of the Border Area, a Military Department and a "Traitor Destroying Department" were founded. It was decreed that the books of the local administrations and of all military units should be constantly open to audit by the representatives of the rank and file and the people.

The slogan under which the conference worked called not only for the consolidation, but also for the extension of the area. The headquarters insisted on the importance of extension. If the base were larger, the people's confidence in it would increase. Militarily, a great area was much easier to defend (using tactics of manoeuvre and attack) than a mere corner of territory.

The Border Area headquarters had authority from the Central Command to unify the anti-Japanese forces operating in the rear of the enemy.

Invitations were issued to all other partisan groups in Hopei to come to Fuping. First to come was Lu Cheng-tsao, a Manchurian ex-officer who had organized a "Common People's Self-Defence Army" in Central Hopei, between the Tientsin- Pukow and Peiping-Hankow railways. Lu Cheng-tsao held seventeen districts,* he was able and patriotic, but he was encountering great difficulties — not only from the Japanese, but of an internal political nature. Many bandits and traitors operated in Central Hopei. The rural gentry had organized a "United Defence Organization" with detachments (remnants

---

* By July 1938, Lu Cheng-tsao held twenty-five complete districts (with their district towns) and parts of four others. The twenty-five were Ankuo, Poyeh, Leihsien, Anping, Shenghsien, Wuehien, Yaoyang, Anhsin, Koyang, Chuhe, Hsiehchen, Taicheng, Ninan, Pahsien, Hochien, Hsinhsien, Yenchin, Yungcheng, Wutze, Chinhsien, Shuning, Tinghsing, Hsiungpsien, Hsushui, and Shengtze. The incomplete districts were Tinghsien, Yungching, Chingyuan, and Kuan, whose district towns were on the Peiping-Hankow railway. Villages a mile from the railway were receiving orders from the Border Government. *Wartime Hopei*, by Mr. Tang Kang, who travelled with Mr. Haldone Hanson, who checked on these facts.

of the old *min tuan*, or landlord militia) in each village. Their slogan was not anti-Japanese defence, but to protect their villages against any and every trespasser. Objectively, this meant that they would give no shelter to the partisans, while, if the Japanese came, they could, of course, never hope to oppose them effectively with their scattered forces. The "United Defence Organization" was thus an obstacle in the path of anti-Japanese resistance. Lu Cheng-tsao had taken effective military action against the bandits, but he was having great trouble with the landlords' self-defence forces. The Border headquarters loaned him a number of political organizers. When they got back to Central Hopei, they introduced the economic reforms which they had previously put through in Shansi. These reforms, as in Shansi, were enforced by the peasants themselves. The people of Central Hopei were united in loyalty to the anti-Japanese struggle and the Border Administration, and the disruptive propaganda and practices of the village gentry died a natural death. The gentry themselves, seeing the strengthening of order and the growth of an effective anti-Japanese defence force, became reconciled to the new situation, and many of them gave their active support to the anti-Japanese armies.

Second to come was Chao Tung, with his "First People's Anti-Japanese Allied Army" of 1,500 men. This detachment, with whose chequered history we are already familiar, had grown in a different manner from the new people's armies springing up in the area. It was strongly disciplined and uncompromisingly committed to the anti-Japanese struggle. Politically, it had achieved the cleansing of its own ranks from bandits and adventurers. But it had not mastered the military or political technique of struggle. Thus far, its encounters with the Japanese had not been sufficiently successful, and because it did not have a positive approach to the people, it had not been able to establish a base. Like Lu Cheng-tsao's army, its training at Fuping armed it with the means of overcoming these defects. Chao Tung's detachment became a part of the army of the Border Military Area. After reorganization it was assigned to garrison six districts west of Peiping — Changping, Wanping (where Marco Polo Bridge is situated), Fangshan, Hsuanhua, Tsoulu, and Hwailai in the provinces of Hopei and Chahar.

Some features of the training the partisans received at Fuping have been described in another chapter. Let us now consider the way in which the partisan armies were supported, and the more concrete aspects of their relations with the people of the areas in which they were quartered.

From the time of the Fuping conference until the summer of 1938, the troops in any particular locality were supported by the district government and the people's organizations. The local administration provided food and a share of tax receipts. Local women would turn out uniforms and shoes (in one district in Central Hopei, the Women's National Salvation Association produced 17,000 pairs of cloth shoes in six months). No requisitioning was permitted. Since last June this system has been changed. With the strengthening of the central power, all questions connected with the maintenance and supplies of the army are handled by a special department of the Border Government. This department buys up locally-produced cotton cloth, and uniforms are dyed and made up in special workshop-factories. The Government purchases arms, ammunition, and scrap metal useful for military purposes from the people at fixed prices. Each detachment requiring supplies submits its estimates to the corresponding department and receives what it needs.

Partisans billeted on the villages must conform with the following regulations:

1. On reaching a village, an officer or representative of the detachment is required to inform the village headman of his intention to enter, and to report the number of men and homes the village is expected to accommodate. No unit has the right to enter a village until these points are satisfactorily negotiated. However, the village headman may not refuse to accommodate the troops unless he has special reasons for doing so.

2. Partisans must make special efforts to avoid disturbing the people in their homes. So far as is possible, they are to quarter themselves in public buildings, such as temples and schools. The villages are responsible for

making these public buildings fit for occupation. If it is necessary for partisans to be billeted directly on the people, they are to be assigned to definite houses. They have no right to impose themselves on any household to which they had not been assigned.

3. Partisans are not permitted to force the villagers to sell them food or clothing if they are not willing to do so.

4. Fodder for the horses must be purchased at the price fixed by the Border Government. The partisans have no right to charge more than the fixed price.

These regulations, too, were a veritable bill of rights for the people who had previously had no rights at all where soldiers were concerned.

If there was much work in the village, as for instance during the harvesting season, the partisans were required to help.

In every way, the people were to be shown that the growth of the anti-Japanese partisan movement would not only not impose new burdens upon them, but would lighten or remove those they already bore.

To satisfy the constant need for new partisan commanders and organizers, a "Military and Political Workers' Academy" was founded at Wutaishan. It graduated a class of 500 every three months. The enrolment for the first term consisted mainly of middle-school and university students, many of whom were refugees from Peiping and Tientsin. There were also fighters from the partisan armies, recommended to the school for special ability. The school was organized on military lines, and the students were split up into small study-groups, which included both the advanced and those of lower standard. A definite plan of work was assigned to them, and those who could master its principles quickly helped those who had more difficulty. There were four hours of class-work daily, after which the students worked over what they had learned and discussed it in their groups. The most important courses were: Political Work in Partisan Units, Problems of the Chinese National Revolution, Guerrilla Tactics, and Fundamentals of Military Science. Military studies were combined with outdoor exercises. Complete unity between theory and practice was aimed at. A new method of teaching was developed. A lecture was immediately followed by practical application of what had been learned. Then faults in execution were criticized and the process was repeated. "Learn — perform, learn — perform, learn — perform until there is not a single wrong move, and thorough understanding is achieved." This was the way one instructor described the system. The third month of the course was devoted almost entirely to practical work. During this period the students camped out and were drilled in the technique of destroying the enemy's communications, rapid advance and retreat, joint manoeuvres, and night attacks. Staff work and command were all in the hands of students, and the conditions of real warfare were reproduced as closely as possible. There was also much field work in political organization. In the lives of the students, maintenance of health, discipline, self-criticism, and co-operative living were stressed. At the end of the three-month course the students immediately joined partisan detachments at the front.

The front was a test of all that had been done, of all that had been built. The Japanese attempts to exterminate the new base of resistance did not cease. The Border Area stood the test. It not only repelled the attacks, but constantly launched attacks of its own. Its method of defence was constant assault on the weak points of the enemy. As time went on, and its organization improved, it came to launch these assaults when the situation demanded that large Japanese forces be tied up in the rear.

During the first campaign of annihilation the partisans launched counterattacks along the Chengting-Taiyuan (Cheng- tai) railway. Large sections of this line were destroyed by partisans and peasants, operating at night. The railway bridge at Fululling was blown up. Twice, in December, workers of the famous Sino-German Chinghsing mines drove the Japanese from their town, demonstrating the traditional hardihood and heroism of miner-partisans the world over, fighting as the miners of Suchansk once fought the Japanese interventionists in the Soviet Far East and the *dynamiteros* of Asturias the Fascist intervention in Spain. Armed peasants repeatedly held up and destroyed Japanese motor caravans on the highways. On December 23, a

Japanese column which hoped to clean up the partisans clustering around the junction of the Peiping-Hankow and Chengtai railways recaptured Hungtzetien* after two days of hard fighting. But they found the town completely deserted and the doors and windows of all houses walled up. While the Japanese vanguards were gingerly wandering through the empty streets, the partisans launched their counter-attack from the hills, catching them unprepared. Realizing that they had walked into a trap, the enemy retreated from the town after holding it for just two hours. Before they left, they tried to set fire to the houses. But they found this hard to do, as all the wooden parts of the buildings had been covered with brick and mortar. Only a few mat-sheds perished. After several days, according to an eye-witness, the people returned and life in the town went on as before. Meanwhile the partisans pressed after the enemy and advanced to the gates of Shihchiachuang, junction town and chief base of the Japanese in the area.

At the beginning of February, when large Chinese and Japanese armies were battling on the Peiping-Hankow railway in North Honan, the Chinese forces in South Shansi launched a counter-offensive against the invaders' right flank. The partisans joined the Eighth Route Army in an operation which resulted in the capture of four important stations along the railway, cutting off the spearhead of the Japanese advance from its base. On February 9, Hsinyao, Tinghsien, Chingfangtien, and Wangtu were taken and their Japanese garrisons annihilated or taken prisoner. Twenty miles of railway were torn up. The important town of Paoting, in South Hopei, was besieged. As a result of these activities the Japanese advance along the main front was held up for some time, the invaders being compelled to send large forces against the partisans to secure their lines of communication. The activities of the partisans became, for the enemy, more than a source of annoyance and expense. They were now beginning to be a menace to his main plan of operations.

---

* Hungtzetien was the partisan capital of Pingshan district, of which the district town (Pingshan) was at that time held by the Japanese.

To counteract this menace, the Japanese concentrated 12,000 men in Paoting and Shihchiachuang, causing the partisans to withdraw from the intervening stations. On March 4 they launched a new general attack on the Border Area, employing mechanized units and airplanes. They came by four routes: from Yihsien to Tzechinkuan, from Mengcheng to Taoma, and towards Fuping from two directions — Tinghsien and Chuyang. They succeeded in reaching and taking Fuping, but they did not hold it for long. The partisan forces of the Border Area proved that with the help of the people and the employment of proper tactics, guerrilla warfare, both defensive and offensive, could be successfully waged even on the flat West Hopei plain. After forcing the Japanese to evacuate Fuping, they continued to harass them incessantly.

In Taishien, which they captured on March 3, the partisans took a "distinguished" prisoner, Wang Huai, a member of the puppet provincial government. The traitor was tried and sentenced to death.

A Japanese attempt to re-take Laiyuan and cut the Border Area in two by creating a fortified belt with blockhouses, artillery and air bases along the Yihsien-Laiyuan highway was frustrated.

This campaign was launched after careful preparation, in the course of which the Japanese had created many strong points and food and supply bases to enable them to hold and consolidate any area they took. Four battles were fought in six days. The enemy broke through and took Laiyuan as planned. But constant guerrilla assaults on their flanks gave the Japanese no peace. Within two weeks they had lost 1,000 men, and on April 14 Laiyuan was again in the hands of the partisans.

In late March and early April, at the time of the great battles of Linyi and Taierhchuang, the partisans began a general attack with the object of disrupting the enemy's communications and tying up as many of his forces as possible to reduce his striking power on the Hsuchow front. They forced the Japanese out of the line they were holding between Chapu and Futouchen, dislodging them from Laiyuan, where they had established themselves at great cost at the end of March. At the same time Lu Cheng-tsao's army advanced on the Japanese garrison posts of Hochien, Kaoyang, Ankuo, Tacheng, and Hsinhsien which guarded the Peiping-Hankow railway in Central and South Hopei. On April 8, they recaptured Ankuo, which has remained in Chinese hands ever since.* The Japanese mechanized units which had been stationed there retreated to Tinghsien. On April 9, Kaoyang fell. On April 11, Tacheng and Hsinhsien were taken. Hochien was recaptured on the 24th, marking the successful conclusion of the operation. Hundreds of rifles, scores of machine-guns, and several cannon were captured during this operation.

Meanwhile, in the areas west of Peiping, the reorganized army of Chao Tung won a whole galaxy of victories. This detachment accomplished the recapture of Laiyuan. On April 6, they surprised a column of 400 Japanese at Erhtaoho, attacking them when they had a mountain on their flank and a river at their backs. With the exception of two who were taken prisoner, the Japanese were annihilated. The partisans captured forty cartloads of supplies, several hundred rifles, and three machine-guns. They themselves lost seventy men, killed and wounded. A Japanese plane came to reconnoitre. The partisans brought it down. On April 10, they destroyed an enemy outpost at Mentouchi. At Toli, on the Peiping-Hankow railway, hundreds of puppet troops killed their Japanese officers and joined the partisans. Advancing rapidly towards Peiping, they established themselves once more on Miaofengshan, scene of their early defeat. All the approaches to Peiping were now subject to guerrilla attack. The city gates were closed and martial law was proclaimed. On May 5, the partisans unfurled the Chinese flag over Marco Polo Bridge. The Japanese became frightened, withdrew their smaller outposts, and concentrated in the larger towns. All through the area, the puppet troops waited to follow the example of their comrades at Toli. Many revolted before the partisans arrived, going out to meet them. On May 13, the partisans took Changping. All they had to do was to send a few men to climb over the wall, frighten the guards away from a telephone booth, and call up the puppet

---

* The Japanese claimed to have retaken Ankuo during a new and greater "annihilation campaign" in March 1939.

headquarters. "We are all around the city. Arrest the Japanese and bring out your arms." Three hundred rifles were brought and eleven Japanese and Koreans were handed over. One of the Japanese was a doctor, and is still working in the detachment. The others were sent to the rear. A group of puppet gendarmes joined the partisans. The railway towns of Lianghsiang, Chochow, and Laishui were taken and held for a short time. Partisan units of all kinds began to operate freely around Peiping, and some regular units of the Eighth Route Army reached the area. They fought the Japanese on the Peiping-Tientsin highway and penetrated into East Hopei, original home of North China puppetdom.

On April 28, when one of the units approached Hangchanghsing, in Suiyuan, it was met by delegates of the "Manchukuo" troops holding the town. "We have killed our officers," they reported as they invited the partisans in.

From Peiping, the foreign news agencies reported Japanese defeats at the hands of the guerrillas, stories of provincial conferences of puppet district magistrates not one of whom had ever dared to set foot in his district city, and, more and more frequently, cases of wholesale defection of Japanese-trained troops to the side of the partisans. These reports confirmed what we were now beginning to hear in Hankow, that desertion had become a mass phenomenon among the puppet levies, who went over in companies, regiments, and even huge formations of 10,000 or more at a time.

It was easy to see why these Chinese traitor troops, many of them forcibly impressed, did not wish to fight their Chinese brothers. It was easy to understand why they hated the Japanese. But what was surprising was that, according to all reports, they did not, in the majority of cases, disintegrate and drift homeward. On the contrary, they retained their cohesion and fighting strength and almost immediately became effective units of the partisan army.

How did this happen? I asked Po Ku, representative of the Eighth Route Army in Hankow, who was well informed concerning events in the Border Area.

"It is because the partisans use the right political approach," he said. "When a unit goes over, they do not disband it and enlist its members individually in their own detachments. This would speed up the political education of individuals, but knowledge of such a practice would tend to make commanders of other puppet units keep their men from going over. To make sure that these men come to them without any apprehension, they take over entire units — Chinese officers and all — transfer them to the rear for a short period of training — and send them into the field with their organization intact. Of course, they are expected to abide by the regulations of the Border Area, part of whose armies they have become. This, as well as contact and co-ordination with other units, is assured by placing a commissar, or political director, from the Eighth Route Army or the Wutaishan training centre in each unit.

"To try to force new ideas or organization on these men at once would be harmful to our own cause," he concluded. "The fact that they have gone over is in itself a serious political step forward. The anti-Japanese struggle will educate them further. That the procedure is correct is proved by the success with which it has been attended in the Northern provinces. It is as a result of these methods that Hopei is fast becoming a second Shansi, that the puppet armies are disintegrating, the enemy's rear is seriously menaced, and that the only result of two campaigns of 'annihilation' has been that the armies of the Border Area, formerly confined to a small territory, are now able to operate in the shadow of the walls of Peiping."

The Japanese drive towards Hsuchow was gaining momentum. The partisan detachments worked and fought with redoubled energy. With captured field radios, they kept in touch with each other and co-ordinated their movements. They got their supplies now not only from the bases of the Border Area, but from the cities of Peiping and Tientsin, where their emissaries established contact with underground sympathizers who included secret workers of the Communist Party and the Kuomintang. Throughout the occupied areas in North China Japanese plans miscarried, Japanese troops were destroyed, and Japanese supplies were lost as a result of constant lightning attacks and ceaseless sabotage.

Mr. Haldore Hanson* has given us a good idea of the extent of the people's sabotage, what it has meant, and the extent to which all sections of the Chinese people have co-operated in carrying it out. He has told of former professors of physics and chemistry who sat in the Central Hopei headquarters and devised ways in which the peasants and partisans could destroy Japanese trains. Lack of dynamite was the besetting woe of the partisans. Even if they held a stretch of railway for some time, they could not destroy important works like bridges and tunnels. So the professors worked out new methods. They instructed the partisans to pull out certain rail-spikes at spots where the tracks curved. When a heavy train went over these curves, the tracks spread — and over the embankment went the train. Days were required to clear the wreckage. So the Japanese tried to outwit them by sending light trains ahead of the loaded ones, running slowly and looking for missing spikes. To counteract this, the partisans began to replace the iron spikes they had removed with wooden pegs appropriately painted, which they placed where they had removed the original iron ones. The light trains ran over the tracks without trouble, and the pegs stood their weight. When the heavies came along, the pegs broke off — and there was another wreck to be cleared. Mr. Hanson reported that thirty trains were derailed on the Peiping-Hankow railway south of Peiping in the course of three months.

In the vicinity of Paoting, wrote Mr. Hanson, several hundred peasants went on railway-destroying parties two nights a week. In a single night they could tear up ten rails and cut down twenty-eight telephone poles. To restore the line, the Japanese were forced to make replacements, which set them back, Mr. Hanson estimated, 4,780 yen — apart from cost of labour. A year of these twice-weekly forays — and the cost would be half a million yen. This was the work of one demolition group. At Lu Cheng-tsao's headquarters in Central Hopei, Mr. Hanson was told that the political workers planned to organize hundreds of such groups among the villagers who were hard-

---

* "Associated Press" dispatches quoted in Time.

working peasants by day, fighting partisans by night. On the morning following a raid the only trace of them was a wreck here and there and a mounting column of figures on the debit side of Imperial Japan, which sought to wage war as cheaply as possible.

The Japanese tried to stop the train-wrecking by terror. As in Manchuria, every village was made responsible for a certain section of line. The peasants were ordered to patrol the embankment at night. They would turn out, help the wrecking groups to rip up the track, then run to the Japanese garrison and report that the partisans had driven them off. When the Japanese arrived, it would be too late. The Japanese caught on. They burned many villages and shot hundreds of peasants out of hand in savage reprisals. But sections of railroad continued to disappear, trains continued to run off the track, and for every region "pacified" ten new trouble-centres arose.

The Chinese people were at home. There were millions of them, and they walked confidently in their own land. How was one to tell of any one of these millions, whether he was a simple farmer or a partisan in disguise? How were the Japanese to know whether the countryside was quiet or a raid on their garrisons was being planned for the morrow? No one would tell them, for who knew what the peasants in thousands of little villages spoke about as they puffed their pipes? The Japanese were few. They were strangers and enemies. Every movement they made was seen, and reported, by the people. These anonymous tall Hopei peasants, who all looked alike, whom the Japanese regarded as cattle and mowed down in mad desperation with their machine-guns, these people now had their own Government and their own army — and they themselves were the Government and the army. Where things were quietest — where trouble was least expected — rapid vengeance descended on the heads of scattered Japanese outposts. Quick death came to the officials the Japanese appointed to administer their will. The amorphous mass which the Japanese had hoped to subdue by terror of their arms was being hammered into iron patterns of organization and struggle. To the Japanese it still looked like the same amorphous mass, only more mysterious and terrible. But the people themselves knew no mysteries. They were learning how to fight for their own with whispered discussions in the farm-houses in which they had lived all their lives, with arms hidden by daylight in familiar fields and groves, with lightning midnight raids executed at quiet words of command which expressed the determination of millions. The Japanese could burn villages and destroy hundreds of men, women, and children with fire and sword. But they could not destroy the people of North China and their new-born consciousness of power. The people were at home. There were millions of them, and they fought confidently for the land that was theirs now more than ever before.

During late April and early May, the Border Area aided the main Chinese armies defending Hsuchow by launching constant attacks on the railway lines. On April 28, a night raid was made on Paoting. On May 3, Nankuan was raided. Other points on the Peiping-Hankow railway attacked at this time were Funghsinchiao, Yuchuang, and Tungchuang. Many Japanese were killed, much ammunition was captured, and several of the enemy were taken alive.

At the end of the last chapter we considered some of the results of the phase of military operations which ended in the capture of Hsuchow. We may now add one more. Throughout the occupied areas, Japanese authority was tottering. A part of the Chinese armies had evacuated, but many units had remained, and now co-operated with the people who were mastering the technique of struggle and pouring into the ranks of new armies. Japanese troops stood along the banks of the Yellow River from the Ordos to the sea. But behind their lines Shansi was still Chinese, Hopei was fast becoming so, and Chinese armed forces were pressing through the old Japanese fiefs of South Chahar and East Hopei towards Jeho — towards Manchuria.

In July, the Border Government decided to commemorate the first anniversary of the outbreak of the war by attacking the enemy and extending the territory of the Border Area. We have already told how Chao Tung's detachment staged a "political" foray towards Peiping, taking the power-plant, plunging the city into darkness, and demonstrating to the foreign diplomats and correspondents in the city, and through them to the whole world, the precariousness of the Japanese hold on North China. But this was only one part of the partisans' general offensive. Along the Peiping-Hankow line, they again reached Marco Polo Bridge, and took and temporarily held Langshan, Yihsien, Mancheng, Hsushui, and a part of Paoting (the West Gate). They attacked Shihchiachuang, at the junction of the Peiping-Hankow and Chengtai railways, and on the latter line they took Pingshancheng. Lu Cheng-tsao's detachments penetrated to the vicinity of Tientsin and took Tengtzeku and Ihsing.

As a result of the July offensive, the authority of the Border Government spread throughout Hopei, to the very borders of Manchuria. Its partisans actually entered the territory of "Manchukuo" in Southern Jehol. Two or three hours' walk out of Tientsin or Peiping would bring one into the partisan area. The cities held by the Japanese were islands in a land that was once more Chinese. Foreign correspondents spread this news around the world.

July 29 was the anniversary of the battle of Nanyuan and the revolt of the East Hopei Peace Preservation Corps at Tungchow. On July 29, 1937, the Japanese had destroyed the 600 policemen at Tientsin. They had taken over Peiping. The Tungchow affair had been a grim warning — but they had been too flushed with triumph to be really concerned about it. They had won the two great cities of North China. They had, they thought, conquered North China itself — its wealth and resources.

On July 29, 1938, this is what *United Press* reported from Peiping:

"The city is still heavily guarded by police. The gates are intermittently shut and people coming in and out are searched. To-day is the anniversary of the Tungchow revolt. The widespread knowledge that numerous guerrillas are around the city fosters the belief that an offensive is at hand. Explosions have been heard near the South Wall of Peiping.

"Many Japanese troops have been sent to Tungchow itself, where several gates have been closed permanently. Sacrifices for the people who were killed in the massacre are scheduled to-day in all districts. But the fact that most of the magistrates have quitted their posts due to guerrilla activity is likely to break the unanimity."

With great fanfare, the Japanese-kept puppet Press announced that the year had been one of peace and prosperity for North China. The Japanese army loved the people. The occupied areas were a paradise on earth.

The Japanese had imposed an indemnity of 1,200,000 yen* on the people of East Hopei, for the "outrages" of the previous year. It may be assumed, however, that they found it as difficult to collect substantial tribute as they had spiritual. The tax collectors of the Imperial Army had presumably left their posts with the magistrates. And that, for the fortunes of Japan's campaign of despoliation, was a more serious matter. But the holiday was a holiday nevertheless, and there was considerable jollification. For a specimen, we may refer to another foreign Press message of the same date:

"United Press, Peiping, July 29. The richest citizen of a small village three miles east of Peiping, having been kidnapped twice and held for ransom by robbers, appealed to the Japanese garrisons for protection. Twenty-seven Japanese soldiers were sent immediately. They obligingly blasted the village with trench mortars, destroying two-thirds of it, although they had been informed that the robbers had already fled. Now he is sorry he asked for protection."

The richest citizen of that small village three miles east of Peiping was now ready for the United anti-Japanese front which rich and poor had joined throughout North China. Like them, he would no longer ask the Japanese for protection. The people of East Hopei had enjoyed Japanese "protection" for five years. In August 1938 the Japanese were finding it necessary to protect — themselves. "Six tanks and several field-pieces were used in a battle against

---

* On December 24, 1938, the *China Weekly Review* reported that the Peiping puppet Government had been compelled to pay a new indemnity of 692,063 yen "for the victims of the revolt". This is one of the ways the Japanese war machine, like Hitler's Germany, replenishes its coffers. To make sure the first indemnity was paid they had imprisoned Yen Ju-keng, noted traitor and formerly head of the "East Hopei anti-Communist Autonomous Government". Another example of how these Chinese who depend on the Japanese are finally hoist with their own petard.

the guerrillas east of Tungchow, on the road from Peiping to Tientsin", reported Reuter on August 7, quoting foreign eye-witnesses. Another Reuter dispatch explained why tanks and guns still found work to do in the "peaceful paradise" of North China. "It is confirmed that 15,000 Japanese-trained Chinese soldiers have deserted to the partisans in the Western Hills, whom they had been sent to suppress in July. The soldiers went over after killing their officers." *United Press* reported that the Eighth Route Army had established a new anti-Japanese training school in Tsunhua, in East Hopei. The schedule of the Peiping-Mukden railway was repeatedly upset by partisan activity around Tangku, port of Tientsin. North of Tehchow, many miles of telegraph wire had been torn down.

On September 8, Reuter reported that an entire division of Japanese troops commanded by a Lieutenant-General had arrived from Japan to deal with the partisans in the Peiping-Tientsin area. Once the Japanese had held all North China with a brigade and had boasted that one division would subdue all China. But here was a new division, "composed of young, fresh, first-line troops", according to the Japanese spokesman — an expensive division, groomed for the Russians, no doubt, and reluctantly sent. But this redoubtable reinforcement to the Japanese armies in China was not going to the front. The Chinese armies on the Yangtze would not feel the brunt of its attack. It bad come for an excursion in the "conquered" and orderly paradise of North China. "Meanwhile", wrote Reuter, "deserters from the Japanese-paid Peace Preservation Corps increased the numbers of the guerrillas. The Peiping-Mukden railway has been cut between Chinwangtao and Shanhaikuan (Shanhaikuan, where the Great Wall runs down to the sea, is on the border of that other paradise — 'Manchukuo'. Small wonder that the Japanese were anxious — I.E.). It is reliably reported that (in Central and South Hopei) a large force of Japanese-trained Chinese troops has joined the guerrillas at Chengting, Tingchow, and Paoting. They drew their August pay and then walked over." Wise Japanese-trained Chinese troops. Unfortunate depleted exchequer of His Imperial Japanese Majesty.

There was only one thing to do, thought His Imperial Majesty's officers:

to tackle the question seriously, and once and for all, to annihilate these bandits. More fresh, new divisions. More red ink in Tokyo ledgers. More misery and suffering for the Chinese people, supposed beneficiaries of Japan's paradise but — unfortunately — ungrateful and inclined to combativeness. What to attack? Wutaishan, seat of the Border Government, seat of the Anti-Japanese Academy (as a measure of their respect for it, Japanese sources always give the number of its students at 5,000, although it never had more than 500 at a time).

For two months, October and November, the attacks on Wutaishan never ceased. They were bitter months for the Japanese troops. They brought mechanized units, but they found no roads. The peasants of the Border Area had ploughed them up, planted crops over them, obliterated them completely. But look, here was a road that was not on the map. It was a good road, built especially for the Japanese. The Japanese took it. In a mountain pass, the "highway" ended suddenly in a cul-de-sac. The road was narrow, it was impossible to move forward, very difficult to turn back. Partisans rushed down from the mountains. Partisan machine-guns opened fire.

This was only one episode. The two-month attack on Wutaishan was neither so simple, nor so easy to deal with. The Japanese were determined to destroy the base of the partisans. They used many airplanes and poison gas. They took the district town of Wutai at the base of the Five Holy Mountains. But finally, like other attacks, this smashing offensive was broken by the iron co-operation between the partisans and population, the initiative and ingenuity of fighters whose whole new lives had taken shape in the struggle, the fusing of the individual wills and hopes of millions into one fighting "fist of the people", the tactics of the people's war.

By mid-November, the Japanese drive had definitely been halted, and of the five heavy columns that had converged on Wutaishan from as many directions, two had been utterly destroyed. The Japanese casualties were more than 10,000 killed and wounded. Twenty tanks, seven mountain guns, 2,000 rifles, and 10,000 tins of concentrated rations were captured by the partisans. For the first time, the Chinese took large numbers of prisoners — not individuals, but whole units. This was due largely to the fact that every partisan now knew a few Japanese phrases, such as, "Japanese brothers, throw down your arms," "we will not hurt you, but will send you home!" "The Chinese and Japanese people must not kill each other." A year before, at Pinghsinkuan, the Japanese remnants had fought to the end rather than surrender because they had been sure that they would be killed if they gave up their arms. In destroying these scattered survivors, the Eighth Route Army had lost more men than in the actual battle. Now the political approach, so effective against puppet troops, was beginning to reap successes in the ranks of the Japanese themselves.

At the beginning of this chapter we asked several questions. Did the Japanese enjoy control of the vast areas behind their lines? Were the people really resisting? How did they resist? Could they stand against major Japanese efforts to consolidate their authority over the "occupied" territories? The reader may judge for himself whether the foregoing pages provide a sufficiently exhaustive answer.

But there were other questions. Was it not necessary for the people to gather their harvest and to take their grain to market? Could the partisan areas withstand the economic pressure that the Japanese were able to exert through their control of the big cities? It was very well to give the peasants new rights, and to reduce their rent payments — but would this compensate them for severance from their markets, and the disorder, famine, and ruin which usually attend constant warfare?

We have indicated that the Border Government recognized, as soon as it was formed, that it would not only have to fight the invaders militarily, but also compete with them politically and economically. Its answer to the puppet State was democracy on the basis of the United Front. Its answer to the savage exploitation of the Japanese, the improvement of the livelihood of the people. Its answer to the Japanese attempt to make of the Chinese people a race of subject beasts of burden, the breaking of the bonds that bound the initiative of the people, the explosive development of the energies and talents of every individual, and the co-ordination of these energies as a basis for the

military, political, and economic power of the fighting democracy it was
building.

But how was this done? What steps were adopted, what institutions
founded? We must have more information about this child of struggle, this
first fruit of the United Front, this vigorous young harbinger of a new China.

To give this information will be the purpose of the next chapter.

CHAPTER X
The Fighting Democracy

THE Shansi-Chahar-Hopei Border Area consists of over seventy districts in the three provinces named. In extent, it is roughly equal to the entire province of Hopei. Its territory is not scattered, but consists of two massive blocks bisected by the narrow, Japanese-dominated corridor of the Peiping-Hankow railway. The western block is mountainous and is bounded roughly by the Peiping-Hankow railway on the East, the Peiping-Suiyuan railway on the North, the Tatung-Puchow railway on the West, and the Chengting-Taiyuan railway on the South. The other block lies immediately east of the Peiping-Hankow railway, which runs parallel to its western boundary. Its northern boundary is formed by the Peiping-Shanhaikuan section of the Peiping-Mukden railway, its eastern boundary by the Tientsin-Pukow railway, and its southern boundary by the new Japanese-built line running from Tsangchow (on the Tientsin-Pukow line) to Shihchiachuang (on the Peiping-Hankow). The western block was the original centre of the area, as established by the Eighth Route Army, and it includes Wutaishan, seat of the Border Government. The eastern block is the extension of the Central Hopei partisan area established by the army of Lu Cheng-tsao.

The Peiping-Hankow railway zone does not in any way isolate the two sections from each other. Not only couriers and small partisan units, but whole armies have repeatedly crossed the railway. Its stations, though well guarded by the Japanese, are subject to constant attacks. The railway between the stations belongs to the Japanese only when their military trains are running over it. At other times it supplies partisan demolition parties with work and partisan arsenals with good rail-steel out of which to fashion rifles and long swords. We have said that the railway is Japanese when Japanese trains are running over it. This statement requires modification. It belongs to them when their trains run over it safely. When they run off the tracks or are blown up by mines and pile up in heaps of wreckage on the Hopei plain — then both they and the railway belong to the partisans, who are never far off and quickly arrive on the scene. Foreign observers tell us that in the autumn of 1938, there were thirty wrecks on the railway within three months. The same conditions prevail on the other railways bounding the area.

Of the area's seventy districts, fifty-three are "full" — that is, partisan control extends over their whole area, including the district towns. They possess district governments taking their orders from Wutaishan. Of these fifty-three, twelve are in mountainous North-east Shansi, two in Chahar, fifteen in Western Hopei, and twenty-four in the flat plains of Central Hopei. A new acquisition to the area is East Hopei — once a Japanese-dominated "Anti-Communist Autonomous State". Here, in the early autumn of 1938, there were already five "full" and ten incomplete districts in the hands of the partisans.* The authority of the command of the Border Military Area extends to partisan units as far east as Shantung and as far north as Manchuria.

---

* All information relates to this period. However, there is no reason to believe that the expansion of the area has been halted. The following is a full list of districts under partisan control within the geographical limits given above:

North-east Shansi: Wutai, Tinghsiang, Fangchih, Taihsien, Hsinhsien, Yangchu, Menghsien, Yinshan, Yinghsien, Hunyuan, Lingchiu, Kuangling, Tatung, Yangkao, Tienchen (three of these are incomplete).

South Chahar: Yangyuan, Weihsien, *Hsuanhua, Cholu, Hwailai* (those in italics incomplete, combined into one "joint district government"). (*See page 230*)

The population of the Border Area is 12,000,000. Its chief crops are millet, wheat, kaoliang (sorghum), and, until recently, cotton. Gold and coal are mined. In Central Hopei, the richest section of the area (and also in Chahar), peaches, pears, and chestnuts are grown. There are large numbers of cattle and sheep. Animal products, exported in large quantities, are furs (chiefly lambskins), hides, and eggs. Factories in the large towns produce paper and cotton cloth. There are a few machine-shops and small arsenals.*

Before they were occupied by the enemy, or isolated by Japanese encirclement, the territories comprising the area had been under the administration of the governments of their respective provinces. In the course of military operations, however, most of the local branches of the civil government had been driven out by the Japanese, had handed over their functions to the military, or had simply disintegrated. For a time, the only governing authority was the headquarters of the Border Military Area established at Wutaishan in October. During the following months, with the Border Area growing as a permanent political and military base of resistance, the local government in district after district was reorganized in accordance with the needs of the war. Where the magistrates had remained and were carrying on the struggle, their authority was confirmed. Where they had been driven out or had run away, new magistrates were appointed — young, progressive men who enjoyed the confidence of the people and were able to awaken and organize them.

The unification of the partisan armies had been successfully achieved at Fuping. Now it was necessary to unify the civil administration, which, while

---

West Hopei: Chingching, Huolu, Pingshan, Lingshou. Hsingtang, Chuyang, Tanghsien, Fuping, *Chengting*, Hsinyao, *Tinghsien*, *Wangtu*, Yihsien, Mancheng, Hsushui, Fangshan, *Lianghsiang*, Changping, *Wanping*, Tienshui, Chochow (those in italics incomplete).

Central Hopei: Lihsien, Shengchai, Anping, Yaoyang, Ankuo, Shenghsien, Poyeh, Yenchin, Hochien, Kaoyang, Hengshui, Suning, Minan, Chingwan, Tunglu, Wuchiang, Chinhsien, Hsinchen, Hsinan, Hsiunghsien, Yungcheng, Phsien, Anhsin, Taicheng (one incomplete — there are few railway towns in this area). Tang Kang, district magistrate of Shenghsien, adds the following names to this total: Tinghsing, Chailu, Wutze, Kuan, Shengtze.

* *H.C.S. Border Area*, and *Wartime Hopei, op. cit.*

the armies fought, would take political and economic measures to consolidate the regions behind the Japanese lines as a part of the territory and administrative structure of the Chinese Republic. Through General Yen Hsi-shan, commander of the entire Western Front, a petition was sent to the Central Government to authorize the formation of a temporary administration, to be dissolved when physical contact was once again achieved with other portions of Chinese territory. The petition was granted. On January 10, 1938, the Border Government, with the official title of the "Provisional Executive Council of the Shansi-Chahar-Hopei Border Area", was formally inaugurated in the presence of 154 delegates representing forty-two district governments, the Kuomintang and Communist parties, the partisan armies, and the national minorities — Mongol, Moslem, Tibetan. There were nine representatives of the Red and Green sects of the Lamaist church. Sung Shao-wan and Hu Yen-Kwei, two old magistrates who had stuck to their posts, were elected chairman and vice-chairman of the Government. Lin Tien-chi, Commissioner of Education, was also head of the Kuomintang Party organization in the area. Other members of the executive council were Nieh Yung-chen of the Eighth Route Army, officially representing the Communist Party, Lu Cheng-tsao, leader of the partisans in Central Hopei, Chang Shu, Sun Chi- yuan, Li Chieh-yung, and Lo Ying-hsien. A declaration was issued containing the following passage: "The Executive Council of the Border Area is a form of political power established by the united nation. It includes all parties, groups, classes, and national minorities. Its purpose is to carry on the anti-Japanese struggle and to realize democracy. It is a local government of the Republic of China, and its formation takes place in accordance with the order of the Central Government." *

The work of the new administration began with a campaign to deepen, extend, and systematize the democratic organization introduced by the Bor-

* Under the general associations were many occupational organizations. For instance, under the Workers' N.S.A., there were N.S. associations of miners, weavers, carpenters, etc.

der Area headquarters. The first requisite of war-time democracy was the education of the people and their mobilization for the twin tasks of self-government and self-defence. To this end, new laws were passed, stating that henceforth, all officials would be elected by popular vote and — if they could not cope with their tasks — would be subject to recall. All accounts were to be opened to audit. To teach the people to exercise these new rights that had been given them, speakers and organizers were sent into all the towns and villages. Everywhere, National Salvation Associations of peasants, workers, merchants, women, young people, cultural workers, gentry, were formed. All these organizations were built from the bottom up. Instead of issuing orders about the organization of the people, the Border Government dispatched men to initiate it at hundreds of points. Only when the village associations had been firmly established did their representatives meet to form a district association. And only after these were effectively functioning did they elect general committees to co-ordinate their activities through the entire area. Each area-wide organization was built upon a firm foundation of hundreds of thousands of human beings. Each local unit existed not on paper but in fact, and was an integral part of the mass base of the power of the Border Government. If the district concerned was temporarily reoccupied by the enemy or cut off from the central administrative bodies, this base nevertheless continued to exist. It was indestructible because the whole population took part in it and because, while the fight went on elsewhere, the people firmly believed that the enemy domination would not last. In January 1938, at the same time as the Border Government was established at Wutaishan, the Japanese had set up their Provisional Government of the Republic of China in Peiping. But three months later, barely one-tenth of the officials appointed by this "Government" had dared to show themselves in their districts — while the authority of the Border Government was operative, in many respects, even within the walls of the puppet capital.

In economic policy, the Border Government aimed at self-sufficiency. Self-sufficiency meant not only independence of Japanese-dominated markets,

but also immunity to blockade.* In the midst of constant warfare, it promul-
gated economic reforms to improve the livelihood of the people, and to ensure a steady supply of food and equipment to the partisan armies. As with
the military and political system, everything was based on the initiative of
the organized people, and full consideration was everywhere given to their
interests. The planting of cotton — raw material for Japan's industries —
was drastically curtailed, not by administrative prohibitions, but by agitation
through the Peasants' National Salvation Association, which already, at that
time, had 600,000 members throughout the area. At the same time, because
most of the peasants lived on the margin of destitution, they were permitted
to dispose of their current crop. Then the cotton-fields were put under food
crops. The Border Area must not be starved out.

To further increase productivity and at the same time better the condition of the land-hungry peasants, unused and waste land was thrown open to
cultivation. There was much such land in the area — left fallow because of
disputed titles, or because it was considered "unlucky" according to the ancient Chinese geomancy. Until the Border Government came, the poor and
the landless had been afraid to work even pieces of land to which nobody laid
claim. If they made them produce, some shark was sure to turn up to dispos-

---

* In November, a blockade was formally imposed by the Japanese. Mr. W. V. Pennell,
writing in the December 1938 issue of *Oriental Affairs*, states that all goods in transit in the
occupied areas must be accompanied by permits signed by the puppet authorities. Those
transporting them must swear they are not taking the goods to the partisan areas, on pain of
severe punishment of themselves and the heads of their villages if the pledge is broken. No
materials suitable for manufacture of munitions, electrical machinery, tools for sabotage,
or (significantly) printing materials may leave the occupied area. Chambers of Commerce
are not permitted to release more than five bags of flour, one bag of salt, one box of matches
(dangerous weapons!), etc., at one time. These rules apply also to transportation by railway.
This, says Mr. pennell, "amounts almost to a divorce between production and distribution.
Two can play the blockade game, and just as the Sino-Japanese regime can control transport of commodities to the Chinese-controlled regions, so can the guerrillas control movement of produce from these areas to the railways. It is a question which is arousing... much
concern among commercial people" (foreign exporters). Mr. Pennell is editor of the British *Peking and Tientsin Times* and has lived in North China for twenty years. He has exceptionally good contacts in the occupied areas. *Oriental Affairs* is a Tory die-hard magazine
which serves as a medium of Japanese propaganda and carries much Japanese advertising.

sess or even punish them — and, of course, they had no recognized rights. Now a law of the Border Government stated that public and private lands not cultivated for two years were to be considered waste land. Abandoned plots, if under 5 mow in area, could be cultivated by the peasant or peasants owning the adjoining fields. If the uncultivated tract was more than 5 mow in area, it was turned over to groups of landless peasants organized under the National Salvation Association. These groups worked on it on a co-operative basis. When the peasants had raised a crop on waste land, they were entitled to claim ownership and to register their title with the Government. Anti-Japanese fighters and their families had the first claim to waste land. However, if any unused tract belonged to a landlord, he could retain ownership by putting it under cultivation immediately.

In many parts of the area rainfall was sparse and the land was irrigated. The Border Government made loans to the peasants to improve and increase the irrigation system, broke up monopolies, and regulated charges. Where seed-grain and farm implements had been destroyed during the fighting and enemy occupation, these were replaced by the Government, the only guarantee required being the good word of the Peasants' National Salvation Association.

As a result of all these measures, the first grain crop, harvested in the summer of 1938, was 70 per cent in excess of that of the previous year — before the beginning of the war. The autumn crop was even better. A Japanese general offensive in September was timed to enable the enemy to disorganize and seize the autumn harvest. By the joint efforts of the soldiers and peasants, this plan was foiled, and the winters' food supply was successfully gathered in and stored.

A remarkable recovery of small industries was also achieved, especially in Central Hopei. The flight of capital was prohibited, and investments in local industries were encouraged. Within a few months, a number of large weaving and tailor shops, for the production of uniforms, were set up in various places. Captain Carlson and Mr. Hanson saw a number of small arsenals and machine shops. Tang Kang, in his article on Central Hopei, mentions soap and paper factories, and oil-pressing mills. Experiments were carried on in the use of vegetable oils for illumination and as fuel for Diesel trucks.

Handicrafts, which had always provided the bulk of the articles in daily use in the interior, were encouraged and developed.

Exchange of products within the area was given every encouragement. Trade relations with the Japanese-occupied areas, however, were strictly controlled. The bulk of imports and exports was handled through the "Yu Min Company", a concern established by the Border Government which had branches in every district, but which did not enter into price competition with private merchants. The export of food products was strictly prohibited, and attempts to smuggle them out of the area were punished by confiscation and a fine of ten times the value of the foodstuffs seized. Inspection and control were carried on by the local mass military organizations — the Self-Defence Corps — which also checked the credentials of every person entering or leaving towns and villages in the area. No Japanese goods of any kind could be brought in. The import of articles of military value — such as metals, flashlight and radio batteries, chemicals and medical supplies — was encouraged. Other imports were heavily taxed, especially where they competed with articles produced within the area. An excess of exports over imports was aimed at, so as to enable the area to absorb national currency from the occupied territories.

The financial basis of resistance was the Government's income from the progressive land tax, import and export duties, the sale of National Salvation Bonds, and the note-issue of the Border Area Bank. At its inception, the Border Government had abolished many miscellaneous surtaxes which previous administrations had collected. Now it initiated widespread propaganda showing that prompt payment of the land tax was the best way to strengthen the Border Area, the fighting outpost of Chinese sovereignty in the rear of the enemy. The Peasants' National Salvation Association organized competitions — which village would pay its land tax first? Without a hierarchy of tax collectors, the Government was able to secure universal and early payment of the levy.

Several million dollars' worth of bonds were sold in the course of an area-wide campaign. General Yen Hsi-shan, commander of the second war zone, set a good example by buying $100,000. The gentry and rich farmers and townsmen did their share. Peasants bought bonds for grain, landless peasants did extra work on the landlord's tracts, and workmen laboured overtime. Old women brought their earrings and rings. They were supporting their own Government, and they had faith that the resistance would continue, victory would be won — and the bonds would be redeemed as promised — in 1942. Speakers from the National Salvation Unions pushed the sale of bonds in every market-place, in every village. Bonds were even sold secretly in the occupied areas, in Peiping and Tientsin.

The pride of the Border Area Bank is that it emerged victorious from a currency war with the "North China Federated Reserve Bank" established by the Japanese. This bank issued huge quantities of notes, which the puppet Government decreed to be the only legal tender in North China after June 10, 1938. The aim of this operation was to collect Chinese national currency, which the Japanese then hoped to dump on the world's markets to collect foreign exchange for themselves and at the same time undermine the financial structure of China. From the first, the people of the occupied territories sabotaged this plan by refusing to use the new notes in their daily transactions, and the great "financial reform" of the Japanese has not been accomplished even now, in 1939. Failing to force the "Federal Reserve Notes" upon the people, the Japanese began to print the authorized notes of various Chinese banks — from plates which had been left behind when the Chinese administration collapsed. Besides this, they simply counterfeited national currency. To fight this new and "subtle" version of "rehabilitation", the Border Government published decrees prohibiting the circulation of the new Japanese emissions and telling the people how to recognize them.* The export of national currency from the Area was forbidden and smugglers were treated as traitors. At the same time, the Border Area Bank printed its own neatly lithographed notes. These notes were backed, dollar for dollar, with national

---

* For instance, in the case of notes of the "Hopei Provincial Bank", the dies of which the Japanese had seized, only such of these notes as bore numbers consisting of six figures were permitted to be circulated in the Border area. This was because the legitimate emission of the bank, before the occupation had amounted to $900,000 one-dollar notes. Notes bearing numbers of seven digits were printed under the Japanese.

currency.* Ready exchange on demand at the bank's local branches convinced the people that the Border currency was safe, and the notes achieved
universal circulation in the area. What is more, the people in the occupied
territories accepted them on the same basis as national currency and in preference to the puppet notes. Even under the heel of the Japanese, Border notes
can be exchanged on demand. Patriotic merchants accepting them can get in
touch with secret representatives of the partisans who are pledged to redeem
them. Not only has the Japanese economic offensive against the Border Area
failed, but the agents of the Border Area systematically expose every machi-
nation of the "Federated Reserve Bank" to absorb national currency from the
occupied areas, and, final and greatest insult, circulate Border notes with
ease where the puppet issues made no headway.

The political and economic measures described above not only exist on
paper, but, according to the testimony of hard-headed foreign eye-witnesses,
have actually been carried out throughout the far-flung territory of the Shensi-
Chahar-Hopei Border Area. The will of the Border Government is felt in every
village — to a much greater extent than that of any administration before it. Yet
the Border Government does not have hordes of officials and an imposing and
complex administrative machine. It has only the unceasing efforts of overbur-
dened military and political workers who go about the countryside and teach
the people how to tackle their own pressing problems. And it has the people,
who recognize the truth that the organizers bring, and the fact that the decrees
of the Border Government mean not simply, "Here. Do this!", but "If you want

---

* "Already it is difficult to find a satisfactory medium in which to effect purchases in the
interior. And this not because of the limits imposed on the carriage of currency from the
main centres like Tientsin, but because producers in the Chinese areas will not take Federated Reserve Bank notes, while Central Government notes are being hoarded to an extent
which is making the whole situation here precarious," writes Mr. W. V. Pennell from
Tientsin (*Oriental Affairs*, December 1938). A testimonial to the patriotism of the "conquered" Chinese in the subject areas and their faith in the final victory of their Government.
To complete the picture, it must be remembered that central notes cannot be converted into
foreign currency anywhere except at Chungking, and there in limited amounts (one of the
Chinese Government's measures to prevent the Japanese from dumping the notes they
have managed to secure). Chinese in Tientsin and Peiping have no access to Chungking —
yet they hoard these, not puppet notes or even Yen.

to save yourselves and improve your lives, this is how you can do it." The law of the Border Government is not imposed upon the people by any official bureaucracy appointed from above: it is enforced by the people themselves through their mass organizations. And the people arc everywhere.

Let us take, for instance, the Peasants' National Salvation Association with its hundreds of thousands of members.* This Association carries on election campaigns. It sees that the laws concerning rent-reduction and limitation of interest are carried out. Its representatives audit the books of the local government. In several instances it has initiated agitation resulting in the removal of corrupt and incompetent officials. It promotes and supervises the substitution of food crops for cotton. It organizes special co-operative groups of 200 or 300 poor peasants for the cultivation of waste land, and there are at least ten such groups in each area. It also organizes voluntary units to work on the land of fellow-villagers serving in the partisan armies. The Peasants' National Salvation Association has set up hundreds of credit co-operatives, which loan money, seed-grain, and farm implements to their members to tide them over hard times. It pushes the sale of National Salvation bonds in every village. It is in charge of the collection and storing of the harvest, and prevents the export of foodstuffs in contravention of the regulations of the Border Government. In the sphere of internal trade, the Association arranges the exchange of products between different parts of the Area, thus making it unnecessary for the peasants to seek markets in the occupied territories. On the other hand, when there is anything to be bought, or any message to be delivered, in the territory of the enemy, the Government seeks the aid of the peasant organizations, since their members know the country and can go anywhere. From the ranks of the Association come most of the recruits for the defence formations. Its members carry on daily and systematic sabotage of the enemy's communications. When partisan detachments operate in the vicinity, they can satisfy their need for transport crews, stretcher-bearers, and parties to attack the enemy's flanks or divert his attention by getting in touch with the local

---

* According to the decree issued by General Yen Hsi-shan: "Those who take part in farming can enter the Peasants N.S.A." This included poor, middle, and rich peasants but not landlords — who had their own National Salvation Association.

committee of the Peasants' N.S.A., which calls for volunteers, and always gets them.

When Pingshan was captured by the Japanese, the neighbouring Associations called a mass meeting and demanded that the partisans re-take the town, offering to immediately provide them with 4,000 armed peasants to participate in the operation. "Without the peasant movement there would be no Border Area. The partisan army is a product of the peasant movement," writes the *New China Daily News* reporter. No wonder the Associations are given all encouragement and "repression of the National Salvation movement" is the most serious sin that can be charged against an official in the territory of the Border Government.

The Youth National Salvation Association is the carrier of progress in the region. Its 240,000 enthusiastic young men and women are the ferment of the Area, its reserve fund of organizers, educators, leaders, and commanders in all fields. Mr. Haldore Hanson speaks of the "fanatical enthusiasm" of the young people of the Area. "The territory is being run by keen and active young men... doing a remarkably good job of rehabilitation and reorganization," admits a pro-Japanese publication, quoting a missionary observer.* After completing their training courses at the Anti-Japanese Academy or National Revolutionary Middle School at Wutaishan, the most able among these sons and daughters of the people came back to their own homes to lead their elders and neighbours through the struggle to a new way of life.

The "Anti-Japanese Youth Vanguard", a mass organization of young men and women between the ages of fifteen and twenty-five, organizes brigades to lead the sowing and harvesting campaigns, provides groups of orators to tell the people the meaning of the anti-Japanese struggle and the political and economic reforms of the Border Government, and has charge of the education of the children — most of the teachers in the village primary schools being Young Vanguards, many of them former Peiping and Tientsin students. The young men of the Vanguard receive military training and often participate in guerrilla

---

* W. V. Pennell in *Oriental Affairs*.

operations. The girls participate in all the activities of the organization outside of actual fighting, besides which they nurse the wounded, work with small children, and lead and organize the village women. Besides the Youth National Salvation Association and the Anti-Japanese Youth Vanguard, each occupation N.S.A. (peasants', workers', etc.) has its own youth groups.

The Workers' National Salvation Association is another pillar of the Area. Though industrial workers are few, their role is exceptionally important. They run the arsenals for the production of small arms and ammunition and the uniform factories. They set up the Area's superb telephone network (2,000 miles of lines, according to Mr. Hanson) and operate the numerous field radio stations by means of which the partisans keep contact with each other. They are the greatest experts in railway and highway demolition, and they manufacture the grenades and improvised bombs and mines which play such an important role in partisan warfare. Without its backbone of mechanics and technicians, the partisan movement would not have possessed a fraction of the military efficiency which it has now achieved. The workers' organization (many of whose members have come from the conquered cities to work in the Area) carries on ceaseless campaigns for increased production. It acts as a general labour union representing the rights of the labourers in relation to their employers. From its ranks have come not only heroes of labour, giving every ounce of their energy to the production of weapons with which to destroy the enemy, but also outstanding organizers and military leaders. The railwaymen's partisan detachments of the Chengting-Taiyuan line are famous throughout the whole Area and throughout China. So are the fighting companies of miner-partisans, of whom Agnes Smedley has given an inspiring account in her *China Fights Back*.

In the last chapter we mentioned the heroic struggles of the workers of the Sino-German Chinghsing mines. Their story, as told by the *New China Daily News* correspondent, cannot be omitted from any account of the partisan movement in North China.

When the Japanese captured these rich anthracite mines, they tried to work them to supply coal for their military trains. The mines had 5,000 workers, probably the most underpaid and oppressed miners in the world. For twelve hours a day underground they received (before the war) a wage so small that besides their labour in the pits they had to work in the fields to make up the sum needed to keep themselves and their families. During the revolutionary days of 1925-7 they had organized and fought for a better life, but fierce and ceaseless repression during the next ten years had seemingly cowed them into submission. The Workers' National Salvation Association of the Border Government determined to put an end to the exploitation of the mines by the Japanese. It sent two worker-partisans to organize the men of the Chinghsing mines and raise them against the enemy.

One organizer, Yao, found four bold men and armed them with pistols. He did not at first enter the mine, but worked outside. To show the miners that the Japanese were not as strong as they seemed and that the partisan movement was near and powerful, this group staged nightly attacks on the sentry-posts guarding the mine. It terrorized the traitors by killing one of their number and leaving on the wall of his room a notice signed "The Traitor Sweeping Society", and, by loosening the rails, wrecked a military train on the nearby Chengting-Taiyuan railway. Meanwhile, the other organizer, Su, worked inside the mine. He agitated among the workers and secretly hammered together a small armed detachment. The work of Yao and Su was like two gigantic hands moulding the 5,000 workers of the mine into a fighting unit.

One night the Japanese surprised a secret meeting in the mine, caught five workers, and shot three. The movement continued to grow. The workers formed friendly relations with the puppet police and brought some of them over to their side. Yao and Su brought from the partisan area propaganda materials printed in Japanese. Some Japanese soldiers took the leaflets and read them. When this was discovered, the garrison was changed.

Attacks on the Japanese troops began. Miners by day, the workers became partisans at night. Every morning Japanese guards were found dead. Every morning, new rifles lay in the miners' secret arms-hoard. Within two months, it contained seven heavy machine-guns, one light machine-gun, 100 rifles, 26,000 rounds of ammunition, and 1,000 hand-grenades — captured during night raids on the Japanese or secretly handed over by the puppet troops. At dead of night, the miners made away with the Japanese field radio. Systematically, they removed lathes from the mine's machine-shop. In the mountains above the mine, a new arsenal was established. Many young workers left the mine for the mountains. Here they drilled and worked, even producing new rifles. Thus the Chinghsing Miners' Partisan Brigade was formed.

The Japanese attacked the new base. The miners kept them off with fierce machine-gun fire, and they retired with many losses. Then one day the Japanese troops in the mining town went a few miles outside the walls for an inter-unit shooting competition. The miners swooped down from their hills on the practice-range, and while some fought the disorganized enemy troops, others made off into the hills with armfuls of rifles and ammunition which had been stacked near by.

Meanwhile, constant propaganda among the puppet troops caused them to rise against the Japanese. With their arms, they went over to the partisans. The Japanese never used puppet troops to guard the mines again.

Work in the mines was constantly being disrupted. The partisans came down from the hills every night and roused the miners from their beds. Together they fought the Japanese. One night, in February, the workers left their hovels and stole into the pits, every passage of which they knew perfectly. At a given signal, they turned off the lights, cut the telephone wires, and took the elevators down to the bottom of the shafts. Some Japanese troops were stationed inside the mines. The workers ran towards these in pitch darkness shouting and firing. The Japanese were seized with panic, cried out wildly, and ran hither and thither. Meanwhile the miners systematically gathered guns, telephone wire and instruments, steel rails, and other articles that they needed. Their comrades on the surface engaged the guards, and the whole operation ended successfully, the booty being taken to the hills. On the next morning, the surviving Japanese in the mine were still hiding, disarmed and shivering, under the coal-cars. Many of the raiders of the night before found them in this condition when they came back, as usual, for their day's work.

The Japanese did not know who was attacking them — the partisans

THE FIGHTING DEMOCRACY

from the hills or the docile-appearing miners who had remained at work. They strengthened their garrison, shot many workers out of hand, forbade more than three men to foregather at any one time, and swooped down on the miners' homes at night to see if they were in their beds. But the workers responded with closer-knit organization. They deceived the Japanese, and the nightly raids continued, flaring up at a new spot each time. By day, the Japanese stalked about proudly. At night, they huddled together in strongly-fortified blockhouses. There was no doubt as to who were the actual masters of the mines. Gradually, all the machinery was put out of commission. Work was suspended.* The Japanese got no more coal. The partisan movement was enriched by new iron battalions and a strong base in the mountains of Chinghsing. This was only one episode in the anti-Japanese struggle of the Workers' National Salvation Association of the Border Area.

Then there is the National Salvation Association of the women. In the feudal darkness of North-east Shansi, women were even more downtrodden than their men. Their feet were bound so tightly that by the age of thirty they could no longer walk, but had to labour on their knees. They killed their girl babies because a female was less than nothing. Into this atmosphere came the straight young uniformed girl organizers of the Border Government. The Shansi women were afraid of them. They barred their doors and mumbled to each other in awe and fear, "Here come the terrible women soldiers." The girl organizers tried again. They put on peasant clothes. They made friends with the peasant women by coming up to them as they worked and quietly and competently helping them mow their crops, wash their clothes, and care for their babies. They talked to the young girls and persuaded them to unbind their feet. They encouraged browbeaten young wives to stand up to their husbands — and told them that under the new law they could divorce a man who did not treat them well. They found that in many cases the friction be-tween young couples was due to the fact that they lived with the groom's parents and the bride was subjected to the unbearable feudal tyranny of the

---

* Confirmed by Mr. Pennell.

mother-in-law, who was all-powerful according to Chinese custom. The girl organizers persuaded the young people to leave the homes of their elders and break away from this oppression. "You are workers like your men," they told the women of North-east Shansi. "Organize to gain equality and to defend your new freedom."

So the Women's National Salvation Association was formed. To-day, its members perform a multitude of tasks. They organize brigades to make cloth shoes for the defenders of their new world. In one district alone, 17,000 pairs of shoes were presented to the army. They form groups for the care of the wounded, groups to provide water for passing troops, and "sewing and washing groups" to take care of the army's clothing. In the spring of 1938, when the men were sowing and had no time to do sentry duty in the villages, the women took their places. If a newcomer came into the village, an old dame peacefully sewing on her doorstep might rise and say: "Let me see your road pass. Let me see if you are carrying prohibited goods."

The women are learning to read and write. They give plays and entertainments. And they have begun to vote and to take part in the administration of their villages, these former creatures without rights. In the district of Tanghsien, twenty women have been elected to be heads of villages. In Fuping district, there are more than ten who hold this office. To their new tasks, the emancipated women bring an impressive conscientiousness and seriousness. They walk miles through snow rather than miss a meeting to which they are delegated. For the first time in centuries, the women of North-east Shansi can hold up their heads. Equal citizens, they are marching in step with the men out of feudalism and oppression. They have their rights now and they acknowledge their responsibilities, which they bear proudly and with honour.

The Merchants' National Salvation Association encourages its members to trade in the domestic products of the area, carrying handicraft and industrial products to the villages and grain to the towns. The more perfect the circulation of goods within the area, the less the dependence of any part of it upon the territory in the hands of the enemy. The merchants and gentry of the area have loyally supported the Border Government and have bought up hundreds of thousands of dollars worth of its National Defence Bonds.

The Cultural Workers' National Salvation Association includes the teachers, with whose work we shall deal later, and the artists and journalists. The artists draw posters and cartoons which may be seen on the walls of every village in the area. As for the Press, the Border Government considers its work to be of exceptional importance. The fighters at the front must be regularly supplied with news from the rear, so that even when they are operating far from their bases they will feel that they have not lost contact with their homes, and know the meaning of their own struggle in relation to other military campaigns going on throughout the country. With the help of the field radio, this has become possible.

The fighting partisans have their own papers. *The Firing Line* (Huohsien Pao) and *Struggle* (Chantou Pao). In the rear, the newspaper serves as the contact between the Government and people. The weekly *Border Government Guide* (Piencheng Tao Pao) communicates the decisions, decrees, and appeals of the Government to the population. *Resist the Enemy* (Kangti Pao) is the oldest and most popular newspaper in the area. Its circulation is 2,500 copies. Recently a new paper has been set up, the *New North China Daily* (Hsin Huapei Jihpao), which will operate on an even larger scale.

Each newspaper tries to enlist hundreds of correspondents from the ranks of the various National Salvation Societies and partisan units. These correspondents, not casual visitors but men and women familiar with every detail of their territory, give accounts of the work of the people and criticize the local administrations. They are the voice of the people to whom they belong. By comparing the reports of its local correspondents with those of the administration, the leaders of the area can tell where fine words have taken the place of action, where organization is deficient and the interests of the population are not fully taken into account. In this way, reports in *Resist the Enemy* led to the remedying of many defects in the administration of West Hopei.

Despite the fact that the Japanese have placed printing materials on the list of prohibited goods which may not be moved out of the occupied territories because they are "of military use to the enemy," *Resist the Enemy* managed to secure a number of presses and a sufficiency of lead type, as well as several months' supply of newsprint. In addition to the paper (three times a week), it now publishes a fortnightly magazine in Central Hopei. On its staff are journalists from Peiping and Tientsin. Indicative of the importance attached to the work of the Press, newspaper-men and printers receive the highest wage paid in the area — $20 a month (the members of the Government draw only $18). Each issue of the *Resist the Enemy* and *The Border Government Guide* is eagerly awaited by the population and is speedily delivered by couriers to the remotest sections of the area. Pingshan, 100 miles from Wutaishan, over trackless mountainous country, receives its *Guide* after only three days. Copies of the Border Area newspapers are eagerly sought for, carefully read, and reproduced for further circulation by patriotic Chinese in the occupied territories — where large numbers are smuggled.

The work of education is in the hands of the Cultural Workers' N.S.A. and the Youth N.S.A., under the direction of the Government's Education Department, headed by Liu Tien-chi, head of the Border Kuomintang. In the area, there are no less than 20,000 lower primary schools, a number of senior primary schools, the Anti-Japanese Training Academy, and the National Revolutionary Middle School at Wutai. The teachers in the thousands of village schools are young men and girls who see their work among the children as a part of the national struggle, not simply a means of filling their rice-bowls. The old parrot-like, sing-song repetition of the classics which once filled the air around the typical dark, hovel-like village schoolroom has now disappeared. So has the decayed scholar who ruled his pupils with a rod of iron, although many of the old primary schools teachers have been re-trained and continue their work. Education is now free, and the poorest can go to school. As a result of this, the number of school-children in the area has more than doubled since the advent of the Border Government.

The curriculum is simple — consisting of reading, writing, arithmetic, "talks on the national crisis" and "general knowledge in national defence". Textbooks are mimeographed, competently illustrated by artist members of the Cultural Workers' N.S.A. Elementary readers consisted not of "I am a little boy, you are a little girl" phrases, but of short stories entitled: "Why Japan Fights China", "Good Men Go to the Front", "Comfort Our Wounded Warriors". In arithmetic the children do not count in abstract figures, but thus: "Four Manchurian provinces plus five North China provinces make nine of our provinces invaded by the enemy." Most of the studies take place in the open air and are combined with games. When the pupils are taught the subject of self-defence, they take little swords and do sentry duty around the village. Soldiers are often quartered in the schools. The children make friends with them, bring them water and towels, and learn in practice how to achieve "Co-operation between the army and the people". Patriotism is not taught by abstract lectures. The children are told stories of heroes of the anti-Japanese, and in particular of their own Border Area. The essays they are asked to write must deal with concrete problems. "How Our Fighters Took Pingshan", "Why We Must Produce a Bigger Crop". During the sowing and harvesting campaigns, the children work in the fields with their teacher at their head. Like their elders, they do their part in the work of resistance and reconstruction. A little boy spotting a stranger will ask him for his passport.

In the Border Area, not only do adults teach children, but children teach adults. Primary school pupils conduct reading classes for illiterate peasants. At noon, one can see scores of boys and girls pouring out into the fields where the men are resting from their morning's work. They carry small blackboards under their arms and chalk in their pockets. They give short talks, each one to a group of from five to fifteen men, lead the peasants in mass singing, and teach them a few characters every day. Both the men and their little teachers are serious in their attention to the business in hand. At the same time, there is an intimate atmosphere and much joking. The men look proudly at these boys and girls who have grown up before their eyes. This is the "Little Teacher System", which has already achieved a great increase in literacy among the inhabitants' of the area.

Throughout the area there are classes organized by the Peasants', Workers', Women's, and Youth National Salvation Association for their own members.

Hundreds of thousands of men, women, and children are learning — and it is recognized that the duty of everyone who has improved his knowledge is to hand it on to others. A teachers' training school has been established at Wutai. Medical organization in the area is better than it was before the war. There are several large hospitals for wounded fighters. Every effort is made to relieve the shortage of medical supplies, and risky expeditions to Peiping and Tientsin are undertaken to buy what is needed. The wounded partisans are given every possible care. Delegations from people's organizations visit them constantly. Women come to nurse them, teachers to instruct the convalescents, youth groups to present plays for their entertainment. They are kept in the hospitals until thoroughly recovered. "We patiently strive for full recovery so that we can again fight the enemy," is the slogan of the Wutaishan hospital. Here the noted Canadian surgeon, Dr. Norman Bethune,* works with a number of Chinese doctors. He is a world authority on blood-transfusion techniques, and before coming to China saved the lives of many fighters for freedom on the battlefields of Spain. To the wounded partisans, he has given all his efforts and much of his own blood. In this, he is only following the example of self-sacrificing labour set by the entire medical service of the Border Government. The fighters of the Border Area know that if they are wounded, they will not be abandoned. They know that they will be surrounded by the care of the entire population until they regain their strength. The soldier of the old war-lord armies avoided fighting and robbed the people not because he was naturally a coward or a brigand. He did it because he was a wanderer on the face of the earth, with every man's hand against him. His officers robbed him. He robbed the people. If he did not take care of himself, no one would do it for him. If he was wounded, he would be left to die. But the partisans of the Border Area are fighters of the people. They are fighting for something of their own, something which they, in

---

* Dr. Bethune and Miss Jane Ewen, a nurse from the Medical Mission of the American and Canadian Leagues for Peace and Democracy. The International Peace Campaign undertook, early in 1939, to sponsor the Wutaishan hospital as the "International Peace Hospital", and the China Campaign Committee, through the China Defence League, has contributed to its support.

common with the whole people, have created. They have no worry about their families, no fear of abandonment if they should be hit. They protect the people, and they know that the people will stand guard over them and theirs when it is their turn to need protection.

We may end our survey of the institutions of the Border Area with an account of the people's military organizations which form the reserve and auxiliary power of the partisan armies.

The immediate reserve is made up of the "Principal Self-Defence Detachments" established in every district. These formations are made up of the strongest and most capable young peasants, workers, and students. They spend all their time in physical drill and military training. Their function is that of a territorial army, and they are responsible for local defence. They are not, however, called upon to participate in campaigns in districts other than their own.

The second line of reserves is the "People's Self-Defence Army", a mass military organization to which all men between twenty-five and forty-five years of age may belong. The training of these men does not interfere with their regular pursuits, and they wear no uniforms. They are called upon chiefly to perform auxiliary duties, but are trained in the use of arms and fight when their homes are attacked. The "Young Men's Anti-Japanese Vanguard", comprising men between the ages of fifteen and twenty-five, also receive similar training. They are more active, however, than the "Self-Defence Army", and from their ranks come the most active political and military organizers in the villages.

Of the auxiliaries, the most important are the "secret partisans". These wear no uniforms, carry concealed arms, and operate in small groups of three or five. They slip into the Japanese-occupied territories to do secret-service work and execute and arrest traitors — demoralizing the puppet officials and demonstrating to the people that resistance goes on. When the partisans are forced to withdraw from any area, numbers of these small units are left behind to organize the population for revolt. When the partisans approach to recapture such an area, the "secret partisans" become active, embarrassing the enemy's rear.

Participation in the auxiliary and reserve defence formations is purely voluntary, yet they embrace the larger part of the population. Not to belong to any of them is to brave the censure of public opinion in the towns and villages. The nature of the help they give to the partisan armies has been discussed in our account of the activities of the Peasants', Workers', and Youth National Salvation Union, with which their membership is to a large extent coincidental.

The Kuomintang and the Communist Party each have their local organizations in the area and co-operate in all respects.

As a result of the consolidation of Chinese authority in the Border Area, the Central Government decided, last summer, to appoint a new governor of Hopei province, lying wholly in the rear of the enemy. General Lu Chung-lin, a veteran army commander who was named for the post, set out from Hankow, slipped through the Japanese lines, and eventually arrived at his destination.

Before reaching Hopei, General Lu and his entourage of newly-appointed officials of the Hopei Kuomintang passed through Eighth Route Army territory in South-east Shansi. Here a great welcome meeting was held on August 20. The speeches at this meeting were indicative of the reality and strength of the United Front.*

"Comrades," said Peng Teh-huai, vice-commander of the Eighth Route Army to the massed throngs of partisans and people's representatives who attended the outdoor rally, "let us welcome Lu Chung-lin, chairman of Hopei, commander-in-chief of the Eighth Partisan War Zone, and chief secretary of the Hopei Kuomintang. Let us also welcome the Hopei Kuomintang Committee and the new head of the political department, Sun Pai-hsin. General Lu was a commander in the national revolutionary campaigns of 1925-7, when our two parties fought together against the Northern militarists. Let us now carry on in the spirit manifested at that time.

"For long years, as a result of Japanese pressure, the Kuomintang has not been able to work openly in Hopei. The Communist Party has been compelled to work underground for a much longer period. Now our parties have united for common struggle against the enemy. Only if we fight and shed our blood together can we build a strong democratic China.

---

* Speeches condensed from an eye-witness report in *Wen Hsien*, November 1938.

"Knowing that the United Front is growing stronger and that it forms the chief obstacle to their plans, the Japanese are trying to stir up dissension between our parties. We must give them no opportunity to do this. Let us say clearly who to-day are our friends and who our enemies. Whoever fights the invaders, no matter to what class of party he belongs, is our friend. Whoever talks of capitulation or seeks to break up our unity is our enemy.

"There are petty people of all kinds who do not understand the United Front. They think that the progress of the Kuomintang will be detrimental to the Communist Party, or that the enlargement of our party will hurt the Kuomintang. But in reality each party has a contribution to make to the struggle in which victory means victory for both, defeat — extinction for both. I heartily hope that the Kuomintang in Hopei will enlarge its organization and admit thousands upon thousands of new members to add to our common fighting strength.

"Let us remember the decisions of the First Kuomintang Congress, held fifteen years ago. We can now resume our co-operation for the carrying out of these decisions, which have been neglected for a decade. The honest completion of the task will be sufficient to win the war.

"In Hopei, we must work together to achieve democratic reconstruction, the mobilization of all the people, true wartime education, and the improvement of the people's livelihood. 'Resist the enemy' is our central slogan, and to it everything else must be subservient. Our two parties should work with each other, and help each other by pooling their experience and offering constructive criticism.

"Build up the North China defence line in the rear of the enemy! Prepare the base from which we can advance to the reoccupation of our lost territories! We welcome General Lu, the members of the provincial Kuomintang, the new headquarters of the Eighth Partisan Area, and the new Hopei Peace Preservation Headquarters. But our welcome must not be expressed in words alone but in action. Let us continue our fighting resistance. Let us strengthen the anti-Japanese United Front throughout North China."

General Lu Chung-lin replied:

"Many people still misunderstand the United Front. They are afraid of working together with the Communists. But here we have come, as officials of the Kuomintang, to take up our posts in large tracts of territory recaptured from the enemy under the direction of the Communist Party. We see that their party has won the full support of the people. This proves that its methods are correct, and that our former suspicions were unfounded.

"The Japanese militarists have invaded China. It is clear that everyone must assist in the struggle to repel them. Only in this way can we win the final victory. To-day, we have achieved unity. All parties are working and fighting together. This is not empty shouting. It is a fact.

"The enemy fights us not only with airplanes, tanks, and heavy guns. What he fears most is our unity, and he tries to stir up dissension among us. But these efforts are useless. We refuse to be either terrorized or misled. With every day our unity grows."

Han Mei-hsin, an official of the Hopei Kuomintang, spoke on behalf of his party organization:

"Since we have come here we have seen Kuomintang and Communist comrades working harmoniously and self-sacrificingly for the national cause. As a Kuomintang member, I salute the revolutionary comrades of the Communist Party.

"If China perishes, no party can continue to exist. To defeat Japan is our common responsibility. We are allies. In war, to strengthen an ally is to strengthen one's self. Those who forget this are consciously or unconsciously helping the enemy intrigues to break up the anti-Japanese United Front and secure our defeat.

"I agree with Commander Peng Teh-huai that we must co-operate in the spirit of the First Kuomintang Congress. Our responsibility is not only to defeat Japanese imperialism. We also have the common responsibility to build a new, strong, democratic China. We know that our victory in this war cannot be achieved in a short time. Victory in the battle for national reconstruction requires an even longer time. Therefore I say that the co-operation between our two parties must be long-term co-operation.

"We have seen, that in North China, real co-operation between the Kuomintang and Communist Party has been achieved. Let us work faithfully together, correct each other's shortcomings, and give all our strength to the fight for victory."

General Lu Chung-lin reached his post shortly afterwards. Meanwhile, the authority of the Border Government continued to spread. We have seen that spirits were high among the partisans. Let us now see how, in spite of strict Japanese censorship, the situation looked to a British newspaper editor in the occupied city of Tientsin:

"In my opinion", wrote Mr. W. V. Pennell in September, "the position of the Japanese is worse on all counts than it was before the military operations began... On all sides, the attempt to secure a solution of 'the Northern problem' by armed force has failed. That is as plain as a pikestaff. It literally hits one in the face.

"The pro-Japanese Governments have been a terrible disappointment. Their prestige is negligible, so negligible that they are now completely ignored by the common people.... The only people talked about nowadays are the Reds and the Guerrillas and the Hopei Governor Lu Chung-lin whose writ runs virtually throughout this province, all the way from the Yellow River to the Great Wall Passes in East Hopei."

"The Great Wall Passes in East Hopei" lead to Manchuria. Sometime in the autumn of 1938, the partisans marched through them and established contact with the volunteer armies which had been defying the Japanese there for seven years. In November, a new border military zone was established, at the meeting-place of the boundaries of Hopei, Jehol, and Liaoning. Shortly afterwards a large body of partisans, led by a detachment from the Eighth Route Army, actually appeared near Mukden, where two divisions of Japanese troops were hastily ordered out to keep them at bay.

In early January of this year, the Central Government took official cognizance of the recapture of new territories and the re-establishment of contact with the lost lands of Manchuria. It appointed General Shih Yu-san to be chairman of Chahar. And it revived the Manchurian provincial governments of Jehol, Liaoning, Kirin, and Heilungkiang — extinct since 1932.

Such were the services of the fighting democracy of the Shansi-Chahar-Hopei Border Area to the cause of China's national liberation in the course of fifteen months of its existence.

CHAPTER XI

New Fourth Army

W HEN the Chinese Red Army set out on its 8,000-mile "Long March" from Southern China to the far North-west, it left a number of detachments behind it in the provinces of Fukien, Kiangsi, and Anhwei. These detachments were too small to retain control of any significant portion of the former Soviet territory. Their function was to force the kernel of a new movement and to keep alive the revolutionary traditions of the people. Split up into small guerrilla units based on inaccessible mountain areas along the provincial borders, these groups of hardy fighters kept the flag of the Chinese Soviets flying at many widely-scattered points in the South-eastern and Central provinces of China.

Then the Marco Polo Bridge "incident" plunged China and Japan into open war. The Communist Party was officially recognized as an ally of the Kuomintang in the struggle against the invading enemy. The Chinese Red Army, which for years had been offering to make common cause with any armed force undertaking operations against the Japanese, placed itself under the orders of the commander-in-chief of all China's armies and became the Eighth Route National-Revolutionary Army of the Central Government. Orders were given that the Red partisans in the South-east and in Northern Hupeh should also be incorporated in the military system of the united country.

Coming down from their fastnesses, they assembled at various points for reorganization and training.

It was hard to concentrate the 15,000 partisans who had been operating in small groups in the hilly regions flanking the Yangtze valley. Many were inaccessible, and it took time for the tidings of the new United Front and the orders of the Government to reach them. In some cases, the provincial military authorities pounced on them when they came down from the mountains for reorganization, and, unable to believe that the era of civil war was over, confiscated their arms. Some of the partisan units themselves had long been out of touch with the world and could not understand the new line of their party. It was January before their forces were finally concentrated* and the creation of the New Fourth Army was decreed by the National Military Council of the Chinese Republic.

General Yeh Ting, one of the outstanding commanders of the famous "Ironsides" who fought in the national revolutionary campaigns of 1925-27, was appointed commander of the new army. Although he took part in the revolts which finally led to the creation of the Red Army, General Yeh is not a member of the Communist Party. During the ten years previous to the outbreak of the Sino-Japanese war, he lived in retirement. On the other hand, Hsiang Ying, a worker, who was appointed vice-commander of the army, had a record of party activity dating back to the great Peking-Hankow railway strike of 1923, had been vice-chairman of the Soviet Government, and was the most important of the Communist leaders left behind in South China when the Red Army commenced its great march to the North-west.

In January 1938, I interviewed General Yeh Ting in Hankow. Ironically enough, his headquarters was located in a former Japanese residence, the

---

* The following forces were incorporated into the New Fourth: 2,000 men under Chang Ting-cheng, from West Fukien; 1,500 men from South Kiangsi, under Chen Yi, ex-chairman of the Kiangsi Regional Soviet; 1,200 men from East Hunan, under Fu Chiao-tao, a former subordinate of Ho Lung; 2,000 men from the Chekiang-Fukien border, under Lia Ying; 4,300-5,000 men from North Hupeh, under Kao Chung-ting, ex-chairman of the Anhwei-Hupeh-Honan Soviet Government. All had maintained small Soviet areas. (Information from personal interview with Yeh Ting.)

floor was covered with *tatami* matting, and a charcoal brazier ineffectually fought the damp chill of the Yangtze winter. A smooth-faced, vivacious, thick-set Cantonese, noted for his spectacular personal courage, General Yeh marched up and down the room as he described the importance and nature of the new military force:

"Our men are old fighters, used to hardship. They are accustomed to facing tremendous odds in equipment and arms. During the past few years they have often gone without food, sometimes living for days on grass. But under all circumstances they have known how to retain their close contact with the people. That is the secret of their survival.

"The New Fourth Army is being organized as a mobile force designed to carry on partisan warfare on the banks of the Yangtze. The men are now gathering here for training and co-ordination before taking the field. As a military force, the New Fourth Army has no connection whatever with the Eighth Route Army. Both are under the direct control of the National Military Commission. But, of course, many of our commanders and rank and file are linked with those of the Eighth Route through common membership in the Communist Party."

During the early spring, one could occasionally see small units of the new army marching through the streets of Hankow. The men were weather-beaten, bare-footed, and bare-kneed, and they walked fast, with the swinging stride of the mountain warrior the world over. Their grey, coolie-cloth uniforms bore no insignia. As they marched, they shouted slogans or sang.

At the beginning of May, when the Japanese were converging on Hauchow, the New Fourth Army was assigned an area of operations in Eastern Anhwei, both north and south of the Yangtze River. It was limited to this area, which was a small part of the South-eastern or Third War Zone, under the command of General Ku Chu-tung. While the region north of the Yangtze is mountainous and well suited to guerrilla warfare, the part of Anhwei south of the great river is a flat dissected plain, studded with lakes and criss-crossed by waterways. This is difficult country for partisan fighters. It offers few natural hiding-places, and the flat terrain makes it possible for the Japanese, with their motor-boats and mechanized land transport, to go practically where they please. From their airplanes, they can spot and destroy any obvious concentration of partisans, spy out their bases, and harry them incessantly. Seventy per cent of the strength of the Fourth Route Army is concentrated in this risky region. Here the army has established its main bases, training-schools, and hospitals, and here it has engaged the enemy in at least one battle a day during the past year in a constant struggle which has often brought it within sight and earshot of the great cities of Shanghai and Nanking.

Unlike the Eighth Route Army, which numbers hundreds of thousands of men and operates mainly in areas which it has recaptured from the Japanese, the New Fourth Army must function within a definite allotted territory, under military and civil administrations which were there before it arrived on the scene. In many parts of North China, the Eighth Route Army and the partisan armies which have formed themselves around it operate alone. The New Fourth Army is one of several military forces in the Eastern War Zone. It must de-pend upon the War Zone headquarters for its general orders, finances, and supplies. It has not the freedom of the Northern partisan armies with regard to recruiting. Moreover, in its campaign for popular support, it cannot carry out democratic administrative reforms or decree the reduction of the rent and tax burdens borne by the people, as was done by the Border Government. The New Fourth Army shows the people, by instruction and example, how the Japanese can be fought, it teaches them how to increase and improve their crop yield, and it gives them free medical service. Where rents and usury have been excessive, and the landlords and money-lenders have re-fused to reduce them, the army has encouraged the Peasants' Anti-Japanese Association to institute rent-strikes,* on the ground that the rich are not bear-ing their just share of the burden of war, which should fall equally on all classes.

All visitors to the New Fourth, both Chinese and foreign, have reported

---

* Jack Belden, in his series of articles on the New Fourth Army in the *Shanghai Evening Post* mentions such a case.

that these activities have won for the army the wholehearted support of the people. But democratic reforms, mass organization, war-time education, and the people's participation in the struggle are all at a less advanced stage than in the Shansi-Chahar-Hopei Border Area, which is a model of what can be achieved with the real carrying out of the slogan of united struggle against the enemy.

The limitations imposed on the natural spread of democratic anti-Japanese mass organization in the Eastern War Zone are responsible for the persistence of a serious problem — the problem of banditry, which was settled so early and so successfully in the North. After the main battlefields of the war had shifted westwards, there remained in the lower Yangtze valley a great number of semi-gangster "partisan" bands, which were often in the pay of the Japanese, occasionally fought against them, but inevitably preyed upon the people. The New Fourth Army found that to win the people's confidence, it had immediately to do something about this problem. In the early months after it began operations, it launched a number of simultaneous attacks against the bandits and the Japanese. Like the Eighth Route Army in the North, it began also to try to split the ranks of the bandits and win over the rank and file by political means. But the New Fourth Army achieved little success in this work, mainly because of the lack of universal mass organization, but also as a result of the fact that the robber bands of the lower Yangtze were often not simply large formations of disbanded soldiers, as in the North, but small, compact gangs led by racketeers from the big cities. Within its own area, the army quickly succeeded in suppressing or driving out such gangs. But in other parts of the Eastern War Zone, banditry continues to flourish.

Within the units, there were also many difficulties. "One of our greatest successes", General Yeh Ting said to me when I saw him again a year after our first interview, "was the welding of the partisan groups into one united army. Our men had for years been fighting in small detachments which were run on a purely democratic basis. Everyone knew everyone else, plans were discussed in common, and there was practically no formal discipline. In the New Fourth Army, the partisans had to recognize different degrees of authority in people they did not know and to obey their orders. Their daily life was subject to strict military routine, something they had not been accustomed to before. Most of the men were peasants, to whom the whole conception of large-scale organization was foreign. Among the old fighters, many were found who objected to these 'infringements of democracy'.

"To cope with this, we started a campaign of political propaganda and education throughout the army, from top to bottom. Our political workers explained to every fighter that the transition from the small-scale partisan tactics of the last years of civil war to the formation of large anti-Japanese mobile armies was a progressive step in our national revolution, and that it was their revolutionary duty to adapt themselves to this new organizational form. These methods were very successful. Our discipline is not mechanical and arbitrary. It is voluntary discipline, based on the national consciousness and class consciousness of our fighters.

"Nevertheless," he said, "it is not true to say that we have completely overcome the psychology of the old partisan period. We still have our problems."

When I asked him for more details of these problems, and of how they were being tackled, Yeh Ting looked at me and smiled.

"Did you see the film, 'Chapayev'?" he asked. "Well, that is how we do it too."

All units of the New Fourth, from the company up, have their political directors (commissars) or political departments. The system followed is the same as that of the Eighth Route Army and the partisan armies in the North. The political commissar is the organizer and educator of the unit to which he is attached. It is his responsibility to see that the unit is a conscious and healthy fighting organism. He has the right of control not only over the men but over the commander, and tactical decisions are never made without his participation. He has not only great powers, but also great responsibilities. Once a plan is decided upon, the military commander gives the orders. The political commissar is answerable for the execution, and must take the lead in carrying them out.

Jack Belden, a well-known American war correspondent, thus describes the beginning of a typical New Fourth Army attack:

"The company commander snaps an order. The political director takes out his Mauser and shouts, 'Follow me.' Then he starts at a full run forward. The soldiers come after him...."

Why do political commissars participate in military decisions? Hsiang Ying, himself not a military man, but a worker and labour union organizer, told Jack Belden:

"Revolutionaries in their work learn tactics and strategy similar to the tactics and strategy used in military operations. Therefore a good political strategist may make a good military strategist. Technicians, on the other hand, work only within certain limits and cannot be real strategists. But a political man learns military strategy quickly, though he must learn from the technician the use of infantry and artillery.

"Because we are a revolutionary army, our leaders feel their responsibility and are anxious to do their duty, and will therefore use all their energy to accomplish their tasks. This is the reason why graduates of military schools are not so skilful as we. They act according to plan and feel that the plan is responsible, not that they themselves are responsible."

According to Yeh Ting, while 90 per cent of the officers in other Government armies originate from well-to-do and intellectual groups of the population, fully 70 per cent of the commanders and political commissars of the New Fourth Army are workers and peasants. This is the chief reason why, in the New Fourth Army, fighters and commanders find no difficulty in living on the same scale. Pay in the Army ranges from $1.50 to $5.00 a month. All ranks receive ten cents a day for food. In the $5.00 category, besides the highest command, are a number of Japanese prisoners working in the Army's Propaganda Department.

The Army receives a very meagre financial allowance from the Government. "If we were to be treated equally with other armies", said Yeh

Ting, "we would receive double or treble the amount which comes to us now. It is only because our Army is based on the toiling population that we can make ends meet. The appropriation only covers the cost of our food and part of our equipment. The budgets for political work, field and rear hospitals, and education, we cover ourselves." Since the New Fourth Army has no direct contact with the local civil administration and does not receive any share of its revenue, the funds for its special services must come from the voluntary contributions of the rank and file, and from sympathizers throughout China and in foreign countries. The aggregate of all these contributions is very small.

There is no conscription. Enlistment in the Army is voluntary. Many applicants are rejected because they belong to other armies, because they come from areas other than those from which the Central Government has authorized the Army to accept recruits, or because the Army is not sure that they are enlisting as the result of a genuine desire to drive the Japanese out of China. Recruits are given a thorough medical examination before being allowed to join. If they are found to be unfit, they are given work which their physical condition will allow them to do.

Every New Fourth Army fighter is educated to understand the aims of the anti-Japanese struggle and never to forget that he is fighting for the people.

Jack Belden has translated into English the rules and regulations which fighters in the Army are expected to obey, and which he was convinced from personal observation that they do obey. Of the three basic rules of the army the first is: "Fight against the Japanese to the last. There must be no surrender to the enemy and no compromise with him." The second enjoins obedience to orders. The third stresses that all fighters of the New Fourth must love the people and respect their interests and feelings as they would their own.

Six regulations state that the men must guard and care for their weapons, be careful of furniture and crockery in houses in which they are billeted, and be active, orderly, clean, and polite.

Ten "points of conduct", which the New Fourth, like the Eighth Route Army, has inherited from the Red Army, deal with personal behaviour and relations with the people.

"1. When you leave a civilian's house, put the doors (which have been used for beds) back in the right place. Put things in order and bind the straw (bedding) into a bundle, and send it back to the people you borrowed it from;

2. Sweep the floor clean;

3. Speak kindly, don't shout;

4. When you buy something, give the normal price. Don't haggle.

5. Return whatever you have borrowed from the people;

6. If you break something which you have borrowed, you must pay the owner;

7. When you wish to relieve yourself, you must use the toilet;

8. When bathing, avoid letting the women see you;

9. Engage in propaganda work everywhere, both in and out of the ranks;

10. Don't kill captives."

The last point is considered very important. A man violating it may be shot. All the fighters are taught Japanese slogans to shout to the enemy in the hope that they will surrender. These slogans state that the Chinese and Japanese peoples are brothers, that the Japanese militarists are the enemy of both, and that prisoners will not be harmed. There are a number of Japanese captives in the hands of the New Fourth Army. They are treated well, and given more pay and privileges than many of the army's members. Some of them are engaged in turning out written propaganda materials and letters in Japanese telling their compatriots not to fight the Chinese people.

We have dealt briefly with the origin, formation, tasks, difficulties and training of the New Fourth Army. Let us see now how the Army fights and what it has accomplished during the nine months' career as an active anti-Japanese partisan force.

Having completed its training, the New Fourth Army, now organized into four divisions designated by the characters for Unity, Forward, Daring, and Resistance, left its base at Yinshui, Western Anhwei, on April 27, 1938, and moved towards the front. On May 10, it arrived at Nanling. On May 16, it had its first encounters with the Japanese when it filtered, in small units, through their lines along the Nanking-Wuhu railway. This was easy to do. The Yangtze garrisons had been depleted to provide troops for the major operations going on around Hsuchow, and the Japanese were occupying only the larger towns, leaving cavalry and armoured cars to patrol the tracts of road and railway between them. When the New Fourth Army penetrated into the vicinity of Nanking, the Japanese were not even aware of its presence, and it was only when the plain-clothes men of the Army penetrated into the fallen capital itself and placarded its walls with posters that they realized they were faced with a new and formidable menace to their occupation of the area.

From May 16 onwards, the record of the New Fourth Army was one constant activity, featured by daily skirmishes with the enemy and ceaseless political work among the people. The areas around Nanking and Wuhu had been subjected to indescribable devastation. Their people had suffered the worst excesses of the Japanese and the depredations of bandit gangs which scoured the countryside like wolves. They wanted only to be left alone, and the sight of a uniform, of whatever kind, meant nothing to them but woe. It took the New Fourth Army time to persuade the people that its ways were different; that it had really come to fight for them and to teach them to fight for themselves. It convinced them of this not by words, but by actions. When one of its units approached a village, it did not bluster in, bristling with rifles, to demand food, shelter, and men for labour. It avoided the tragic conflicts which arise so often in China between the fighters of her armies, who come into the village exhausted, battle-worn, and hungry, and the people who lock their gates against them because their food too is limited, because it is a case of either the soldiers going hungry or they themselves starving. When the New Fourth Army came to a village, it sent one man forward to talk with the people, and the man went unarmed. It promised to pay for everything it needed, and it kept its promise. When the people brought the commanders presents of pigs and chickens, they found, to their surprise, that these presents were refused. Instead, the army bought food, and invited the peasants to banquets, at which its leaders asked them if they had any complaint to make of the

THE NEW FOURTH ARMY ATTACKS A TRAIN ON THE SHANGHAI-NANKING LINE

army's behaviour. They, the people, were the masters, and the New Fourth Army was responsible to them and acknowledged its responsibility.

From sporadic clashes with the Japanese, the New Fourth Army proceeded to systematic attacks on their lines of communication and destruction of their equipment. Between May and October, it set itself the special problem of impeding the great Japanese advance towards Hankow. I have before me as I write, a mimeographed rice-paper booklet, with a black- and-white drawing of a partisan on the cover. This is the official report published by the New Fourth Army Headquarters for these months. On its first page, there is a statistical table summarizing the military activities of the army between May 16 and September 27, 1938, based on the reports of individual units.

Three points stand out from this table. The first is that the partisans of the New Fourth harass the enemy ceaselessly and unrelentingly. Yeh Ting had told me that the Army participated in an action practically every day. The table bears him out. In the 130 days under review, there were 108 clashes with the enemy.*

The second point is that, as the fighting was confined to skirmishes along the lines of communication, the casualties on both sides were relatively small. Moreover, as a result of the New Fourth Army's tactics of ambush and surprise, its own losses were far less than those of the Japanese. The table states that during the four months under review 892 Japanese were killed and 583 wounded. The partisan losses are given as little more than a tenth of this number.

In the light of the fact that foreign military observers have stated their conviction that this was the true proportion of losses in partisan warfare in the North, there seems no reason to doubt that the New Fourth Army, with similar tactics, has achieved similar results.

The third point, and the most important, emerges from the figures given of the enemy's material losses. These figures show conclusively that the value of guerrilla warfare against a modern mechanized force lies not only in the number of human casualties it can inflict, but in the extent to which it can

---

* Before the end of the year, this number had grown to 170.

destroy the enemy's expensive equipment, nullify the conditions which make it possible for him to take advantage of his superior mechanical power, and generally frustrate every attempt of a force victorious in formal warfare to assert effective control over the territory it has "won". From May to September 1938, the New Fourth Army destroyed two enemy trains, 120 trucks and staff cars, and six launches. It blew up sixty-four bridges, tore up more than five miles of railway track, and destroyed fifty miles of highway. It captured 1,281 rifles, 47,000 rounds of ammunition, large sums of money, many truckloads of military supplies, and 590 Japanese and "puppet" prisoners. By December, Jack Belden was reporting that officers at the New Fourth Headquarters claimed the destruction of 150 trucks north of the Yangtze alone, while Yeh Ting, whom I interviewed in January, gave the number of rifles captured as 3,000.

The record of the individual detachments is impressive. The Unity division, for instance, destroyed nine highway bridges near Nanking between July 11 and 16. On July 30, it routed and disarmed a force of Japanese-paid police at Kaochih and dynamited a section of the Shanghai-Nanking railway, causing all traffic between Chinkiang and Tanyang to be suspended for ten days. On August 12, in one of the few direct attacks made by the army on a fortified Japanese stronghold, it entered Chuyung, a town situated a short distance from Nanking, and on August 24 it reached the Ginling gate, three miles south of the city, retreating only when a force of twenty tanks was sent out against it. On the following day it first blew up a section of the highway, then attacked again and destroyed the small group of Japanese army engineers sent to repair it. The subsequent history of the division was characterized by the same ceaseless activity. Of the 108 skirmishes reported by units of the New Fourth between May and October, the "Unity" division fought forty-eight.

During the month of August alone, the men of the "Forward" division derailed a military train, sank a number of steam launches, and forced a punitive column of 2,000 Japanese troops to return to its base without having fulfilled its mission. In the area where it operated, the Japanese had cut down all the crops and set fire to every village within sight of the railway to eliminate any possibility of partisan attacks on the line. While carrying out this "civilizing" measure, they shot hundreds of peasants and raped their women. The "Forward" division helped the enraged people to organize themselves so that they could strike back at the enemy. Foreign visitors to the New Fourth report that the peasants said to them: "Formerly, two or three Japanese soldiers could come into a village and demand, and receive, women. Now they don't dare to approach, except in large numbers with machine-guns, and even then we give them such a hot reception that their visits are far more rare than they were. When a small force of Japanese approaches, the peasant self-defence units call up their full strength and surround them. If the enemy force is large, the peasant partisans split up into small groups and divert its attention to give the village population a chance to flee to safety and remove all food and personal belongings."

A part of the "Resistance" Division operates north of the Yangtze. On September 15, it dynamited a number of Japanese tanks on the Anking-Hofei highway. On the next day it again held up a long convoy of supply trucks, destroying forty of them. The success of the New Fourth Army in disrupting road communications between Anking and Hofei and Hofei and Huangmei had the effect of slowing down for weeks the operations of the right flank of the Japanese forces advancing towards Hankow.

A high officer of one of the auxiliary services of the New Fourth Army who recently visited Hongkong* thus summarized the results of the nine-month activity of the New Fourth Army on the lower Yangtze:

"In the first place, the presence of a strong and well-organized army ready to strike at any weak point in the Japanese defences has forced the invaders to station major forces along their lines of communication, as well as at strategically vulnerable points. These are the forces which would otherwise be available for west-ward penetration along the Chekiang-Kiangsi railway. In the second place, wherever the army extends its activities, the local villagers and townspeople are trained and organized into self-defence

---

* Surgeon-General Sheng, head of the Medical Department.

bodies which carry out a census and other measures which make it impossible for any renegade to come spying into these regions. Moreover, where local opinion has been brought to wholeheartedly support the struggle against the invaders, the Japanese find it increasingly difficult to form puppet governments in the places which they succeed in capturing, for the simple reason that the village elders and propertied classes would lose the leadership of their communities if they subscribed to the Japanese schemes. Thus, although a region may be occupied, it can never be politically consolidated. In the third place, the army also takes on itself the task of leading the population in matters of culture and health. The Political Departments of the various divisions see to it that the cultural level of the people is raised. Schools are established and illiteracy is combated with a vigour surpassing that of the old days. The Army Medical Service not only establishes hospitals for the sick and wounded, but also promotes health movements among the people.

"A partisan force cannot operate effectively in a region where the population is allowed to lead an ignorant and passive existence. To raise the cultural level of the general population is to strengthen the fighting power on which we depend for final victory. Finally, the courage with which our fighters carry on the struggle and their ability to steal victories from the invaders in spite of long suffering and hardship have won the intense admiration of other troops stationed in the neighbouring areas. We have created a model army from which other armies draw their inspiration, and thus have actually caused an improvement in their fighting qualities. The value of such 'competition' and comparison cannot be over-estimated."

The New Fourth Army is, in a very real sense, an army of the United Front. Its fighting rank and file is composed mainly of former Red partisans. But its subsidiary enterprises, which account for a large measure of the army's effectiveness and have enabled it to transform the whole region in which it operates, combine all the vital elements of the new China. Of these subsidiary activities, four especially deserve our attention. The first is the network of small industries being established by the army — a result of the efforts of Shanghai workers and technicians who have trekked inland rather than stay in a place where they would be forced to sell their skill to the national enemy. The second is the army's training-school, which turns out commanders, political commissars, military engineers, and other army workers. This school is staffed not only by the New Fourth Army's own commanders, but also by progressive educators from all parts of the country. The third is the Army's Political Service Corps, the carrier of culture to the people, which is made up of young men and women, most of whom were once students in China's great cities. The fourth is the medical service. In the face of many hardships, a group of devoted doctors have created what has been described as the best military medical service in China.

The story of the army's industrial base is in itself an epic of living China. It is being built up almost literally out of nothing. In many cases, both machinery and raw materials have had to be improvised. For the production of cloth, there is only coarse, short-staple cotton, ordinarily not used for textile purposes. Metals must be collected in the form of scrap or captured from the enemy. But the co-operative workshops of the New Fourth, owned in common by those who labour in them, function nevertheless. From them, besides a variety of other commodities, the army gets its rifle ammunition, hand grenades, and land mines, and the hospitals get medical cotton, blankets, lint bandages, and some surgical instruments. The small machine-shop that turns out the latter is the pride of the New Fourth Army, which it provides with one fine new rifle a day. Doctors, desperate for vaseline (needed for sulphur ointment to treat the scabies universal among the under-fed fighters and refugees), founded a "chemical industry" which manufactures an acceptable substitute from the bean of the wax tree. Co-operative printeries produce propaganda materials, textbooks, the army newspapers *Resist the Enemy* and *Firing Line*; and *Salvation*, the organ of the people. The workers who have built these industries are real heroes of labour. They go to their shops as the fighters go to the front, knowing that they must fight the enemy's superior power with increased output and increased initiative and inventiveness. Their work forms one of the main bases of the army's munition supply, its political and educational activity, and its medical service. They are true comrades in arms of the front-line fighters of the New Fourth in the people's struggle for liberation.

Yeh Ting told me that the Field Military and Political Academy attached to the New Fourth Army's headquarters has almost 1,000 students.* These students, the future commanders and political workers of the army, include old fighters who have proved themselves in battle and are studying to acquire the theoretical basis for advancement, and new recruits from every Chinese province south of the Yangtze. More than half of the total enrolment consists of industrial workers from Shanghai. Students training for military leadership give 70 per cent of their time to tactical studies and practical exercises in the art of mobile warfare, the rest to political schooling. For those who look forward to a political career the proportion is reversed. The larger part of their efforts is given to the acquisition of a complete understanding of the aims of the Chinese revolution, the theory and practice of the United Front,** and the international political situation. But they too devote 80 per cent of their time to intensive military training. The organization of the academy is military. It is divided into nine companies, five for military and two for political cadres, one which trains engineers, and one, composed of women and adolescents ("little devils"), which prepares workers for essential services such as nursing, sanitation, and propaganda.

As in the Eighth Route Army, however, only a small part of the educational activity of the force is represented by the formal instruction in the academy. In the New Fourth Army everybody studies. The illiterates learn to read and write. Those who have already mastered the rudiments go on to

---

* Belden gives the exact number as 840.

** Belden: "Through slogans, newspaper editorials, wall posters and songs, the New Fourth Army is carrying on a strong United Front campaign in its own ranks.... They are taught that China can never attain victory without political unity, that there must be total resistance throughout the whole country, and the Communists alone cannot win the war, and finally that 'we should wish not only for our own progress but for that of every army fighting against Japan'. Membership of the New Fourth Army is not limited to any faith. Members of the Kuomintang and even downright *bourgeois* are fighting in its ranks."

more advanced study. All, whether literate or not, listen to political lectures and learn the technique of guerrilla war. And all learn a required minimum of Japanese to enable them to do propaganda among the enemy. Educational work goes on not only at the bases, but also at the front. Between skirmishes the latest news is read and ceaseless open-air classes and discussions are held.

The Army's Political Service Corps consists of 300 young men and women and some thirty children. It brightens the life of the fighters with dramatic performances and mass singing. It produces striking posters and writes wall newspapers for troops in the rear and on the march towards the front. It educates and entertains the wounded in the hospitals and carries the message of anti-Japanese struggle to the people in the form of colourful songs, narrative ballads, and one-act plays. When these forms of propaganda have aroused the interest of the people, the Political Service Corps helps to initiate mass organizations of the peasants, workers, merchants, women, and youth. The plays and songs deal with methods of struggle and organization, with the bravery of anti-Japanese fighters (usually the heroes of the army itself), the signs by which traitors may be recognized, the ways in which the army helps the people, and the ways in which the people can help the army. The art of the Political Service Corps is true art. It is close to objective reality, to the burning questions of the hour, and to the hearts of the people. It broadens understanding and leads to action. And the playwrights, singers, actors, artists, and writers of the corps find joy in their work and make really creative use of the limited technical facilities at their disposal, because they feet deeply that their activity is a part of life and of the struggle around them.

Finally there is the Medical Service, which in this partisan force is better organized than that of any other army in China. The core of the service consists of eight well-trained and experienced doctors and a number of qualified nurses from the great Central Hospital at Nanking. From this small nucleus and the miserable sum of 600 dollars which the first eight doctors brought with them has grown a medical organization which includes a base hospital at headquarters, a medical training-school, and several divisional hospitals, with an aggregate capacity of several hundred beds, laboratories which carry out blood and urine tests and microscopic examinations, a scientific dietetic kitchen, and X-ray and surgical apparatus donated by sympathizers. This result has been achieved by endless self-sacrificing work, infinite resourcefulness, and maximum utilization of the tiny budget the service is forced to work on. The hospitals are in draughty old temples, the beds are boards on trestles, the laboratories are in huts. There are no bottles — they have been improvised from hollow bamboo. Tinsmiths were mobilized to build, with primitive tools, a distilling apparatus, incubators and sterilizers.

The New Fourth Army is a people's army. It fights with and for the people, and its medical service serves not only its own needs, but those of the whole region.

Miss Agnes Smedley, now with the New Fourth writes:

"Only one hospital has wounded alone because the chief problem is sickness. The army brought the first medical service into this region, and people come carrying the sick and injured from scores of miles away. On the army itself, years of under-nourishment have left a heavy mark. I find the following chief cases in the hospitals — malaria, tuberculosis, dysentery, small-pox, stomach ulcers, leg ulcers, upper respiratory infections, scabies (90 per cent of the army has scabies), trachoma and hookworm."

The service works in conditions of extreme poverty and scarcity of the barest essentials. Dr. Sheng, the army's surgeon-general, tells the story:

"Our hospitals are established in old, disused temples. In winter, with clothing scarce and bedding, if any, rarely sufficient to protect the sick from the intense cold, a doctor's role is not to be admired. We are left helpless to watch the patients wear away or take much longer to recover because of insufficient clothing."*

This terrible scarcity is universal in the New Fourth Army. One fighter in three has a blanket. An overcoat may be the common property of a whole squad, to be used by the man on sentry duty. Food is poor. Yet in the face of these difficulties the New Fourth Army not only fights, but is transforming the whole region in which it operates, giving it new confidence, reduction of rents, the beginnings of co-operative productive organization which will in the long run allay the acute shortage of necessities, an active political and social life, education, and a health service.

Inseparable links have been forged between the people and the army. They are sharing struggle and poverty, and the beginning of democracy and reconstruction. And they are building up together on the Yangtze, on the basis of the United Front, one of those indestructible strongholds of resistance that arises everywhere where the people are fighting for themselves.

"Can you outline for me the present situation of the New Fourth Army and the prospects of partisan warfare in the Nanking-Shanghai-Hangchow area?" I asked Yeh Ting.

"We have completed our reorganization and are remedying our internal faults," he said. "If you will compare our situation with that of the other forces operating in the area, you will see that it presents a totally different picture. They are well supplied with rifles, but have difficulty in finding recruits. We have educated the people in our area and convinced them both that they have something to defend and that they can defend it successfully. Everyone wants to join our army. But we have not sufficient arms, receive an appropriation so small that it is difficult for us to make ends meet even on our present scale, and are not permitted to advance farther east than Wusih in the direction of Shanghai. Nevertheless, we have already succeeded in making ourselves a serious obstacle to the plans of the enemy.

"We still have many weaknesses which we must overcome. But what we

---

* The China Defence League, Hongkong, receives contributions for the medical service of the New Fourth.

have succeeded in achieving has proved that all the forces in the area can do much more than they have done if they base their work and organization on the principles which we apply. One of the best-financed forces of the region, for instance, is well provided with arms and equipment, but can muster only 2,000 men. The same is true of other detachments which have been unable to establish close contact with the people, and this is unfortunately a common situation in the eastern partisan area. I must say that there are detachments which are different. A former political prisoner named Liu who was released at the beginning of the war after spending eight years in jail in Nanking has succeeded in organizing between 30,000 and 40,000 peasants. Unfortunately, they have only 1,000 rifles partly picked up from the battlefields after the struggles for Shanghai and Nanking, and partly captured from the enemy. They, and another similar unit operating near Haimen, on the north side of the Yangtze, have won the confidence and co-operation of the people and are doing good work.

"The effectiveness of partisan warfare in the Nanking-Shanghai-Hangchow triangle is much less than it might be. But it is clear that even with the present situation, the Japanese cannot possibly 'pacify' the area with the forces they have stationed in it. We may therefore expect that a determined extermination campaign will be launched by them after they have gained control of the entire length of the Nanking-Changsha railway. That will be a major test both for us and for the other partisan forces in the eastern zone."

Temporarily exhausted by their campaigns against Hankow and Canton and the entire eternal search for victories which should win the war but somehow don't, the Japanese waited many months before resuming their operations along the railway. Finally, in March 1939, they took Nanchang and cut the last Chinese rail link between the hinterland and the sea. The "clean-up" campaign of which Yeh Ting spoke is now an immediate menace. Meanwhile, the New Fourth Army continues fighting and working to create a strong nucleus of popular resistance in the rear of the enemy. It is giving an example of effective struggle by which all the forces in the Eastern War Zone may benefit. And it is building up on the granite foundation of voluntary mass organization the base of the future Chinese counter-attack in the lower reaches of the Yangtze.

CHAPTER XII
Universal Resistance

WE have devoted much space to the Border Area and the New Fourth Army because they are more than examples of the will of the Chinese people to resist. While they form the spearhead and the most effective section of the great Chinese partisan movement, their significance is not for to-day alone. In the rear of the enemy, they are already building and expanding models of the democratic China of the future.

But it is not only the conscious vanguard of the future China that is resisting the Japanese. The significance and strength of the Chinese people's war and of the national United Front, the guarantee that the victory in the present struggle will belong to China, lie in the fact that nowhere has any section of her armies surrendered to the enemy. And nowhere have her people quiescently accepted the domination of the invader. Isolated, loosely linked with other armed detachments, or operating under the orders of the Central Command, mobile units of Chinese soldiers constantly harass the rear of the Japanese forces. Throughout the occupied territories, the peasantry of China, in its traditional secret societies, village defence organizations, or newly-organized armed formations, carries on the struggle against an enemy under whose rule normal existence has proved to be impossible.

Why the Japanese advance has everywhere aroused the fierce hatred and desperate opposition of the peace-loving population will be readily understood by those who have read such books as H. J. Timperley's *What War Means* and Amleto Vespa's *Secret Agent of Japan*. These books give a vivid picture of the full horror and depth of moral perversion that characterized every step of the Japanese adventure in China. Murder and rape are mass phenomena in the Japanese army not because all Japanese soldiers are beasts. They are the logical actions of men who have been brought to believe in the righteousness of the imperialist rape of a whole nation — just as the individual brutalities of Nazi pogrom-makers are logical results of the whole system of German Fascism.

Japanese looting, also, is not a fortuitous circumstance. The invasion of China was avowedly begun with the object of seizing raw materials and trade for Japan's top-heavy economy. But this economy has proved so weak that it cannot afford to take over, invest in, and develop, the country by "normal" imperialist means. It must tear from the body of China immediate profits to pay for its military adventure. So, in the captured cities, the army systematically loots scrap iron and all Chinese private property convertible into cash. In the country it "requisitions" the last grains of the peasants' rice. At the bottom of the line, individual officers and men are encouraged to fill their pockets at the expense of individual Chinese. Looting is not an offence in the Japanese army. It is the raison d'être of the army's activity.

These are incontrovertible facts, confirmed by every independent observer of the Sino-Japanese hostilities. The Japanese military expedition in China is a predatory raid in the style of Genghis Khan, carried out under modern conditions. It has proved itself to be a menace not only to the sovereignty and territorial integrity of China, but also to the safety and personal and property rights of every Chinese, old-fashioned or modern, peasant, worker, intellectual, merchant, or soldier.

Two things enable the Chinese people to resist the horror that has descended upon them. The first is the length of the Japanese battle line and the impossibility of the invader's garrisoning the territory away from their lines of communications with the small forces they have at their disposal. The second is the fact that the Chinese people throughout the country are to some extent organized and armed. The old peasant self-defence organizations, such as the "Red Spears", still survive everywhere in Central China — with an estimated 1,500,000 members in the province of Honan alone. Years of civil war have scattered rifles throughout the Chinese countryside. They have also accustomed literally millions of men to the use of firearms, through intermittent service in the provincial armies, constant conflicts between village militia and bandits, and class battles between the peasantry and the armed guards of the landlords.

Since the beginning of the war, rifles and men have been combined into militia groups which receive intensive training in all parts of the country. These, stiffened by groups of regular soldiers left behind during retreats or specially assigned for the purpose, form the backbone of guerrilla bands in every province. And the final ingredient in the typical guerrilla band, even of "Red Spears", is the political propagandist. It is a rare unit that does not have its fighting speaker or cartoonist, though he may be no more than a traditional story-teller, chanting the deeds of the band in the sing-song of the ancient martial tales. As time goes on, more modern groups of political workers tend to seek out the detachments which manage to survive the inevitable early trials, or the detachments themselves form contact with organized centres.

Let us make a rapid survey of the main partisan groups in the country, their strength and history. For convenience, we will start from Manchuria, swing through Inner Mongolia, then South and East along the Yellow River to Central China. We will also consider guerrilla activities along the Yangtze, in the vicinity of Shanghai, and in the occupied area around Canton.

Manchuria

Organized Chinese resistance in Manchuria continued from 1931 to 1933, when the last troops under Generals Ma Chan-shan, Su Pingwen, Li Tu, and Wang Teh-lin were forced across the Soviet border. During the next two years, numerous independent partisan armies waged sporadic warfare against the invaders. These partisan forces were of all kinds. Some were led by landlords and old Manchurian generals. Others had a large percentage of workers and were under the influence of the Communist Party. Still others were largely composed of "Red Spears" and "Red Beards", peasant partisans and the traditional mounted frontiersmen-bandits of Manchuria. The Japanese launched numerous "bandit extermination campaigns" against them, but, as later in China, succeeded in exterminating only the innocent population. To consolidate their control over the country they resorted to wholesale massacres (Ilan, Fushun) and insanely severe administrative measures — such as burning all villages in a given area and forcing the population to concentrate in one "consolidated village" which could be watched by a single garrison.

Nevertheless, the partisan armies grew. In harmony with the development in free China, they moved towards a political United Front and unity of command. Between 1934 and 1936, the Communist-led "People's Revolutionary Army"; the "Anti-Japanese Federated Army" composed of former Manchurian troops; the "Self-Defence Army" of Hsieh Wen-tung, a landlord who led his tenants against the Japanese oppressors; the "Iron and Blood Army", and the "National Salvation Army", were all merged into one Anti-Japanese United Army under the command of General Li Tu, who was confirmed in his post by the Chinese National Government at Nanking in 1937. This united force now numbers a total of 150,000 regular and guerrilla fighters, Chinese, Mongols, Manchus, Koreans, White Russians living in Manchuria who have turned against the Japanese, and even deserters from the Japanese Army. It has been newly sub-divided into twelve armies, one of which, the second, is composed largely of Koreans. Its ammunition and supplies are captured from the Japanese or surreptitiously delivered to it by friendly "Manchukuo" troops. The tactics of the anti-Japanese armies are mobile, based on the sympathy of the people and the experience of seven years of warfare against a garrison force of hundreds of thousands of Japanese. The armies have political departments in which many anti-Japanese intellectuals, escaped from the cities, do valuable work in organization and propaganda.

The basic policies of the Anti-Japanese United Army are simple. They are: to regain the lost territories, aid the Chinese national armies in their struggle against Japan, and confiscate the property of the Japanese and their puppets to finance anti-Japanese activity. The military operations of the twelve army corps, according to decisions adopted at a joint conference after the Marco Polo Bridge incident, are carried on in four military areas — in each of which the anti-Japanese armies hold much territory. The first area, under Yang Ching-yu, concurrently commander of the First Army, covers East Liaoning province. The second area — Kirin east of Harbin — is under Li Yen-Lui, concurrently commander of the Fourth Army. South Kirin forms the Third Area, under Chao Paochung, commander of the Fifth Army. Chao Shang-chi, commander of the Third Army, heads the Fourth War Area in North Heilungkiang.*

The Manchurian partisan detachment formerly under the command of Chao Tung, whose adventures around Peiping are described in an early chapter, operates in East Liaoning. It is not part of the United Army, although it co-operates with it. At present it is under the command of Chao Tung's wife. Due to its isolationist policy, this group has decreased considerably in numbers and influence.

A Japanese writer (Eitaro Ito in *Sekai Shishiki*, Tokyo) states:

"According to an official communiqué 1,850 battles were fought between the Japanese Army and the volunteers in the three years following the Manchurian incident. If we collect the data from newspaper reports, then the battles fought from 1935 to 1938 must exceed the total number fought in the previous three years."

The Manchurian volunteers were the pioneers of the people's anti-Japanese resistance in China. During the years of capitulation, they held high the torch of struggle, inspiring a whole heroic generation of China's youth. First

---

* Another large force, under Sun Yung-chin, operates in Jehol. Japanese sources admit that it has a strength of 40,000 men.

of all China's armies, the Manchurian volunteers achieved and consolidated their United Front. The great song of China's resistance is the song of the Manchurian volunteers.

The Japanese seek to hold Manchuria in a grip of iron. They make the populations of whole villages responsible with their lives for volunteer activities. The country is honeycombed with new roads, railways, and fortresses. The garrisons total 400,000 men. "Bandit-extermination campaigns" never cease. Yet even pro-Japanese publications are forced to admit that the population remains staunchly Chinese in sympathy and that amazingly bold and telling blows are constantly being struck at the Japanese at the very centres of their power.

"The War 'Inside the Great Wall' as the resident natives describe the rest of China", writes W. A. Mitchell in the August 1938 issue of *Oriental Affairs*, "profoundly affects everyone in Manchuria.... When a foreigner with knowledge of the language travels through the country, farmers, business men, labourers and representatives of all classes take the first opportunity of inquiring about the War.... The native has learned that he must describe himself as a subject of Manchukuo... yet in an astounding number of cases we find that his sympathies are entirely with the Central Government of China.... In some strange manner the spirit of unity which we hear has been manifested in China has spread in no small measure to her sons in the North-east."

Mr. Mitchell also informs us that the Japanese Army admitted 1,300 casualties during 1937 operations against "bandits" in Manchuria. Anyone familiar with Japanese military arithmetic (see Mr. Amleto Vespa's *Agent of Japan*) will know that this means actual losses of many times this figure.

Another writer, in the same magazine for December, states:

"The burning (by incendiaries) of the Japanese army's winter supplies, uniforms, etc. in Mukden, undoubtedly influenced the embargo (on wool) introduced in Manchukuo...."

The people of Manchuria are doing their part!

Towards the end of 1938, there took place an event full of human and historical drama.

The partisan armies of the Shansi-Chahar-Hopei Border Area and regular units of the Eighth Route Army crossed the Great Wall into Jehol and Liaoning, the first Chinese national troops ever to *advance* into the lost territories of Manchuria, and established contact with the volunteers. Somewhere on those snowy hills and plains glad shouts rang out, grim fighters ran towards each other with smiling faces. The Hopei-Jehol- Liaoning Border Military Area was formed on November 14.*

In accordance with a decree of the Central Government at Chungking issued at the beginning of 1939, the provincial governments of the four North-eastern provinces Jehol, Liaoning, Kirin, and Heilungkiang — all in abeyance since the Japanese invasion, were formally reconstituted. This, admittedly, is still a paper measure. But the foundation for its realization has been laid by the two iron streams of partisans which have at last met across a border that has now ceased to exist.

Inner Mongolia

In the notorious Tanaka Memorial, the secret *Mein Kampff* of Japanese

---

* This brief account of the recent history of the volunteers in Manchuria is compiled from the following sources:

"Volunteers in Manchuria During the Past Seven Years," Yu Ping-jan, *Singtao Jihpao* September 18 1938;

"September 18 and the Anti-Japanese Allied Army," by General Li Tu,the army's commander-in-chief. Written on September 18, 1938;

"Struggle of the North-eastern United Armies," Eitaro Ito, *Sekai Chishiki*, a Japanese account translated in *Pacific Digest*;

"Anti-Japanese Activities of the People of the North-eastern Provinces," by Wang Ai-hua, *Counter-Attack*, Hankow;

"Letters from Manchukuo and North China," in various issues of *Oriental Affairs*, a British publication with a violent anti-Chinese and pro-Japanese bias in its editorial policy.

imperialism, "Manchuria and Mongolia" are always spoken of together as the base which Japan must seize before she can advance her further ambitions on the continent of Asia. And, in fact, no sooner had Japan established the domination of her arms over the Manchurian provinces, than she began extending her tentacles to the Mongolian steppe — just as the octopus-arms of Hitler's Germany work their way slowly towards the rich Ukraine. After Manchuria in 1931 came Jehol in 1933. Then the Japanese annexed "autonomous" Mongol corridor of six South Chahar counties in 1935. In 1936, a halt was called to this creeping aggression. General Fu Tso-yi destroyed bands of Japanese-Mongol "self-determinationists" at Pailingmiao, arousing enthusiasm throughout China.

While Chinese-administered Inner Mongolia was only beginning, at long last, to resist, the Mongol People's Republic in Outer Mongolia already stood as a stumbling-block in the way of the Japanese dream of a Mongolian empire. The M.P.R. acknowledged Chinese suzerainty, but its frontiers were also guarded against aggression by a mutual assistance pact with the Soviet Union. When the Japanese attempted, in 1935, to encroach upon its territory, the new Mongol army taught them a lesson at Buir Lake which they were not likely soon to forget.

Thus it was, that after Marco Polo Bridge, the Japanese carried on their campaign of conquest in Inner Mongolia alone. Very early in the war, they forced their way to the terminus of the Peiping-Suiyuan railway at Paotou. But until the present time, they have gone no farther. Constantly raiding their communications, wiping out garrisons, and recapturing town after town is the guerrilla cavalry of wily, wiry, hard-riding General Ma Chan-shan, who once gave them a merry time in Manchuria.

General Fu Tso-yi, the victor of Pailingmiao, left his Inner Mongolian province for Shansi in October 1937 and was in charge of the heroic defence of Taiyuan, praised even by the Japanese themselves. But now he is back, and his troops envelop the slender Japanese lines. From the neighbouring Border Area and the nearby former Soviet regions in North Shensi, Eastern Kansu, and Southern Ninghsia, units of the Eighth Route and its related partisan armies lend their experience to the struggle. And not only Chinese fighters participate in the operations. Large Mongol detachments, many of them originally trained by the Japanese, now form part of the anti-Japanese armies. A few miles west of the farthest Japanese outposts at Paotou, the bearded semi-Turkish Mongol cavalry of General Ma Hung-kwei is encamped.

In our survey of the Hsuchow campaign we have indicated how much the constant raids of Ma Chan-shan's cavalry in the rear of the enemy contributed to the slowing-up of the Japanese advance and the immobilization of large sections of their forces. Since then, these raids have continued without a break. The bold horsemen have penetrated into Paotou and Kweihua, seized Japanese supplies and artillery, and generally assured that the Japanese "spearhead" in Inner Mongolia will long concentrate not on penetrating farther, but on preserving its present precarious position. And how the Japanese would like to advance, if they could do so with anything like their present forces, may be seen from just these two facts. Not far away to the South-west lies North Shensi with its centre of Yenan, "capital" of China's Communist Party, seat of the Anti- Japanese Military and Political Academy, epitome of everything that the Japanese militarists hate most. Through Ninghsia to the West, the main route of war supplies from the Soviet Union is also geographically accessible. But still, for over a full year now, the Japanese have hugged the railway and advanced not an inch.

Before we leave the Inner Mongolian plains, one more significant fact must be noted. Not only Chinese troops from "Manchukuo", but Japanese-trained Mongol soldiers are constantly deserting to the Chinese side. These desertions culminated in November 1938 in the revolt of an army of 10,000 Mongolian cavalrymen near Kalgan, who killed their Japanese officers and galloped to the West to establish contact with Ma Chan-shan. The Japanese have not only failed in their strategy of "using Chinese to fight Chinese": they have even failed to enlist the Mongols, who have undoubtedly suffered much national oppression from the Chinese war-lord misrule of the past and were at one time inclined to listen to their blandishments. But no longer. Reality is teaching the tribesmen of Inner Mongolia, princes, lamas, and commoners, that it is only by wholeheartedly joining in China's fight that they can save themselves from being made nationally a pawn in Japan's game of power politics and individually the slaves of every Japanese with a gun. Meanwhile, in the representative bodies of the Shensi-Kansu-Ninghsia Special Region and the Shansi-Chahar-Hopei Border Area, groups of Mongols are experiencing the future, a future in which they will take their rightful place as equal members of a democratic federation of China's peoples. They see also that it is in the process of the joint struggle against Japan that this future is beginning to take shape.

Shansi

South of Suiyuan, westward limit of the Japanese advance in Outer Mongolia, lies the province of Shansi. We have dealt elsewhere with the extensive campaigns in this province during the first eighteen months of the war. The Shansi highlands, storehouse of mineral wealth and key to the domination of the North China plain, have from the beginning eluded the grasp of the Japanese. It was here that the United Front of the Central, Provincial, and Eighth Route Armies, employing the tactics developed by the latter, proved the weakness of the Japanese in mountain warfare and their vulnerability to guerrilla attacks. All this happened in a province in which the usual rent was once 75 per cent of the crop, the usual interest on loans 100 per cent a year, the typical financial institution — the pawnshop, the chief source of revenue — opium, the army — an ill-fed poorly equipped horde of men considered a rabble even among the inferior provincial forces. Even after the outbreak of the present war, the Shansi peasantry evacuated their villages at the approach of their own troops just as they did when they heard that the Japanese were coming. To-day, both armies and people have changed.

After the fall of Taiyuan, General Yen Hsi-shan, for twenty years military leader of Shansi, realized that only widespread guerrilla warfare could prevent the Japanese from consolidating their influence. He authorized the opening of a Military and Political Academy at Linfen, in which progressive leaders from all parts of China taught the political principles of resistance and commanders of the Eighth Route Army acted as instructors in partisan tactics. Students, political workers, and army officers flocked to this school. Meanwhile, a circular was sent to all district magistrates inviting those of them who did not feel competent to actively lead the people of their districts against the Japanese to resign immediately. New regulations were issued, which constituted a long-overdue Bill of Rights for the people of Shansi. While calling upon them to co-operate with the army, they expressly forbade requisition without payment, press-gang methods of conscription, and billeting without consent.

After the fall of Linfen, the armies operating in Shansi did not retreat across the Yellow River, but doubled back along the western boundary of the province and took up positions on the flanks of the Japanese. Shansi was divided into first seven, then nine, partisan districts. With the north-eastern part of the province, seat of the Wutaishan administration, we are already familiar. We have also seen how the Chinese troops remaining in South Shansi held out against repeated Japanese campaigns and continued to prevent the enemy from crossing the Yellow River at Tungkwan. In North-west Shansi, the 120th Division of the Eighth Route Army under Ho Lung, co-operating with other forces, stood as a wall against Japanese attempts to thrust westward toward Shensi.

Between January and April 1939, several new Japanese attempts to move westward towards Sian were decisively smashed. To-day "conquered" Shansi is a Chinese and not a Japanese stronghold. A year and six months after the fall of Taiyuan, only 10 per cent of the area of Shansi province is in the hands of the enemy, and this 10 per cent, is a narrow zone along the railways.

The Taihang Mountains

In an early chapter, we mentioned the Tientsin Professor Yang Hsiu-ling and his group of student guerrillas in the Taihang mountains, on the border of Shansi and Honan. During the past year and a half this group has grown to an army of tens of thousands working closely with the Eighth Route and the Manchurian troops of General Wan Fu-lin, formerly stationed in South Hopei. Strategically situated, it dominates an entire section of the Peiping-Hankow railway in North Honan as well as the rich coal-mining belt along the short Toaching railway, where the important enterprises of the Anglo-Chinese Peking Syndicate once functioned. Its work is to prevent the smooth running of Japanese communications and the Japanese exploitation of the mining area. This work has been carried out successfully. Railway sabotage is carried on by skilled train-men, organized into workers' partisan brigades. And the coal-miners not only refuse to give their services to the enemy, but play grim hide-and-seek with them through the shafts after the manner of their comrades at Chinghsing. The Taihang mountains are to the Shansi-Honan border what Wutaishan is to the boundary of Hopei, Charhar, and Shansi. From this impregnable stronghold the partisans swoop down on the Honan plain, and to it they retire in the face of strong punitive expeditions. Here arms and supplies are safely stored. Politically, too, the Taihang range is a centre. In all respects, it forms one of the bases of the future general counter-attack of the Chinese armies.

North Honan

Honan itself bristles with guerrillas. This dry, dusty province is the heart of China. In it, China's civilization grew through the centuries. Here, too, the ancient trade-routes of China and of Asia meet — from the bare northern tundra to the lush south, from the domes of Samarkand to the Pacific. A large part of the population is Moslem. There are remnant colonies of Chinese Jews who came originally as carriers of the Roman trade early in our era.

Militarily, Honan is the great battle-ground of China. Throughout the ages, rival armies have manoeuvred on its flat surface for historically decisive battles. The population has much experience of civil war. Its traditional self-defence organizations are strong — the Red Spears alone boast 1,500,000 members. The civil wars left another legacy. There are 600,000 rifles in the province.

A missionary from North Honan told me of conditions there after the occupation: "The people endured murder and looting and all the routine atroci-

MA CHAN-SHAN'S GUERRILLA CAVALRY CROSSES THE GREAT WALL

ties of the Japanese Army. But when the Japanese began to confiscate their choice seed-grain, the reserve that determined whether they would eat or starve during the next year, and to feed it to their big Australian artillery horses, the people could stand it no longer. 'They rape women and give seed to beasts' was the phrase that spread like fire throughout the countryside, and everywhere the peasants revolted. Not a day passed without an attack on some Japanese garrison. Along the roads, trucks and military transport were waylaid and destroyed. The Japanese burned whole villages and killed all the inhabitants each time this happened. But this did not help. Political agents arrived to work among the rebel peasants. Now the guerrilla movement is organized and universal."

For centuries, banditry has been an ever-present scourge in Honan, and the civil wars of the present century have increased the number of wandering predatory gangs. When the Japanese came, they gathered these groups together, formed them into armies, and gave their leaders titles. At last, they thought, they had discovered the loyal Chinese forces for which they had been looking. They spoke joyfully of "Chinese Francos". The end of their daydream was described as follows by a British writer in North China:

"There has been only too much evidence of the untrustworthiness of such forces. One of the few semi-military formations created under the present regime (the Peiping puppet government — I.E.), if not the only one, furnished a case in point. Li Fu-ho, commander of the First Anti-Red Army directly under the Public Safety Ministry, was killed at Suitehchen, in North Honan, early in August, when inspecting his men on his return from Peking. The men who attacked him were guerrillas who had enrolled themselves in his army: a device which it is hard to prevent....

"The Japanese originally had much hope of him. He had quite a triumphal entry into North Honan after his visit to Peking and the formal recognition of his status by the Japanese there. He was known locally as the Franco of the East. As the story goes, an Italian military officer went into Honan, saw Li Fu-ho's troops in manoeuvres, and was so impressed that he gave him the above description." *

In Honan, as elsewhere, the traitors perish, and the resistance of the Chinese people continues to grow and flourish. In "Japanese occupied territory", the mere fact of being "recognized by the Japanese" means death. The glory of a would-be Franco is short in present-day China, whether he struts in the occupied areas or plots in Chungking, whether he dies in Honan or flies to Hanoi, whether his name is Li Fu-ho or Wang Ching-wei.

The last guerrilla area we shall consider on the North Bank of the Yellow River is the territory of the re-established Chinese administration of Western Shantung. Here, the guerrilla movement began much as in North Honan, but was soon stiffened by workers' battalions from the labour unions of the Tientsin-Pukow railway and by groups of political organizers from the Border area. Although the entire province is technically in Japanese hands, the provincial administration, under Governor Shen Hung-lieh, continues to function.

According to the most reliable sources, the number of Chinese troops and organized partisans at present operating behind the Japanese lines in China north of the Yellow River exceeds 600,000. The largest regular forces are the Eighth Route Army, with 100,000 men, the troops of Yen Hsi-shan and Fu Tso-Yi in Western Shansi and Suiyuan, numbering about 70,000; 50,000 German-trained Central Government troops under Wei Li-huang in South Shansi; and several Honan and ex-Manchurian divisions in the Taihang mountains. Of the new forces that have grown up since the beginning of the war the largest is the 100,000-strong partisan army of the Border Area. The figures here given do not include guerrilla bands and local self-defence units, but only formations operating under central command and control, although they may be split up into small groups for partisan operations.

---

* W. V. Pennell, "North China Correspondence," *Oriental Affairs*, October and November 1938.

These forces have nullified the attempts of the Japanese puppet Government to establish its dominion anywhere in the occupied territory. They have limited the control of the Japanese themselves to a precarious foothold on the railways. To maintain even this foothold, eleven Japanese divisions, numbering 300,000 men,* are immobilized in North China. They are costing the Imperial Treasury huge sums, but they do not secure any return beyond loot. Militarily, they are not available for new Japanese drives against China or the Soviet Union, and must be subtracted from the sum total of Japan's offensive armed strength.

SOUTH OF THE YELLOW RIVER

East Honan

In East Honan, along the Lunghai railway, south of the Yellow River, the partisan movement began after the fall of Hsuchow. A good deal of mass organization work had been done in this area before the Japanese came, and on the day after the fall of its centre, Kweiteh (May 23), the militia in the region were reorganized into the People's Self-Defence Army. On the same day, under the leadership of a certain Chang, district magistrate of Shayi, they attacked an enemy detachment and managed to put two tanks out of commission. On June 1, Magistrate Tsai of Niuchen recaptured his district town, which had previously been entered by 200 Japanese. These and other successful actions were of great moral importance in stimulating the formation of new units in the rear of the enemy.

It was early summer and the crops stood high in the fields. This made it easy for the partisans to move about unobserved by enemy planes. Everywhere, they launched surprise attacks. Embarrassed by lack of men, the Japanese used their old device of stationing "sentinels" of inflated rubber and "cannon" of the same material along the walls of towns and villages

---

* The estimate of eleven divisions is made by Commander Yeh Chien-ying, principal of the Chinese army's new school for the training of regular officers in guerrilla warfare.

which they held with small squads. This worked until a watching guerrilla, surprised, saw a dog dragging away what had appeared to be a heavy gun. Perhaps another, emboldened, stuck a pin into a "guard" who burst. Tidings of these tricks, together with the burning indignation caused by Japanese kidnapping of women, led to general risings all over East Honan. By the end of September, twenty districts had been recaptured. The "People's Self-Defence Army" had grown to 100,000 men, had established a headquarters, and had been recognized by the provincial Government. The army is composed chiefly of local militia, with a stiffening of army men acting as instructors.

During the winter of 1938, the Central Command began to put into effect, in Honan as elsewhere, its policy of sending large numbers of regulars to operate in the rear of the enemy. On these flat plains, on which everything can be observed and tanks can move anywhere at will, both the initial infiltration of such forces and their subsequent activity are greatly hampered. Nevertheless, Honan, too, has become the scene of incessant partisan warfare — and in April 1939, guerrillas and regulars together had mustered sufficient strength to recapture the railway station of Kaifeng, the provincial capital, and even to enter, for a time, the walled city itself.*

Anhwei

Very different geographically is the region of the Anhwei-Honan border, lying farther to the East. This region is mountainous, and is dominated by the massive Tapieh range. One of the greatest actions of the Hankow campaign was fought here, and partisans, including detachments of the New Fourth Army, have found conditions ideal for their activity. Both during the large-scale battles of September 1938, and in the months since, they have given the enemy ceaseless trouble — dynamiting highways on mountain shelves in places where repairs are most difficult to carry out, and launching constant

---

* This victory was achieved by the troops of General Sun Tung-hsuan, Shantung army units detailed for work in the rear of the enemy which at the time of the battle of Taierhchuang had made a daring and successful attack on Tsinan.

attacks on Japanese outposts and communications. They have reduced to a science the procedure of holding up motor convoys, and their success in this form of interference with the plans of the enemy may be gauged from the fact that, early last winter, the northernmost outposts of the New Fourth made a grand haul of 120 trucks all at once.

Not geography alone, however, has made Northern Anhwei a region of effective resistance behind the enemy lines. The major part of the credit belongs to the campaign of mass organization that began in the province before the Japanese occupation and has continued at an increased tempo since.

The work was begun by the Mass Mobilization Committees of General Li Tsung-jen, who, while he commanded the Fifth War Zone, held concurrently the civil post of governor of Anhwei. We have seen, in the chapter on Taierhchuang, the effective work of these committees in maintaining the amazing spirit of the people of Hsuchow and the front-line areas in South Shantung. In Anhwei, the same atmosphere of self-confidence and self-help was fostered.

Middle-school graduates throughout the province were registered, and from their number, more than 2,000 were trained to hold the triple post of village head, primary school teacher, and militia commander according to the Kwangsi system. Another thousand were formed into Mass Mobilization Squads, each composed of between fifteen and twenty young men and women, every one of whom had a separate responsibility within the group. The programme, within the limits of the general instructions issued by the Mobilization Committee, was determined democratically, by majority vote. Once a decision was taken, military discipline was applied in its execution. Members received $12 a month, from which they were expected to feed themselves and cover all expenses.

The squads suffered severely after the fall of Hofei, several being caught and destroyed by enemy cavalry. Work did not cease, however, and the groups quickly adapted themselves to these conditions. Some of the young men continued to carry on the work of propaganda and organization. Others themselves took up arms and became the nuclei of new partisan detachments.

One squad operating near Fengyang managed to organize a force of 3,000 Red Spears within a few weeks after the occupation of the town. The members of another, near Hofei, voluntarily cut their individual expenses from $12 to $3.50 a month, devoting the remaining funds to the purchase of arms, which they used to good effect when the time came. In Hohsien, the district in which the survivors of the attack on the U.S.S. *Panay* first found shelter, a former student of the Central University at Nanking gathered his fellow-townsmen into a unit which succeeded, using forty old flintlocks, in beating off the first Japanese scouting parties to appear in the area. At Liuan, a twenty-five-year-old graduate of the Eighth Route Army's National Revolutionary Middle School in North Shensi, organized a "Young Men's United Service Group", which recaptured the town from the Japanese and grew into a partisan force which fought throughout the province, from the Yangtze to the Tapieh mountains. A "Women's Service Corps" organized by a girl normal school student followed this group to the rear of the enemy, doing propaganda work in the villages.

As in other places where the people themselves have been made the basis of the struggle, the United Front is strong in Anhwei. Old line regulars, the New Fourth Army, and the numerous guerrilla detachments co-operate well.

Three names popular with China's youth occur in connection with the resistance in Anhwei.

Mr. Chang Nai-chi, the patriotic Shanghai banker who was one of the seven National Salvationist leaders arrested for anti-Japanese activity before the war, is now Finance Commissioner of the province and attends to the sinews of partisan warfare.

Miss Hu Lan-chi, a young progressive writer who as a student in Germany saw the inside of a Nazi prison, leads a group of Shanghai working girls which, like Ting Ling's column in the North-west, is a combination propaganda team, mobile theatre, and travelling school. In her *One Fifth of Mankind*, Anna Louise Strong tells of how this unit teaches co-operation between the army and the people. My own most vivid impression of Hu Lan-chi was formed when I met her, small, plump, cheerful, helmeted, and uniformed, in Hankow and she described to me, with great emotion, how, at an early stage of their work, the girls caught their first glimpse of anti-Japanese partisans on the opposite bank of the Yangtze, and, unable to cross because there were no boats, sang to them across the broad river. No rivers separate the group from the partisans now.

Finally, there is Fang Tsao-chen, an old man, though a hero to China's youth, the leader, at seventy-two, of a large guerrilla detachment. Holder of a classical degree under the Manchu dynasty, commander of the rebel forces in North Anhwei during the first revolution of 1911, he had retired long before the Japanese invasion. The men of Fengyang and Tingyuan had known and respected him all their lives, and sprang to arms at his first call. "We know the use of weapons, and we know our own mountains and streams," he told them. "Why should we become slaves in our own homes?" When more than 4,000 fighters had joined, Fang led a counter-attack against the important railway town of Pengpu. The detachment has fought many other engagements, inflicting heavy losses on the enemy, and, on occasion, itself suffering severely.

Before the fall of Hankow, the family of this fighting patriarch lived in a refugee camp in that city. The Government undertook to take better care of them, but the old commander refused even the small routine subsidy given to the dependents of military officers. His men were not well fed or equipped and had no opportunities of getting medical treatment when wounded. He saw clearly that the Government must finance guerrilla resistance more adequately, and went specially to Hankow to plead for this. So when the subsidy for his family was offered, he replied: "I hope, rather, that you will use it to supply our partisans with the bare necessities of existence and struggle."

That is the spirit of the white-bearded leader of the guerrillas of Fengyang and Tingyuan, the grand old man of Anhwei.

Kiangsu

Kiangsu, the long coastal province which includes Shanghai and Nanking and sprawls northward as far as Hsuchow, is, with the exception of the towns on her many railways, still in Chinese hands. In the North of the province, the whole area traversed by the eastern section of the Lunghai line to Haichow on the sea, is held by an army of 60,000 regulars who have been there since the fall of Hsuchow. In the South, there is the headquarters of the Third War Area under General Ku Chu-tung, while various guerrilla forces, including the New Fourth, constantly threaten the captured capital and China's greatest port.

General Han Teh-chin, one of the divisional commanders who remained when the main forces defending Hsuchow retreated to the West, is now chairman of Kiangsu, with his seat at Funing. General Li Ming-yang, successful organizer of Hsuchow's Mass Mobilization Committee, also stayed with the people he had summoned to carry on the struggle even after the regular army left.

The existence of a pocket of Chinese regular troops in North Kiangsu, no less than the activities of the New Fourth in the South, is a constant source of irritation to the Japanese. Until early this year, however, no major campaigns were undertaken against either, since the enemy was busy elsewhere. The New Fourth has still to face its "campaign of extermination". The army in North Kiangsu has already gone through one — during February and March 1939. The Japanese took Haichow, marched up and down the area, announced themselves victorious, and removed their main strength elsewhere. The Chinese promptly emerged and recaptured everything that they had lost, and to-day the area is not much the worse for its experience. A Japanese dispatch of April 14 declared that the guerrillas in North Kiangsu have now been reinforced by units of the Eighth Route Army. It is certainly true that detachments of the Eighth have operated in Shantung. Whether they have actually entered Kiangsu is questionable, but in any case the *Domei* message proves one thing. The Japanese only christen a force "the Eighth Route" when they find it adept in all the arts of the people's war of guerrilla resistance. The Kiangsu partisans evidently satisfy these conditions.

Shanghai Area

The New Fourth Army holds the area south of the Yangtze from Nanking to Changchow. East of Changchow, and towards Shanghai, there is the "Brave and Loyal National Salvation Army" of General Tai Li.* This force has jurisdiction over the guerrillas in the outskirts of the great port and at Pootung, across the Whangpoo river from the city. It is composed of members of the Blue and Red Rings, two powerful Chinese secret societies formerly notorious in Shanghai municipal politics. Since the war began, the "rings" have proved themselves to be ardently anti-Japanese. Although they have not been able to organize mass formations based on the people, their flying pistol columns have destroyed many an unwary Japanese outpost. It is these men, too, who enter the city individually and carry out terrorist acts against puppet officials, spies, and traitors. So efficient have they been in this field, that few have been caught, although the number of their victims has exceeded 100. To-day, to accept office under the Shanghai "Great Way" Government or to fall in in any way with the schemes of the enemy is to invite certain death in Shanghai. In this occupied city, retribution comes to national traitors more swiftly and surely even than in the areas in which the Central Government is in absolute control.

On August 13, 1938, first anniversary of the outbreak of the Shanghai war, the "Brave and Loyal Army" startled the city by penetrating to the Japanese military airdrome at Hungjao and hoisting over it the Chinese national flag. In the western outskirts of Shanghai and in Pootung, fierce guerrilla warfare is constantly going on. Heavy columns, comprising thousands of troops, supported by tanks, airplanes, and artillery, are constantly being sent against the partisans, but the only effect of these efforts visible to the citizens of Shanghai is the steady stream of trucks bringing Japanese wounded into the city. After each campaign, the complete extermination of the elusive enemy is claimed by the invaders. But within a few weeks, the necessity arises for a new drive — again and again and again.

---

* In nominal command.

Pootung is one of the few places in China which has witnessed, in the course of the present struggle, a minor "civil war" between patriotic detachments and Chinese traitor forces. Indicative of Japanese desires, rather than of any accomplished fact, the commander of such a group in Pootung was hailed for a time (like Li Fu-ho in Honan) as the "Chinese Franco".

Hsu Hsing-fa, would-be *El Caudillo* of Pootung, was once a bandit, and when the war broke out was serving a sentence of twelve years for armed robbery. Freed under a general amnesty, he joined a guerrilla unit near Shanghai, fought his way to a position of leadership in a force of former gangsters, and, when he had 1,000 men under his command, launched out as an independent war-lord seeking power and wealth through co-operation with the Japanese. Having assumed the title of General in command of a puppet "Self-Defence Army", he sent an ultimatum to all the guerrillas in the region to place themselves under his orders.

When the ultimatum was rejected, he called in the Japanese, guiding them to the partisan headquarters and giving directions for the operations of their bombing planes. Reinforced by mechanized units of the Imperial Army, he began a campaign of encirclement and annihilation against his former comrades. The campaign was a complete failure. The armies of the puppet Franco were scattered and he himself was severely wounded. To-day, the main section of Pootung remains in Chinese hands with regular civil administrations functioning and an army of partisans holding off the enemy.

South China

In South China, partisan activity began immediately after the fall of Canton. No difficulty was experienced in raising guerrilla detachments from the ranks of the people's militia with its 300,000 men and rifles organized before the Japanese landing. Experienced commanders, like Tsai Ting-kai, who conducted the heroic defence of Shanghai by the Nineteenth Route Army in 1932, were assigned to lead these detachments, and patriotic workers of all types, from the subordinates of old feudal militarist Li Fu-lin to emissaries of the New Fourth Army, devoted themselves to the task of preparing for guerrilla resistance throughout the South.

The East River District, over which the invading Japanese columns had marched to Canton from Bias Bay, was quickly recaptured. It was here that the first peasant unions had been organized in 1923 and the first Chinese soviets had been established — and the memory of those revolutionary days was strong in the minds of the people. After many encounters with the newly-formed partisan detachments, the Japanese decided that it would be too difficult to hold open this line of communications to the sea and retired upon Canton, where they could receive reinforcements and supplies directly by the West (Pearl) River. Since then, they have been content cautiously to expand the area under their control by moving westward along the river banks supported by their fleet. Strong Chinese forces of regulars and partisans have deterred them from even attempting to consolidate their hold over the entire Canton-Kowloon railway. The only reason that the partisan movement in Kwangtung has not grown to proportions comparable to the great anti-Japanese bases on the north and on the lower Yangtze is that the Japanese have not attempted to occupy the entire province, but have remained concentrated in a small fortified section around Canton, the command exercised by their fleet over the waterways freeing them from the necessity of depending on the overland communications so vulnerable to guerrilla attacks. The counter-attack in Kwangtung, therefore, will have to be carried on by the regular army and the air force, which has already operated with considerable success against enemy warships and transports.

This ends a brief and fragmentary survey of the guerrilla movement in the occupied territories. Enough has been written, however, to indicate how great and how insoluble are the difficulties facing the Japanese army in imposing its will on the Chinese people, even in those parts of the country in which it is long since deemed to have attained formal military supremacy.

CHAPTER XIII
Fight for Hankow

H SUCHOW had fallen. The Japanese forces held a more or less unbroken line from Hangchow Bay to Inner Mongolia. There was not a single Chinese railway north of the Yangtze on which they did not have a foothold. From three directions — along the Lunghai railway west from Kaifeng; by highway from Hofei, in Anhwei province, to Sinyang on the Peiping-Hankow line; and directly from Nanking along the Yangtze — the way to Hankow lay open. The stage was set for another major campaign.

Strategically, the Japanese were much worse off after the fall of Hsuchow than they had been after the fall of Nanking. After the retreat from Shanghai, the Chinese army had been badly shaken, and the Japanese advance towards the capital could properly be described as the pursuit of a fleeing enemy. Not only the Japanese and their allies, but also Great Britain, and the still influential pro-Fascist elements in the Chinese Government itself, had thought the moment opportune to end the war. The mediatory endeavours of Dr. Trautmann, although they did not meet with any success, had had the serious attention of some Kuomintang leaders — and responsible Government spokesmen went out of their way to express their "appreciation of the German efforts to arrange a just peace". Now, after Hsuchow, the atmosphere was very different. The Chinese armies were intact and were fighting successful rear-

298

guard actions. The Japanese had gained positions on all the main approaches to Hankow; but the actual distance of their vanguards from the city was hundreds, not scores, of miles, interspersed with by no means contemptible Chinese defences. Moreover, there was now no alternative to military action. The "cheaper way" of political intrigue was meeting greater and greater obstacles, and the efforts of the capitulation- mongers, though they continued, were recognized as futile even by those who most wished to see them succeed.

Having failed to win the war at Nanking, the Japanese had subjected the people of the city to the most barbarous mass terrorism ever to disgrace modern history. Their record at Nanking was substantially repeated at Hsuchow. And ten days after Hsuchow fell the high-minded Samurai who had failed to "beat China to her knees" (Premier Konoye) by decisively defeating her Army, attempted to "demoralize China's population" (Mr. Yoshida, Japanese Ambassador to the Court of St. James) through the mass slaughter from the air of the defenceless people of Canton.

Canton is the home of China's resistance to foreign domination. Here, 100 years ago, old Commissioner Lin burned cargoes of Indian opium and brought on China's first armed clash with England. From Canton, Dr. Sun Yat-sen began the movement that was to overthrow the corrupt Manchu dynasty and found the Chinese Republic. Canton was the birthplace of the Kuomintang and of its first anti-imperialist United Front with the Communist Party, the revival of which now ensures for the China people both the possibility of further struggle and the certainty of final victory. First source of progress in China, the province of Kwangtung has itself often fallen into the hands of feudal reaction. But among its sons, the tradition of national revolutionary Canton has lived on with a persistent, unextinguishable life.

To break the spirit of the Cantonese has been the ambition of every imperialism that has ever knocked at the gates of China. In May 1938, in the minds of the Japanese militarists, this aim was expressed in practical terms. The thousands of bombs they had dropped on the Canton-Hankow railway, main route of China's munition intake, had not interrupted the flow of supplies to the front. The poor marksmanship of their airmen had not been able to cope with the problem of destroying a single major bridge. (What damage they did do to rails and roadbed was invariably repaired within a few hours by the heroic army of railway workers which won daily victories over tremendous odds on the front of China's national transportation.) This was why they decided to batter the population of Kwangtung into a frame of mind in which it might be disposed to accept a guarantee of safety in return for "autonomy" which would involve the suspension of arms shipments to the North. But there was little hope of this scheme succeeding, and the Japanese knew it. There was desperation in the unreasoning and indiscriminate fury with which they rained high explosives on the heads of the defenceless Cantonese — in the imbecile savagery which made them designate the most crowded city in China as a training-ground over which their youngest and rawest aviators were sent to gain experience.

On May 28, 1938, 600 people were killed in Canton and more than 900 were injured by Japanese bombs. Many of the missiles appear to have been aimed at the Wongsha station, terminus of the Canton-Hankow line.* Within the station, a passenger train was wrecked. But most of the bombs felt several hundred yards away, in the dwellings of the railway workers. Hundreds of small houses were destroyed. Acres of ground were covered with a grotesque mixture of brick, mortar and flesh, dust and blood. Rescue workers, middle-school boys and girls trained in First Aid rushed out to the scene. Dressed in blue, with Red Cross flags plainly displayed, they began to extricate the dead and wounded. The Japanese planes came over again. They flew low and machine-gunned the boys and girls and their ambulances. Forty were killed and fifty injured. The children did not stop their work. Those who were carrying stretchers did not drop their burdens, but tried to bear them to safety.

------

* The much-bombed Wongsha station was in no sense an important military objective. It was a terminus, not a junction, and the war supplies from Hong-kong to Hankow flowed past it, along a loop line connecting the Canton-Hankow and Canton-Kowloon railways several miles to the north-east. There is every indication that the Japanese concentrated on Wongsha precisely because it was in the heart of the city. They hit it relatively seldom and it was finally destroyed, not by Japanese bombs, but by Chinese sappers who blew up near-by munition dumps during the evacuation of Canton.

Some succeeded. Others were killed, together with their charges. On the same day, the Japanese bombed the great Sun Yat-sen Memorial Hall. One bomb went through the roof and exploded on the stage. There was no one in the hall. The Japanese were bombing a symbol, the symbol of Chinese revolutionary nationalism.

On May 29, 250 were killed and 450 wounded in two Japanese raids on Canton. Many of the casualties were children. None were soldiers.

On May 30, the planes killed 100 people and wounded 200.

On May 31, acting on the assumption that the Chinese air fleet had hurried South to defend Canton, fifty-four Japanese aerial raiders attacked Hankow. They met with an unpleasant surprise. Fifty Chinese pursuits engaged them in a thrilling battle which could be seen from the city. Fifteen of the raiders were shot down, and the rest returned to their base without having dropped a single bomb on their objectives. The victory of Hankow was celebrated by the people of Canton who knew that China's Air Force was weak, that to split its strength in the name of the defence of any one city was to play into the hands of the enemy, and that every plane was needed in the battle area of which Hankow was the hub. Japanese attempts to stir up dissatisfaction with the Central authorities on the ground that they had "left Canton defenceless" met with complete failure.

In reply to horrified international protests, Tokyo's spokesmen announced that the bombing of Canton would continue. Acting on the assumption that the Japanese air terror over the South was the prelude to a large-scale landing, the *United Press* transferred me from Hankow to Canton.

I arrived in the city on June 3. On the next day I witnessed a new blood-bath, the most disastrous of any Canton had yet experienced.

Over 2,000 were killed and wounded on June 4. For the first time, all parts of the city received their quota of bombs. During the past week of horror, the population had come to regard the river-front and the business section as not likely to become targets. Now the Japanese bombed the river-front and the business section. Every one of the 2,000 human beings slaughtered on June 4 was killed at a spot which he or she had picked out for safety. The Cantonese did not know about the Douhet theory. They did not know that masses of civilians, schools, hospitals, and the sources of light and water are also "objectives".

I had seen air raids in Nanking and Hankow and many other places in China. The Japanese planes had come, dropped their bombs, and gone. Their bases had been relatively distant, and they were not able to loiter long. In Canton it was different. The planes came from the coast in twenty minutes. They dropped their bombs and returned for more. Meanwhile other planes carried on their work. On June 4, the murder squadrons spent five successive hours over the city.

On June 6, fifty planes raided Canton and killed and injured 1,500 people in four hours, climaxing ten days of sustained horror such as no other city has yet experienced. The streets of Canton were littered with dead. Waxy-white corpses, victims of concussion, lay with no sign of injury beyond a trickle of black blood flowing from blue lips. Closer to the explosions, men, women and children were turned into un-identifiable slabs of meat, which were piled up and taken away in baskets. Quivering wounded moaned, pinned down under heavy concrete beams. Grotesque wrecks of houses bled from broken water-pipes as human victims bleed from torn veins and arteries. Huge weary crowds stood night and day on the banks of the creek which encircles the Anglo-French concessions of Shamen (at the gates of which armed Indian and White Russian police were stationed to keep out refugees). For five successive nights, following on long days of slaughter, the Japanese came again after dark to murder the sleep of the city. They could not hit anything in the pitch darkness, and generally contented themselves with circling interminably and nerve-wrackingly overhead for hours. This was part of the plan "to demoralize the people of Canton".

But the Cantonese people were not demoralized. During every raid, volunteer Red Cross and fire-prevention squads worked heroically under the bombs. All the essential services functioned. Newspapers appeared regularly. Between alarms, tea-houses were full and moving-picture houses showed, endlessly, the same American films (the suppliers in Hongkong refused to risk their valuable commodities by hiring them out to Canton theatres after the first raids). On June 6, the artist, Jack Chen, gave an exhibition of American graphic art and posters from Republican Spain in a building at the doors of which many people were killed on the same day. Japanese planes were over the city at the hour when the Mayor was scheduled to open the exhibition. The Mayor came. Hundreds attended the showing. There was promise, in the behaviour of the people of Canton, of the great upsurge of popular organization which the city would witness during the following months.

In mid-June the raids subsided. Attention, both local and international, shifted to the front where the great drive against Hankow was beginning. Before we leave the subject of Canton, however, it may be well to consider a few figures published by the Kwangtung Provincial Government on the Japanese air-terror over the province:

"Number of civilians killed in Canton. 500 approx.
Number of civilians injured ... 5,500 approx."

The following figures were also released:

"Between August 31, 1937, and June 7, 1938, there were 1,400 air raids over Kwangtung province. In the city of Canton, the air-raid alarm was sounded 800 times. The total number of Japanese planes participating in these raids was 5,986. The number of bombs dropped was 10,292. In the province, 5,027 houses were destroyed, 4,595 civilians were killed, and 8,555 civilians were injured."

On June 3, as a result of a Cabinet re-shuffle in Tokyo, General Itagaki, the defeated "hero" of Pinghsinkuan and Taierhchuang, was appointed Japanese War Minister. Itagaki is a notorious fire-eater, and, like Doihara, he has been identified with Japan's continental adventure ever since its beginning in 1931.* His entry into the Cabinet meant firstly that the drive on Hankow would be pushed immediately and with great vigour, and secondly that the Japanese finance-capitalists, whose representatives sat quite comfortably in the Government as colleagues of this rabid "National Socialist", would support the most intense prosecution of the campaign in the belief that it would give them control of the economic centre of Central China, while at the same time hastening the end of the war and the beginning of "peaceful reconstruction" (read "undisturbed predatory exploitation") of the territories** occupied by the army.

The Hankow campaign began with a resumption of the Japanese push along the Lunghai railway, westward from Kaifeng. But on June 10, the Yellow River dikes were opened between Kaifeng and Chengchow and the level plain over which the Japanese army had hoped to advance was turned into a vast lake. In this lake, a certain amount of mechanized equipment was lost, and the whole Lunghai campaign came to an end. The laments of Japanese propagandists over the "inhuman atrocity" of the Yangtze were loud and long. And well they might have been, for the floods caused them to change their whole plan of operations.

The change was accomplished quickly. Within a few days the main theatre of war shifted from the south bank of the Yellow River to the valley of the Yangtze, where fierce fighting was to continue unbrokenly for four months.

On June 13, Anking, capital of Anhwei province, was occupied by a

---

* Since then, Itagaki has developed rapidly in the direction of a political and military conservatism almost indistinguishable from that of the financial elements. Between January and May 1939, he made several speeches advocating consolidation of the occupied areas and caution with regard to further advance on the main fronts.

** On June 13, General Itegaki and Premier Konoye discussed "the full exploitation of the Japanese victories in China" as the pressing problem of the hour. On June 18, Finance Minister Ikeda, a representative of the big financial interests announced the begininng of a nation-wide economy drive to finance the new campaign. Those who were expected to "economize" were, of course, the Japanese people, already labouring under a serious shortage of commodities and steeply rising prices characteristic of the beginnings of malignant inflation. On June 21, the Japanese Budget figures were announced. The total exceeded 6,000,000,000 yen of which 4,850,000,000 yen were earmarked for military expenditures, making a total of over 8,000,000,000 yen spent on the China adventure since its beginning.

Japanese landing-party, the first large city on the Yangtze to fall into enemy
hands since the capture of Nanking and Wuhu in December. Anking was not
seriously defended, being garrisoned by inferior troops — badly trained and
worse equipped. It lay less than 200 miles east of Hankow.

At the end of the next week, when it became apparent that the floods had
made operations in the North impossible, twenty transports, a large number
of naval units, and aircraft-carriers bearing a total of 150 planes, steamed
upriver from Shanghai for the grand Hankow offensive. As the Japanese
planned it, the Yangtze campaign would be carried out by the co-ordinated
action of the navy, the ten Japanese divisions pushing along the north bank
of the great waterway, and landing-parties to be disembarked at strategic
points on the south bank. Together, these forces formed the left flank of the
Japanese advance on Hankow, of which the central column was pushing across
Anhwei province from Hofei to Sinyang on the Peiping-Hankow railway,
and the right flank was immobilized by the Yellow River floods. Since the
left flank was both the strongest (having the aid of the navy and assured river
communications) and the least impeded by natural obstacles (the central
column, for instance, would have to negotiate the great Tapieh mountain range
before reaching Hankow), it became the spearhead of the entire Japanese
advance.

The Chinese Army disposed its forces along the lower slopes of the Tapieh
mountains north of Hankow, and along both banks of the Yangtze river. The
southern forces were under the general command of General Chen Cheng,
whom we have met as head of the Political Department at Hankow. They
included the Cantonese armies of General Hsueh Yoh, which were to distinguish themselves in the fighting south of the river, and the troops of General
Chang Fa-kwei, once commander of the far-famed "Ironsides" of the 1927
revolution. North of the Yangtze, the Chinese forces were commanded by
General Li Tsung-jen, just recuperated from a slight wound received during
the retreat from Hsuchow. They were substantially the same armies that had
fought on the Tientsin-Pukow railway — crack Kwangsi divisions, Chiang
Kai-shek's own units under General Tang En-po, and the Second Group Army

of General Sun Lieh-chung which had won the victory of Taierhchuang.

The advancing Japanese forces were well equipped with artillery, and they were supported by the navy and an adequate air force. They were accompanied by chemical warfare units, and, both on the south and north banks of the Yangtze, they were to make frequent use of gas.

The Chinese Army had much less artillery than the enemy. Its air force was in slightly better condition, and was to play an active, and effective, part in making things unpleasant for the Japanese Navy. Of chemical weapons and means of defence it had none, lacking even the simplest gas masks.

The object of the Japanese, as in the Hsuchow campaign, was not merely to reach and take its objective, but mainly to draw the Chinese Army into battle and annihilate its main force, thus abolishing its future striking power and (they hoped) bringing an end to the war.

The Chinese, on the other hand, proceeded from the beginning on the assumption that Hankow would finally be lost, but that the war would continue. They believed that the final stage of the war would see a general counter-attack by new and well-equipped Chinese armies. They planned to preserve the core of their army intact, and to use only a part of their mechanical equipment for the defence of Hankow, keeping the rest in the hinterland to become the basis of a future accumulation of sufficient striking power to launch the final counter-offensive. This counter-offensive would come at a time when the Japanese armies were strung out over a tremendous territory, none of which they effectively occupied, due to guerrilla activities, when their morale was beginning to break, and when the strain on Tokyo's exchequer became so great as to make large-scale reinforcements of men and supplies extremely difficult.

Hankow would be defended tenaciously. Many local counter-attacks would be launched, so that the Japanese would have difficulty in concentrating their mechanized forces for a break through at any one spot. Not an inch of ground would be yielded without fighting. On the other hand, there would be no second Shanghai. There would be no risking the strength of the entire Chinese Army in tactically unfavourable circumstances.

Fierce fighting broke out on the north bank of the Yangtze, at Taihu. On June 23, this front was immobilized, like the Lunghai sector, by floods. For a time it looked as though China's two great rivers would between them abort the plans of the Japanese high command.

But the high water on the Yangtze, unwonted at this time of the year, helped the Japanese as much as it hindered them. Heavy ships which in the normal course of events could not have moved until the river rose in the early autumn, were now able to proceed in the direction of Hankow. The navy took up the advance, and began a general assault on the Matang boom, below Kiukiang, while a large force of soldiers was landed at Tungliu, on the south bank of the river, to attack the forts and shore batteries which formed the boom's land defences.

This was the opportunity for the Chinese Air Force to prove to the nation just why it had preserved its forces instead of splitting and exhausting them in the simultaneous defence of Hankow and the martyred population of Canton. On June 25, it successfully bombed the Japanese naval concentrations on the Yangtze, forced them to scatter, and set fire to several transports. On June 26, two Japanese warships were hit and several planes shot down. On June 27, three more Japanese warships were claimed to have been sunk. Twelve Japanese bombers which had just landed at Anhing and had had no time to refuel were destroyed on the ground. There was jubilation all over free China.

Unfortunately the Chinese successes in the air were not duplicated on land. On the contrary, there occurred one of those throwbacks to the old war-lord China which only a few years ago would have been taken as a matter of course, but now stood out in lurid relief against the background of united national resistance. When the Japanese attacked the Matang forts, the general in command was not at his post, but feasting at Kiukiang. The assault was sudden, and there was no one to give orders. The forts were reduced within a day. The general was shot, but one of the strong points of the Yangtze defence system had gone.

On June 29, the Japanese fleet steamed through the Matang boom, which proved to have been of amazingly flimsy construction. After a few days of fighting west of Matang, the Japanese landing force penetrated a few miles south-west to Hukow. Here again they were halted, and it was almost a month before they reached Kiukiang — a month during which they suffered heavy casualties. Advancing down the Kiukiang-Nanchang railway to Tehan, they met stiff opposition, which they could not overcome for fully two months.

The Chinese air fleet repeated its record of the previous month. During the first three days of July it sank or disabled an aircraft carrier and more than ten naval craft of various kinds. The small, swift Thornycroft torpedo boats which China had been buying for some years for river defence also did good work, it being claimed that they destroyed several gun-boats near Kiukiang. The Japanese strenuously denied all these losses, even while they were towing the battered hulks of their disabled warships down through the lower Yangtze plain for all to see.

The positions established south of the Yangtze at the end of July remained practically unchanged through August and the greater part of September. These months were months of diversions, both in China and on the international arena.

Faced with the necessity of rushing more troops to the front to overcome the strong Chinese resistance, the Japanese found to their dismay that they not only could not withdraw a single soldier from North China and the Shanghai-Nanking area, but were actually compelled to take men away from the main theatre of war to deal with the partisan activity which was spreading like wildfire through the occupied territories. Already during the Taierhchuang campaign, partisans all over the country had done much to slow down the enemy advance. But this was nothing to the systematic operations which the guerrilla forces now undertook to impede the Japanese progress towards Wuhan.

From Inner Mongolia to the islands off the coast of Kwangtung, the occupied territories were in turmoil. Taking advantage of the serious weakening of Japanese garrisons in North China, the partisans of the Border Area, with units of the Eighth Route Army as their backbone,* extended their activities, as we already know, to the gates of Peiping and Tientsin and beyond these cities to East Hopei and the Manchurian border. In Shansi and Honan, twenty-eight divisions of Chinese regulars still remained, and they took advantage of the general preoccupation with the Yangtze to recapture scores of towns. In Shantung, 1,000 men of the mobile army of Shih Yu-san actually entered, and held for a couple of days, the city of Tsinan itself. To the disgust of the Japanese, guerrillas briefly took over Chefoo at a time when the American Far Eastern Fleet was anchored there. Hsuchow, so recently captured, was repeatedly threatened by the troops of Han Teh-chin, based on Eastern Kiangsu, which formed an unconquered pocket of China in the midst of the occupied areas. On the lower Yangtze, a new force of former Red partisans, the New Fourth Army, made its appearance. In the very outskirts of Shanghai, firing was constantly heard. Guerrillas recaptured many towns in Pootung, across the river from the city, and on August 13, anniversary of the beginning of the Shanghai hostilities, a partisan unit actually ran up the Chinese national flag over the Japanese military airfield. Far to the South, Namoa Island, which the Japanese had occupied in late June, was re-taken by tough armed fishermen, maddened by the murder of their fellow toilers, the destruction of their junks and nets, and the raping of their women. Troops from the mainland reinforced them, and it took the Japanese a month to reassert their control.

At the end of July, "incidents" began occurring on the "Manchukuo"-Soviet border. While Europe seethed with the explosive potentialities of the Spanish and Czech situations, the Japanese military clique, with the new War Minister, General Itagaki, at its head, decided to "feel out" the readiness of the Soviet Union to fight. The U.S.S.R. showed no disposition to knuckle under to provocation, and troops and ships began to leave the Yangtze for Manchuria. But by mid-August, everything was quiet

---

* On August 25, Chu Teh, in a statement commemorating the anniversary of the Eighth Route Army, stated that during the elapsed year the army had participated in 600 engagements, inflicted 34,000 casualties on the enemy, and taken 2,000 prisoners.

again.* Driven off Changkufeng hill, Japanese commanders on the border lamely told Reuter's correspondent that they were "proud that the Japanese soldiers could withstand a bombardment such as that to which they have been subjected by Russian guns". It was a new thing for the Imperial Japanese Army to boast of such passive virtues. Having satisfied their curiosity and lost a good half of their prestige and every bit of their taste for further "incidents", the Japanese hastened to withdraw. Their defeat at Changkufeng was a shock to the whole Rome-Berlin-Tokyo axis. Germany indicated clearly that she was not ready to back her Japanese allies in an immediate large-scale campaign against the Soviet. She renewed her pressure on Tokyo to refrain from wasting further energies in China, while herself turning to the bullying of the more tractable west.

During July and August the international aspect of the Far Eastern conflict again came to the fore. Early in the summer the Japanese had made a feint at Hainan, and had been warned by London and Paris,** in seemingly unmistakable terms, that the occupation of the island would be regarded as an unfriendly act. France, as a counter-measure, occupied the Paracel islands on July 3. The Japanese protested loudly, staged a naval demonstration, and in their turn grabbed the island of Weichow in the Gulf of Tongking. But the French held fast, and the Japanese both formally stated their consent to the Paracels *coup* and evacuated Weichow. This was before Munich, and the actions and utterances of Britain and France were taken seriously, both by the Japanese, who knuckled under, and by the Chinese Government, which decided that Tokyo would not aggravate the Western Powers by ordering an

---

* The Japanese people, less sanguine than their militarists, were greatly alarmed by the border provocations from the beginning. An uncensored, undated *United Press* mail release from Tokyo read: "If the Japanese Government wanted to find out what the people of Japan thought about a possible war with Soviet Russia, they chose an excellent trial balloon in the Changkufeng affair. The answer was that the Japanese people had enough war on their hands already, and wanted no more of it ... the thought of adding more burdens through a war against the Soviet was dismaying... businessmen suspended pending deals... the Stock Exchange slumped."

** An earlier gesture towards "recognition of realities" had been made by London on May 3, when the Anglo-Japanese Customs Agreement, (*See page 311*)

attack on South China, and accordingly moved the best Cantonese troops to the Yangtze front. On August 16, Secretary of State Hull delivered a strong speech against the aggressor states in which he reaffirmed the vital interest of the United States in seeing that international law was not further violated. This was interpreted as a further stiffening of the international front against Japan.

Then, seemingly out of a clear sky, but actually out of the muddy waters of Cliveden diplomacy, the King Charles's head of "peace" negotiations again appeared. First there was a question in the House of Commons to which Mr. R. A. Butler, Under-Secretary for Foreign Affairs, replied that His Majesty's Government would be glad to undertake the task of mediation in the Far East. While it was generally stated in Hankow that the British Ambassador was urging Chiang Kai-shek to defend the city with all the forces at his disposal, his colleague in Tokyo launched highly friendly conversations with Foreign Minister Ugaki.* And when a loan to China was discussed in Parliament, Mr. Chamberlain and Sir John Simon very successfully squashed the whole matter.

"Mediator! Mediator! Who'll be the mediator?" The unborn spirit of Appeasement was casting long shadows forward. At the first session of the People's Political Council, held in July, Mr. Wang Ching-wei had introduced a resolution "for the improvement of friendly relations with Italy and

---

regulating the division of Chinese Maritime Customs revenues in occupied ports between British bondholders and Japan, was concluded in Shanghai, and the Chinese Government — because, most awkwardly, it still had legal existence — was invited to give its formal consent to this amiable arrangement. Hankow protested instead of acceding; and, to keep the goodwill of the bondholders, undertook to itself meet loan service charges for occupied stations out of the meagre revenues it still retained.

* Sir Archibald Clark-Kerr is openly and sincerely pro-Chinese. Sir Robert Craigie, on the other hand, is a thorough Japanophile. The appointment of these two ambassadors was no accident. Each, in his own post, would be cordially received. As for reports, those of the envoys themselves carried less weight in Whitehall than the communications of subordinates and attachés, presumably more "neutral". The sincerity of an envoy did not mean the sincerity of the government that sent him. Chamberlain and Simon saw in the maintenance of good relations with both sides the guarantee that Britain could smoothly undertake mediation when the time came.

Germany". Then the ubiquitous German correspondents, fairly quiet since January, once more descended on Chiang Kai-shek with questions on what he thought of peace by negotiation. He replied, in effect that he did not think of it at all so long as any Japanese troops remained on Chinese soil.

At the same time a laconic message stated that the Chinese Government was showing great apprehension as the result of reports that Japan and Mr. Chamberlain might come to an agreement on their respective spheres of influence in China. So serious was this apprehension, that the Chinese ambassador in London felt impelled to ask for reassurances which he received.

This was all before Munich. The Soviet Union had just shown clearly (and evidently dangerously, in the opinion of Mr. Chamberlain and the axis) that it could be relied upon to pay any aggressor back in his own coin. Soviet prestige was high in China. Mr. Sun Fo was freshly back from a very satisfactory visit to Moscow and a series of disappointments in London. It was natural that Chinese public opinion should note, and draw conclusions from the comparison. The sympathy of the British people for China was known and appreciated and Sir Archibald Clark-Kerr, who did not conceal his pro-Chinese views, was personally popular. The attitude of the Chamberlains and Simons, on the other hand, was deeply resented. It was the policy they represented which made the personality and preferences of the liberal ambassador misleading and dangerous. While Sir Archibald encouraged resistance in Hankow, Sir Robert Craigie, his colleague in Tokyo, was discussing the possibility of compromise with General Ugaki, the Japanese Minister of Foreign Affairs.

In this welter of uncertainty only two solid beliefs remained. The Yunnan-Burma road was giving Britain a new interest in the preservation of Southwest China from Japanese domination. And even if Britain had made a deal with the Japanese, surely such a deal included a Japanese undertaking to leave South China alone and refrain from choking off Hongkong. On the basis of this "axiom", Canton was taken to be "diplomatically defended", and its military establishment was seriously weakened to provide fresh levies for the Yangtze — where, with a new Japanese offensive under way, they were urgently needed.

The offensive began on August 22. This time the Japanese central column, operating in Central Anhwei, a good 100 miles north of the Yangtze, took the initiative, thrusting westward towards the Peiping-Hankow railway. Although the Chinese fought back strongly, and even won a minor victory in the re-capture of Susung, it was in this sector that, two months later, the fate of Hankow was ultimately decided.

Stopped on the Yangtze, the Japanese had tried to turn the flank of the Chinese and crumple their lines by attacking far to the North. Now, halted in Anhwei, they again began fighting for a break-through on the south bank of the great river.

The beginning of September saw epic battles south of Kiukiang, for the towns of Tehan and Juichang. These engagements were the most intense of any that had taken place since the fight for Shanghai. Heavy artillery, hundreds of airplanes, and gas were used. In one place, a whole regiment of Cantonese troops fell victim to the choking horror. But the Chinese lines held. Chinese artillery and airplanes engaged in duels with Japanese warships. The battle of Juichang, on September 2, was the greatest Chinese victory since Taierhchuang, the Japanese casualties running into thousands.

Fierce fighting on all fronts and in the rear of the enemy continued all through September.

On the Yangtze, Matoucheng, a fortress on the south bank which was one of the strong points of the Hankow defence system, fell on September 15, after a week-long battle. Tienchachen, which played a corresponding role on the north bank, was taken on September 30. The struggle for these two points was unprecedented in its severity, and casualties on both sides ran into tens of thousands, the proportion being at least one Japanese to every two Chinese losses — a better ratio than had hitherto been achieved by the defenders in positional fighting.

In the middle of the month, the Japanese right flank, which had been considerably strengthened, resumed its advance through Anhwei and Central Honan towards the Peiping-Hankow railway. Before the end of

September, the Japanese had reached the line.

At no point, however, had the enemy come within fifty miles of Hankow, and at no point had they passed any but its outermost defences. Not only the strong Chinese resistance at the fronts, but also intensive guerrilla activities seriously impeded their advance and upset all their schedules.

What finally decided the Hankow campaign in favour of the Japanese was not any local development, but the capitulation of Munich. When Britain and France betrayed democracy in Europe, the Japanese not only intensified their drive on the existing fronts and sent their bombing squadrons for the first time to hammer the new south-western bases of resistance, but they created a new front in South China.

On September 29, when the practical meaning of "appeasement" began to be clear, General Ugaki, the Japanese Minister of Foreign Affairs, was forced to resign. Ugaki had been a partisan of Anglo-Japanese *rapprochement* in the Far East. He had opposed the navy's policy of "Southward Expansion", and seen the future of Japan's continental programme in terms of a division of spheres of influence in China — the North for Japan and the South for Britain — with the City of London financing and consolidation of the Samurai conquest. The Yangtze, in his eyes, constituted the chief axis of British influence in China. After the fall of Hankow, Japan would be in control of the main portion of the river. She could use the promise to reopen this great artery to the trade of third nations as a bargaining counter to secure British recognition of her gains in the northern provinces. Ugaki wished to avoid provoking Britain into further opposition to Japan's schemes. He wished to flourish, rather than to use, the manifest Japanese ability to do great harm to British interests in China, at the same time holding out hopes of a "reasonable arrangement" which would be necessary to include British pressure on China to concede through mediation the Japanese demands in respect of the northern provinces.

Responsible sources claim that when the crisis was at its height, Japan massed large bodies of troops in Formosa for an attack on Hongkong. It is probable that, had war broken out, these forces, in conjunction with the navy, would have taken the opportunity to attack the almost defenceless British and French bases in the South Seas. But certain it is also that there was a strong section of opinion in Tokyo — to which evidently Ugaki belonged — which advocated not military action, but a judicious mixture of neutrality and armed blackmail, at least until the outcome of the conflict in Europe could be predicted with some degree of accuracy. Such "malevolent neutrality", as one observer called it, might exact as its price at least the complete withdrawal of Anglo-French support — such as it was — to the Chinese Central Government.

Mr. Chamberlain's behaviour at Godesberg and Munich, however, proved to the satisfaction of the Japanese militarists that Britain did not have to be courted — that she could with impunity be bullied.* The concentration of ships, troops, and military supplies in Formosa, said to have been prepared for Hongkong, was diverted to Canton. The blow to British commerce and prestige was almost as effective as if Hongkong itself had been occupied.

At a moment when China's strength was becoming apparent to the world and her weaknesses were half forgotten, another great city fell as Peiping and Tientsin had fallen — without effective resistance. Like the loss of the northern cities, the rapid fall of Canton was due to weaknesses inherited from the era of internal division and external capitulation. But there was a difference. At the beginning of the war, these weaknesses were obvious and widespread. To-day, they are fast disappearing, and it is not unlikely that Canton will be the last price China will be called upon to pay for the decade of calamity that ended with Marco Polo Bridge.

China's weakness has been due to the fact that she did not begin earlier to organize and use the chief source of her power — her 450,000,000 people. Only the people of China can defeat Japanese aggression. Only the people

---

* Unfortunately, the Chinese Government did not foresee this inevitable result of Munich. A high Kwangtung official told me months later: "If the Japanese had landed a forthight later, they would have found even less forces opposnig them. Two more divisions were under orders to go to the Yangtze in mid-October."

of China can assure for her a place as a free and independent nation. So long as the Chinese Government saw resistance to Japanese encroachment in terms of financial and diplomatic arrangements with a third Power, suppressing the while the popular anti-Japanese movement, the enemy continued to advance. But when, goaded beyond endurance, it unfurled the banner of resistance and sent its armies to defend Nankow and Shanghai, even the defeat of these armies did not halt the wave of confidence in victory that swept the entire country. A China basing her struggle on an armed and democratically organized people can use every scrap of foreign aid that she is able to obtain to strengthen her power of resistance. A China which did not develop her own strength and had no faith in her own ability to defend herself could not be saved from enslavement by any amount of outside help.

It is true that steps were taken to organize and arm the people of Kwangtung. According to official figures, 300,000 civilians in the province possessed rifles and had been trained to use them. But this great force was not made part of the plan for the defence of South China. Political work for the awakening of the people, which was enthusiastically and successfully carried on, was not effectively linked with military preparation for repelling the invader. As a result, the depleted provincial garrisons, outnumbered by the Japanese, were unable to defend Canton. The militia was mustered. But there was no one to tell it what to do. The Kwangtung authorities played at mobilizing the people, but left them out of their calculation when the crisis came. However, the work of training and organization had not been meaningless and was not wasted. Such work never is. To-day, the civilian militia forms the backbone of widespread guerrilla resistance in Kwangtung. The people of the province take themselves more seriously than their leaders did. They have more faith in their capacity for struggle.

At the time of the invasion, the province of Kwantung was governed by a triumvirate. After the flight of Canton's semi-independent militarist ruler, Chen Chi-tang, in 1936, that Central Government appears to have decided that no one man should be allowed to make himself master of

Kwangtung. It therefore gave military command in the province to Yu Han-mou, a feudal-minded general of the old Cantonese army who had helped to drive out Chen Chi-tang. The civil governorship went to Wu Teh-chen, former mayor of Shanghai and a Central Government career man. The financial power was placed in the hands of Tseng Yang-fu, mayor of Canton and finance commissioner of the province. The division of authority between the three men was not clearly defined, and, to make matters worse, each controlled a military force, General Yu Han-mou commanded the Fourth Route Army. Governor Wu Teh-chen had authority over a large force of Peace Preservation Corps, or soldier-police. Mayor Tseng was commander of Kwangtung's 300,000 newly trained militia. This delicate system of checks and balances was meant to keep the province on even keel in peace time, representing, as it did, a nice adjustment of local to central authority. Under war conditions, the arrangement was a factor only of delay and sabotage. The Central Government made a decision. Immediately the question arose — who would carry it out, and if all three, how would the responsibility, and credit, be divided among them? Excessive dependence on Britain, failure to utilize the fighting resources of the province, and bureaucratic division of power in the administration were responsible for the collapse at Canton. All three faults stemmed from one poisoned roof the remoteness of authority from the people and the lack of confidence in the people as the basis of resistance. Under a greater measure of democracy, none of these faults would have existed. We have only to remember the relations of the army, the people, and the civil administration in the partisan areas to be convinced of this.

I spent five months in Canton witnessing the worst of the terror-bombings, the subsequent resurgence of popular organization for resistance, and finally the evacuation and fall of the city. Before the invasion, I made trips into various parts of the province of Kwangtung, so that my observations were not confined to Canton. Following the landing, I travelled to the front and was able to get a glimpse of the military causes for the rapidity of the enemy advance. After the occupation I again spent several days in the countryside, observing at several points the arrival of the Japanese and the reactions of the rural population. Besides this it was part of my duties to interview numerous foreign and Chinese eye-witnesses of different phases of the campaign and occupation.

All these observations on the spot convinced me that the rapid fall of Canton by no means signified the collapse of the resistance of the Cantonese people. Nor did it discredit it any way the work of organization which had been gaining impetus during the preceding three months. We have analysed the causes which led to the Cantonese army's being taken by surprise by a better organized, more mobile, and possibly more numerous Japanese force equipped with weapons which gave it terrific striking power. The success of the evacuation, when evacuation became inevitable, was due to the intensive political training which the people of Canton had been receiving since the bombings. Other results of this training were the rapid formation of guerrilla units, the staunch defence of individual villages by the people's militia, and the absence of any significant group in the province willing to lend itself to the aims of the Japanese.

Had the invasion come before the heavy bombings of last May, June, and July, the loss of Canton might have been a far more serious blow to resistance in the province than it has since proved. The Japanese air terror against Canton's population was a failure from the military point of view. But it proved to be a political factor of the first magnitude. Instead of striking fear into the hearts of the Cantonese, it evoked the most striking growth of patriotic sentiment and organization hitherto seen in any of China's great cities.

Paralysed by the suddenness of the attack from the sky during the last days of May, Canton quickly rallied to give its answer to the bombers. Evacuating at first after every heavy raid, the people soon came face to face with the fact that this was not economically feasible. With grim determination they returned to take up their normal activities, reacting with less fear and more hatred to every new visit from the raiders.

July 15 witnessed the inauguration of the political Department of the

Fourth War Area (Kwangtung, Fukien, and part of Kwangsi)* whose work of political organization was soon brought to the attention of the world by a series of monster demonstrations the like of which had perhaps never before been seen in China. Those who were in Canton at the time will never forget the "Offer Gold to the State" campaign on the anniversary of the Shanghai war, the parade of 150,000 organized and partly armed Cantonese citizens on September 18, and numerous other manifestations culminating in the huge torchlight parade of 100,000 volunteer militia four days before the fall of the city. The power of the armed people so impressively demonstrated at that time is still there, and it is this that is preventing the further penetration of the Japanese into the heart of South China.

Behind the demonstration lay a wealth of constantly expanding activity, the object of which was to draw ever wider groups of the people into participation in preparations for defence. In July 10,000 citizens were trained in the use of arms. Huge mass rallies were held for the singing of patriotic songs. A number of new student service groups left Canton for the Yangtze front. Party and Government organs issued orders defining the duties of individuals in case of invasion. On the one hand, leaders of social organizations were forbidden to leave the city to escape from bombing, on pain of being deprived of their positions. On the other, it was decreed that prominent citizens of points under threat of Japanese invasion be required to leave before enemy occupation so that the Japanese could not, by threats or any other means, secure their services in their puppet regimes.

In August 7,000 senior middle-school students and university lower-class men were called up for military training. One hundred thousand signatures were collected for a letter to the World Youth Congress in Poughkeepsie, appealing for a firm stand against Japanese aggression in the Far East. Dur-

---

* Taking its orders partly from the Central Political Department, partly from Yu Han-mou, the head of the Fourth War Zone, this organ was hampered in its work by uncertainty as to its status in the administrative setup of Kwangtung. Nevertheless, its activity was greater than even that of the parent body in Hankow. The blame for the failure to make use of the forces which it evoked did not lie with the Political Department.

ing the week beginning August 13 the "Offer Gold to the State" campaign became the setting for an inspiring demonstration of defiance by the entire population of the city. "This is our answer to the bombs," cried impassioned orators — and when the bombers came over, the disciplined crowds in the streets sang patriotic songs, drowning out the wail of the siren, the hum of planes, and the whistle of bombs.

On August 20, a survey was made of all arms in the possession of the people of Canton. The Canton branch of the Sino-Soviet Cultural Association was formed. Printers, newsboys, hotel employees, postal workers, oil-mill workers, and ricksha pullers were organized into war-time education groups for political and military training. New regulations were issued for the apprehension and suppression of traitors. At the end of August Madame Sun Yat-sen paid a visit to Canton, the first in ten years. Her arrival gave a new stimulus to the activity of patriotic women's associations, all of which were shortly afterwards unified into one city-wide organization.

Three important mass campaigns took place in September. The "Write to the Front" movement produced 250,000 letters to the armies on the Yangtze. The anniversary of the Japanese invasion of Manchuria on September 18 was marked by the inauguration of a universal food, fuel, and clothing economy drive. On September 9, the day on which the League Assembly met to consider the application of sanctions to Japan, 101 delegations of people's organizations, comprising a total of over 100,000 persons, marched in a gigantic parade through the city.

On September 16, Madame Sun Yat-sen returned to Canton to open the Overseas Mobilization Conference, attended by hundreds of delegates from Chinese communities all over the world. With her came old Madame Chao, "Mother of the Guerrillas" — the sixty-year-old peasant woman whose exploits among the partisans in Manchuria and the northern provinces have become a legend in China to-day. Her numerous public appearances stimulated widespread interest in guerrilla warfare and discussion of partisan tactics to be adopted when the Japanese invaded South China.

The increasing participation of the Cantonese people in preparations for resistance and the general enrichment of social and political life in the province were reflected also in the work of intellectual and artistic groups. Mid-September witnessed a striking exhibition of war-time graphic art which attracted thousands of people. Patriotic drama flourished and performances were given nightly on illuminated outdoor stages set up at different points within the city. The mass-singing movement developed to such an extent that, walking through the streets of Canton, it was impossible even for a moment to be out of hearing of the stirring strains of popular war-songs.

There can be no doubt that in the course of these activities tremendous numbers of people were stirred to a consciousness of the tasks facing them as Chinese and as citizens of Canton. Within the space of several weeks quiet shop clerks and garage mechanics changed into talented orators and organizers. Every parade and rally brought out new groups, new faces, and new leaders. After a year of silent acceptance of ruthless bombing, the people of Canton could at least speak out, organize, prepare for their own defence — the activities of the three summer months were illuminated with passion.

The civil and military authorities of the province lagged far behind the people. For the late emergence of mass activity, and for the failure to utilize the great human reserve which the campaigns of July, August, and September made available for the defence of the city and province, they alone must be held responsible.

In view of the free use the world Press has made of the terms "collapse" and "sell-out", it would be well to briefly survey the military history of the Japanese advance on Canton as I gathered it from my own observations in and around the city, and from subsequent conversations with informed observers.

The Japanese landing at Hachung on the morning of October 12 was not resisted, because Hachung, a shallow beach facing high hills and fairly remote from any road, was the last place where an attack was expected. Two things helped the Japanese to land there. One was the use of a new type shallow-draft landing-boats equipped with air propellers. This is the type of boat which, when the British learned of its existence, revolutionized all plans for the coastal defence of Honkgong. The second was the employment of Chinese traitors. There is no road from Hachung to Tamsui, on the highway ten miles from the coast, but there is a country path known to local smugglers. The Japanese took this path, and within several hours of landing had surprised and defeated the small Chinese garrison at Tamsui,* thus gaining a foothold on the main road to the coast. Japanese tanks and heavy equipment were landed at Autao, coastal terminus of the road, following the fall of Tamsui.

From the first moment of the landing, Japanese aircraft began systematically surveying, bombing, and machine-gunning all avenues of communication along which Chinese reinforcements would have to come. On October 12, the air-raid observation stations reported that 138 naval planes were over the province. Waichow, directly in the path of the Japanese advance, was bombed for twelve successive hours. A British engineer who was there at the time told me: "Innumerable planes, criss-crossing over Waichow for twelve hours in groups of six and nine, reduced the town to a complete ruin. During the two hours from noon to 2 p.m. I could swear that a bomb fell every ten seconds. As refugees surged out along the highway, Japanese planes flew low over them and machine-gunned." Everything that moved along the roads and waterways and every concentration of human beings, whether soldiers or civilians, was attacked. In several cases crowds of refugees and groups of peasants attending village fairs were ruthlessly destroyed. Troops unfortunate enough to be caught along the roads were wiped out. Japanese aerial activity in this campaign was the most intensive of the war, and possibly the most intensive in history.

While aircraft kept the meagre Chinese forces from moving towards the coast, Japanese tank columns forced their way along the highways, and reached

---

* The commander at Tamsui was Mo Hsi-teh, a feudal throwback even in the Cantonese provincial army. Mo had a reputation for reckless courage, cultivated personal loyalty among his men, and made them go through military exercises in long gowns. The other side of this "picturesque" facade was the preoccupation of the majority of his officers with tungsten smuggling to Hongkong (and ultimately to Japan). Mo's men were taken by surprise at Tamsui. Mo himself was in Canton. Placed under arrest and sent to face a court-martial at Chungking, he is now serving a 10-year sentence.

the defences west of Waichow before the Chinese had had an opportunity to bring up troops to man them. Heroic resistance was offered by small units along the way, but at no point was the number of Chinese troops sufficient to stop the advance of the enemy. As the Japanese mechanised units made their way towards Canton, the defenders, unable to hold the road, did not retreat upon the city, but retired to the hills along both sides.

In the East River area the Japanese troops actually out-numbered the Chinese. The bulk of the Chinese forces had been disposed along the Canton-Kowloon railway, the cutting of which was thought to be the main Japanese objective. The Japanese skirted this concentration and made straight for Canton.

In the city the evacuation was ordered, first of the women and children, and then of the entire population. The army, when it retreated, did not pass through Canton. On the night before the Japanese entry the majority of the Cantonese army's artillery and mechanized transport was successfully removed by train. This was imperative because the Japanese were already threatening to cut the railway north of the city.

The evacuation of Canton was perhaps unprecedented in history. Within a few days a city of 600,000 (the normal population of Canton is over a million) became an uninhabited desert of brick and mortar. It is estimated that on the day of the Japanese entry (October 21) there were not more than 10,000 people in Canton.

The completeness of the evacuation, the willingness of the Cantonese to leave their homes rather than submit to the invader, and the fact that for months after the occupation there was no sign of any large-scale influx of returning inhabitants (the Japanese had, perhaps on purpose, left several avenues open) provide full proof of the unbroken spirit of the people of Canton, of their unquestioning acceptance of a life of hardship and struggle as preferable to a life of slavery, and of their conviction that the Japanese victory was not final and that the fight would go on.

On the morning of October 21 the streets were deserted and the Chinese rear-guard was busy dynamiting the nerve-centre of the city. Within two hours the Pearl River Bridge, the city power-station and waterworks, the radio-station and a number of industrial enterprises — all of which the Japanese bombers had for months been vainly trying to hit — were destroyed or ir-reparably damaged. When the Japanese entered they found not the rich me-tropolis which they had set out to capture, but a wilderness of houses without light or water, people, or food.

On the following night the wilderness became a sea of flame. Terrific explosions shook Canton as ammunition dumps blew up. For two days the city was empty. The Chinese had gone. The Japanese, frightened, retired to a suburb, waiting for the flames to subside. They did not begin patrolling the streets until weeks later, when they set about their usual work of terrorization, scavenging for metals, promotion of narcotics, gambling and prostitution, and establishment of a puppet administration. To-day, six months after its fall, Canton remains an empty shell.

The capture of Canton accelerated the long-planned evacuation of Hankow. Once more, as after Nanking, the whole machinery of the Chinese Government shifted far to the West, and the roads, railways and rivers, were crowded with countless thousands of refugees. But whereas the evacuations of the capital had been carried out while the main forces of both sides were still engaged a good distance from the city, the civilian and military with-drawal from Hankow took place simultaneously — and the entire strength of the Japanese air force was free to harass it with bombs and machine-gunning.

The retreat from Hankow was entirely successful. Military equipment, a large part of the industrial plant, and large stores of commodities were all removed beforehand. Buildings likely to be of use to the enemy were blown up. The entire Japanese concession was levelled with the ground. After a maximum of effort, the capture of the city brought the enemy a minimum of material profit.

The Japanese were unable to proceed immediately to the consolidation of their gains, which should have taken the form of a simultaneous advance from Hankow and Canton to win control of the entire railway between the two cities. Had they pushed on with sufficient forces, they could probably have achieved this object without much difficulty — just as they could have reached Hankow many months earlier than they did, had they launched their drive on the Yangtze immediately after the fall of Nanking. But, as after Nanking, they suspended their military offensive in favour of new "peace" intrigues. The Chinese armies were thus enabled to take up strong positions in the mountains of Northern Kwangtung and Southern Hunan, after which the junction of the Canton-Hankow railway began to present, for the Japanese, a problem more difficult of solution than the junction of the Tientsin-Pukow railway at Hsuchow had been. At the beginning of May 1939, six months after the fall of Hankow, the Japanese were not yet ready to begin large-scale operations along the Canton-Hankow line.

They advanced far enough in early November, however, to bring about a new catastrophe — the destruction of Changsha. This great city, the capital of Hunan, was burned to the ground by misguided officials while the Japanese were still the best part of 100 miles away. No warning was given to the population, and thousands, who shamefully included a large number of wounded soldiers, perished in the flames. It is noteworthy that the responsibility for this act lay with men who were historically the enemies of progress in China, and even during the months of war had done all they could to sabotage the United Front in the province of Hunan. Even more noteworthy is the fact that swift justice overtook them at the hands of Chiang Kai-shek, who rushed to the stricken city and ordered their immediate execution, despite the fact that several of their number had long been his close retainers and had carried "faithfulness to the leader" as a banner to cover a long series of crimes against the Chinese people.

With the retreat from Canton and Hankow, the conditions under which the war between China and Japan was being waged underwent a sharp change. Hankow had been the hub of China, with excellent communications with the provinces of the North, South, and West. Its position had made it the great military, political, and trading centre of the entire country after the fall of Nanking. After its fall, there was no point that could take its place, and the great blocks of Free China which were destined to face the next wave of

Japanese attacks — the South-west and North-west — could communicate physically only by a thousand-mile detour over indifferent highways centring on Chungking, far, far to the West. Kweilin, Chungking, and Sian had therefore to share between them the military and administrative offices that had hitherto been centred in Hankow.

The Canton-Hankow railway had been the chief avenue of sea-borne imports from abroad. Now its place had to be taken by the railway from Hanoi to Yunnanfu, the road between Langson, in Indo-China, and Lungchow in Kwangsi, and the new highway which had been built with prodigious effort between Burma and Yunnan. Haiphong, Saigon, and Rangoon became ports of entry for goods destined for China. But the French authorities banned the import of war materials and imposed heavy duties and restrictions on articles such as trucks, even when they were destined for the Red Cross. The Burma road was not yet fit to take heavy traffic. Only the long Russian route through Sinkiang was fully open, but it was a difficult route with limited accommodation.

How to carry on the struggle under these new conditions was the problem before the country. *Whether* to go on fighting, was a question not asked by anyone. If the period between the fall of Nanking and the fall of Canton and Hankow had demonstrated that the advantage in formal warfare was on the side of the Japanese, it had also shown that Chinese armies could fight successful delaying actions, and, on occasion, launch effective counter-attacks. The core of the Chinese fighting forces was still intact, and was fast being stiffened with new arms and new methods of training. And, most important of all, the partisan movement of the armed people had proved its ability to prevent effective Japanese control of any of the "conquered provinces". The term "occupied territories" disappeared from the Chinese Press, and the words "guerrilla area" took their place. This was not empty boasting: it was a fact — a fact that the Japanese themselves acknowledged by launching a huge new "extermination campaign" against the partisans in which almost as many troops took part as had been necessary to consummate the great drive on

Hankow. Unlike the drive on Hankow, however, this campaign, even after three months, achieved no tangible objective.

An army still essentially undefeated. A partisan movement actively challenging Japanese control of the occupied areas. Unprecedented development of internal communications, of industry in the hinterland, and of new routes connecting China with the rest of the world. A national United Front which, though still insufficiently strong, stood firmer than ever before for resistance to the ultimate victory. This, despite the fall of her greatest cities, was the spectacle that China presented to the world after the first fifteen months of the war.

CHAPTER XIV
Transition

THE strength of the national unity of the Chinese people and of its political cornerstone — the collaboration between the Kuomintang and the Communist Party in the anti-Japanese struggle — is indicated by the fact that, despite waverings and slowness of development, it has always been most effective in times of crisis and decision. The fall of Nanking had been one great turning-point in China's fight for survival. The fall of Hankow was another. Each time, the two parties conferred, pooled their experience and effort, and contributed equally to the framing of plans to meet the new situation facing the country.

In a manifesto to the nation after the Japanese capture of Nanking, Chiang Kai-shek had announced that resistance would be continued, that the true strength of the Chinese people lay not in the coastal cities and towns, but in the great hinterland. On October 31, 1938, after the enemy took Hankow, he again called attention to this fact in a new "Declaration of Policy", and stated with satisfaction that the protracted defence of the city had given time for the consolidation of new military and economic bases in the deep rear. Calling upon the people to continue their struggle, and reiterating the national confidence in ultimate victory, he quoted the examples of the American War of Independence, the military campaigns of the French Revolution, the October

328

Revolution in Russia with the subsequent victory of the Red Army over the intervention, and the fight for the creation of modern Turkey as proving that an unwavering determination to continue the war was the only alternative to slavery, the only course that would lead to the creation of a China that was fully independent and fully free.

Just as after Nanking, highly significant military and political discussions were held, so the end of the Yangtze campaign was the occasion for a series of important conferences. Simultaneously with the evacuation of Hankow, the Enlarged Sixth Plenum of the Central Committee of the Chinese Communist Party concluded in Yenan, with the passing of a series of resolutions outlining the party's programme, and making recommendations for national policy, for the next stage of the war. During the city's last days, Chu Teh flew down from the North for a series of talks with the Generalissimo. In Chungking a session of the war-born People's Political Council issued a ringing call to the nation to go on fighting. A general military council held at Nanyo, Hunan, in early November, reached decisions as important as those of the great military conference in Wuchang which had mapped the strategy for Hsuchow and Taicrhchuang. In January, the Kuomintang held all extraordinary plenary session. Shortly afterwards, the People's Political Council assembled again. The proceedings of all these discussions, which took place during a period of rapid changes in internal, military, and international situation, are of great interest and importance.

Uniting them, and characterizing each one separately, was an atmosphere of absolute determination to carry on the struggle and of increased confidence in China's final victory. There was essential unity also in the concrete methods advocated for carrying on the war, and in every case the decisions reached were based on the lessons learned by both parties, and by the nation as a whole, from common experiences in the united struggle for existence.

In a long speech delivered before the plenum of the Central Committee of the Communist Party of China, Mao Tse-tung gave the fullest exposition and explanation of the three-stage theory of the protracted war* which, after the fall of Hankow, became the established basis of the military and diplomatic policy of the Chinese Government. Briefly, this theory may be stated thus. Japan, a small but highly-developed and well-armed imperialist State, attacked China, a vast but relatively unorganized, and semi-colonial country. Her superior military power enabled her to advance rapidly to gain control of China's great cities and modern communications, taking full advantage of her own strength and of China's many weaknesses. This constituted the first stage of the war, which approached a close with the fall of Hankow.

The reason that the war did not end in this first stage with a complete Japanese victory was that China was politically united in her determination to resist, that in the course of the war she was progressing towards external liberation and internal political and social democracy, and that her struggle for independence was increasingly based on the broad masses of her people. These circumstances made it possible for her to take advantage of her great size to retreat without demoralization, to carry on resistance which was increasingly exhausting the enemy and slowing down his advance, and at the same time to build up her own strength. The second stage of the war would therefore necessarily be a comparatively long period of stalemate, with China's power not yet sufficient to turn the tide, but able now, with the assistance of geographical factors and greater international support, to prevent the enemy from making new gains and to undermine those which he had already won. This stage would be protracted and difficult, so that the wavering and defection of some elements might be anticipated, but if

---

* Mao gave, as an example of a one-stage war — the Russo-Japanese War of 1904-5, which ended with the success of the Japanese offensive and a Russian retreat. The Franco-Russian War was a two-stage struggle — consisting of Napoleon's offensive and the Russian retreat and a Russian counter-offensive and Napoleon's defeat. Three-stage wars included the Seven Years War, the Thirty Years War and the Great War in Europe. A attacked B, who retreated; there was a long period of stalemate during which B gathered his potential forces and reformed his methods and organization; B counter-attacked and finally won the war.

national unity and political progress were maintained and the mass base for the struggle extended, it would see a great increase of China's power leading to the stage of counter-attack.

The third stage would come when Japan was at the end of her resources and China had developed hers sufficiently to launch a general counter-offensive. It would result in the complete defeat of Japanese imperialism and the emergence of China as a strong, democratic, and completely independent state, with the foundations of her future political, economic, and cultural development already firmly laid.

The immediate prospect was a period of transition from the first stage to the second. This period, according to Mao Tse- tung's speech and the resolutions published at the conclusion of the plenum, would see an increase of the hardships facing China. After the fall of Hankow and Canton, the struggle would be hampered by "the loss of our big industries and trade, the occupation of the country's main railways, the geographical separation of the political administration from the fighting areas, the occupation of the coast, the temporary decrease of foreign aid, stringency of finance, and dislocation of the national economy, disruption of transportation, and the consequent inadequacy of military supplies". To take advantage of these difficulties, the Japanese would not only strive anew for a military decision, but were planning to organize a central puppet Government claiming authority over the entire country and to intensify their efforts to alienate the Kuomintang from the Communist Party, and to cause an internal split within the Kuomintang itself on the question of peace. The increased strain on the nation would give the enemy an opportunity to "create disappointment and pessimism among the people, to sow dissension in the anti-Japanese camp, to cause some elements to waver and others even to betray".

But there was another side to the picture, a side which made it possible to say that, despite all these hardships, the objective situation would become more and more favourable to China. Why? Because, while the new obstacles facing China would to a large extent be paralleled by new difficulties arising in the path of the enemy, her internal progress would create conditions in her favour which the Japanese militarists could not duplicate. What were the difficulties of the enemy? "For the Japanese, the lengthening of the fighting line means the disposition of fewer troops over greater areas. Once away from the coast, river, and railways, operations in the mountainous regions of the interior will be much more difficult. The spread of guerrilla warfare in their rear will slowly reduce the enemy to a state of exhaustion. The Japanese attack on South China tends to sharpen Anglo-Japanese, American-Japanese, and Franco-Japanese conflicts. The further aggression of the Japanese militarists and China's determined resistance will make the war seem endless to the Japanese people, thus stimulating the growth of an anti-war and anti-Fascist movement in Japan."

What were the factors favouring China? "China is increasing in unity and becoming more democratic. Generalissimo Chiang and the people throughout the country are holding rigidly to resistance. Co-operation between the Kuomintang and the Communist Party and the unity of the whole nation are progressing. Both parties are growing in numbers and political influence. The Chinese people hate the Japanese invaders and are strengthening their solidarity. China still holds large areas (in the North-west and South-west) as her general bases for the war of resistance. At the same time, in the enemy's rear, widespread guerrilla warfare is gaining momentum and new anti-Japanese bases are being consolidated and enlarged. Chinese troops have accumulated valuable experience in the war and are strengthening their fighting power. The national political system is proceeding step by step towards greater democracy (particularly in the anti-Japanese bases in the rear of the enemy) and the broad masses of the people are being mobilized and organized."

How could the scales be further weighted against the enemy? How could the favourable situation be maintained? How could China make sure that the stage of stalemate would not become permanent, that she would not, at the conclusion of hostilities, remain half slave and half free? Mao Tse-tung's answer was that she could do this by further developing those sources of strength which had enabled her to delay the enemy's advance in the first stage to a point where they could halt it in the second, and turn in into a route in the third.

"The central pivot upon which hinge both the determined prosecution of our war of resistance and successful conquest of our difficulties is the further consolidation of the unity of the Chinese people." The fundamental tasks facing the nation were, therefore, to maintain resistance and to strengthen and enlarge the anti-Japanese United Front.

After the outbreak of the Shanghai war, the co-operation of the Kuomintang and Communist Party had been formally announced. After the fall of Nanking, the Communist Party had declared that this co-operation was not for the period of the war alone, but also for the subsequent period of reconstruction and the building of a democratic republic. Long-term co-operation between the two parties required an organizational form. Boldly the Communists announced — the best such form is to turn the Kuomintang into a national-revolutionary alliance of all anti-Japanese parties, which all their members, without sacrificing their own allegiance, could openly join. "The... Communist Party of China formally resolves not to build secret organizations of the Communist Party in the Kuomintang and its armies and declares once more its sincerity in support of the Three People's Principles, of Generalissimo Chiang, and of the National Government. It solemnly declares... that it considers it to be the best form of co-operation to have members of the Communist Party join the Kuomintang and the Three People's Principles Youth Corps. It will hand over to the leading organs of the Kuomintang the names of its members who have joined the party and the corps, and it will refrain from recruiting new members for itself from within their ranks. The second (alternative) proposal is that the two parties shall form joint committees of all grades (town, district, provincial, national) to lead all activities in which the two parties co-operate.... The proper solution of the organizational form of co-operation between the two parties is of tremendous significance in the improvement of relations and to guarantee long-term co-operation between them."

Why did the Communist Party now wish for such close organic contact with the Kuomintang, its enemy of ten years' standing and only recently an ally? According to Mao Tse-tung's speech and the Resolutions, it was impelled to do this in the first place by its Marxist analysis of the historical stage at which China found herself. "The internal condition of the nation (the war of resistance and national reconstruction through the efforts of an anti-Japanese National United Front of all parties, groups and classes), as well as the international situation, all show us that at this historical stage it is impossible to establish a one- party dictatorship, a Soviet state, of a socialist system." For the common effort of many forces whose chief impulse was now not conflict among themselves but a common battle for self-preservation and reconstruction, the only form of government was "a democratic republic in its new form, a new China of the Three People's Principles, whose foundations will be laid in the difficult and protracted war of resistance".

That this conclusion flowed inescapably from the situation was proved by the following "substantial evidence of the development of the State towards democracy since the outbreak of the war; the proclamation of the Programme for the War of Resistance and National Reconstruction, the convocation of the People's Political Council, the establishment of provincial and municipal People's Political Councils; the legalization of the various anti-Japanese parties and groups; the gradual realization of freedom of speech, publication and association for the people; the realization of democracy in the anti-Japanese bases in the Shensi-Kansu-Ninghsia and Shansi-Chahar-Hopei Border Regions; and the improvement of the people's livelihood".

All these things, representing the framework, the first beginnings of democracy in China, had been realized with the Kuomintang in control of the Central Government, in which the other parties, although legalized, still played no official part. It was obvious, therefore, that the Kuomintang itself had altered its stand of the last ten years, and that it would continue to go forward still further under the stress of the war of resistance. That was why Mao Tse-tung had argued that "the Kuomintang has a brilliant future", and had wished for an increase of its anti-Japanese strength, as well as that of his own Communist Party. In this anti-imperialist war, in which China was emerging from her semi-colonial status, the two parties were allies. In all severe struggles, said the Communists, the strengthening of an ally is equivalent to an addition to one's own strength, and close co-operation between allies is the secret of victory over a common enemy.

Did the Communist Party offer to give up its organizational independence and political principles? On the contrary, its members maintained that only its organizational independence and its adherence to its own principles made it possible for it to march boldly forward, proposing new measures for the consolidation of the common anti-Japanese front. The Communist Party was not afraid of losing its own identity in such a front. It was the party of the Chinese working class, and it believed that this class (and therefore its political party) not only had a glorious future before it, but was already the vanguard of the nation. "The posts for Communists are in those places where blows can be most severely inflicted on the enemy," stated the resolutions of the Plenum and the armies in which the Communist Party provided the leadership, the Eighth Route and the New Fourth, exemplified this statement by being constantly in the van of the struggle in its most difficult and dangerous sectors. Now the Central Committee called upon all Communists to be not only model fighters, but also model builders of the United Front, the chief guarantee of success in the anti- Japanese war. At the same time, it urged them to raise the level of their own theoretical knowledge, "to learn the theories of Marx, Engels, Lenin, and Stalin, to learn the experience of Marxism-Leninism and of the Comintern, to apply them actively in the struggle in China, to study the Three People's Principles and Chinese history". In its own ranks, the party sharply denounced both the "Left" deviation, whose adherents "do not understand that the only way to emancipate the Chinese people is to strengthen and enlarge the National Anti-Japanese United Front..." and the Right opportunists, who "execute the tactics of the United Front at the expense of the independence of the party, politically and organizationally distorting the policy of the proletariat in building an anti-Japanese National

United Front so that the working class and the Communist Party drag at the tail of the bourgeoisie, rather than hold their position as the vanguard". Confirming the expulsion of Chang Kuo-tao, a former leader who had belonged, at different times, to both the "Left" and the Right dissidents from its policy, the Communist Central Committee pointed out that all attacks on the solidarity of the party and attempts to split it from within were assaults on an important bastion of anti-Japanese resistance, and were therefore of concern and danger not only to Communists, but to the entire nation in its struggle against the invader.

The exposition of the theory of the three-stage protracted war and the proposals for an organizational formulation of the United Front, together with the clear re-statement of the Communist Party's position within that front, were the most historic features of the plenum. Its other resolutions concerned the strengthening of the anti-Japanese unity of all parties, factions, classes, and nationalities in China through democratic reforms and a struggle against economic and national oppression; the improvement of the political and military training of the army and its technical equipment; the development of guerrilla warfare, the institution of wartime financial, economic, and educational reforms; the suppression of traitors and Trotzkyites;* the strengthening of China's ties with the anti-Fascist Powers; and the establishment of a

---

* The Chinese followers of Trotzky (organized into the so-called "Communist Revolutionary League") have played a sinister role in the war of resistance, standing in the same line with the Japanese and with Chinese traitors in their opposition to the National United Front. In Kwangsi, one of them, Huang Kung-tu, attempted an armed rising at a moment when the provincial troops were fighting the enemy on the Northern Front. Chang Mu-tao, another, who, as a subordinate of Feng Yu-hsiang during the Chahar anti-Japanese military movement in 1933 urged his chief to "establish a United Front with the Japanese against the counter-revolutionary Chiang Kai-shek government" and later, at Sian, advocated the execution of Chiang, attempted to organize a rebellion in Shansi soon after the fall of Taiyuan. Chen Tu-hsin and Yeh Ching worked actively against the unity of the Chinese nation in Hankow, the latter being responsible for the bitter attacks on the Communists in the Kuomintang Press in January 1938. In Shanghai, the Trotzkyists went into the refugee camps to recruit workers for Japanese industries, telling them that by returning to the factories they would "strengthen the revolutionary ranks of the proletariat". All these cases are well known in China and were exposed by non-Communist quarters.

United Front against the Japanese military fascists by the peoples of China, Japan, Korea, and Formosa.

Finally, at the conclusion of its deliberations, the plenum sent telegrams of greeting and solidarity to Generalissimo Chiang Kai-shek, who "leads the whole nation in a war of prolonged resistance which has achieved the unity of the Chinese people, dealt a severe blow to Japanese imperialism, and established the foundations of our final victory and national reconstruction"; to the Kuomintang; the Eighth Route and New Fourth Armies; the people of Manchuria; the Communist Party and heroic people of Spain; the underground Communist Party of Japan which was leading the struggle against Japanese military fascism; and to the Communist parties and progressive peoples of the world. In this last message, the plenum stressed the organic connection of China's fight with the anti-Fascist struggle everywhere. Deploring the assistance Japan was still receiving from the democratic Powers, it called on all friends of China to put pressure on their Governments, to apply sanctions against Japan under Article XVI of the League Covenant, to agitate for an embargo on exports of war supplies and raw materials to the aggressor, intensify the boycott of Japanese goods, organize seamen and transport workers to refuse to handle Japanese imports and exports, and campaign for aid to China in the shape of funds, medical equipment, and supplies. "With a powerful National United Front," it declared, "and with the assistance of the international working class and of all progressive people, the Chinese people will win the ultimate victory in their war of prolonged resistance."

During the week that saw the fall of Canton and the evacuation of Hankow, the reactionaries and defeatists who had worked for "peace" after the loss of Nanking tried their utmost to again develop their activity. Wang Ching-wei, high priest of capitulation, flew a "peace" kite in all interview given to Reuter in which he declared that China was ready for mediation and was waiting only for acceptable terms from Japan. Fiercely attacked especially by the Overseas Chinese for making such a statement at such a time, Wang hastily swallowed his words. A few days later, Chiang Kai-shek reiterated the national determination to fight on, not only to the world at large, but also privately to the British Ambassador, who had rushed to his field headquarters in Hunan to learn the real situation with regard to the future of Chinese resistance. Finally, the People's Political Council, of which Wang Ching-wei was the unpopular president, concluded its session in Chungking by passing a series of resolutions which reflected not Wang's treasonable "pacifism", but a stubborn confidence in the future of China's struggle and national reconstruction.

At a time when in Japan the people had lost even the few democratic rights they had once possessed, the People's Political Council of China found it possible to resolve the abolition of all censorship of books, magazines, and other publications and the drastic liberalization of the censorship of the daily Press.

Japanese oppression of the Korean and Formosan peoples was increasing. In China, the Council voted to establish closer relations with the national minorities and to correct the injustice previously suffered by the Mongol, Moslem, and Tibetan peoples under Chinese rule.

The Tokyo Government, waging an unpopular war, saw salvation only in rigid centralization of all political control. In China, fighting for her life against the Japanese onslaught, the Government could depend on its people. By a great majority, the Council voted for acceleration of local autonomy for various regions and the expansion of the functions of regional administrations.

Financial stringency in Japan had led to severe restrictions on the movements of foreign exchange, the only imports on which precious gold was spent being those considered to be immediate military necessities. China also was conserving her gold. But the People's Political Council passed a resolution calling for the release of substantial sums for the purchase of scientific and educational equipment to replace that lost in the fire of war, so that cultural progress could continue.

Other resolutions dealt with the broad development of popular education and the energetic promotion of internal trade.

During the first week of November, Chiang Kai-shek called a grand military council of all China's chief commanders at Nanyo, in Hunan. The unanimous stand of the Chinese Government, the Kuomintang, and the Communist Party on the question of further resistance had been made completely clear. Japan had also announced her intentions. "If necessary, we will march to the remotest sections of China," her War Minister, General Itagaki had said to Reuter's representative on October 26. The military struggle would continue. The task of the Nanyo Conference was to decide on the principles and methods which would govern China's strategy in its next phase.

Speaking to the assembled commanders, Chiang Kai-shek expressed his conviction that henceforth the entire Chinese Army would have to depend more and more upon the tactics of the people's war. Many of his officers had been trained in the formal Prussian military tradition. Now he invited them to consider an entirely new set of principles of warfare, which he phrased thus:

"The people are more important than the army;

"Guerrilla warfare is more important than positional warfare;

"The political education of our soldiers is more important than their military education;

"Propaganda is more important than bullets."

These slogans were propounded with a definite purpose in mind. They did not mean that the military education of the army, preparations for positional warfare, and the manufacture of arms would receive less attention than hitherto. They did indicate, however, that the highest command of the Chinese forces realized that the "political reserves" of China's strength, which had previously been sadly neglected, should now be released. Hence the striking emphasis placed on these aspects of resistance by the chief of China's armies.

To give concrete effect to these slogans, political departments were organized in all military units down to the company. By the order of the Generalissimo, a school of guerrilla tactics was established, with attendance obligatory for all army officers, who would be withdrawn, in rotation, from their units, to under- go an intensive three-month course in partisan warfare. Yeh Chien-ying, once chief of staff of the Red Army, and later the Eighth Route Army's delegate at Nanking and Hankow, was named dean of the school. Thus there was created, on a national scale, an academy of the political and military principles of partisan warfare, with courses paralleling those of the famous anti-Japanese University at Yenan and the training school for commanders and commissars founded a year previously at Wutaishan, the capital of the Shansi-Chahar-Hopei Border Region. All China was learning the tactics of the people's war, tested and proved under the most severe conditions in the new bases of resistance which unswerving determination to fight on, hard work, and complete faith in the people had created in the rear of the Japanese in North China and on the lower Yangtze.

Finally, to carry out the new strategy, the strength of the Chinese Army, amounting to more than 200 divisions, was fundamentally redistributed. One-third of the total forces were assigned to the various fronts where they would continue to impede the advance of the Japanese vanguards. One-third were allocated to the rear, for re-arming, mechanization, and training which would increase their striking power and fit them for the shock tasks of the future anti-Japanese offensive. And one-third of the total regular strength was ordered to filter through to the rear of the enemy, to carry on the struggle by guerrilla methods, reinforce existing partisan armies, and form the nucleus for the creation of new detachments.

Thus the first phase of partisan warfare came to an end, and the gulf between the operations of the regular troops at the fronts and the activities of guerrillas in the enemy's rear was formally bridged. The so-called "lost territories" were re-named "guerrilla areas", and their defence, like that of other sections of the country, was recognized as being one of the duties of the National Army, which, more than ever before, was becoming the army of the united Chinese people.

As Chiang Kai-shek and other leaders of her resistance had always confidently predicted, China's international position improved with every new manifestation of her steadfast will to continue the struggle. Ever since the League of Nations, in October 1937, had recommended that its member States give individual assistance to China, constant and valuable aid had been forthcoming from the Soviet Union, which took seriously its obligations under the Covenant and was, moreover, the only country in the world whose foreign policy called for assistance to any and every people whose independence was menaced by armed aggression. The democracies of Western Europe had been backward with their help, chiefly as a result of the dreams Mr. Chamberlain and his friends in the City continued to entertain of the possibilities of Far Eastern "appeasement". The United States had gone beyond Britain by issuing pronouncements in which she officially branded Japan as a law-breaker. But the law-breaker still committed his felonies with the aid of American oil and scrap iron. It was only after Munich and the invasion of South China, that Britain, France, and the United States dealt their first counter-blows against the Far Eastern partner of the axis, who, while perhaps the most favourably placed of the Fascist Powers with regard to swift military action (British, French, and American forces in the Pacific being, at that time, relatively negligible), was at the same time the most vulnerable to economic pressure.

Since Japan had not made any perceptible move towards compromise with foreign interests, but, on the contrary, was attacking more and more boldly the remaining spheres of Western influence and trade, the Powers were driven, towards the end of 1938, to supplement their strong (but disregarded) diplomatic notes to Tokyo by new loans to the Chinese Government, which had proved itself to be the only available bulwark against Japanese expansion. On December 16, it was announced that the British Export Credits Department had granted credits amounting to £10,000,000 for the development of the Burma road, and the American Export and Import Bank, the sum of $25,000,000 for the purchase of trucks and other non-military equipment. Thus, the continued struggle of the Chinese people provided the base for other efforts to curb the Japanese drive for domination in the Far East. These efforts were different in kind and intention. The political philosophy and the interests of the Soviet Union led it logically, as we have seen, to back China to the full in her fight for complete independence and the defeat of the aggressor. The Roosevelt administration in Washington had, at this stage, also arrived at a full realization of the importance of placing the entire weight and resources of the United States on the side of world peace and international order, although the strength of isolationist reaction within the country still prevented it from taking any really effective action.* Finally, Chamberlain and his echo Daladier desired to put pressure on Tokyo, not in order to help China *per se* or to curb aggression generally, but to defend their threatened possessions and to "bring Japan to reason", as they were still trying to bring Hitler and Mussolini to "reason" in Europe. China's internal political and military progress made it possible for her to turn all these motives to advantage, to utilize to the full the positive aspects of the increased international aid she was receiving, and to fear no disaster from the manoeuvres of the betrayers of Czechoslovakia.

During eighteen mouths of war, China had withstood the assault of the Japanese military machine, the "peacemaking" efforts of would-be mediators, and the enemy's indefatigable attempts to exploit every evidence of wavering and every potential source of disunity in her rear. Now, in spite of greatly increased difficulties, her strength was growing, her confidence in victory greater than ever before. The Japanese, who had never given up hope of conquering China by political means, their German and Italian allies, and the capitulationist faction in Chungking itself all felt, in December 1938, that the position was growing desperate. In joint consultation they decided to launch a new political offensive, to bring about a conflict between the new China and all the remaining forces of the old, and to cause the magnificent resistance of the Chinese people to collapse in internal disintegration and civil war.

The functions in this offensive were divided as follows: Tokyo was to

---

* The rulings curtailing aircraft exports to Japan were a step forward. The "cash and carry" provisions of the Neutrality Act, however, operate in favour of the aggressive states, whose chief source of essential raw materials the United States still continues to be.

produce a new and "moderate" set of peace terms. The axis Press was to tout the prospects of a "settlement". Wang Ching-wei was to present the terms to Chiang Kai-shek. Should they be rejected, he was to muster his own political forces for a movement against the Government.

It is definitely known that before they were publicly issued, the Japanese proposals later embodied in the declaration of Prince Konoye were submitted to Wang Ching-wei for approval. Some say that this was done through Wang's connections in the puppet administrations, others through the Italian Embassy at Chungking. In any case, by mid-January the terms were in his hands. They provided for China's adherence to the Anti-Comintern Pact; full freedom of residence, travel, and trade for the Japanese in all parts of China; economic and political "co-operation" between China, Japan, and "Manchukuo"; and the "temporary" stationing of Japanese troops in Inner Mongolia "to prevent the spread of Communism". In return for China's placing all her resources at the disposal of Japan for the furtherance of her ambition to achieve complete economic, political, and cultural control of the continent of Asia, the pundits of Tokyo offered to "surrender" the tiny territorial concessions and the extra-territorial rights which they had possessed before the war.

When Wang Ching-wei tried to urge these conditions on the Generalissimo, the latter practically threw him out, the interview lasting only five minutes. On the following day, Chiang Kai-shek flew to Sian to inspect the North-western bases of resistance and the military roads to the Soviet Union.

Wang had played his first card and lost, lost so utterly that he considered it dangerous to remain in Chungking. Privately, his followers were informed: "Our leader is in peril. We must get him out of the capital." Peng Hsueh-pei, Vice-Minister of Communications and a member of the capitulationist group, secretly provided the plane in which he left, on December 18, for Yunnan. (Peng was later arrested.)

Then Wang Ching-wei played his second card — the feudal backwardness of the rear-line provinces to which the Government had been forced to retreat. Szechuan, for instance, had for thirty years been bled white by the internecine struggles of rival satraps, having seen no fewer than 200 civil "wars"

since the Revolution of 1911. Now that the Central authorities had moved to
this province, the power of the local commanders was curbed, and a certain
amount of resentment was known to exist among them. Yunnan, too, had been
practically independent for a long period, and had come under the Government's
complete control only after the beginning of the war. Months before the Generalissimo and the active leaders of the Government had left Hankow, Wang
was already working in Chungking to bring these potentially rebellious elements under his control. He placed his subordinate, Chen Kung-po, in charge
of the Kuomintang headquarters at Chengtu, Szechuan's provincial capital.
His own wife and a number of his trusted followers spent much time in Yunnan.

Arriving at Yunnanfu, Wang immediately went to see Lung Yun, the provincial chairman, who, he had been given to understand, had already been
brought around to the "peace bloc". He told him of Prince Konoye's terms and
pointed out that the Japanese had never menaced Yunnan, that the war had
meant to the province only the loss of its autonomy, the destruction on many
far-flung fronts of most of the troops that had once formed the basis of Lung
Yun's power, and the horror of air raids over its titles.* Proposing that Lung
Yun side with him against the Central Government, he at the same time instructed Chen Kung-po in Chengtu to make similar approaches to the regional
militarists of Szechuan.

This effort to throw united China back into the not-so-long-dead days of
inter-provincial civil wars failed completely. Lung Yun's answer to Wang Ching-
wei was to ask him whether the Generalissimo was aware that he had left
Chungking and come to Yunnan with such proposals. If not, he said, he would
immediately inform him. Wang Ching-wei fled forthwith to Hanoi, and Lung
Yun made a full report to Chiang Kai-shek. The intrigue in Szechuan fell through
just as ignominiously, and Chen Kung-po followed his master to Indo-China.

It is an interesting study in the anatomy of treason to consider the careers
of the men who accompanied Wang Ching-wei on his flight. All were political

---

* Early in May 1939, Lung Yun revealed that Wang continued, from Hanoi, his efforts to
alienate yunnan from the national cause. In a letter dated March 30, he again called upon
Lung to rebel.

adventurists who had attached themselves, like barnacles, to the body of the Chinese national revolution, seeing in its progress opportunities not of service to the people, but only of personal advancement. All had a long record of waverings and betrayals. Chou Fu-hai, who as chief of the Central Publicity Board, had long sabotaged China's internal and foreign propaganda,* and Chen Kung-po, Wang's Man Friday in Chengtu, had been among the earliest members of the Communist Party at a time when to be a Communist was intellectually daring rather than physically dangerous. After turning their coats at the first whiff of adversity, they spent ten years following Wang Ching-wei in his shabby shuttlings from the extreme "Left" to the extreme Right of the Kuomintang. Finally, they ended by betraying the Kuomintang and the Chinese people. Tseng Chung-ming, Vice-Minister of Railways (later assassinated), had a history that was different in its details, but not in its nature. Tao Hsi-sheng we have already met as the professor who helped the police hunt down his own anti-Japanese students during the Peiping demonstrations of December 1935. These, and one or two more, were Wang's followers.

Outside China, this unsavoury pack took up the task of proving the benevolent intentions of the Japanese imperialism that had taken the lives of millions of Chinese men, women, and children, and the dangerous criminality of those who were still leading China in what they termed her "suicidal" struggle for existence. Liberally provided with funds by the Japanese, they bought up newspapers in overseas centres, hired scoundrels of the pen to argue that Britain, France, the United States, and the Soviet Union were the worst enemies of Far Eastern peace, and organized a widespread net of espionage. At the same time, they strove to create the impression that they were still a power within the country and that there was a wide following for their "policy". This was designed mainly to increase their status in the eyes of their new masters.

* An idea of what this double renegade considered effective propaganda for China may be gleaned from the fact that when he first assumed office early in 1938 he amazed foreign correspondents by making his first general Press reception a Sino-German friendship demonstration, at which several speakers stressed the good relations between the two countries. This was only three weeks after Hitler had openly expressed his desire for a Japanese victory and announced Nazi recognition of "Manchukuo"!

The Japanese, however, understood very well that they had been misled as to the strength and influence of the capitulationist clique. They were furious with Wang Ching-wei for having exposed himself and left Chungking where, even if his political importance was small, his high posts would have enabled him to advance the future intrigues of the Axis. Now that his usefulness was so greatly reduced, they showed no enthusiasm at all for the numerous grandiose declarations which Wang took to issuing "to the Chinese people" (although they distributed them mechanically, like their own propaganda, throughout the occupied territories), and made contemptuous remarks about him in interviews with foreign pressmen. Prince Konoye, the Japanese Premier, who had placed so much faith in Wang's ability to secure the defection of Szechuan and Yunnan and thus deprive the Chinese Government of its chief territorial bases, was forced to resign, and a new Cabinet was formed, led by Baron Hiranuma, an appointee of the army. But this Cabinet too could not recover from the final shock that had been administered to Japanese hopes of an easy victory in China. To date, it has not produced a clear foreign policy nor made a statement of its intentions convincing to the world or to the Japanese people.

The consciousness that they had failed completely in their attempt to stir up internal dissension in China did not prevent the Japanese and their friends from trying to lead the world to believe that in reality it was not a handful of bankrupt careerists but Chiang Kai-shek and the entire Kuomintang who had tired of the struggle and desired to exchange the fight for freedom for co-operation with Japanese militarism and the resumption of civil strife. Only the Communists, they maintained, now had an interest in resistance.*

Chiang Kai-shek himself answered these insinuations when, on De-

---

* At the moment of Wang's defection, Chang Chun-mai, one of his associates and leader of the National-Socialist Party, launched an attack on the Communist party in a letter to the *Central Daily News*, the Kuomintang's chief organ which was still in the hands of Wang's followers. Characteristically, he argued that the existence of the Communist Party made not capitulation, but resistance more difficult. This was only another aspect of the disruptive activity of Wang Ching-wei's claque. If these gentlemen could not destroy national unity in the name of peace", they would do it in the name of patriotism. (It is not only in China that those, who want to open the gates to the enemy operate under the cloak of "anti-Communism".)

cember 26, he launched a devastating oratorical attack on the "moderate" proposals of the maladroit Prince Konoye, and, rejecting the deceptive phrases in which they were presented, struck straight at their true essence.

"Konoye's statement," he said, "can only be considered in connection with the enemy's words and deeds during the past months. In this way we can see it for what it really is, the complete self-exposure of the fantastic Japanese plan to annex China, dominate East Asia, and go on to the conquest of the world. It is a complete revelation of our enemy's scheme to destroy our country and exterminate our people.

Point by point, the Generalissimo analysed the inner meaning of the so-called "conciliatory" terms:

The Japanese talked ceaselessly of their desire to "create a new order in East Asia" which they officially defined as consisting of "Japan, Manchukuo, and a reborn China assisting each other and co-operating closely in politics, economics, and culture to combat the Red peril, protect Oriental civilization, remove economic barriers, and help China to rise from her semi-coloniai status."

"Let all observe", said Chiang Kai-shek, "that by China reborn they mean that independent China must perish and an enslaved China be created in its place. This enslaved China will then be tied by 'close links', which remind one of nothing so much as of the links of heavy chains, to the Japanese-created 'Manchukuo' and to Japan herself. What is the significance of the other points? Under the pretext of opposition to the 'Red peril', Japan seeks to control China's military affairs. Claiming to uphold Oriental civilization, she aims at uprooting China's national culture. By urging the elimination of economic barriers, she hopes to exclude American and European influence and to dominate the Pacific. Under the so-called economic unity, she understands a Japanese stranglehold on the sources of our economic life.... Finally, by the rebuilding of China she means the destruction of our free country and the 'construction' of a nation of slaves."

The speech dealt just as summarily with Japan's demagogic slogan of the return of the Western concessions. "What has been called the rendition of the concessions would be the surrender of them all to the Japanese." As for Japan's offer to give up all claims for reparations as well as her own concessions and extra-territorial rights, it was "natural that since the Japanese want our entire resources and population, they are not interested in any part of our territory or substance as a mere concession or indemnity".

The points concerning "joint defence against Communism" were also mercilessly exposed.

"It is pointless for us who are carrying out the Three People's Principles", said the Generalissimo, "to discuss 'co-operation against Communism'. Suffice it to say that, on the part of the Japanese, this pretended motive is a screen for a desire to dominate our military dispositions and to proceed from this to the management of our internal politics and culture, and even our external diplomacy. This is the same demand that Japan was consistently urging upon us during the years before we began our armed resistance. It was because we were unwilling to concede these very things that we first endured a multitude of hardships and then, finally, were forced to call the whole nation to struggle and sacrifice.

"The truth for us to remember is that Japan entered the Anti-Comintern Pact not in order to combat Communism or Soviet Russia, but to use it as a pretext for destroying China. If the point at issue were really Japan's national defence against the Soviet, then why, after the Changkufeng affair, did the Japanese Ambassador at Moscow yield so ignominiously to the Soviet Foreign Minister? No, Japan's 'anti-Communism' is only a ruse to deceive world opinion and her own nationals at home."

Commenting on the demand of the Japanese that they be allowed to station troops in Inner Mongolia, Chiang Kai-shek declared that the Tokyo militarists were evidently in the habit of hoodwinking themselves as well as other people. A China that had been aroused to battle for its freedom was evidently something of which they could not conceive. This was certainly indicated by their demand that such a China should acquiesce in any infringement of its integrity.

Concerning the right of Japanese to reside and trade in the interior, he declared scathingly that, on the surface, this demand appeared quite harmless. But in making it, Prince Konoye did not "seem to be aware that the mere mention of Japanese residents reminds our people only of the spying activities of the Japanese special service, the exploits of the *ronin*, opium smuggling, the peddling of morphine and heroin, the operation of gambling dens and houses of prostitution, the training of traitors, and all the other Japanese devices to secure their degradation and enslavement".

"We have now covered the principal points of Konoye's statement, which he describes as a collection of 'minimum demands'. If these are 'minimum demands', I should like to ask what more he wants. Compared with Hirota's 'Three Points', they are many times more comprehensive and virulent. Let me ask: If we could not accept Hirota's 'Three Points' before the commencement of hostilities, how can the enemy entertain the hope that now, after eighteen months of struggle, China will accept these terms of national extinction?"

Finally, Chiang Kai-shek expressed confidence that Japanese militarism was proceeding blindly towards its own destruction. In the meantime, however, it remained a menace not so much to China, which had awakened, as to the other Pacific Powers, who were still largely asleep.

"The gallant sacrifice of more than a million of our men at the front and of countless numbers of our people in the rear has saved the country from destruction. Strong bulwarks have already been erected to safeguard our national existence. On the other hand, our unyielding stand has made it impossible for the enemy not to reveal his every vicious intention.... Japan's continental policy has now broadened into an oceanic policy. Having first advanced northward, she is now also moving southward. Besides attempting to annex China, Japan is trying also to overthrow the international order in the Far East and to banish from the entire Pacific the influence of Britain and the United States.

"The nations of the world, which are bound by treaty obligations, should long ago have applied punitive measures against the aggressor. But they have hesitated and looked on, while China has taken upon herself the immense responsibility of curbing the Japanese militarists.

"Our object in prosecuting this war of resistance is to complete the tasks of our national revolution and to secure independence, liberty, and equality for our country. Internationally, our aim is to support righteousness and justice and restore the distinction between good and evil in dealings between nations. Ours is a war between right and wrong, between justice and force, between a country that abides by the law and one that has broken it. Ultimately, this will have its effect and the world will rise to support us. In the meantime, we must hold fast to our stand and fix our eyes steadfastly on our goal. Our determination should be steeled by each new difficulty, and our courage increase as resistance is prolonged. The final victory will be ours. I urge my comrades in the party, our army and our people to redouble their efforts towards its achievement."

A few days later, Chiang Kai-shek's clear statement of policy found its echo in formal action by the party of which he was the head. On January 1, at an extraordinary session of the Standing Committee, Wang Ching-wei, and those who had followed him, were formally deprived of all their posts and expelled for life from the ranks of the Kuomintang.

In mid-January, the Fifth Plenary Session of the Central Executive Committee of the Kuomintang met to consider the tasks facing the country and its chief party during the forthcoming second stage of the war of resistance. As a result of the most important of its decisions, a supreme National Defence Council was founded, in which was vested the final authority over all political and military affairs, as well as the internal party affairs of the Kuomintang, for the duration of the struggle. In recognition of the opening of China's great West and the necessity, recently stressed by the People's Political Council, of improving relations with the national minorities in these areas, a new organ of the Government, the Ministry of Frontier Affairs, was brought into being. Other important measures dealt with the control of industries, the improvement of financial administration, the promotion of foreign trade, and the encouragement of co-operatives as a form of war-time economic rehabilitation.

The discussion of the proposals for the organizational formulation of the United Front advanced by the Communist Party was not published, but the other decisions, and the composition of the National Defence Council, indicated that they had not been accepted. At the same time, the pronouncements of the session on the question of prolonged resistance, the condemnation of capitulationist tendencies, and the military and economic measures it adopted, demonstrated that the unity of the two parties on basic questions of national policy was greater than ever. This was further emphasized by a message which the Communist Party sent to the session, pledging anew its support of Chiang Kai-shek and the Kuomintang in the anti-Japanese struggle.

The best proof of the solidarity of the entire Chinese nation came, however, not from within the country, but from the reactions of the Japanese.

On the one hand, the realization that, having shot off all her military and political big guns, Japan was still as far as ever from achieving the subjugation of China caused profound confusion and discouragement in Tokyo. Even so bellicose a sabre-rattler as General Itagaki stopped talking about marching to Chungking, and assured the worried financial interests (and his country's equally worried Fascist allies) that the Imperial Army would henceforth concentrate on the strengthening of its control over the "occupied territories", in which many new fronts were springing up. Just as after attempting to probe the strength of the

Soviet Union at Changkufeng, the Japanese Army hastily transferred its attentions to South China, which was much easier going, so now it preferred, rather than launch a new major campaign on the continent, to seize Hainan, blockade the concessions, and otherwise trample on the rights of the foreign Powers whose entire attention was taken up by the recurrent crises in Europe. At the same time, the "elder statesmen" in Tokyo were a little frightened by adventures of their military bad boys in the pursuit of Japan's Manifest Destiny on the shores of the Pacific. Discreetly, they approached Mr. Chamberlain's ambassador, Sir Robert Craigie, on the subject of mediation. Rumour said that these approaches had the approval of the Emperor himself.

On the other hand, the new threats hurled by the Japanese militarists at a China which would not submit revealed how deeply right Chiang Kai-shek had been in his analysis of the soft words of Prince Konoye. In contradistinction to the former Premier's disclaimer of territorial ambitions, War Minister Itagaki declared, at the end of January, that the Japanese army had no intention at all of ever evacuating Central and South China, much less the North. Forgotten too, were the flattering words that had been addressed to the Kuomintang when the Japanese had entertained the hope that it would follow "its leader" Wang Ching-wei. Instead, General Araki thundered again that the "Three People's Principles" must be uprooted and the Kuomintang (no less than the Communists) utterly destroyed. In token of the everlasting friendship of Japan towards the downtrodden people of China, Chungking, Kweilin, Ichang, Wanhsien, and many other important cities were subjected to new terror-bombings in which many thousands were killed.

Against this background of the growing exasperation, waverings, and exhaustion of an originally far more powerful and dangerous enemy, China's growing strength and unity stood out in bold relief. Japan was increasingly enmeshed in internal and international contradictions. China, on the other hand, was marching confidently forward not only to a new stage of her war of resistance, but also towards a new stage in the century-old struggle which she has waged for the fight to develop as a modern and democratic nation, able to take its place among the free and independent peoples of the world.

CHAPTER XV
China Marches On

D R. SUN YAT-SEN was the founder of modern political thought in China, the initiator of her national revolutionary movement, and the father of the Republic. When he died, on March 12, 1925, he left behind him as a legacy his San Min Chu I, or "Three People's Principles", in which the tasks before the country were defined as the achievement of full national independence and equality, the realization of internal democracy, and the improvement of the livelihood of the Chinese people. Dr. Sun stressed that these three tasks were closely inter-connected, and that the national emancipation of the Chinese people could not be fully achieved until they were all successfully accomplished.

For forty years, this great national-democratic leader stood at the helm of the struggle to free the Chinese people from the shackles which impeded the development of their great capabilities and of the rich resources of their country. With a small group of followers, he overthrew the Manchu dynasty which had long hung rotten-ripe on the tree of history, and threatened, in the last stage of its decay, to bring the whole nation to destruction through its endless surrenders of Chinese territory and sovereign rights. After the fall of the Empire, the progressive movement which he led found itself faced by a new enemy, the compradore-militarist reaction which was based on the feudal backwardness of the country and backed by contending foreign imperialisms. For more than a decade the war-lords, who were united only in their hostility to the forces of progress, tormented the nation with endless civil wars. At the time of Dr. Sun's death, this phase of modern Chinese history had not yet ended.

The thing that enabled Dr. Sun to stand for four decades in the van of the national revolutionary movement was his extraordinary capacity to learn from experience and to alter his methods of work in accordance with changing historical demands. After the disappointment of the early years of the Republic, he came to understand that the compact conspiratorial organization that had sufficed to bring about the downfall of the Manchus could not hope to face the new tasks of the national democratic revolution without the conscious and organized support of the masses of the Chinese people. He learned, too, that the revolution must have its own strong army, and that this army must be thoroughly imbued with its political principles. Finally, he realized the identity of the interests of the people of China with the interests of historically progressive forces all over the world.

On the basis of these lessons, Dr. Sun laid down the foundations of the internal and international strategy of the Chinese people's struggle for liberation, which was responsible for the phenomenal success of the northward march of the national-revolutionary forces in 1925-7. Under his guidance, and with the collaboration of the Communist Party, which he regarded as indispensable, the Kuomintang undertook the organization of the people for the coming fight, supporting the demands of the peasantry for agrarian reform and the efforts of the workers to achieve an eight-hour day and a fair wage. For the training of strong and politically-steeled leaders for the national army, the Whampoa Military Academy was established. Finally, in foreign affairs, the Kuomintang in those days followed the principle of friendship with the peoples of the entire world and with those governments which were prepared to deal with China on a footing of complete equality. The British Government of the time, whose policy acted as a pattern for the other Western Powers, fomented revolts against the new national administration in Canton, ordered its troops to shoot down Chinese workers and students, and gave its full support to the Northern militarists. As a result, the Kuomintang maintained official relations only with the Soviet Union, which had renounced the concessions and extra-territorial privileges held by imperial Russia, and did not hesitate to demonstrate its full sympathy with the new national democracy. Besides this, delegates were exchanged, and close contact maintained, with the trade union movements and progressive parties of the United States, Great Britain, France, India, and Japan.

The charge then levelled at China's first United Front — that it was unconditionally hostile to Western interests, was malicious and untrue. In *The International Development of China*, published in 1922, Dr. Sun invited the Powers to invest in a gigantic programme of national reconstruction, involving the building of several new ports and tens of thousands of miles of roads and railways. Little attention was paid to this programme because, firstly, its author was regarded (with the dense blindness of wishful thinking) as the bankrupt doctrinaire of a lost cause, and secondly because Dr. Sun insisted that the projected increase in foreign economic activity should not be accompanied by any impairment of China's sovereignty, but, on the other hand, could only take place when the country had achieved complete independence. That the reasonable and just ambitions of the Chinese people were branded as Communism, brigandage, and worse, was a reflection not of the facts of the situation in China, but of the policy of the Chamberlains of the day. It was the age of the forged "Zinoviev letter".

The policy of the Chamberlains of that time (when Sir Austen graced the Foreign Office) succeeded only too well. The unity of China's national forces was broken, her strength was spent in new and greater internal blood-lettings, and the menace of Japanese imperialism threatened not only utterly to destroy her independence, but also to sweep Western interests from the country. To-day China has returned again to what is for her the only path of survival and progress. And the Chamberlains of to-day, faced with a danger far more real than the bogey they laid in 1927, have perforce to admit that the fate of their own stake in the East lies, with many other things, in the hands of the fighters for China's reconstituted United Front.

It is not my purpose to make further excursions into history. But in summing up correctly the fundamental results of the first stage of China's war of national emancipation, the events of 1924-7 constitute a necessary point of reference. To-day, as then, the "Three People's Principles" of Dr. Sun Yat-sen form the basis of a national united front of the Kuomintang and Communist Party. As then, again, the political goal of the struggle is the establishment of a San Min Chu I republic. By the progress made during the war in the achievement of the "Three People's Principles" we may gauge how much China has advanced. By the tasks which still remain unaccomplished we can explain the reasons for China's failures and perceive the outlines of the long road that she still has to travel before the final victory is achieved.

Let us take the principle of Nationalism.

Before the outbreak of the war, the independence of China was in deadly danger. Three years ago, when the Japanese wave threatened to engulf the unresisting Northern provinces, only the students of Peiping offered articulate protest. The civil war between the Kuomintang forces and the Red Army ended only at the end of 1936. In many provinces, rival satraps ruled, waiting eagerly for the disintegration of the Central power. The anti-Japanese movement was banned and patriotic workers were jailed. A growing gulf separated the people, who realized the peril of subjection to Japan, from a Government that pleaded rearmament for future resistance as an excuse for a policy of "appeasement" in relation to an insatiable aggressor. Lacking faith in its own forces, Nanking saw in diplomatic and economic pressure on Tokyo by England and America the sole hope of checking Japan. Whether China would survive seemed to lie in other hands than her own.

To-day China is more truly independent not only than at the beginning of the war, but also than at any time in her modern history. Everywhere that the Japanese have penetrated, resistance is being offered. No recognition is given to their "special rights", and they have no safety even in their old bases. In regions from which the regular armies have retreated, not parading boys and girls, but strong partisan forces dispute Japanese control. Civil war is a vague memory, and Kuomintang and Communists stand together against the national enemy. Armies from every province have shed their blood at the front. The Japanese and their ally Wang Ching-wei tested the loyalty of previously rebellious regions and found it proof against their every intrigue. The slogans of the patriotic movement have become the guiding principles of the nation. The Government has the complete support of the people in the anti-Japanese struggle. China is fighting with more and more confidence for her own future. Not only does she realize that her survival depends upon her ability to utilize her own reserves of strength, but the countries on whose protection she once based all her hopes now recognize this strength, and see it as the only power able to conduct the defence, on the spot, of their own Far Eastern holdings.

After the fall of Hankow, Japan took advantage of the protracted European crisis to refuse to reopen the Yangtze and Pearl rivers to neutral navigation, increase her pressure on the foreign concessions, and seize Hainan and the Sprattley Islands as bases for further attacks on British, French, and American positions in the Pacific. China's continued resistance became more and more important to the Powers menaced by these developments. Support of the Central Government, which had clearly manifested its determination and ability to carry on the struggle, presented itself as the most readily available to strike back at the encroaching Japanese. Looking back at the record of China's pre-war relations with the West, we see at once a difference in the circumstances in which this support is given. In the past, most international aid to China has not only been accompanied by attempts to control her policy, but foreign loans have been secured by the presence on her soil of foreign troops. To-day, all the old strongholds of foreign influence are in occupied areas and face only one enemy — Japanese monopoly. The loans granted to China at the beginning of this year, while giving the Powers a share in her new economic development, have had the political effect not of impairing her independence, but, on the other hand, of helping her to struggle for it. By fighting for herself, and at the same time carrying on reconstruction, China has taken the most decisive steps in her modern history towards emerging from her semi-colonial status and making sure that she will never again be a passive prize in the struggle for the control of the Pacific. This has been further proved by the failure of all "mediation" efforts, from whatever quarter they have come.

Even before the war, public opinion in the West and, to a lesser but nevertheless appreciable extent, the Governments of the countries concerned, understood that the unequal treaties imposed on China during the nineteenth century and following the Boxer Rebellion would finally have to go. It is very likely that, as Dr. Sun Yat-sen insisted, foreign participation in the gigantic reconstruction that will follow the war will be conditioned on their total abolition. Serious difficulties on this account are extremely improbable if the present tendency in international affairs continues, particularly because the last two years have already seen them disappear, one by one, as living factors in the relations of Chungking with Washington, London, and Paris. This has been due to one circumstance alone — that China has continued to resist. Any concession to the elements sighing for a Far Eastern Munich — and there are such, not only in Downing Street, but in the inner recesses of the State Department of the progressive American democracy — and she will roll back towards the bad old days of tutelage, consortia, and "spheres of influence". But while such tendencies undoubtedly exist, history, both Chinese and international, has gone beyond them, and it is extremely unlikely that they will ever again dominate the Far Eastern scene.

What about democracy?

In these pages we have already discussed in detail what has been accomplished in this field. In certain areas in China, complete popular democracy is a fact. All over the country, freedom of speech, Press, and assembly have been recognized as the right of every shade of political opinion that does not oppose the war. Every anti-Japanese party can openly exist and propagate its viewpoint. Representatives of all parties, of the professions, and of the people's organizations have a voice on questions of national policy through the People's Political Council. Of course, all this falls far short of real democracy. The names of candidates for the Council are handed in by the various organizations, but their appointment comes from above. No elected body proposes or passes legislation, and Central Government posts are monopolized by the Kuomintang.

There is no need to minimize these shortcomings. They will be remedied. As the course of the war thus far has convinced the entire nation, as well as its ruling party, of the necessity of broadening the political basis of the struggle, so the long fight ahead will lead to a further development of this tendency. In this regard, the living example of the partisan areas, where the most determined attacks of the enemy have been overcome by the widest extension of democracy, is of particular importance.

The recognition of the limited nature of the democracy at present existing should not, moreover, blind us to the great progress it represents. It was only three years ago that liberal thought was classed as "cultural banditry", publications were suppressed, the people's anti-Japanese movement was allowed no liberty, national salvation workers were imprisoned, and membership of opposition parties was legal ground for the imposition of the death penalty.

The livelihood of the people?

The "Three People's Principles" called insistently for agrarian reform, decent working conditions for industrial labour, the limitation of private economic enterprise, and control of the basic industries by the State.

Agrarian reform is, of course, one of the fundamental needs of modern China. It is also one of the basic conditions of the war of resistance, because the Chinese peasant is, more than anyone else, the man who is fighting the war. The peasantry is called upon to produce recruits for the national armies. On its efforts depends the nation's supply of food. It is largely from the land taxes that the struggle is financed. Wherever the battle for China's independence is being waged, it rolls over the peasant's fields. The peasant's muscles have levelled China's airdromes and built her new international roads. With every month of the war, new burdens and new responsibilities fall on his toil-bowed shoulders.

For an example of what a serious approach to the problem of improving the lot of the peasantry can do for the war we must turn again to the Border Areas. There, scrupulous regard for the peasant's rights, the reduction of rents and interest, and the turning over for tillage by the village poor of the temple and waste lands and the estates of runaway landlords have produced bulwarks of resistance which have stood against innumerable Japanese "campaigns of extermination". In other parts of the country, much less has been done. But in the front-line districts taxes have invariably been remitted. Usurer's interest has been reduced. Conscription methods have been regularized and the organizations of the peasantry, long suppressed, have been allowed to reappear. In the account of the battle of Taierhchuang we have seen how the national armies are improving their treatment of the people, and how the people respond.

The fact that no national land policy for the period of the war has yet been enunciated by the Government remains, however, one of the flaws in the general picture of progress presented by China to-day. The absence of such a policy has led, in some places, to the unmitigated continuance of the old abuses, abuses of which the Japanese have been quick to take advantage. The invaders realize the importance of the peasantry. While destroying with fire and sword whole villages suspected of harbouring partisans, they attempt to bribe the country-folk to abandon resistance by exempting them from taxes and issuing loans of money, farm animals, implements, and seed. The fact that in certain sections of the lower Yangtze valley these methods have, despite the savagery and indiscipline of the Japanese army, led to some measure of "pacification", is directly traceable to backwardness of neighbouring Chinese forces and administrations. The peasant has borne the bloody outrages of invasion. There is no doubt of the fact that he wants to fight; if there were, there would have been no war of resistance. But in order that he may fight, it is necessary that he be given the opportunity to both fight and live. This means the lifting of his heavy burdens.

In the prolonged deadlock that is likely to mark the next stage of the war, with increased Japanese attempts to organize the territories behind their lines, the comparative welfare of the population in areas under Chinese and Japanese control will assume even greater importance. The Chinese peasant has given much to the war. Except in the Border Areas, he has received little. The Chinese landlord, on the other hand, has most certainly not given enough, in many cases refusing to lower rents even where military operations have devastated the land. This must be changed, and certainly will be in the course of the struggle. At the same time, there is no reason why, at the present time, class conflicts in the countryside should become dangerously acute. Certainly, so long as the whole nation is united against the invader, the interests of the national struggle will overshadow all else. What is needed is that all sections of the population should make equal contributions to unity. The experience of the Border Areas has shown that where the Japanese menace is immediate, the village gentry have been ready to grant the concessions demanded of them by the law and the peasants' organizations, realizing that such concessions strengthen resistance and are the best insurance against an enemy victory. The adoption of a resolute land policy by the Central Government, to be carried out by the local authorities supported by the people's organizations, is a necessary step that would immeasurably enhance the military effectiveness of the national army as well as increase the agricultural yield.

For the industrial workers of China, life has changed drastically since the beginning of the war. In Shanghai alone, 70 per cent of China's machine industry was destroyed by bomb and shell or dismantled by the Japanese following their occupation of the city. The Chinese working class, however, was not destroyed. Through two years of struggle, Chinese working men and working women have toiled to maintain production, carrying on until the last moment in factories that were the targets of enemy airplanes, and moving, when these were destroyed, to the new industrial areas in the West. The railwaymen of China, by maintaining a full service on lines menaced not only by bombing and artillery but also by the direct attacks of enemy tanks and infantry, have written a new and bright page into the annals of labour heroism throughout the world. Skilled workers follow the partisan armies, supplying them with arms and ammunition and guarding their mobile arsenals with their lives. In this book we have read how industrial workers fought, shoulder to shoulder with the soldiers, during the great battles for Shanghai. We have read of the miner partisans of Chinghsing, the railway workers' demolition brigades in Shansi, Hopei, and Shantung. Workers are the backbone of China's new mechanized divisions. Han Ying, vice-commander of the New Fourth Army, is a worker from Hankow.

During the anti-Japanese struggle the Chinese working class has won back its freedom of organization. In Hankow, in 1938, May Day was celebrated as a national holiday for the first time in Chinese history.

For the first time since 1927, the organization of the people and the thorough political training of the army, both so strongly advocated by Dr. Sun, are recognized as the bases of successful defence of the country's freedom. It is hard to imagine the war of resistance without the popular enthusiasm, the wealth of voluntary effort and initiative, and the flowering of the creative powers of the people which it has brought in its train. This is a measure of the great changes which have taken place in a country in which, only three years ago, no non-official body could afford to be suspected of being actively interested in the ultimate destiny of the nation.

The army, long bred in the Prussian tradition, or in blind personal allegiance to provincial militarists, has to-day its United Front guerila school which all officers must attend, its political workers in every unit. The soldier is no longer, to the people, merely an instrument of compulsion or a tax collector: he is the conscious defender of their rights. The personnel of the army has changed also. No longer does it consist mainly of the declassed elements of town and village. The man who carries a rifle to-day was a hard-working peasant, city labourer, or shop apprentice only a few months ago. He is one in background and desires with the vast majority of the Chinese people.

This much has been achieved. Where both popular organization and the army fell short of the demands of the struggle, the responsibility lies with the heritage of the past. As in the case of Canton, the awakening and arming of the people often have no effect on the military strength of a given point because they are looked upon as a symbolic war-time exercise rather than a vital part of the country's system of defence. The approach to the task of creating a mass basis for resistance is too often purely formalistic. People are registered, organizations are named with pomp and ceremony, and the whole "movement" then goes to sleep until the next anniversary parade, because it is built not on the initiative of the people, but on the paper plans of "leaders" who consider that everything necessary has been done when the required number of names has been entered on the membership rolls. Needless to say, this is not the general rule. The reader of the previous pages will see the tremendous amount of real work that has been accomplished and its importance to the success of resistance thus far. Everywhere in the country, efforts are being made to deepen and extend the participation of the organized people in the war.

The Chinese Army has improved beyond recognition. In the chapters dealing with the major campaigns of the past two years the process of this improvement has been discussed at some length. We have seen that the tactical programme adopted by the army is correct. Why, then, although the Japanese advance has become progressively more difficult, has the tide not yet decisively turned? Part of the answer lies in the political field, in the tasks that must still be tackled in the realm of political and economic reforms. The rest must be referred to the technical and organizational backwardness which the army itself has inherited from the past. Uniformity is still lacking in trading and equipment, in degree of initative and political education, and in the quality and method of the command. Some of the provincial military leaders have proved to be brilliant strategists in the war of resistance, as for instance Li Tsung-jen and Pai Chung-hsi of Kwangsi, Li Han-wan, Chang Fa-kwei, and Yeh Shao of Kwangtung, Sun Lien-chung, Chih Feng-chen, and Chang Tze-chung of the old Kuominchun. Among the Generalissimo's direct subordinates, Tang En-po, Wei Li-huang, Chen Cheng, and many more have distinguished themselves. But many of the old generals have been unable to adapt themselves to the new situation, and have turned out to be lacking in initiative and unfitted to handle large armies under the complex conditions of modern warfare. Some of these men have been shot for dereliction of duty, others have been removed, but not a few still remain in command.

Has the Chinese Army, apart from the partisan areas, developed no List-ers and Campesinos, no military talents forged from the midst of the people in the fire of war? Of course it has. But they are still in the ranks or among the younger officers. They stage the forays that so often disrupt Japanese mili-tary plans, and command the heroic battalions whose courage in the face of overwhelming odds amazes the world and makes it wonder why, with such an army, China has not long since fought the invader to a complete standstill. One of the problems that must be solved before the war is much older is how to provide more scope for the initiative of these leaders, how to ensure that they will bring their qualities to the larger tasks of the struggle, instead of dying at the head of small units to cover the mistakes of their superiors. We can say with confidence that this question will find an early solution, as it has in all the people's wars of history.

As a political force, the Chinese Army is a factor of prime importance. It is unanimously in favour of determined and unwavering resistance, and its confidence in China's final victory is complete. Long before it came into the open, the capitulationist faction of Wang Ching-wei found its way blocked by the united opposition of the military group. After Wang's treachery, the army was loud in its demands for his punishment and for the purging of all Government organs of the remnants of his influence.

The launching of counter-attacks on all fronts during April and May 1939, hailed by the foreign Press as the beginning of a general counter-offensive, is of prime significance politically rather than militarily. It cannot yet achieve the military turning of the tide, because the balance of available striking power is still in favour of the Japanese. But it does demonstrate that the determination of the Chinese Government to carry on the struggle has not only not been shaken, but has grown stronger. It shows that the armed forces of the country have made gains in strength since the fall of Hankow compa-rable to those which took place between the loss of Nanking and the victory of Taierhchuang. Most important of all, it dashes the political initative from the hands of the enemy.

Japan wants desperately to stabilize her front and to consolidate her control of the territories already occupied. Dissatisfaction at home, the grumblings of her anti-Comintern allies, and the necessity of creating a clear position for ultimate bargaining with the other Powers all dictate that this be done. But all the paper plans and schedules devised in Tokyo towards this object are based on one assumption — that the military situation will remain fully under Japanese control. The Imperial army must be able at all times to chose where to advance, where to halt, and where to retreat. That is not the position to-day. To-day the invader, must fight where they are attacked, not where they themselves want to attack. The disposition of their forces is determined not by Japan's complicated internal and international situation, but by the wishes of the high command in Chungking. Until the strength of the Chinese army is destroyed, Tokyo cannot guard against such disruptions of its military and political designs. On the other hand, a new offensive to smash the Chinese forces is certainly not likely to have any better results than previous efforts having the same object. A repetition, at this stage, of the Hsuchow and Hankow campaigns is undesirable from the point of view of the Japanese themselves, as well as detrimental to the larger aims of the axis.

Externally, Japan's position is no better. Most luckless of the Fascist Powers, she could not match Hitler's Czechoslovakia and Memel and Mussolini's Albania with even a clear-cut victory in tiny Kulangsu. It cannot be said that her forces are exhausted. They are not. But Chinese resistance has already placed her in a position in which she does not know how to use them and cannot confidently depend on them for the achievement of ally of her strategic aims. War is the armed pursuit of policy. It is hard to say what Japan's policy is to-day.

Progress towards the achievement of Dr. Sun's injunctions on foreign policy has had its rewards. These were summed up as follows by Dr. H. H. Kung, in his report to the People's Political Council in February 1939:

"The international situation has changed in our favour. The friendly Powers and their peoples now have a better understanding of the object and spirit of our resistance, and consequently are showing greater sympathy with us and are giving us a larger measure of assistance.

"The 104th Session of the League Council resolved to give China continued moral support. The U.S.S.R. has helped us unceasingly, as a member of the League and in fulfilment of the spirit of the resolutions passed by the League. Both England and America have likewise materially aided us. The United States has purchased much silver, thus stabilising our currency. Recently America and England have granted us commercial loans."

The peoples of the world have shown the greatest solidarity with China. The London boycott conference, the formation in America of the Committee for Non-Participation in Japanese Aggression, headed by Colonel Stimson, the progress of the boycott and embargo movements, the work of organized labour in refusing to load and transport war cargoes to Japan, and the existence of numerous organizations for aid to China throughout the world — all these have been a source of great encouragement to the country in its struggle.

The closer collaboration between the peoples of China itself and the institution of a more enlightened policy with regard to the national minorities have already been noted. The Western marches are playing a more and more important part in China's political and economic life. Sikang, on the borders of Tibet, has been reorganized from a territory into a province. In his report to the People's Political Council, Dr. Kung described as "a cause for gratification, the remarkable progress of Sinkiang (Chinese Turkestan), a province of many races which have been welded into a solid bloc by General Sheng Shih-tsai, the Pacification Commissioner". A conference of national representatives held in its capital, Tihua (Urumchi), at the end of 1938, disclosed truly amazing advances. This remote region, in the heart of Central Asia, has for the first time really entered the current of Chinese life. It has contributed funds and airplanes and is mustering soldiers for the anti-Japanese fronts. Its flying-schools are training China's aerial cadets, and its new university, publishing houses, and cultural development projects have attracted many of the intellectual leaders of the pre-war National Salvation Movement in Shanghai, among them Mao Tun, China's most famous novelist, who is dean of arts in the new seat of learning. Moslem and

Mongol are fighting in China's war.* Tibet is showing more interest than ever before in her destiny.

More features of Dr. Sun's programme of national reconstruction have seen materialization during the two years of the war of resistance than during the previous ten. Air communication has developed to an unprecedented degree. New highways have been built linking China, through Sinkiang, with the Soviet Union, and through Burma with the Indian Ocean. Railways are being pushed southward through Kwangsi to Indo-China, south-westward from Yunnan to Burma, westward along the Soviet route, and to linkup internal communications in Szechuan, Kweichow, and Kwangsi. Plans made long ago and shelved for decades are at last seeing the light. New industries are growing in the deep rear. The Chinese Industrial Co-operatives, an experiment of great promise, have within the short space of a few months set up 500 of a projected 30,000 small manufacturing units, mobile and ubiquitous, to maintain the supply of essential commodities even in areas near the front.

War-time industrial reconstruction is controlled by the Executive Yuan, through the Ministry of Economics, the National Resources Commission, and other Government organs. Transportation along the new roads is operated either directly by the State or under special charter.

China's chief banking and industrialist groups, as well as Chinese capitalists overseas, are financing these developments, and thereby actively supporting the war of resistance. Apart from this, they have invested heavily in national bonds, thus showing their confidence in victory. Unfortunately, there is also much "refugee capital" being invested in mushroom real estate booms in Shanghai and Hongkong, or simply hoarded to await hoped-for quick profits under safe conditions during the country's post-war reconstruction. The na-

---

* Complex Japanese intrigues in this province were defeated during 1935-7, in the course of a fierce civil war. It is indicative that one of the exiled rebels who, in 1938, was "representing" the Uigurs of Sinkiang in Hankow, told me that Wang Ching-wei had promised him the chairmanship of the province after the war. This gentleman was much sought after by German news correspondents in the war-time capital who publicized with glee his attacks on the provincial government and the Soviet Union.

tional income tax still awaits thorough and effective application.

Good harvests, the tapping of the natural riches of the South- west and West, an able financial policy, international support, and the patriotism of her people have kept China's currency stable, while the yen has had to be bolstered with numerous artificial restrictions and Japan's puppet "Federal Reserve" currency balances crazily on the brink of complete worthlessness.

Economically, as politically and militarily, China is holding her own.

How "Red" is China?

The summary given above should go far to answer this. It should be read with particular attention by all those who have been misled by Japanese propaganda concerning the "bolshevization" of the country. During the past two years, the Republic has moved more rapidly than ever before in its history, but still too slowly in relation to the pressing demands the war, towards the realization of the "Three People's Principles" of Dr. Sun Yat-sen. Far from nearing Communism, however, it has not yet shaken off all the feudal trammels which hinder the advent of even the Western type of Parliamentary democracy.

Like many other countries, China now has a strong legal Communist Party. It is the second largest party in the country, but is inferior in numbers to, for instance, the Communist Party of France. The Chinese Communists support the Central Government, which is leading the nation in its struggle against extinction. They do not, however, hold any ministerial posts in this Government, and they are not represented on the new Supreme National Defence Council formed in February 1939. In one respect, the position of the Communist Party in China is unique. As a result of special historical circumstances, it controls armies which forms approximately 10 per cent of the total military forces, and a special administrative district in which live 1,000,000 of China's 450,000,000 people. Apart from this district, its influence is greatest in the Shansi-Chahar-Hopei Border Area and a small sector of the lower Yangtze valley, these regions having been recaptured from the enemy respectively by the Eighth Route and New Fourth Armies.

Throughout the country, the prestige of the party is far in advance of its numbers or power. This is because it has demonstrated, both on the battle-field and in the areas in which it has had a hand in the determination of policy, the soundness of its analysis of the situation facing the country and the effectiveness of its methods of carrying on the national struggle. The widespread recognition of this fact not only sends students flocking to the anti-Japanese university at Yenan, but causes the General Staff (whose chief concern was once the war against the Red Army) to welcome Communist commanders to its deliberations and embody their suggestions in the funda-mental strategic plans for the conduct of the anti-Japanese war. All officers of the Chinese Army now undergo training in partisan tactics under one such commander, General Yeh Chien-ying. On the other hand, the National Gov-ernment has been slow in adopting the political and economic reforms which the Communist hold to be an essential factor in successful partisan warfare, and to which can be ascribed the magnificent record of their own armies, which is recognized by both friend and foe.

What of the future?

It is safe to say that China will go on fighting, that the war will be a protracted one, and that as it goes on the "Three People's Principles", form-ing the basic programme of the Chinese people's struggle for national emancipation, will continue to approach full realization. More and more of China's reserve forces will be thrown into the fight, the awakening of her people will continue, more and more new leaders will be produced.

The Governments of the world will have increasingly to reckon with a new factor in international affairs, a China reborn which will be an important ally of the democracies and a formidable enemy to the forces of Fascist aggression.

For the peoples of all countries China's struggle holds rich meaning and a message of hope.

China is fighting Fascism. In the three years that have seen the final act of the Abyssinian tragedy, the disappearance of Austria and Albania, and the shameless betrayal of Czechoslovakia and Spain, she has gone not back but forward. Fascist barbarism has engulfed country after country, destroying the national independence, democratic rights, and human dignity of people after people. But it is not on all fronts that the forces of progress have suffered setbacks. China is one-fifth of mankind and China fights on. Capitulation would have sealed her fate as a nation. By resistance the Chinese people have not only retained but are strengthening their independence. For the first time in their history they are approaching democracy. As always when peoples fight for freedom, the stress of the struggle has forged new men and women faster than new institutions — men and women who have grown from darkness and serfdom to full human stature, who do not know surrender, but defend with arms in their hands what is dearest to all mankind.

There is no need to enlarge on the significance of this fact, on the supreme necessity that this front shall hold. The fighters who man it are doing their part. To help them against the common enemy is the responsibility of the world's free peoples.

A few hours before these lines were written, the Press brought to China the news that her latest appeal to the League of Nations had been shelved. We know how little China would have profited even if, in the present state of affairs, her requests had received full endorsement. But this did not occur. The proposal was blocked, and Lord Halifax, the Foreign Secretary of a democratic nation, has again offered to China the gratuitous insult of empty words of sympathy coupled with a refusal to even consider the possibility of collective aid.

Such signs are dangerous — and not to China alone. The peoples of the world must remedy this situation. They must make sure that those who speak in their names also carry out their will. It is their responsibility to the fighters on the Far Eastern front of the struggle against Fascism. It is their responsibility to themselves.

图书在版编目（CIP）数据

人民战争 / 爱泼斯坦（Epstein, I.）著.
－北京：外文出版社，2003.12
（中国之光）
ISBN 7-119-03471-5

I.人… II.爱… III.抗日战争－史料－英文
IV.K265.06
中国版本图书馆 CIP 数据核字（2003）第 091248 号

外文出版社网址：
　http://www.flp.com.cn
外文出版社电子信箱：
　info@flp.com.cn
　sales@flp.com.cn

中国之光丛书

人民战争

作　　者　爱泼斯坦（Epstein, I.）
责任编辑　蔚文英
封面设计　蔡　荣
印刷监制　冯　浩
出版发行　外文出版社
社　　址　北京市百万庄大街 24 号　　　邮政编码　100037
电　　话　(010) 68996121 / 68996117（编辑部）
　　　　　(010) 68329514 / 68327211（推广发行部）
印　　刷　三河市汇鑫印务有限公司
开　　本　小 16 开
印　　数　1000 册
版　　次　2003 年第 1 版第 1 次印刷
装　　别　精装
书　　号　ISBN 7-119-03471-5 / Z·671（外）
定　　价　80.00 元